Managing the Bucket List: the Journey Begins

Volume I

Carol McIlwain, PhD

Table of Contents

Introduction

Why the Journey?

By reading this book, you will embark on a literary journey of travel with the intent of learning more on bucket list type locations and activities. Through this journey though, you will also acquire knowledge, some new and some re-examined. The journey is accomplished by walking in my figurative footsteps as I explore new countries, cities, and activities, some considered lifetime experiences. This journey is accomplished within about a year's timeframe, with the first trip in November 2022 and the last one in December 2023, challenging the physical and mental stamina of repeated travel conditions. At the end of this year, I integrate the knowledge gained and synthesize it with basic principles of international relations to answer some questions and provoke more questions on how specific countries are doing and then collectively how the world is doing. Volume I includes Part 1 and 2. Part 1 of this book describes a bucket list, why someone should have one, and some well-known bucket list options such as the various Wonders of the World, UNESCO World Heritage Sites, Museums of the World, World-Renowned Religious Sites, and Magnificent Castles.

Part 2 of the book describes my trips during this period. Although I retired on March 31, 2023, I took trips to Portugal in November 2022 and Patagonia in January 2023 just prior to retirement. The Portugal trip clinched my desire to see the world, thus ending one career and starting another. Although I have completed a doctorate majoring in Project Management from the University of Maryland, I found myself seeking further education in International Relations. The question I posed myself: do I want to take additional courses to learn more about the world or do I want to learn by firsthand experiencing the world? Well, that was an easy answer, experience the world but do it expeditiously. I retired after thirty-nine years with the Department of the Navy, spending the last seven years as a senior executive, and was ready to start the next chapter of my life.

A bonus with accelerating my adventure is that group tours were offering big savings to lure potential travelers back into traveling after the COVID-19 pandemic. The price cuts wouldn't last forever and so traveling sooner allowed this cost savings advantage over traveling later. Looking into 2024 and 2025, the prices are increasing in double-digit percentages. In other words, I could save enough in a couple trips in 2023 to pay for a trip in 2024. So, prices are going up based on inflation and more people are back traveling again, supply and demand economics.

The movie *The Big Year* starring Steve Martin, Owen Wilson, and Jack Black as the main characters depicts the annual competition in birdwatching to discover the most different types of birds in a year. The three competitors travel around the United States to catch glimpses of birds in their known or migratory locations. An alert system allows the competitors to know when someone has spotted a rare bird fueling a mass scrambling to airplanes and cars to get to the location before the birds disappear and also ahead of their competitors. Borrowing from the premise of wrapping an adventure around a search or exploration, I turned my bucket list into an expedited *Travel Big Year*. I had a tentative list of places that I wanted to visit, but when I started planning the *Travel Big Year*, the list grew dramatically. In addition, as I started taking trips, I found myself extending the one year into a second year quickly and then even a third year and possibly a fourth year. I was bitten by the travel bug.

Volume II includes Parts 3, 4, and 5. Part 3 describes some previous personal trips taken that were part of my bucket list: Caribbean Islands, Mexico, Dominican Republic, Israel, Egypt, Greece, and Peru. Some I solely planned, while others were a combination of an organized tour and some planning on my part.

Part 4 includes trips taken as part of my work life: Puerto Rico, United Kingdom, Japan, Haiti, France and Romania, Australia and Solomons Islands, and deployments to Iraq and Afghanistan. Always looking to expand my knowledge, these trips for work also included venturing to sightseeing places within the country and learning more about the culture and the people. I've included these to provide a richer picture of the international scene to investigate common themes, problems, and potential interdependences between countries.

All chapters are then explored further in Part 5 with general information on international relations taken from renowned authors on the subject. This concluding chapter integrates information and knowledge across all trips. I can't take credit for the concept or analogy of looking at information through a lens that is readily used by academia to filter information through one's knowledge, whether learned or experienced, for understanding. Based on my knowledge-set acquired through multiple academic degrees, training certification curriculums, multiple experience in government service, and an abundance of reading, the neurons in my brain are representative of that knowledge and reflect the interconnections of information. An avid reader, my library holds more than 500 books with most being non-fiction. In other words, the knowledge retained within the brain is what limits one to interpret the world around them. Sensory inputs are the five senses: hearing, seeing, smelling, tasting, and touching. This book is written with my very diverse knowledge-set seeking to complement existing knowledge with that of the new trips in the year.

In order to manage the reader's expectations, I need to discuss what the book covers and what it does not. This book isn't is a travel reference book describing where are the best places to go, where to eat, or what to see. I've encountered numerous blogs, books, and magazine articles which provide an abundance of information on many countries for this purpose. I'm not seeking to replicate that resource. Through my travels, I will describe places that I visited and activities that I did that are noteworthy, but they are not all inclusive. Descriptions are more for a human-interest perspective than a *how to travel* perspective.

Although many of the trips were through a tourist organization, I will not provide information on any specific tour company; therefore, this book is not intended to make a comparison of travel companies. However, I will describe the planning needed to accomplish the aggressive travel and any problems and solutions encountered. I will describe the pros and cons of group travel versus self-planning trips, having accomplished both.

When I stumble across a diamond in the rough, a special hotel, restaurant, or activity, I will share that discovery in the book. I also reference movies and television shows that provide a unique perspective to culture and history. Some are filmed at locations around the world. This tends to be a significant point of interest for tour managers to enlighten their tour group. Most tourism ministries in a country are well aware of this information. Local tourism organizations usually have tours specifically for this purpose. I remember my trips to Hollywood, California and the celebrity tours, learning who lives or lived in which house. Tours of Miami City, Florida are quite similar.

Basically, simple project management is applied to aggressive travel planning. Largely, an excel spreadsheet is my master travel document. Most group tours, whether one or two weeks, are a sprint. They are not a leisure vacation spent sitting on the beach in a single location merely for rest and recuperation. Group tours typically encompass a country or parts of a country or multiple countries. There is a lot of action visiting sites or doing activities, but this activity is good for the body and mind. My decision to expedite travel was to make sure that I would still be capable of accomplishing some of the more aggressive trips, long-distance flights, hiking in the mountains, all day sightseeing, and long travel days, while I'm still physically able. This is a comment that many mature travelers have conveyed on my trips; they want to travel while they still can and can still enjoy it.

A word of warning with respect to any travel information, it is time sensitive. Almost everything changes whether it's guidance on where to go, what to do, dos and don'ts on travel, advisory guidance on countries, problems with traveling, airline issues, etc. When it comes to where to go, for United States citizens check the State Department website for country advisory advice. Many other countries also have their version of country advisories for their citizens. Previously as a United States government employee, I was required to follow their recommendations to avoid places that were considered to have unreasonable risk.

For those who like to play it safe, read the guidance and plan accordingly. Also register your trip with the Smart Traveler Enrollment Program (STEP). The State Department then sends updates on the locations that you have registered.

The world can be a volatile, dangerous place. The only way to manage this is to keep updated with timely information. When I went to Machu Picchu in 2019, I never imagined that it would be closed a couple of years later because of protests in Peru. Hopefully, we have figured out how to manage the variants of COVID-19 so as not to shut down travel and all social contact again, or at least not for a very long time.

In any writing venture, one asks who is my audience? The easy answer is people that are interested in traveling whether current travelers or want-to-be travelers. The book provides information on my traveling experiences; helpful tips through lessons learned; information on the countries visited including history, culture, environment; and the benefits gained as a citizen of any country for being a more knowledgeable person of the world. My last point relates to how through traveling one becomes more knowledgeable and therefore acquires a better understanding of foreign policy in addition to domestic policy and how it relates to decision-making. Although historically the United States has adopted at times an isolationist policy, it wasn't effective prior to World War II. Japan decided that the United States shouldn't sit on the sidelines for the war. Fortunately, the country rallied to the cause in a very expeditious and sacrificial way. My father always talked about two timeframes of his life: before World War II and after World War II. He was entering his teenage years when the United States entered the war, and it made a lifetime impression on him.

Part 1 – The Concept of Bucket

As of this writing in late 2024 and early 2025, there are two significant wars, (1) Ukraine and Russia and (2) Israel and Palestinian terrorists, that have been ongoing for months driving global regional instability. I haven't been fortunate to visit Ukraine or Russia yet, but I have visited Israel with two of my sons and traveled near both the Gaza Strip and the West Bank. I'm sure both sons feel that they connect with the plight of both the Israelis and the Palestinians from our trip. The birth of Christianity through the birth of Jesus Christ lies in the religious center of Israel. Before Christianity, Judaism formed this land. Islam also lays claim to the territory. Does the expression *The Holy Land* embrace all three Abrahamic Religions? Will there ever be true world peace if three major religions cannot figure out how to share such sacred ground?

Through the age of discovery, European nations expanded their sphere of influence through colonization. These countries overextended their reach and could no longer wager control over those territories after considerable investment resulting in some progress in the lives of the inhabitants whether willing or not. De-colonization turned into war and destruction with either the colonized country fighting for independence such as the United States and England in 1776 or internal civil war over factions controlling the country. The twentieth century, although deemed the Industrial Age, was also the Age of De-colonization.

In the situation of Russia and Ukraine, is Ukraine an isolated case or is Russian expansion part of a grander strategic plan? What impact does this have on international stability? On my travels, I learned a lot about the history of countries which is crucial for understanding the problems of today because they are rooted in the actions of the past. In Samuel Huntington's bestselling book, *The Clash of Civilizations and Remaking of World Order*, published in 1996, he cites three outcomes for the precarious relationship between Ukraine and Russia: (1) conflict between Russia and Ukraine; (2) Ukraine splits apart; and (3) Ukraine remains independent but cooperates closely with Russia.

Why does he raise the potential for conflict between Ukraine and Russia in 1996? At various times in its history, Ukraine was independent but for most of later history it has been governed from Moscow. In 1654, the Cossack leader Bohdan Khmelnytsky swore allegiance to the Russian tsar in exchange for assistance in its uprising against Polish rule. Besides a brief independence from 1917 to 1920, Moscow largely politically controlled Ukraine. In the past, western Ukraine has been part of Poland, Lithuania, and the Austro-Hungarian empire. Culturally, western Ukraine has acclimated one-way towards European Slavs; eastern Ukraine has acclimated the other way towards Russo-Slavs, creating cultural splits between the regions. So over centuries of border shifts occurring, which footprint does the country, and the world accept as the appropriate one. Regardless of the actions of history, is the differentiating factor on policies what people want today?

The Israeli and Palestinian conflict has raged for decades. What solution will make both people whole since both lay claims to the same sacred ground? If God or Allah does exist, have the children created a world over a couple of millennia that now meets the vision of faith. Learning about history in the Middle East affords one to understand the conditions for which faith-based religions derived and possible connections into the state and actions of today.

The outbreak of COVID-19 and the transference across national lines taught the world interconnectedness and vulnerability. Do international organizations such as the United Nations have the right clout to resolve international problems, problems that do not recognize boundaries?

Whether designated a United Nations Education, Science, Cultural Organization (UNESCO) World Heritage Site or recognized as a Wonder of the World, does the international community have a voice in the protection of these historically significant structures to ensure their protection and at what cost? Although the nation holds claims to its territory, does the safety of these treasures elevate to a higher level of responsibility. Once they are gone, the door is closed forever for further discovery and understanding of the global past.

The Buddha statutes in Bamiyan, Afghanistan were destroyed by the Taliban government in 2001 based on their religious beliefs. Since then, UNESCO has made the Bamiyan Valley a World Heritage Site, one of the few in Afghanistan. Ironically, now that the Taliban is back in power, they have turned the site into a tourist attraction charging the equivalent of $5 to wander around and take photos of the giant holes left in the cliffs where the ancient statues existed. The two sixth century statues, one at 180 feet (54.9 m) tall and the other at 124 feet (37.8 m) tall, towered over the valley and represented the Buddhist holy site on the ancient trading route, the Silk Road, between China and Europe.[1]

UNESCO's vision is truly worthy for an international organization focused on the betterment of all countries and their people.

Since wars begin in the minds of men and women, it is in the minds of men and women that peace must be built. UNESCO uses education, science, culture, communication and information to foster mutual understanding and respect for our planet. We work to strengthen the intellectual and moral solidarity of humankind and bring out the best in our shared humanity.[2]

UNESCO originated on November 16, 1945, growing to have 195 Members and eight Associate Members that govern by a General Conference and an Executive Board.

Learning to live with history, good or bad, is a quest for all governing nations, both its citizens and leadership. The United States has gone through a period renaming federal buildings or federal complexes that were originally named after a Confederate leader of the Civil War. This Civil War will always be part of history of states in the north and south of the United States. Through my trips, I've learned the difficult histories of other countries and how they are reconciling that today.

Although the United States fought England during the American Revolution, it has maintained a good relationship with the United Kingdom for decades. Although the United States fought Japan during World War II, a good relationship developed and has lasted for decades. The European Union has brought a more integrated Europe than ever before, although during the medieval period Western Europe was in constant conflict. There is hope that adversaries can become allies because history reflects this outcome. Is the ability to deal with ambiguity one of the most critical attributes for people to acquire to develop peace and maintain it? Is ignorance a core element for individual's misconceptions of the difference in social or cultural aspects?

My trips over the past year were a journey in knowledge, adventure, exploration, and most importantly learning. I documented in a written journal as much information as I could remember during the trip and then researched the various topics to ensure my understanding and accuracy of information. Sometimes interpretations of information can be different which leads to a different perspective and conclusion. I hope by reading this book you are on a third-party journey of exploration and learning by making your own sense of the information provided. A life-long reader, I have included information from the many books that I have read over decades to gain a greater understanding of the information acquired during my trips.

Since the information provided in this book is through my lens of knowledge acquired through my five senses, a review of my background is beneficial to the reader. I was selected in 2016 as a Defense Intelligence Senior Leader to the Naval Intelligence Activity, previously serving as the Director for Acquisition and Contracts at the Office of Naval Intelligence. I previously deployed supporting *Operation Enduring Freedom* as the Senior Advisor to the Afghan National Security Force from 2012 to 2014 for acquisition and logistics. I also deployed as the Senior Advisor for acquisition to the Iraqi Ministry of Defense from 2010 to 2011, focusing on improvements to their acquisition processes supporting *Operation Iraqi Freedom* and *Operation New Dawn*.

Throughout my thirty-nine years with the United States Navy as a civilian, I served in several positions both engineering and program management, starting my career at the Naval Air Development Center in Warminster, Pennsylvania as an engineer in life support systems conducting over forty engineering and accident investigations in oxygen systems and identifying and resolving problems. I also led research and development and science and technology programs for oxygen and life support systems.

As part of the Capitol Hill Fellowship Program in 1998, I served as the Military Legislative Assistant to Congressman

Patrick Kennedy, a then-member of the House Armed Services Committee. The areas that I provided guidance to the Congressman were on defense, intelligence, budget committee, government reform, and women's issues. I also spent eighteen months as an action officer/policy analyst in the Office of the Deputy Assistant Secretary of the Navy (Air Programs) from 2000 to 2001. As part of a Government Affairs Institute legislative course, I drafted the paper *Presidential and Congressional Relations: The Conflict of Vieques Island* requested by Chief of Naval Operations (CNO)(N87) on the issue of live fire training on the Vieques Island range and recommendations on strategic solutions between the United States and Puerto Rico.

I hold a Bachelor of Science in Engineering Technology from Temple University and several master's degrees: Master of Engineering from Pennsylvania State University; Master of Art in International Relations from Salve Regina University; Master of Science in Business Administration from Temple University, majoring in Management Science/Operations Research; and Master of Science in National Security Resource Strategy from Industrial College of the Armed Forces. I also hold a Doctoral degree in Civil and Environmental Engineering with a major in Project Management from the University of Maryland (UMD).

My dissertation titled, *Defense Institutional Building-Integrating the Work*, is a deep and wide-dive assessment in combining campaign planning and project management planning to achieve performance in asymmetric warfare. I proposed a system approach to leverage network theory and complexity science strengthened through centralized planning but optimized through de-centralized execution. Managing and leveraging the interdependencies of activities (work) creates exponential performance (S-curve model). I have continued my technical learning through courses in areas of information technology and artificial intelligence.

To supplement my academics, I acquired additional coursework at the graduate-level and accreditations in multiple areas. I graduated from the College of Command and Staff of the Naval War College, received a Master Certificate in Legislative Studies from Georgetown University, a Master Certificate in Contract Management from George Washington University, certification in Agile Project Management from UMD, and certification in Executive Data Science from John Hopkins University. I completed the Fundamentals of Neuroscience Xseries and China Xseries from HarvardX online courses.

I have also completed leadership and management programs in government and academia: the Department of Defense (DoD) Acquisition Professional Community, Senior Acquisition course, Naval Air Systems Command Senior Executive Management Development Program, the United States government Executive Potential Program, DoD Defense Leadership and Management Program, Leadership in the Intelligence Community, and Sloan Executive

Certification of the Massachusetts Institute of Technology in Advanced Certificate for Executive in Management, Innovation, and Technology.

Through this period of time, I received several recognitions and awards: two Joint Civilian Service Commendation awards, two Global War of Terrorism awards, North Atlantic Treaty Organization (NATO) medal, Naval Air Warfare Center Innovation Award for Program Management, and the Daniel S. McCauley Professional Achievement Award for Engineering. I have also published several papers on system mathematical modeling, maintenance data and reliability, project management, international relations, intelligence, and leadership.

The knowledge and experiences acquired through travel are viewed through this knowledge lens and combined to develop new insights and perspectives. Every traveler will synthesize their new knowledge through their own lens. Yes, I have a very diversified education and experience background. So, I hope you enjoy walking in my literary footprints while getting inside my head as I explore new and old places over the year. After reading this book, many a traveler will associate themselves to being an intellectual traveler with the purpose to better understand the world and the people and places that are in it.

Part 1

THE CONCEPT OF BUCKET LIST

This section will set the stage for the rest of the book providing the description and foundation for bucket list travel activities. Although bucket lists can encompass more than just travel, this book limited the scope to travel related bucket list activities. One might be surprised with the numerous options.

Part 1 – The Concept of Bucket

Chapter 1

The Rationale of a Bucket List

What is a bucket list? Why make one? And what are potential man-made bucket list sites? As cited by Stanford Medicine's Letter Project, a bucket list is several experiences or achievements that one hopes to have or accomplish during their lifetime or before they *kick the bucket.*

The focus of a bucket list is to live a life with hopes and aspirations. Making a bucket list allows us to reflect on our values and goals and identify important milestones and experiences that we want to have in our lifetime.[3]

Although the definition includes lifetime, I've never heard a ten-year-old or eighteen-year-old refer to a bucket list of experiences or achievements over a lifetime. Most are more focused on short-term goals, getting through school and entering the workforce. People in their twenties are probably starting to think about what lifetime experiences or achievements they want outside of getting married and having a family. Traveling is one such experience that many people tend to focus a little later in life. Although, there are some younger people that put travel first before starting their career or family. For this reason, there are tourism organizations that cater to the younger crowd designing tours that provide a more active experience that may be challenging for the older generation. I caution one when searching for an organized tour group to ensure alignment with your physical capability and interests.

Let's back up, where did the phrase *kick the bucket* originate? Well, like other expressions, it has several legendary origins. According to the experts on information, Wikipedia has a couple of possibilities.[4] It possibly originated from Medieval hangings when the bucket was kicked out from someone or under suicide circumstances when one stepped from a bucket with a rope around their neck. Another possibility has to do with a pig suspended from a beam or bucket as it was referred to and the pig sometimes still struggling during the slaughter therefore referred to kicking the bucket.

None of these possible origins bring a very good feeling to be associated with the more positive feelings of a bucket list. A third refers to the Catholic practice of holy water buckets positioned at the feet of the corpse for people to sprinkle holy water over the body. Well, this one brings a little more optimism. Regardless of which derivation one accepts, the phrase has come to symbolize one's limited time on earth and the eventual end of the physical being.

For all those familiar with the Myers-Briggs personality test, the concept of making a list of objectives and goals and checking them off will entice the combination of a thinking and judging person. This type of personality is driven to planning and meeting objectives. A defined bucket list of life objectives and accomplishments fits their calling in life. An excel spreadsheet is a useful approach to manage the bucket list, one column for the activity, one column for the date of accomplishment, a column for notes, and any other columns that provide detail for the undertaking.

The flip side of judging is the perceiving person who does not like to be tied down with plans but prefers to be spontaneous. Although this can provide excitement for any occasion, it can be counterproductive to making the most out of experiences by leveraging the planning element. For example, planning and getting tickets for venue admissions can reduce waiting in line or even guarantee admittance versus showing up at the last minute and waiting a long time for no ticket. This next statement will make perceivers cringe, plan for spontaneity. In other words, the activities one most wants to do need to be planned but one should allow time for spontaneity to embrace what happens and be adaptable in the moment. Being tied to a plan for an entire vacation can feel like work or a chore, so allowing time for whatever just happens to be available allows one to be freewheeling, a bohemian.

Wonders Lists

So, you have decided that you want to add travel to your bucket list. The world is a very big place, so how do you decide where you want to go. Here are the wonders lists that no traveler would want to miss.

With respect to traveling, there are many approaches to

borrowing bucket list goals, such as the seven wonders lists. These lists are not part of the United Nations Educational, Scientific and Cultural Organization (UNESCO) effort although there are UNESCO sites that happen to be on a wonders list. The original list of the seven wonders, now referred to as seven wonders of the ancient world, was constructed by Philo of Byzantium written in 225 BC.

Philo of Byzantium, also known as Philo Mechanicus, was a Greek engineer, physicist, and writer on mechanics, who lived during the latter half of the third century BC.[5] Although he was from Byzantium (Türkiye today), he lived most of his life in Alexandria, Egypt. No surprise that the list compromises structures in Greece, Turkey, Iraq, and Egypt. Talk about someone being ahead of their time.

More recently, organizations have established their own lists to include Seven Wonders of the Modern World, Seven Wonders of Nature, seven wonders of cities, Seven Wonders of the Underworld, Seven Wonders of the Industrialized World, Seven Wonders of the Solar System, seven wonders within various countries, and the list goes on. Clearly, it's a case of jumping on the Philo bandwagon and making your own list of seven wonders of anything. The magic number of seven probably relates to the original list having seven items. Seven has become the magic number for wonders.

If Philo had constructed the list with ten, lists would be generated with ten wonders versus seven wonders. All those in favor of the metric system would raise the fact that standardizing on the number ten is just a foundation of civilization, whether a measuring system or a rewarding system, factors of ten typically designate an optimal number to be recognized. These ancient wonders represent structures that achieved a level of creativity and capability of their time centuries ago. These amazing works serve as a testament to the ingenuity, imagination, persistence, and commitment of early mankind. The only structure still existing today is the Great Pyramid of Giza in Egypt. Meanwhile, the other structures were verified through documentation but have either disappeared through natural phenomena, such as earthquakes or hurricanes; destruction through wars; or deterioration through time.

The locations of these wonders are known except the Babylon Gardens. The specific site of the gardens is not known but Babylon ruins are in central Iraq about 50 miles (80.5 km) south of Baghdad on the Euphrates River.

The Seven Wonders of the Ancient World

When modern historians wanted to introduce a list of sites more modern like after the time of Christ, they needed to differentiate between Philo's list and the new list, thus the original Seven Wonders of the World became the Seven Wonders of the Ancient World. I think National Geographic, the world expert on the study of nature and people, said it best:

The Seven Wonders of the Ancient World, selected by

Hellenic travelers and noted in poetry and other arts, tell the stories of human imagination and technical aptitude, and how civilizations left their marks on the world and culture. Amid the march of progress throughout the modern world, evidence of Earth's rich past exists in historical constructions that tell stories of human achievement. Among these, seven were deemed "wonders": hallowed examples of the contributions of ancient Mediterranean and Middle Eastern civilizations.[6]

To watch an informative video on the seven ancient wonders of the world, see the Ancient History Encyclopedia website link: https://youtu.be/1YWPMZ6pHm8. I've provided an overview of these significant accomplishments of world history.

The Great Pyramid of Giza, Egypt

A trip to Egypt can arguably be one of the most memorable events in one's life. It should include visiting the Great Pyramid of Giza, located about ten miles southwest of Cairo. One may even enter it through the middle of the north side and climb the ramp to the top chamber. Beware, there is no picture-taking allowed in the top chamber. There is also no ventilation so it can be very hot and stuffy, especially in the summer. I checked this ancient wonder bucket list box in February of 2019.

According to archaeologists' estimates, the Great Pyramid was completed around 2560 BCE, taking 20 years to build and rising to 482 feet (147 m) high, although settling has reduced the size to 451 feet (138 m). To understand the magnitude of its size, it is made from 2.3 million large, cut-stone blocks weighing about 2 ½ tons each, totaling 5.75-million-tons (5.22-million-metric-tons). It is believed that Napoleon Bonaparte visited the Great Pyramid in 1798 and calculated that there were enough stones to build a one- foot-wide (0.3 m), 12-feet-high (3.7 m) wall around France. Although sources conflict with the actual dimensions of Napoleon's estimate, he did provide an assessment before the Battle of the Pyramids. Sounds like Napoleon had a budding civil engineer within him. Maybe if he had channeled his energies in that direction, he would not have tried to conquer all of Europe. For those interested in project management in an ancient construction application, an interesting paper is *The Pyramids and Implementing the Project Management Process* by Dr. Alaa A. Zeitoun and Dr. Ahny W. Helmy.

The Great Pyramid was not only the largest pyramid ever built but remained the tallest structure in the world until the late nineteenth century. Philo got it right with this selection for one of the seven ancient wonders. It is believed that it was built as a burial site to honor Pharoah Khufu. Khufu was the second king of the fourth dynasty in ancient Egypt, ruling for 23 years in the late twenty-sixth century BCE. He was the son of Pharoah Sneferu and Queen Hetepheres I. Pharoah Sneferu built previous pyramids, but his son Khufu outdid the father building his larger and remaining the largest. Was this the battle of egos?

Little is known of the builder of the Great Pyramid. He became pharaoh and had two children, Djedefra and Khafre, and had at least three wives. Khafre built one of the other two pyramids next to his father's and the Sphinx. Khafre's son, Menkaura, built the third pyramid. So, this complex includes three generations of pyramid building.

More is known about the Great Pyramid which covers a little over 13 acres. Although each side is not the same length, they are about 756 feet (230 m) long. Each corner is nearly an exact 90-degree angle. Each side is also aligned to face one of the directions of north, east, south, and west. Inside the Great Pyramid are three burial chambers, one below ground, one just above ground, and one in the heart of the structure. It is believed that Khufu was buried in this chamber in a heavy, granite coffin. In 818 CE, the Arab ruler Caliph Ma'mum attempted to loot the pyramid but found that the Grand Gallery and granite coffin had already been emptied of treasure. In a rage, he had the limestone covering removed and took about 30 feet (9.1 m) of the cut-stone blocks off the top to use for building. Wow, as far back as the ninth century, robbers were breaking into pyramids to steal relics to make a quick buck.

The Great Pyramid of Giza is located about ten miles southwest of Cairo. Recently, the Grand Egyptian Museum was built near the Giza necropolis with a bypass road around Cairo establishing a route from the airport to the pyramid complex. The original Egyptian Museum is in Cairo near Tahrir Square, the location of the January 25, 2011 protest, known as the Day of Revolt, against the Mubarak government. The three pyramids were added to the UNESCO World Heritage List in 1979.

The Lighthouse at Alexandria, Egypt

The Lighthouse of Alexandria was built between 285 and 247 BC on Pharos Island standing at a height of at least 350 feet (107 m). For centuries, it was considered the tallest building in the ancient world; however, it did not pass the test of time, nor was it built to be earthquake-proof, falling into ruin in 1375 AD. Although the lighthouse no longer stands, some of its materials still reside in the area. In 1480, lighthouse materials were used to build the Citadel of Qaitbay, a fortress on Pharos Island built for the Sultan of Egypt. Lasting over 1500 years is an exceptional feat. In 1994, Jean Yves Empereur, a French archeologist at the French National Research Center, investigated the Alexandria harbor and found at least a few of the blocks still reside in the water.

The city of Alexandria located in northern Egypt on the Mediterranean Sea was founded in 332 BC by Alexander the Great. Alexander's successor, Ptolemy Soter, ordered the lighthouse constructed to assist sailors navigating the Alexandria harbor, taking 40 years to complete. It comprised three sections: the bottom section was square and held government offices and stables, the middle section was an octagon and held a balcony for observers to admire the view, and the top section was cylindrical and held a fire that was continually lit to provide a light for sailors to avoid the rocks. At the very top was a large statue of Poseidon, the Greek god of the sea. The lighthouse was a trendsetter with many of the lighthouses today constructed with a similar design.

I checked this box on the same trip to Egypt in February 2019 but not through the organized group tour, which was focused on Cairo and the southern Nile River. I added a few days on the end of the trip to travel to Alexandria for its Roman ruins and locate the spot where the lighthouse resided. When planning a trip to Egypt, it is worth spending some time in Alexandria.

Hanging Gardens of Babylon, Iraq

Babylon ruins are in central Iraq about 50 miles (80.5 km) south of modern Baghdad along the Euphrates River. Babylon was the largest city of the Babylonian empire, founded more than 4000 years ago, becoming one of the most powerful cities under King Hammurabi. Centuries later, the Neo-Babylonian Empire expanded to encompass the Persian Gulf to the Mediterranean Sea. During this period, Babylon became a city of beautiful architecture with the hanging gardens, Ishtar Gate, and the Tower of Babel.

During the Neo-Babylon period, King Nebuchadnezzar (605-562 BCE) had the hanging gardens built as a gift to his wife Amytis, a Persian princess, to comfort her homesickness for the green forests of her homeland of Media, a city in the northwestern part of modern Iran. To ensure adequate water supply to the gardens, an engineering wonder needed to be constructed. Scientists believe a system of pumps, waterwheels, and cisterns were employed to raise and deliver the water from the Euphrates River to the top of the gardens.

In 539 BCE, Persian ruler Cyrus the Great conquered Babylon during the Battle of Opis. Since Babylon's walls were considered impregnable, the Persians diverted the flow of the Euphrates River so that it fell to a crossable depth. Although Babylon fell to Persian control, the city flourished as a center of art and education. Babylonian mathematics, cosmology, and astronomy were highly respected with Pythagoras developing his famous mathematical theorem based on a Babylonian model.

By 331 BCE, Alexander the Great conquered vast areas of the Persian empire including Babylon. History created the question of whether there were one or two gardens. An Oxford historian found evidence that a garden existed in Nineveh located 300 miles (483 km) north of Babylon, but other site references include documents of Alexander's time, denote gardens in Babylon during his rule and death in 323 BC.

Since the question of the exact location of the hanging gardens is a mystery, I'm checking this box based on my experience in the Defense Department. I spent 15 months in Baghdad, Iraq as part of the Ministry of Defense Advisor program in 2010- 2011 advising the Iraqi Ministry of Defense on acquisition and logistics. That's probably closer than most people will get to the origins of the Hanging Gardens of Babylon with Iraq still a security risk for travel.

The Statue of Zeus at Olympia, Greece

Most trips to Greece's mainland will include a trip to Olympia. I checked this box during August 2017 when touring the Greek mainland. Although the statue of gold, ivory, and wood stood over 40 feet (12 m) tall depicting the Greek god Zeus seated on a cedar throne around 435 BC by the sculptor Phidias, the statue disappeared around the fifth century presumably destroyed. Olympia was a sanctuary, a place of protection, a place to worship, and a place for the ancient Olympic games located on the Greek Peloponnese Peninsula. The first ancient Olympic game was held in 776 BCE with the foot-race winner Coroebus of Elis, a local entry from the town of Elis. Around 600 BCE, a temple was built for Hera, the goddess of marriage and wife of Zeus. It was at this spot that the Olympic torch was lit in ancient and modern times.

To celebrate their triumph of the Triphylian War, the people of Elis built a new more elaborate temple for Zeus at Olympia. Although construction started in 470 BCE, it did not finish until 456 BCE depicting Doric architecture, a rectangular building with a platform-oriented east-to-west. One side of the rectangular building held 13 columns while the other side had six columns. The columns made of local limestone were covered with plaster and supported by the marble roof. The exterior of the temple was detailed with sculpted scenes from Greek mythology while the interior was kept simpler to emphasize the Zeus' statue. True of Greek mythology, stories are documented on structures. Over the entrance to the temple on the east side sat a chariot scene from the story of Pelops and Oenomaus. The western side depicted the battle between Lapiths and the Centaurs. Although the temple was considered impressive, the selection for wonders of the world specifically cited the statue's magnificence.

It was designed by sculptor Phidius, whose works include the large statue of Athena for the Parthenon. It is the description of the statue left by the second geographer Pausanias in the second century CE that is noteworthy. Zeus, the king of all Greek gods stood 40 feet (12 m) tall with a beard sitting upon a royal throne, in his right hand holding a figure of Nike, the winged goddess of victory, and in his left hand, a scepter topped with an eagle. The statue sat on a three-foot (1 m) pedestal. Although the size was unequaled, it is the beauty instilled from rare materials that elevated it above all others. Zeus' skin was made of ivory, and his robe made of plates of gold decorated with detailed animals and flowers. The throne was made of ivory, precious stones, and ebony.

The life of an artist in ancient times can be rather precarious. Phidius was later jailed on the offense of including his and his friend Pericles' images within the Parthenon. He died in prison awaiting his trial. The Zeus statue lasted for

800 years being oiled regularly to avoid damage by the humid climate. In 393 CE, the Christian Emperor Theodosius I banned the Olympic Games. Emperor Theodosius II ordered the statue destroyed by setting fire to it, the remnants were then later destroyed by earthquakes. Excavations in Olympia have uncovered the base of the temple and the workshop of Phidius. Although Christianity brought the spirit of love, hope, and charity through Jesus, it also resulted in an intolerance of pagan beliefs of Greek and Roman culture. Unfortunately, the destruction of temples and statues resulted.

The Colossus of Rhodes, Rhodes, Greece

I checked this box as part of a Mediterranean cruise through the Greek Isles in August 2017. If you are specifically looking to see this sight, then you want to plan a trip to Rhodes or ensure a cruise to the Greek Islands includes Rhodes. Again, one can only stand at the harbor and look out over what was there and not what is there now. The bronze and iron statue of the Greek sun-God Helios stood 110 feet (33 m) tall, about the size of the Statue of Liberty. It finished in 282 BCE but stood for only 56 years before it was destroyed by an earthquake. For 900 years, the remaining huge pieces stayed on the beaches as a tribute to the work of man or possibly too cumbersome for man to remove. What is the story behind the purpose of the statue?

For a year, the city of Rhodes had been at war caught between the rivals of Alexander the Great's successors:

Ptolemy, Seleucus, and Antigonus. It was Antigonus' son, Demetrius, who attacked the city for supporting Ptolemy. One could say that Demetrius's approach was one of overwhelming force: 40,000 troops (more than the population of Rhodes), catapults, and special engineers adept at designing weapons for attacking Rhodes, such as a 150-foot (46 m) tower mounted on iron wheels to hold the catapult. The shrewd Rhodians flooded the area around the city, causing the tower to get stuck in the mud. Demetrius's sluggish attack allowed sufficient time for Ptolemy to send reinforcements from Egypt. Demetrius fled the city leaving his massive weaponry behind. The Rhodians so enthralled with their success decided to build a giant statue in honor of their patron god, Helios. Is this a case of mind over matter? Although a sophisticated weapon for its time, the townspeople succeeded by introducing a mere flood.

To build the statue, the Rhodians used Demetrius' abandoned weapons for material or sold parts for funding. Of, the irony to construct the monument of victory using the parts or funding from the defeated weapon. Rhodian sculptor Chares of Lindos, a pupil of Alexander the Great's sculptor Lysippus, was chosen to design and build the massive statue. He would die before completing it. Exactly how it was built and what it looked like are debatable. The exterior consisted of an iron framework covered in bronze plates with an interior of two or three stone columns as the main support. Iron rods provided the connection between the stone columns and the iron framework.

In 654 CE, Rhodes was conquered by Arabs and after 900 years with the ruins lying dormant, the Colossus remains were shipped to Syria for trade. A myth of the Middle Ages is that the statue straddled Mandrákion Harbor. This is dismissed by experts who believe the lack of engineering proficiency at the time could accomplish the large span. This seems like a challenge for civil engineers to explore the possible construction based on engineering acumen of the period.

The Temple at Artemis at Ephesus, Türkiye

Türkiye is still on my bucket list but planned for Fall 2024. The Temple of Artemis, also known as Artemisium, was located near the current town of Selcuk in western Türkiye to honor the Greek goddess of hunting. The original temple existed before the seventh century when it was destroyed by flooding. A second temple existed from 550 BC to 356 BC, when it was burned to the ground by the arsonist Herostratus on July 21, 356 BC. The third temple was then destroyed by the invading Goths in 286 AD. The second version of the Temple of Artemis was built as a place to worship near the port city of Ephesus. It was the rebuilt version Philo awarded a place on the Wonders of the Ancient World list.

The Greek Artemis or Roman goddess Diana was the virgin goddess of hunting and wild animals and the twin sister of Apollo. She was often depicted with a bow and an arrow.

Combined with the local, pagan goddess of fertility, Cybele, known in Ephesus, she symbolized athletics, health, and fertility. Artemis was also the patron deity of the city of Ephesus. It was King Croesus of Lydia who commissioned the statue built on the previous version dating as early as 800 BCE.

The king wanted a temple more magnificent than the previous one. The new temple met his desires built to be larger than an American-football field at 350 feet (107 m) long by 180 feet (55 m) wide made from white marble. With 127 Ionic columns in two rows all around the structure, it reached 60 feet (18 m) in height, nearly twice as high as the columns in the Parthenon in Athens. Also, there was a notable change of the period, even the columns were covered in exquisite carvings. Inside this magnificent temple stood a life-sized statue of Artemis.

Sculptures that remain depicting Artemis illustrate her with her legs tightly wrapped together with a long skirt covered with animals, such as stags and lions, and her arms in front of her. A garland of flowers is around her neck and upon her head is either a hat or headdress. Most unusual is her torso covered with numerous breasts or eggs. Coincidently, the timing of the temple's burning and the birth of Alexander the Great on the same day created the legend that the goddess was too busy attending Alexander's birth to save her temple.

The story continues when Alexander the Great arrived in

Ephesus in 333 BCE, he offered to pay for rebuilding the Temple but was declined by the Ephesians so they could retain ownership. After the destruction by the Goths, the Ephesians now under the growth of Christianity chose not to rebuild the temple. The ruins of the Temple of Artemis were plundered for its marble and the site along with the city of Ephesus would succumb to swamp hiding the site for centuries. In 1864, John Turtle Wood, funded by the British Museum in London, excavated the area hoping to find the ruins. After five years of exploring, he found the remains under 25 feet (7.6 m) of swampy mud. Further excavations in 1904 would reveal more of the site. The artifacts found reside in the British Museum in London, of significance is a Hellenistic column drum of the sixth century CE with carved figures of Hades, Persephone, and Hermes.

The Mausoleum at Halicarnassus, Türkiye

Again, Türkiye is still on my bucket list but currently Bodrum is not part of the tour I planned for 2024. The Mausoleum at Halicarnassus, originally called the Tomb of Mausolus, was built around 350 BC. The Mausoleum was built to honor and retain the remains of Mausolus of Caria who died in 353 BCE; the construction was ordered by his wife Artemisia, who was also his sister, and she would eventually be buried there two years later. Artemisia commissioned five sculptors to design and build the tomb: Bryaxis for the north side, Scopas for the east side, Timotheus for the south side,

Leochares for the west side, and Pythis for the chariot atop the structure. The structure consisted of a square base, 36 columns arranged as nine on each side, and then topped by a pyramid with 24 steps. The chariot sat atop made of marble standing 25 feet (7.6 m) high with statues of Mausolus and Artemisia riding in the chariot pulled with horses. The entire structure was covered with lavish carvings. Wow, that would be really striking to see.

Although the grand structure survived for 1,800 years, it was earthquakes in the fifteenth century that would bring it down. The material of the ruins was used for building other structures in the area such as the Crusader fortress for the Knights of Saint John. It was in 1522 CE that the crypt was looted. The Mausoleum of Halicarnassus was forgotten, the area becoming more residential for the town. In the 1850s the British archeologist Charles Newton recognized some of the artifacts at Bodrum Castle, the new name for the Crusader fortress, could be from the lost mausoleum. Newton went on to excavate the area and found the original site. The British Museum in London retains these findings.

The Seven Wonders of the Modern World

In the year 2000, a Swiss foundation launched a campaign to create a new list for the Seven Wonders of the Modern World, since only one site remained from the original ancient list. This new list was compiled in 2007. They kept the magical number seven but reduced the list down to 21 finalists with the winners for the Seven Wonders of the Modern World: Chichén Itza, Mexico; Colosseum, Italy; Machu Picchu, Peru; Christ the Redeemer Statue, Brazil; Petra, Jordan; Taj Mahal, India; the Great Wall of China, China. Yes, I intend to visit all these sites. My bucket list includes visiting all the runners-up too listed below in alphabetical order. Many tours include these places in their tour itinerary, so it is not that hard to put a dent in the list if one just starts traveling.

- Acropolis, Greece
- Alhambra, Spain
- Angkor, Cambodia
- Easter Island Statues, Chile
- Eiffel Tower, France
- Hagia Sophia, Türkiye
- Kyomizu Temple, Japan
- Kremlin, Russia
- Neuschwanstein Castle, Germany
- Pyramids of Giza, Egypt
- Statue of Liberty, United States
- Stonehenge, United Kingdom
- Sydney Opera House, Australia
- Timbuktu, Mali

Chichén Itza, Mexico

Chichén Itza is located on the Yucatán Peninsula in

Mexico. It originally was a Mayan town called Chichén Viejo settled in the fifth century with most of its significant archeological constructions from the sixth to the tenth century such as the Nunnery, the Church, Akab Dzib, Chichan Chob, the Temple of the Panels, and the Temple of the Deer.

The second settlement constituted the migration and inclusion of the Toltec warriors in the tenth century. According to legend, the King of Tula, Ce Acatl Topiltzin Quetzalcoatl, or Kukulkan as the Maya translated the name, reportedly took the city between 967 AD and 987 AD. After the thirteenth-century, construction was curtailed, and the city rapidly declined after 1440 AD. It wasn't until 1841 AD that the site was excavated.

The complex includes many monuments and temples, with the most significant being El Castillo or the Castle with a height of 79 feet (24 m) above the Main Plaza. It's always amazing the astronomical capability of ancient peoples to include this structure built with 365 steps equivalent to the number of days of the solar year. On par with an India Jones adventure, during the spring and autumn equinoxes, the sunset casts shadows on the pyramid that gives the appearance of a serpent slithering down the north stairway. A stone snake's head resides at the base.

Another significant attribute of Chichén Itzá is that it has the largest tlachtli at 545 feet (166 m) long and 223 feet (68 m) wide, a type of sporting field, in the Americas. The field was used for a ceremonial ball game popular throughout pre-Columbian Mesoamerica. It has been a UNESCO World Heritage Site since 1988, for the fusion of construction techniques within the Mayan and Toltec civilizations. Besides El Castillo, the Warrior's Temple, and El Caracol, the circular observatory survived.

Surrounding El Castillo are terraces where the major monumental complexes were built: on the north-west are the Great Ball Court, Tzompantli or the Skull Wall, the temple known as the Jaguar Temple, and the House of Eagles; on the north-east are the Temple of the Warriors, the Group of the Thousand Columns, the Market and the Great Ball Court; on the south-west is the Tomb of the High Priest.[7]

Chichén Itzá or translated *at the edge of the well of the Itzaes* denotes the name of the settlement for its underground water resource.

Colosseum, Italy

A trip to Rome necessitates a tour of the Colosseum. I checked this off my bucket list on my trip to Italy in April 2023 which is described later in the book. The Colosseum, also named the Flavian Amphitheater, was built under the ruler Emperor Vespasian in the first century between 70-72 CE. Like all Wonders of the Modern World, it is an engineering feat for the period. The amphitheater measure 620 feet by 513 feet (189 m by 156 m) with a complex system of barrel and groin vaults built as freestanding and made of stone and concrete.

The structure can hold 50,000 spectators with 80 entrances to watch combat events for entertainment. Is the beauty of the structure marred by the activities that partook there? Possibly 500,000 people died in the Colosseum, including public executions, with the legend that Christians were martyred here by the Roman pagans. Besides the gladiators who fought each other, the destruction of animals for entertainment also provided carnal enjoyment, possibly yielding the extinction of some species. Is this where the enthusiasm for boxing or bullfighting originated? Does human nature drive an internal thrill for violence? If so, is humanity forever rooted in emotional violence or will humanity evolve to a better compassionate species?

Although the interest in the brutality of combat games diminished, it was the fall of the Western Roman Empire that initiated significant decline. The Colosseum started its deterioration with earthquakes in the fifth century damaging much of the structure. By the twentieth century, nearly two-thirds of the original structure were destroyed. A restoration project in the 1990s saved the structure from further decline and made it a bucket list check for travelers to Rome.

Machu Picchu, Peru

Machu Picchu is the Incan site located near Cuzco, Peru. Discovered by Hiram Bingham in 1911, he believed it to be Vilcabamba, a secret Incan stronghold used during the sixteenth-century rebellion against the Spanish rule. That claim has since been disapproved but the purpose of Machu Picchu still confounds scholars. Some theories are the home to the Virgins of the Sun, women who lived in convents under a vow of chastity; a pilgrimage site; or a royal retreat. Regardless of its purpose, it is one of the few major pre-Columbian ruins that remain largely intact. It has agricultural terraces, plazas, residential areas, and temples.

Even today, the site can only be accessed by train or on foot, no roads lead to the small- town Agua Caliente located at the base of the mountain. The train ride from Cusco through the Andes Mountains is an enjoyable ride. In the book *Turn Right at Machu Picchu* by Mark Adams, an archaeologist enamored with Hiram Bingham's trek, he documents retracing Bingham's expedition in 1911. I made this trip to Machu Picchu in May 2018 with my twenty-something son. More information on this trip can be found in the chapter for my trip to Peru.

Christ the Redeemer Statue, Brazil

Christ the Redeemer, a massive statue of Jesus, presides atop Mount Corcovado overlooking Rio de Janeiro and became a Wonder of the Modern World in 2007. Its construction was originally proposed in 1850 by priest Pedro Mario in honor of Emperor Pedro II's daughter, Princess Isabel. Its planning dates to World War I when Brazilians feared a period of godlessness. The statue was designed by

Frenchman Paul Landowski with Brazilian engineer Heitor da Silva Costa to symbolize peace, protection, and blessing. The construction started in 1926 and took five years to complete. The statue stands 98 feet (30 m) tall with a base of 26 feet (8 m) high and outstretched arms span 92 feet (28 m). Its ultimate claim is that it is the largest Art Deco sculpture in the world. The statue is made of reinforced concrete covered with approximately six million tiles; now I know why it took five years. Ironically, Christ the Redeemer is a lightning rod for God since it has often been struck. In 2014, Jesus lost the tip of his right thumb during a storm. Christ the Redeemer has been a UNESCO World Heritage Site since 2012 as part of the Rio de Janeiro: Carioca Landscapes between the Mountain and the Sea.

A good idea spreads. While visiting Lisbon, Portugal, I noticed a version of the Jesus statue that stands next to the 25 de Abril Bridge as our coach drove across the bridge. In fact, you can't miss it. The Portuguese version, Christ the King or Cristo Rei, is on the banks of the Tagus River. The bridge is designed similar to the Golden Gate Bridge in San Francisco, California in the United States. The bridge connects Almada and Lisbon with the statue 436 feet (133 m) above the sea. After the Cardinal Patriarch of Lisbon visited Christ the Redeemer, he supported a version for the Portuguese adopting its purpose for gratification that Portugal was spared direct destruction during World War II. The statue was inaugurated on May 17, 1959. The statue is part of the

Sanctuary of Christ the King, a Catholic monument and shrine in Almada.

Petra, Jordan

Petra is literally an Indiana Jones adventure. The site was used in the 1989 film *Indiana Jones and the Last Crusade* with Harrison Ford's quest to find the Holy Grail. Other movies that used the deserts of southern Jordan for filming are *Lawrence of Arabia* (1962), *The Martian* (2015), *Aladdin* (2019), and *Dune* (2021). Petra is located within a remote valley nestled among breathtaking mountains and cliffs between the Red Sea and the Dead Sea. During the Exodus of the Israelites, Moses passed through this area. It is believed to be the location at Wadi Musa (Valley of Moses) where Moses struck a rock and water gushed forth creating a spring from the barren land. As depicted in Numbers 20:10- 11 in the Bible: *And Moses and Aaron gathered the congregation together before the rock, and he said unto them, Hear now, ye rebels; must we fetch you water out of this rock? And Moses lifted up his hand, and with his rod he smote the rock twice; and the water came out abundantly, and the congregation drank; and their beasts also.*[8]

The Arab Nabataeans made it their capitol becoming an important trade center, especially for spices. A crossroads for Arabia, Egypt, and Syria-Phoenicia. The Nabataeans carved beautiful dwellings and rock formations into the sandstone causing the colors to shift with the sun. Even more impressive was the irrigation system that provided for lush gardens and farming. The most photographed area of Petra is called the Treasury or Al- Khazneh, carved into the rock with intricate carvings of the afterlife. It was built to be a mausoleum and crypt holding the remains of Nabatean King Aretas IV. It acquired the name treasury based on local Bedouins who believed the structure contained riches.

Petra's population peaked at 30,000 but eventually declined when the trade routes shifted. A major earthquake in 363 CE created problems in the city then eventually abandoned after a tremor in 551 CE. Although the city was discovered in 1912, archaeologists did little until late in the twentieth century. This became a UNESCO World Heritage Site in 1985.

The fusion of Hellenistic architectural facades with traditional Nabataean rock-cut temple/tombs including the Khasneh, the Urn Tomb, the Palace Tomb, the Corinthian Tomb and the Deir (monastery) represents a unique artistic achievement and an outstanding architectural ensemble of the first centuries BC to AD. The varied archaeological remains and architectural monuments from prehistoric times to the medieval periods bear exceptional testimony to the now lost civilisations which succeeded each other at the site.[9]

I have this trip planned for December of 2024 and I can't wait. I'll pack my Indiana Jones hat and plenty of suntan lotion for the desert climate. Any trip to Jordan should include a visit to Petra but also Wadi Rum for an overnight glamping excursion. What is more adventurous than camping on the sand in the desert? I hope a camel ride is also part of that trip.

Taj Mahal, India

The most romantic Wonder of the Modern World is the Taj Mahal in Agra, India built by Emperor Shah Jahān who reigned between 1628-1658. He built the structure to honor his third of eight wives Mumtāz Maḥal who died in 1631 giving birth to their fourteenth child. The love story reads that the couple were inseparable since their marriage in 1612. This structural dedication to love took 22 years with 20,000 workers and includes a vast garden and reflecting pool over a 42-acre site. Of course, gardens and pools reflect love. To further accentuate romance and a feminine mood, the mausoleum is made of white marble with semi-precious stones in geometric and floral patterns. The structure is situated on the eastern part of the city and the southern bank of the Yamuna River; it is considered the finest example of Mughal architecture with a blending of Indian, Persian, and Islamic designs.

The white marble of the mausoleum reflects hues according to the intensity of the sunlight or moonlight. The structure stands at 23 feet (7 m) high with four similar facades encompassing a wide central arch rising to 108 feet (33 m) at the apex and slanted corners with smaller arches.

The grand central dome stands 240 feet (73 m) to the top of its finial with four lesser domes surrounding it. A most interesting note, the acoustics inside the dome cause the single note of a flute to reverberate five times. Cenotaphs or false tombs reside for Mumtaz Mahal and Shah Jahān with the true sarcophagi lying beneath the tombs at the garden-level.

The structure became a UNESCO World Heritage Site in 1983. What made it so captivating as a UNESCO-selected site: *the Taj Mahal is considered to be the greatest architectural achievement in the whole range of Indo-Islamic architecture. Its recognised architectonic beauty has a rhythmic combination of solids and voids, concave and convex and light shadow; such as arches and domes further increases the aesthetic aspect. The colour combination of lush green scape reddish pathway and blue sky over it show cases the monument in ever- changing tints and moods. The relief work in marble and inlay with precious and semi-precious stones make it a monument apart.*[10]

How does this love story end? It is believed that Shah Jahān intended to build another mausoleum made from black marble across the river for his remains. The two symbols of love would be connected by a bridge across the river. Unfortunately, he was deposed by his son Aurangzeb in 1658 and served the rest of his life in prison at Agra Fort. I guess the son was not as much of a romantic as the father.

The Great Wall of China, China

Part 1 – The Concept of Bucket

Although internet sites boast that the Great Wall of China can be seen from space, this is a fallacy. The wall blends into the landscape and therefore is not visible. But it still would be impressive to see first-hand. It is one of the world's largest construction projects at 13,170 miles (21,196 km) long; however, the most preserved section built during the Ming dynasty (1368-1644) is 5,500 miles (8,850 km). The construction started in the seventh century BCE and continued for 2000 years.

Parts of the wall contain two parallel walls with watchtowers and barracks. Designed for protection from invasion, the size may have achieved political propaganda and intimidation to rivals.

Early sections of a wall date back to 770-221 BC when small states or princedoms built walls to denote and protect their borders. It was under the Qin Dynasty (221–206 BC) when Qin Shi Huang conquered and unified the states instructing the walls be joined together for a unified defense against Mongol invasions from the north. This unification constitutes the first Great Wall. During the Han Dynasty (206 BC-220 AD), the walls were reinforced and lengthened to further guard against the Mongols in the north. The wall spanned from the North Korea coastline near Pyongyang in the east to Jade Gate Pass in the west; it includes not only the fortified wall but branching walls, natural barriers such as rivers, and trenches.

During the Yuan Dynasty (1271-1368), China was

48

controlled by the Mongols, not the Han people, therefore China and Mongolia were one and the wall became obsolete. However, with the Ming Dynasty (1368-1644), China regained its independence, and the wall flourished with a 100-year rebuild project to protect it from further northern invasions. The Great Wall sections built near Beijing, such as Badaling and Mutianyu, were built during the Ming period. A breach in the wall at Shanhai Pass in 1644 by Manchu forces led to the end of Han control. The Qing Dynasty (1644-1911) ended with the Chinese Revolution when a nationalistic democratic revolt overthrew the dynasty and created a republic. With the death of Empress Dowager Cixi in 1908 and the succession of the child Emperor Puyi, his regency was unable to ward off unrest in the country. Eventually, the Badaling section was restored by the government of the People's Republic of China and opened to the public for tourism in 1957. The Great Wall became a UNESCO World Heritage Site in 1987.

Seven Wonders of the Twentieth Century

The American Society of Civil Engineers felt compelled to comprise their own list of Seven Wonders of the Twentieth Century in 1994. The factors judged were pioneering of design and construction, contributions to humanity, and engineering challenges that were overcome. As experts in man's modern capability to push the limits of construction, those listed below reflect achieving what was considered impossible:

- Channel Tunnel connecting France and the UK

- The CN Tower in Toronto
- The Empire State Building
- The Golden Gate Bridge
- The Itaipu Dam between Brazil and Paraguay
- The Netherlands North Sea Protection Works
- The Panama Canal

Well, this list just got added to my bucket list. I can check off the Empire State Building based on a Girl Scout field trip as a child to New York City. The Panama Canal is described later in Volume II of the follow-on book.

Chapter 2

Potential Natural Wonder Bucket List Items

Seven Natural Wonders of the World

How did the list originate? An investigative reporter working for CNN conducted a study on the world's most incredible natural wonders. The generated list includes atmospheric phenomena, harbor, canyon, mountain, volcano, reef, and waterfall. The Seven Natural Wonders of the World are Northern Lights or Aurora Borealis; Harbor of Rio de Janeiro, Brazil; Grand Canyon, United States; Great Barrier Reef, Australia; Mount Everest, Nepal; Paracutin, Mexico; and Victoria Falls, Africa.

Northern Lights or Aurora Borealis

The elusive Northern Lights may require a few quests to finally see this natural phenomenon. Although I traveled to Alaska during this year, the Northern Lights eluded my observations. While in the Anchorage area, it was too cloudy for viewing. The Fairbanks area had forecasted a better opportunity. With a trip planned for Iceland next year, specifically a quest for the Northern Lights, I hope to check this box. This is a bucket list item that one may want to check a few times; I don't think that one will get bored looking at this natural atmospheric phenomenon.

The Northern Lights or Aurora Borealis is seen in many countries in the aurora zone or northern lights belt, the oval-shaped region around the North Pole between 65– 72°N. Here are some countries where you can frequently see the northern lights: Iceland, Greenland, Norway, Finland, Sweden, Scotland, Canada, and Alaska of the United States. The Northern Lights are a natural light display caused when charged particles from the sun collide with gases in the Earth's upper atmosphere. The collisions produce flashes that fill the sky with colorful light.

With billions of flashes occurring in sequence, the auroras appear to move or dance in the sky. The stronger the solar storm, the brighter the light. Because the magnetic field of the Earth redirects the particles toward the poles, there are Southern Lights, Aurora Australis, too. However, there are fewer people living in these areas of the southern hemisphere to see them. The bright colors are dictated by the chemical composition of the Earth's atmosphere. The more dominant colors seen are red produced by nitrogen molecules and green produced by oxygen molecules.

Skywatching the Northern Lights is rather elusive because one can only marginally predict their visibility. Cloud cover will shield the show. The National Oceanic and Atmospheric Association (NOAA) Space Weather Prediction Center provides forecasts. To increase the chance of an Aurora Borealis sighting, plan a stay for a few days in one of the areas where frequent activity occurs. Many hotels specialize in viewing such as providing glass igloos for night observance and alarm systems to wake hotel occupants. Tour packages also specialize in maximizing the opportunity for Northern Lights encounter by allowing backup nights for failed attempts.

Harbor of Rio de Janeiro, Brazil

Some items on the natural wonders list are noteworthy for their size or magnitude, such is the case with the Harbor of Rio de Janeiro or Guanabara Bay in southern Brazil. It is the world's largest natural bay by volume. The bay covers 159 square miles (412 square km) with depths up to 56 feet (17 m). The entrance is framed by granite rock formations and monoliths. With notable landmarks such as Sugarloaf Mountain and Morro Cara de Cão, it draws millions of tourists a year. The initial arrival of the Portuguese colonialists to the harbor in 1502 makes it a significant historical site too. The backdrop of the city of Rio de Janeiro and its vibrant cultural life enhances the beauty of the bay's scenery for an urban setting. With Christ the Redeemer watching over the beautiful harbor and the vivacious city of Rio de Janeiro, God blessed Brazilians with a world-class landscape.

Despite the harbor's evolution into a major economic and human activity hub, featuring key locations in the city and popular beaches such as Copacabana, the bay's natural beauty endures. The way that city life has harmoniously blended with the bay's natural elements remains something of a conundrum. Although Guanabara Bay hosts one of the busiest ports in Brazil, it continues to be rich in biodiversity and wildlife, home to species such as dolphin pods, green sea turtles, jellyfish, tropical sea fish, Capuchin monkeys, hermit crabs, seahorses, great egrets, and more.[11]

A trip to Rio de Janeiro provides a double check for one of the Natural Wonders of the World and one of the Modern Wonders of the World. Two checks for the travel cost of one location.

Grand Canyon, United States

I checked this bucket list item in May 2019 when I had a trip to Las Vegas and expanded my sightseeing to southern Utah and a one-day trip to the Grand Canyon's western rim with a day at a ranch. If I could do it over again, I would organize my trip to include a couple of days at the ranch.

Although the Grand Canyon resides within the state of Arizona, it is near the borders of Utah, Nevada, and even Colorado. The Grand Canyon took 1.2 billion years to create through the extensive shaping of the Colorado River. The canyon spans 277 miles (447 km) with 18 miles (29 km) in width, and 1.1 miles (1.8 km) in depth.

To put this depth in perspective, the Empire State Building could be stacked in the Grand Canyon over four times. The canyon's rust-red colors and sediment layers stretch endlessly, while its diverse wildlife includes 1,500 plant species, 355 birds, 89 mammals, 47 reptiles, 9 amphibians, and 17 fish. The canyon is also home to a unique species: the Grand Canyon Pink Rattlesnake, which has a pink hue to blend into the colorful rocks. [12]

It is one of the most popular attractions in the United States with around six million visitors to the Grand Canyon National Park annually. The size of the national park encompasses more than the state of Rhode Island, 1,904 square miles (4,931 sq km); therefore, helicopter rides can provide a more all-encompassing grandeur experience. Hiking and rafting are also a must to experience nature's true grandeur on a more intimate level. I strongly recommend the helicopter ride through the canyon. Although not a fan of heights, within seconds I was so absorbed in the beauty of the scenery that I lost consciousness of the height. I was just in awe of the depth of the mesmerizing landscape.

Great Barrier Reef

I checked this Natural Wonder of the World in August 2023; it was one of my life's truly awesome experiences. I'll elaborate on my adventure in the chapter on my Australia trip.

The Great Barrier Reef, off Queensland, Australia in the Coral Sea is the world's largest coral reef system, with New Caledonian Barrier Reef and Florida Reef coming in second and third respectively. It covers 133,000 square miles

(344,468 sq km) and stretches 1,429 miles (3,701 km) long, considered the largest living structure on earth. Although it is a misnomer that the Great Wall of China can be seen from space as stated earlier, it is true that the Great Barrier Reef can be seen from space according to NOAA.

Known for its biodiversity, it houses over 1,500 fish species, 411 types of hard coral, and a third of the world's soft corals. The reef also supports 134 shark and ray species, six of seven threatened marine turtle species, and over 30 marine mammals, serving as a critical breeding ground for humpback whales and a sanctuary for endangered species like the dugong and green turtle.[13]

With global emphasis on climate change and impacts on our natural resources, is the Great Barrier Reef being affected? The *Nature* journal published a paper in March 2017 stating that huge sections of a 500-mile (800 km) stretch in the northern part of the reef had died. They attributed this to the 2016 high water temperatures which are considered the result of global climate change. These types of changes to the environment can create exponential results across multiple environmental mediums: air, water, and land.

The Great Barrier Reef consists of 3,000 individual reefs with 900 islands. It was declared a UNESCO World Heritage Site in 1981. The closest location for air and hotel travel is Cairns, Australia. Besides being a natural wonder, the area also promotes water recreational activities such as snorkeling, diving, sailing, boating, and helicopter rides.

Mount Everest, Nepal

This trip is probably intimidating for even the most seasoned travelers. One does not need to climb Mount Everest to check this box; a trip to Nepal and visually seeing the great mountain is sufficient on a passing airplane ride.

The Himalayan Mountain range straddles the border of China, the Tibetan area, with Nepal. The summit or very top stands at 29,029 feet (8,848 m) and is the official marking of the border; it also is the tallest peak above sea level. The mountain range was formed from metamorphic and sedimentary rocks over sixty million years ago. It is known for its harsh weather with temperatures dipping below -76°F (-60°C). At this altitude, climbers need to be on supplemental oxygen to ward off hypoxia. The snow melting from these giant peaks feed many of the rivers in Asia, the lifeline for farming. Charles Darwin would enjoy studying the unique wildlife that has adapted to such cold temperatures and high altitudes, such as the snow leopard and the Himalayan tahr.

The number of hikers reaching Mount Everest's summit has exponentially increased over the past few decades. In 1990, fewer than 100 people made the ascent, a minuscule number compared to today's count. In 2023, around 656 people reached the summit, though this is still less than the pre-pandemic peak of nearly 900 climbers in 2019. Local Sherpa communities, who work as guides, heavily rely on mountaineering tourism. However, there is ongoing debate about the ethics of exposing them to danger, especially with increasing tourism numbers and climate change-related disasters. Litter from tourists and microplastic pollution further exacerbate environmental concerns around Everest, leading to many activists questioning the number of hikers allowed to ascend the mountain.[14]

The World Atlas raises the question that many tourist attractions' management are debating, should restrictions be placed on the number of visitors to global natural resources to ensure these treasures are there for generations to come? The balance between economics and preservation can challenge some countries when tourism largely drives their economy or is a significant part of it.

As globally the middle class grows, more people have the deposable income to travel to places that are a Wonder of the World or a UNESCO World Heritage Site. As limits are put on the supply and availability of the sites, prices will increase, eliminating a greater number of people from connecting with the treasures of the globe. This result is merely applying the supply-demand curve basics of microeconomics.

Paricutin, Mexico

Even volcanoes can be natural wonders, and this may be one of the lesser-known Natural Wonders of the World. The Paricutin Volcano in Michoacán, Mexico, considered the youngest volcano on the planet, edged its rating to be in the top Seven Natural Wonders of the World. A series of earthquakes triggered a lengthy eruption for almost a decade from 1943 to 1952. The eruption started in farmer Dionisio Pulido's cornfield causing a cone-shaped cinder reaching a height of 1,391 feet (424 m). With the extensive lava flows covering 9.7 square miles (25 sq m) the village of San Juan Parangaricutiro had to be evacuated. By 1952, the peak reached 9,213 feet (2,808 m). The volcano has been in a dormant state, but the hardened lava and ash has created a unique tourist site with the church steeple protruding from the solidified lava mass.

Victoria Falls, Zambia and Zimbabwe

Victoria Falls straddles the two countries of Zambia and Zimbabwe. It is the largest waterfall in the world measuring 5,604 feet (1,708 m) wide and plunging 354 feet (108 m) in depth. During the wet season, the largest continuous sheet of falling water on Earth occurs with about 500 million liters of water flowing over the edge every minute.

The falls are formed from the Zambezi River with basalt erosion. Locally, the falls are known as Mosi-oa-Tunya or the smoke that thunders with an average of 38,422 cubic feet per second (1,088 cubic meters per second) of water flow. With such hydropower, the falls can be heard up to 25 miles (40 km) away.

Victoria Falls has become a bucket list tourist site with over a million visitors a year. The Scottish missionary and explorer David Livingston of the famous expression stated by Henry Morgan Stanley *Doctor Livingston I presume* was the first European to visit the falls. He named the falls for Queen Victoria. In 1873, Livingstone died in a small village in Zambia, having succumbed to malaria and dysentery. With no waterfalls in the United Kingdom to equal Victoria Falls, he was stunned by its beauty.

Besides walking along the falls, there are other recreational opportunities; both Zambia and Zimbabwe have national parks near the falls. It was declared a UNESCO World Heritage Site in 1989. The other two iconic waterfalls are Iguazu Falls situated between Argentina and Brazil recognized as the largest system of waterfalls and Niagara Falls situated between the United States and Canada recognized with its massive water volume.

The New Seven Wonders of Nature

The original Seven Natural Wonders was created through a CNN poll. The New Seven Wonders of Nature was an initiative started by the New7Wonders Foundation polling between 2007 to 2011. The organization reached out globally to vote from a selection of 28 finalists. The process was internet-based through a dedicated website with phone voting as an alternative. Through the millions of votes cast, a list of the top seven was declared. Our planet earth has far more than seven natural wonders and a means to categorize to achieve slightly different criteria raises the awareness level of the marvels that exist.

Iguazu Falls, Brazil

Iguazu Falls or Iguacu Falls, like other famous waterfalls such as Victoria Falls (Zambia and Zimbabwe) and Niagara Falls (the United States and Canada), borders two countries: Argentina and Brazil with their respective national parks, Iguazú National Park in Argentina and Iguaçu National Park in Brazil.

The waterfall system consists of 275 distinct falls along 2.7 kilometers (1.7 miles) of the Iguazu River. Some of the individual falls are up to 82 meters (269 feet) in height, though the majority are about 64 meters (210 feet). The most impressive of them all, known as the "Devil's Throat," is a U-shaped, 82-meter-high (269 feet), 150-meter-wide (492 feet), and 700- meter-long (3,000 feet) waterfall.[15]

With subtropical rainforest surrounding the waterfalls fed from the constant spray of the falls, there is a thriving biodiversity which includes even some rare and endangered species of wildlife. Wildlife known to be found in the area are South American tapir, giant anteater, giant otter, howler monkey, ocelot, jaguar, cayman, and a variety of rare birds. On my trip to Costa Rica, we found an abundance of howler monkeys. Of course, there are recreational activities available such as hiking, bird watching, and the boat ride that even travels under the falls. Reminds me of the boat ride on Maid of the Mist at Niagara Falls where raincoats are a necessity. These beautiful parks and shared waterfalls made the list of UNESCO World Heritage Sites: Iguazú National Park in Argentina in 1984 and Iguaçu National Park in Brazil in 1986.

Ha Long Bay, Vietnam

Ha Long Bay or Halong Bay is an amazing natural wonder located in northeast Viet Nam, a few hours' drive from Hanoi. The bay contains thousands of towering limestone islands with lush vegetation sprouting out of the rock. According to local legend, a dragon came to protect the people, and the bay was therefore named *"where the dragon descends into the sea"* or Halong. A lot of English words to equate to one Vietnamese word.

The bay is a festive sight with the numerous local junk boats used for day or multi- day cruising. One can explore the many caves nestled within the islands that have been carved from centuries of wind and erosion. Secret beaches are sheltered in isolated areas found with kayaks or tender boats. The bay's largest island, Cat Ba, hosts a national park in addition to an area that has few full-time residents; other sights and activities are hiking at Ti Top Island and exploring Sung Sot Cave, also known as Surprise Cave, which is the largest cave in the bay. Other caves to explore are Thien Cung Cave or Paradise Cave, Dau Go Cave or Wooden Head Cave,

Luon Cave, Trung Cave or Male Cave, and Me Cung Cave or Maze Cave. So, it's a cave exploring adventure. Ha Long Bay became a UNESCO World Heritage Site in 1994.

I have a Southeast Asia adventure planned for 2024 which includes Haling Bay and an overnight cruise in a junk boat, can't wait.

Jeju Island, South Korea

Jeju Island is in the Korea Strait south of the Korean Peninsula and South Jeolla Province. The island spans 707.8 square miles (1833.2 sq km). The island was a volcanic creation with Mount Halla, South Korea's tallest mountain at 6,398 feet (1,950 m), formed at its center. The island is two million years old, created during the Pleistocene epoch, measuring 16 miles (26 km) north to south and 40 miles (64 km) east to west.

The most notable characteristic of the island is the Gotjawal Forest covering about 12 percent (86 square miles or 224 sq km). It remained unexploited until the twenty-first century due to the 'A'a lava base which is not compatible with farming. This type of lava flow creates a rough, broken, jagged surface covered with sharp, angular blocks. The lava flows are hotter and move faster than the pahoehoe lava flows, which have a smooth, billowy, or ropy surface. Other locations where 'a'a lava flows created volcanos is Kilauea Volcano, Hawaii; Sunset Crater Volcano, Arizona; and Mount Nyiragongo, Democratic Republic of Congo.

The flows are very dense and advanced by crumbling at the front therefore forming a rough blockish surface. Both 'a'a and pahoehoe are terms used in volcanology that originated from the Hawaiian language. The island being untouched led to the forest developing a unique ecosystem.

Jeju Island is surrounded by warm currents, and its oceanic climate supports some subtropical plants. The mountain and surrounding area are a national park. As described by the UNESCO World Heritage Site declared in 2007:

Jeju Volcanic Island and Lava Tubes together comprise three sites that make up 18,846 ha (46569.48 acres). It includes Geomunoreum, regarded as the finest lava tube system of caves anywhere, with its multicolored carbonate roofs and floors, and dark-colored lava walls; the fortress-like Seongsan Ilchulbong tuff cone, rising out of the ocean, a dramatic landscape; and Mount Halla, the highest in Korea, with its waterfalls, multi-shaped rock formations, and lake-filled crater. The site, of outstanding aesthetic beauty, also bears testimony to the history of the planet, its features and processes.[16]

Puerto Princesa Underground River, Philippines

The Puerto Princesa Subterranean River also known as the Puerto Princesa Underground River is on the northern coast of the island of Palawan in the Philippines. The underground river spans 5.1 miles (8.2 km) making it the longest navigable underground river in the world. It flows directly into the West Philippine Sea and is surrounded by abundant greenery and the protected area of Puerto Princesa Subterranean River National Park, which encompasses a mountain-to-sea ecosystem. As with other unique ecosystems, this environment promotes various species of trees, birds, mammals, and reptiles. The river flows beneath the Saint Paul Mountain Range and through a remarkable cave system of stalactite and stalagmite formations. Remember both formations are created by calcium salt deposits formed by dripping water. Stalactite forms from the water dripping from the ceiling and grows down; stalagmite grows up from the floor. Frequently the two connect over much time and become a column.

The national park has been a UNESCO World Heritage Site since 1999, also a popular tourist attraction with boat cruises of almost a mile (1.5 km) down the river. I don't think that I have been to a cave that didn't have breathtaking rock formations; nature is truly creative and unique in its wonders below the surface of the earth. Traversing almost a mile makes this a unique experience.

Table Mountain, South Africa

Table Mountain overlooks the city of Cape Town, South Africa. Atop Table Mountain, one achieves stunning views of the city, where the landscape meets the Atlantic Ocean. Its name is fitting since it portrays a flat top like a table, with its highest point at 3,563 feet (1,086 m) above sea level. As part of the Cape Floral Region Protected Area, it was declared a UNESCO World Heritage Site in 2004. Typical of UNESCO sites, the biodiversity is rich and unique; the Cape Fynbos biome includes endemic species not found anywhere else in the world. Fynbos vegetation is a fine-leaved sclerophyllic shrubland plant adapted to both a Mediterranean climate and periodic fires. *It is recognized as one of the world's 'hottest hotspots' for its diversity of endemic and threatened plants, and contains outstanding examples of significant ongoing ecological, biological, and evolutionary processes.*[17] Charles Darwin, if you were to explore this area, would you supplement or modify your previous conclusions in your book, *On the Origin of Species?*

There is a cableway for visitors to ascend and descend the mountain; it provides spectacular views with 360-degree rotation, there is no bad viewpoint. It's also a perfect location for hiking. The Kirstenbosch National Botanical Garden resides at the foot of the mountain and is considered one of the great botanic gardens of the world.

I have a trip planned to South Africa for January 2024 which includes Cape Town and a trip to this amazing mountain, another bucket list check.

Komodo Island, Republic of Indonesia

Komodo Island is one of 17,508 islands that comprise the

Republic of Indonesia with a surface area of 151 square miles (390 sq km) and over 2000 occupants. Komodo Island is volcanic and one of the Lesser Sunda chain of islands that forms part of the Komodo National Park. You probably have heard the word Komodo before and associate it with the Komodo dragon which is an inhabitant of the island. The Komodo dragon is the world's largest living lizard with about 5,700 living on the island. They acquired their name due to their appearance and aggressive behavior. They exist nowhere else in the world therefore of great interest to scientists studying evolution, back to Charles Darwin again.

The island also has a variety of wildlife, the Timor deer, wild horses, water buffalo, wild boar, long-tailed macaques, and goats. Whales, dolphins, and sea turtles navigate the waters surrounding the island. Komodo Island has been a UNESCO World Heritage Site since 1991. The rugged hillsides of dry savannah and sections of thorny green vegetation are a stark contrast to the sandy beaches and blue waters over coral reef. Komodo Island is noted for snorkeling and diving.

In 2020, the Indonesian government considered closing the island to tourism to protect the natural recovery of the landscape and the dragons. However, the government implemented a premium tourism model that limits visitor numbers but still allows access. This is becoming routine practice for the protection of natural and man-made wonders to ensure their existence for generations of the future.

Besides the Komodo dragon, the island is also home to one

of seven rare and intriguing pink beaches of the world, a combination of white and red sand. The others are Pink Sands Beach, Harbour Island, The Bahamas; Spiaggia Rosa, Budelli, Italy; Elafonisi Beach, Crete, Greece; Balos Lagoon, Crete, Greece; Horseshoe Bay Beach, Bermuda; and Great Santa Cruz Island, Zamboanga, Philippines. Minuscule fragments of marine species known as Foraminifera create a reddish tint. The tiny organisms with their vibrant red shells flourish within the surrounding coral reefs. The force of nature grinds these shells into fine particles blending them with the sand creating a shade of pink.[18]

Amazon Rainforest

The Amazon Rainforest resides in several countries: Brazil, Columbia, Venezuela, Ecuador, Bolivia, Guyana, Suriname, and French Guiana. The Amazon River, one of the largest rivers in the world, is the lifeblood of South America. At a length of 4,345 miles (almost 7,000 km), it is the second largest river in the world next to the Nile River in Africa. However, with respect to water discharge into the sea, it is unsurpassed, accounting for 20% of all the freshwater discharged in the oceans worldwide. That truly represents a global interconnectedness. To appreciate its magnitude, the river originates in the Andes Mountains of Peru and traverses through several countries while crossing South America until it discharges into the Atlantic Ocean. Along the journey, it collects water from over 1,100 tributaries of which 17 are over

1,000 miles (1,610 km) long.

The river's diverse aquatic ecosystem constitutes 3,000 known species of fish with many still undiscovered. The feared piranha lives in this ecosystem. The giant arapaima, one of the world's largest freshwater fish, also lives in the Amazon River. The river's basin is also a habitat for a wide array of other wildlife such as jaguars, tapirs, and caimans.

The Amazon Rainforest or Amazonia is the lush, tropical rainforest surrounding most of the Amazon River's basin. It spans over 2.1 million square miles (5,438,975 sq km) and represents more than half of the planet's remaining rainforests. It is recognized as the world's most biodiverse region, supporting millions of species of insects, plants, birds, and other forms of life, again many undiscovered.

The rainforest plays a crucial role in global climate regulation by acting as a carbon sink, absorbing millions of tons of carbon dioxide emissions each year. However, it faces threats from deforestation and climate change, which lead to loss of biodiversity and habitat, and contribute to global warming. Both the Amazon River and the Amazon Rainforest are integral to the Earth's health. They provide a home to a staggering array of wildlife, help regulate the world's climate and serve as a source of livelihood for many local communities. Their conservation is of paramount importance for maintaining global biodiversity and climate balance.[19]

Seven Wonders of Africa

For nature enthusiasts looking for additional variety for their bucket list, I'll add the Seven Natural Wonders of Africa.

Mount Kilimanjaro, Tanzania

Ernest Hemingway wrote a short story about the great mountain to later become a movie. He never climbed the mountain but did take an airplane ride past it. *Kilimanjaro is a snow-covered mountain 19,710 feet high and is said to be the highest mountain in Africa. Its western summit is called the Masai Ngàje Ngài, the House of God. Close to the western summit, there is the dried and frozen carcass of a leopard. No one has explained what the leopard was seeking at that altitude.*[20]

Located in Tanzania near the Kenya border, the dormant volcano is the highest mountain in Africa and the highest free-standing mountain above sea level in the world at 19, 341 feet (5,895 m) above sea level and 16,100 feet (4,900 m) above its plateau base. Trekking organizations provide for a several day trekking adventure to the top, much easier to climb than Mount Everest. The mountain has been a UNESCO World Heritage Site since 1987.

Sahara Desert

Equivalent in size to the United States or China, the Sahara Desert is the third largest desert in the world behind

Antarctica and the Arctic. It is also the hottest desert in the world. It doesn't reside in merely one country but several countries: Morocco, Mali, Mauritania, Egypt, Libya, Algeria, Chad, Niger Republic, some parts of Sudan, a small portion of Nigeria, and a small part of Burkina Faso.

Okavango Delta

The Okavango Delta is a vast inland river delta in northern Botswana known for its grassy plains flooding seasonally. The Moremi Game Reserve resides in east and central areas of the region. Wildlife is plentiful with hippopotamuses, elephants, crocodiles, near the water and lions, leopards, giraffes, and rhinoceros on dry land. The Okavango Delta became a UNESCO World Heritage Site in 2014.

Ngorongoro Crater

The Ngorongoro Crater is a large volcanic caldera located in the Ngorongoro Conservation Area, a UNESCO World Heritage Site in northeastern Tanzania since 1979. A vast expanse of highland plains, savanna, savanna woodlands and forests. This area is also home to much wildlife including globally threatened species. Archaeological research has discovered a long sequence of human evolution and human-environment dynamics to include early hominid footprints that date back 3.6 million years.

Nile River

The Nile River is the major north-flowing river into the Mediterranean Sea located in northeastern Africa. It has been depicted as the largest river in the world, but some researchers suggest that the Amazon River is slightly longer. The river has been the lifeblood for Egyptians dating back to the Pyramid civilizations. Its basin includes parts of Tanzania, Burundi, Rwanda, the Democratic Republic of the Congo, Kenya, Uganda, South Sudan, Ethiopia, Sudan, and the cultivated part of Egypt. For travelers to Egypt, a Nile River cruise transports one to the many Egyptian treasures including Valley of the Kings.

Red Sea Reef

The Red Sea Reef is a diverse reef system located in the Red Sea. The Red Sea Reef extends 1, 240 miles (2,000 km) along the coastlines of Egypt, Sudan, and Eritrea facilitating an abundance of aquatic life. The Red Sea Reef hosts over 1,100 species of fish, 200 soft and hard corals, and 44 different species of sharks. Approximately 10 percent of these are endemic and found nowhere else in the world.

Serengeti Migration

The Serengeti Migration, also known as The Great Migration, is a massive circular migration of wildebeests, zebras, and other antelopes occurring largely in Tanzania and the balance in Kenya. It is the largest terrestrial mammal migration in the world. Although the herds are always moving or migrating, it is in the months of September and October when the migration herd moves north across the Mara River into Maasai Mara Nature Reserve, Kenya that wildlife enthusiasts vie for safari expeditions.

Part 1 – The Concept of Bucket

Chapter 3

Other Bucket List Points of Interest

United Nations Educational, Scientific and Cultural Organizations (UNESCO)

<u>UNESCO World Heritage Sites</u>

On your travels, have you ever noticed a plaque that states this is a UNESCO site? I also mentioned UNESCO during the last two chapters. So, what does that mean? There is a bureaucratic process to review and select these sites. The mission of the United Nations Educational, Scientific and Cultural Organization (UNESCO) is to encourage the identification, protection, and preservation of cultural and natural heritage around the world considered to be of outstanding value to humanity. This is embodied in the international treaty adopted in 1972 called *Convention Concerning the Protection of the World Cultural and Natural Heritage.*

World Heritage Sites have value to all people of the world, irrespective of territory's location. The 2023 list encompassed 1199 properties; they couldn't find one more and make it an even 1200 sites. However, for 2024 the organization added 24 sites now totaling 1223. This list is too long to post here but it can be found at the UNESCO website: https://whc.unesco.org/en/list/ Heritage List. With the list changing over the years, one will need to review and update their bucket list for UNESCO sites. Nothing in life remains stagnant and that includes bucket lists or UNESCO sites; however, Wonders of the World are timeless.

Although included in the introduction of the book, it is important to re-emphasize their worthy vision here. *Since wars begin in the minds of men and women, it is in the minds of men and women that peace must be built. UNESCO uses education, science, culture, communication, and information to foster mutual understanding and respect for our planet. We work to strengthen the intellectual and moral solidarity of humankind and bring out the best in our shared humanity.*[21]

Part 1 – The Concept of Bucket

Number	Description of Criteria
i	to represent a masterpiece of human creative genius;
ii	to exhibit an important interchange of human values, over a span of time or within a cultural area of the world, on developments in architecture or technology, monumental arts, town-planning, or landscape design;
iii	to bear a unique or at least exceptional testimony to a cultural tradition or to a civilization that is living or which has disappeared;
iv	to be an outstanding example of a type of building, architectural or technological ensemble, or landscape that illustrates (a) significant stage(s) in human history;
v	to be an outstanding example of a traditional human settlement, land-use, or sea-use that is representative of a culture (or cultures), or human interaction with the environment especially when it has become vulnerable under the impact of irreversible change;
vi	to be directly or tangibly associated with events or living traditions, with ideas, or with beliefs, with artistic and literary works of outstanding universal significance. (The Committee considers that this criterion should preferably be used in conjunction with other criteria);
vii	to contain superlative natural phenomena or areas of exceptional natural beauty and aesthetic importance;
viii	to be outstanding examples representing major stages of earth's history, including the record of life, significant on-going geological processes in the development of landforms, or significant geomorphic or physiographic features;

ix	to be outstanding examples representing significant on-going ecological and biological processes in the evolution and development of terrestrial, fresh water, coastal, and marine ecosystems and communities of plants and animals;
x	to contain the most important and significant natural habitats for in-situ conservation of biological diversity, including those containing threatened species of outstanding universal value from the point of view of science or conservation.

Description of UNESCO Criteria
(https://whc.unesco.org/en/criteria/)

The UNESCO World Heritage List requires sites to have an outstanding universal value and meet at least one of ten selection criteria. The *Operational Guidelines for the Implementation of the World Heritage Convention* explains the criteria applied. Prior to 2004, World Heritage Sites were selected based on six cultural and four natural criteria. As sited above, this has been revised to include one set of ten criteria. The criteria are a work in progress, routinely revised to be relevant. Listed in the table above are the criteria taken from their website in 2023.

UNESCO List of Intangible Cultural Heritage

The UNESCO World Heritage List reflects either the physical marvels of mankind or nature. The UNESCO List of Intangible Cultural Heritage evaluates cultural aspects that have a significant impact on the world. In my trip to Patagonia, I learned that the Tango dance made this list on August 31,

2009, with a proposal submitted by both Argentina and Uruguay. The dance reflects the area's cultural history and dialogue through music. This list is broken into three categories: List of Intangible Cultural Heritage in Need of Urgent Safeguarding, Representative List of the Intangible Cultural Heritage of Humanity, and Register of Good Safeguarding Practices.

UNESCO List of Biosphere Reserves and Global Geoparks

There are two environmental categories: biosphere reserve and global geoparks.

A UNESCO Global Geopark uses its geological heritage, in connection with all other aspects of the area's natural and cultural heritage, to enhance awareness and understanding of key issues facing society, such as using our earth's resources sustainably, mitigating the effects of climate change and reducing natural hazard-related risks.[22]

On the other hand, biosphere reserves *are an essential component of UNESCO's mandate as the United Nations' organization for sciences. Each biosphere reserve promotes innovative local sustainable development solutions, protects biodiversity, and addresses climate disruption. They also support local and Indigenous communities through practices such as agro-ecology, water management, and the generation of green income. Biosphere reserves contribute to helping achieve the targets set by States upon the adoption of the Kunming-Montreal Global Biodiversity Framework in December 2022, which includes designating 30% of the Earth's land and marine surface as protected areas and restoring 30% of the planet's degraded ecosystems by 2030.*[23]

What better method to unite the world than through such honorable intentions of preserving and restoring nature's complex systems.

Museums

Another type of bucket location that warrants bucket list activity is museums. What is a museum? The Peabody Museum of Archeology and Ethnology at Harvard University put a study guide together to provide information to the students on how to evaluate what they expect from a museum to include its responsibilities and whether the museum met its obligations. The students were to *enumerate the various purposes that we commonly expect museums to fulfill; to articulate the values that are expressed within these assigned purposes; to differentiate between the people and needs affected by each; and to contend with the overlapping, at times conflicting, responsibilities at stake.*[24]

Most museum titles are descriptive, providing some indications of the contents and educational factors for the public to expect. A natural history museum is a scientific institution focused on the environment with a collection of current and historical records of animals, plants, fungi, ecosystems, geology, paleontology, climatology, and others. A history museum will focus on the collection and display of artifacts related to the past, usually presented in chronological order of historical events and culture, showcasing history through objects and information.

An art museum will focus on art exhibits. So, when evaluating whether to visit a museum make sure that your expectation of the focus of the museum aligns with the purpose of the museum.

Name	City	Country	Year
Louvre	Paris	France	1792
State Hermitage Museum	St. Petersburg	Russia	1764
National Museum of China	Beijing	China	1959
Metropolitan Museum of Art	New York City	New York	1870
Museo del Prado	Madrid	Spain	1819
Vatican Museum	Vatican City (Rome)	Vatican City	1506
Tokyo National Museum	Tokyo	Japan	1872
National Museum of Anthropology	Mexico City	Mexico	1964
Victoria and Albert Museum	London	United Kingdom	1852
Humboldt Forum	Berlin	Germany	2020
Kunsthistorisches Museum	Vienna	Austria	1891
Houston Museum of Fine Arts	Houston	United States	1900
National Museum of Korea	Seoul	South Korea	1909
Art Institute of Chicago	Chicago	United States	1879
British Museum	London	United Kingdom	1753

Mystetskyi Arsenal	Kyiv	Ukraine	2006
National Gallery of Art	Washington, DC	United States	1937
MASS MoCA	North Adams	United States	1999
Art & History Museum	Brussels	Belgium	1835
Museum of Fine Arts	Boston	United States	1870
Royal Ontario Museum	Toronto	Canada	1912
Shandong Art Museum	Jinan	China	1977
Israel Museum	Jerusalem	Israel	1965
National Gallery Singapore	Singapore	Singapore	2015
Minneapolis Museum of Art	Minneapolis	United States	1883

List of Top 25 Museums

(https://en.wikipedia.org/wiki/List_of_largest_art_museums)

The above table lists the twenty-five museums of the world ranked by their gallery space. Once the Grand Museum of Egypt is opened then the list will slide down one because it will be at the top unseating the Louvre as the museum with the largest area.

World Renowned Religious Sites

As mentioned earlier in the book, Another Beautiful

Church (ABC) can be a godsend or shortcoming depending on one's perspective for touring across Europe: eastern, central, and western. Religion was an instrumental part of life for centuries creating stunning structures that now require significant investments to maintain. The Renaissance period focused on religious art with greats like Leonardo da Vinci, Michaelangelo, and Raphael commissioned by the Pope. Great masterpieces can be found within some of the most magnificent churches in Europe. In addition, through my travels, I've entered what seems like close to a hundred churches, and I haven't become numb to their beauty or uniqueness yet.

The successive architectural style of European churches consists of early Christian, Byzantine, Romanesque, Gothic, Renaissance, Baroque, Rococo, Neoclassical, various Revival styles of the late eighteenth to early twentieth century, and then modern.

Ken Follett's bestseller, *The Pillars of the Earth*, depicts his admiration of cathedrals depicted through a fictional novel. Although he experienced literary angst in undergoing such change from his former popular thriller writing style, he was driven to research and pursue learning more about one of history's most intriguing endeavors, the age of architectural discovery through churches.

Why were these churches built? There are simple answers-for the glory of God, the vanity of bishops, and so on-but those were not enough for me. The building of the medieval cathedrals is an astonishing European phenomena. The builders had no power tools, they did not understand the mathematics of structural engineering, and they were poor: the richest of princes did not live as well as, say, a prisoner in a modern jail. Yet they put up beautiful buildings that have existed, and they built them so well that they are still here, hundreds of years later, for us to study and marvel at.[25]

A question intriguing many a traveler is what's the difference between a church, a chapel, a cathedral, and a basilica? A church is any place to worship with a permanent congregation and officiated by a pastor or priest. The word church is referred to as the physical structure but also the worshipping event. A chapel is a place of worship that has no pastor or priest and no permanent congregation. Chapels are found in other structures like airports and hospitals. Las Vegas is known for numerous chapels for quick weddings.

A cathedral is a church that is overseen by a bishop within a specific diocese or area of the bishop's jurisdiction. There are two types of basilicas: basilicas major and basilicas minor. Basilicas major are the four personal churches of the pope and are found in and around Rome: Archbasilica of St. John Lateran, St. Peter's Basilica, the Basilica of St. Paul Outside the Walls, and the Basilica di Santa Maria Maggiore. Basilicas minor are found all around the world and have been awarded the status by the pope for some historical, spiritual, or architectural significance.

To sustain spousal harmony, couples should plan upfront church-oriented trips or balance time between churches and other activities. To help with planning, the following lists barely scratch the surface of the world's renowned works of religious architecture. This advice is not gender specific; any couple may have one person more human-constructed focus and the other be more nature-developed focused. I've come across both genders favoring each area.

Wikipedia List[26]

Wikipedia's list for renowned works of architecture include

Saint Peter's Basilica, Italy	Santa Maria Maggiore, Italy
Notre-Dame, France	Basilica of San Vitale, Italy
Cologne Cathedral, Germany	Saint Mark's Basilica, Italy
Salisbury Cathedral, United Kingdom	Westminster Abbey, United Kingdom
Antwerp Cathedral, Netherlands	Saint Basil's Cathedral, Russia
Prague Cathedral, Czech Republic	Sagrada Familia, Spain
Lincoln Cathedral, United Kingdom	Hagia Sophia, Turkey
Basilica of Saint-Denis, France	

Hagia Sophia in Istanbul, Türkiye is now a mosque. A mosque is a place of prayer for Islam. The Arabic word masjid means a place of prostration to God and is the same word in Persian, Urdu, and Turkish. There are two types of mosques: the masjid jāmi or collective mosque, a large state-controlled mosque that is the center of a community, or smaller privately operated mosques.

What is a temple? A church is associated with the Christian faith; a temple is dedicated to other non-Christian faiths such as Buddhism, Hinduism, and Judaism.

Ten Most Beautiful Churches Around the World[27]

This list comes from *Architectural Digest* and with a hint of criteria uniqueness.

Shrine of Our Lady of Las Lajas, Colombia	Chapel of the Holy Cross, United States
Panagía Paraportianí Church, Greece	Stykkishólmskirkja Church, Iceland
Göreme Churches, Turkey	Borgund Stave Church, Norway
Church of St. George, Ethiopia	Cadet Chapel, United States Air Force Academy, United States
Chapel of Saint-Michel d'Aiguilhe, France	Temppeliaukio Church, Finland

Conde Traveler List of Topmost Beautiful Churches[28]

This list of the topmost beautiful churches in the world, from Ethiopia to Brazil was generated according to *Conde Traveler* article on June 7, 2021. Some of these are repeats from *Architectural Digest's* list of the top ten most beautiful churches.

St. Basil's Cathedral, Russia	La Sagrada Família, Spain
Hallgrímskirkja, Iceland	Borgund Stave Church, Norway
Gergeti Trinity Church, Georgia	Church of St. George, Ethiopia
Notre-Dame Basilica, Canada	The Pilgrimage Church of Wies, Germany
Church of the Transfiguration, Russia	Las Lajas Sanctuary, Colombia
Cathedral of Brasília, Brazil	Basilique du Sacré-Coeur, France
Duomo di Milano, Italy	St. Patrick's Cathedral, New York City
Church of the Assumption, Slovenia	Monasteries of Meteora, Greece
Chapel of the Holy Cross, Arizona	

30 Most Beautiful Churches in the World [29]

For those who are looking for one of the most complete lists of the 30 Most Beautiful Churches in the World compiled by David Johnston in a *Road Affair* blog of August 24, 2023. One will see quite a few duplicates from other lists. If one is truly enamored with places of worship and castles, then use excel to create a spreadsheet that provides information on site, location, and a little description. As one is planning their journeys, they can check the spreadsheet for potential bucket list items. Managing implies organizing information in such a way that it is useful. If not part of an organized tour, then one might want to extend their trip to travel to a nearby gem. Also explore locally when on travel because I've encountered real gems that no one put on a top list. Although many now have small fees, it's worth it to help preserve these historic treasures.

Sagrada Familia, Spain	Saint Alexander Nevsky Cathedral, Bulgaria
Notre-Dame de Paris, France	Westminster Abbey, United Kingdom
Santa Maria del Fiore, Italy	Mont-Saint-Michel Abbey, France
Saint John's Co-Cathedral, Malta	Borgund Stave Church, Norway
Saint Basil's Cathedral, Russia	Cathedral of Brasília, Brazil

Saint Peter's Basilica, Vatican City	Notre-Dame Basilica, Canada
Duomo di Milano, Italy	Church of the Transfiguration, Russia
Saint Stephen's Basilica, Hungary	Church of the Assumption, Slovenia
Catedral Basílica Del Pilar, Spain	Church of St. George, Ethiopia
Kölner Dom, Germany	Wieskirche, Germany
Hagia Sophia, Turkey	Las Lajas Sanctuary, Colombia
Saint Stephen's Cathedral, Austria	Church Of the Nativity, Palestine
Hallgrimskirkja, Iceland	St. Patrick's Cathedral, New York
Saint Vitus Cathedral, Czech Republic	Saint Mark's Basilica, Italy
Chapel Of The Holy Cross, Arizona	Sacré-Cœur, France

The 14 Most Breathtaking Mosques Around the World[30]

According to an article in *Veranda Travel* published June 21, 2022, the below table depicts the 14 most breathtaking mosques around the world that they believe should be added to your bucket list. Not all places of worship have the same criteria for entry, especially for visitors. In particular, expect that mosques and temples will have a dress code. I've borrowed a headscarf or long skirt a few times to enter a site, including the Wailing Wall in Jerusalem. It is quite common that shoes are removed before entering a mosque or temple. As with some historic church sites in Europe, mosques may ask guests to respect the sacredness of the building and its worshippers, which can mean no pictures, flash, or video photography. If pictures are allowed, then one should refrain from taking pictures of people unless the person acknowledges that it is acceptable.

Jama Masjid, India	Nasir al-Mulk Mosque, Iran
The Great Mosque of Djenné, Mali	Sheikh Zayed Grand Mosque, United Arab Emirates
Crystal Mosque, Malaysia	Shah Mosque, Iran
Masjid Wazir Khan, Pakistan	Great Mosque of Xi'an, China
Lala Mustafa Pasha Mosque, Cyprus	Putra Mosque, Malaysia
Sultan Ahmed Mosque, Turkey	Sultan Qaboos Grand Mosque, Oman
Hassan II Mosque, Morocco	Tilla Kari Madrasa and Mosque, Uzbekistan

12 Most Beautiful Temples in the World [31]

Veranda Travel also published an article on the 12 most

beautiful temples in the world which should not be missed for your bucket list considerations.

Ranakpur Jain, India	Paro Taktsang, Bhutan
Wat Rong Khun, Thailand	The Temple of Hephaestus, Greece
The Temple of Heaven, China	Seiganto-ji, Japan
Shwedagon Pagoda, Myanmar	Man Mo Temple, Hong Kong
The Temples of Abu Simbel, Egypt	Bửu Long Pagoda, Vietnam
Wat Benchamabophit Dusitvanaram, Thailand	Kek Lok Si Temple, Malaysia

Most Beautiful Synagogues in the World [32]

This series of lists would not be complete without recognizing the most beautiful synagogues in the world according to *Conde Traveler* originally published in 2014 but republished with additional information in 2017.

Neue Synagogue, Germany	Hemdat Israel Synagogue, Turkey
New Synagogue of Bochum, Germany	Ulm Synagogue, Germany

Spanish Synagogue, Czech Republic	Szeged Synagogue, Hungary
Great Synagogue, Hungary	Old Synagogue, Hungary
New West End Synagogue, England	Old Synagogue, Germany
Grand Synagogue of Edirne, Turkey	Grand Choral Synagogue, Russia
Ohel Jakob Synagogue, Germany	Congregation Mickve Israel, Georgia, USA
El Ghriba Synagogue, Tunisia	

My suggestion is to make your own list focused on relevant characteristics in a place of worship or the architectural significance of the structure. This section can also be used for reference to check locations where one might be traveling to determine if one of these gems is on your itinerary or close to places that you will be exploring.

Magnificent Castles

Throughout one's travels, one will inevitably come across magnificent castles, some intact and others in ruins or a mere fragment of their original grandeur. Adding these to one's bucket list will entice your medieval-side for the swashbuckling days of chivalry. For a list based on regions, peruse the link:

https://en.wikipedia.org/wiki/List_of_castles. For assistance in reducing one's research, here are a couple of borrowed sample lists. Also, the acronym ABC can also embody the term *Another Bloody Castle*.

Famous Castles List [33]

This list of castles is differentiated by their construction style, location, use, architecture, and involvement in various historical events. Similar to the religious sites lists, I don't know how anyone narrows down the list with so many candidates.

Alnwick Castle, United Kingdom	Leeds Castle, United Kingdom
Burg Eltz Castle, Germany	Lichtenstein Castle, Germany
Château de Chenonceau, France	Neuschwanstein Castle, Germany
Cité de Carcassonne, France	Tower of London, United Kingdom
Conwy Castle, United Kingdom	Warwick Castle, United Kingdom
Heidleberg Castle, Germany	Windsor Castle, United Kingdom
Highclere Castle, United Kingdom	

This list seems to be Europe-centric with a slight slant to the United Kingdom. For those focused on United Kingdom visits, this list will provide one several items.

Travel Pirate List[34]

This list has a little more diversity across the globe.

Neuschwanstein Castle, Germany	Schönbrunn Palace, Austria
Pena National Palace, Portugal	Alhambra, Spain
Predjama Castle, Slovenia	Hawa Mahal, India
Aït Benhaddou, Morocco	Trakai Island Castle, Lithuania
Vianden Castle, Luxembourg	Mont Saint-Michel, France
Dunrobin Castle, Scotland	Peles Castle, Romania
Castle of Spirits, Slovakia	Castello Scaligero di Sirmione, Italy
Himeji Castle, Japan	Frederiksborg Castle, Denmark
Windsor Castle, England	Topkapi Palace, Türkiye
Moszna Castle, Poland	Prague Castle, Czech Republic

Top Ten List (savingcastles blog) [35]

For those so confused with the abundance of choices, the savingcastles blog has narrowed down candidates to a list of ten that cross Europe and Asia.

Neuschwanstein Castle, Germany	Prague Castle, Czech Republic
Edinburgh Castle, Scotland	Alhambra, Spain
Himeji Castle, Japan	Windsor Castle, England
Château de Chambord, France	Mont Saint-Michel, France
Bran Castle, Romania	Pena Palace, Portugal

Ironically, there are some recommended castles to visit that were never finished for one reason or another, such as Neuschwanstein Castle in Germany. All are magnificent.

The Making of a Bucket List

The 2007 movie *The Bucket List* raised awareness for lifetime goals to achieve outside one's career aspirations. For a collection of 1000 adventures to review check out the book *The Bucket List 1000 Adventures Big and Small*, which starts at the North Pole and works its way down by latitude to the South Pole. Although many of the 1000 ideas are destinations, not all are and one's list should also include activities, some large and some small. This really adds a fun element to adventure. The book provides information snippets on each of the 1000 adventures. While perusing, I learned that drinking coconut water is a bucket list activity just in time to check that box in Costa Rica after a walk in Manual Antonio National Park. The street vendor had coconuts on ice, so the drink was cool, tasty, refreshing, and bucket list noteworthy.

The most important part of a bucket list isn't what you do but expanding your experiences and knowledge. Whether it's learning more about your own country's history, culture, and environment or other countries' history, culture, and environment, the experience expands your knowledge and possibly develops more neurons in the brain or allows more neuron connections across various parts of the brain.

The old expression, *You can't teach an old dog new tricks* is a misnomer. We now better understand that exercising the brain is just as good as exercising one's muscles throughout one's entire life. With some of the trips, one will also exercise one's muscles as well as their brain through outdoor activities or even some indoor activities spending hours wandering through museums.

What are the benefits for bucket list travel items? The most obvious knowledge gained from traveling is a better sense of geography. When one is watching the news and the anchorperson mentions a country, you'll have a better sense of where that country is located, history, and culture if you have traveled there or a neighboring country.

Just like in residential neighborhoods, some neighboring countries get along well, and some do not. Jared Diamond wrote three books related to geographical impacts on the world: *Guns, Germs, and Steel*; *Collapse*; and *Upheaval: Turning Points for Nations in Crisis*. Robert Kaplan wrote *The Revenge of Geography: What the Map Tells us about Coming Conflicts and the Battle Against Fate* also related geography to the destinies of countries.

If you are married, work on the bucket list with your spouse. This is an excellent means to reconnect with the spouse, especially if the couple is approaching the retiring years and needs to reconnect after being offspring and family-focused for many years. One of my travel mates became interested in national parks because her parents after retirement took a trip across the United States touring parks for several months, camping in a tent for some and others springing for the cost of a motel or hotel. Just imagine how adventurous a couple becomes on such a journey. I think I need to add that experience to my bucket list.

Hopefully, the couple are on the same page for what they consider adventures, places, and activities on a bucket list. My friend spent a few vacations with her own children visiting national parks. She and I started traveling internationally but then with the COVID-19 pandemic, we started pursuing national parks in the United States. She got me hooked on experiencing the beauty of the American landscape through state and national parks. I've experienced this with my own children venturing to Seattle and visiting Olympic National Park and Mount Rainer National Park this year. For many countries, national parks are their national treasures.

Part 2

MY BIG YEAR

My *Travel Big Year* largely consisted of 2023 after my retirement on March 31, 2023. It also included two trips: Portugal in November 2022 and Patagonia in January 2023. During these trips, I visited 50 UNESCO World Heritage Sites, one item on UNESCO's Intangible Cultural Heritage List, one Wonder of the Modern World, and one Natural Wonder of the World. Las Torres del Paine National Park is considered the eighth Natural Wonder of the World, so one extra one. As of early 2025, UNESCO has designated 1,223 World Heritage Sites; so, my 50 accomplishments barely scratches the surface of exploring these places.

Then again, checking the box of 50 in a year is an accomplishment. I also did some bucket list checking for museums, places of worship, and castles. The first Big Year added two museums, ten religious sites, and five castles to my bucket list. These are reflected in collected lists depicted in chapter three. Again, the sample lists are just a starting point but can be beneficial in determining where one wants to go. If there are places of religious sites, castles, or museums that one is yearning to visit, then those locations become a higher priority for travel.

Part 2 – My Big Year

Chapter 4

Background Information for Understanding

Before embarking on one's travels around the world, it is beneficial to have some basic knowledge about historical civilizations, political systems, and religious systems that developed because these are the foundations of our world today. When browsing through historical literature, one will find the notations BCE, BC, CE, and AD referring to certain periods of time. What do they mean? The two notations BC (Before Christ) and AD (Anno Domini) were used predominantly by the West. Scholars adopted BCE (Before the Common Era) and CE (Common Era), but both connotations denote the same timeframe. One might also see the letters "ca" before a date; this is an abbreviation for the Latin word *circa* which means *approximately* or *around*.

The terms Medieval Ages, Renaissance, and Enlightenment are used for eras of significant change. What is the difference? The Medieval Ages is the period after the fall of the Roman Empire in the fifth century to the rise of the Renaissance period starting in the thirteenth century. Prior periods reflected advances of the Greek and Roman empires. This Medieval period or Dark Ages reflect the rise of Christianity through the Roman Catholic Church and control through the papacy creating friction with control by monarchies.

The Renaissance period occurred after the Medieval Ages, providing a surge in classical learning and values. During this period, individuals and nations embraced discovery and exploration of new lands. A shift from a Ptolemaic system to a Copernican system of astronomy also reflected significant changes to preconceived thinking, such as the world is flat, and the earth is the center of the universe. Although Nicolaus Copernicus created this concept in the later part of the Renaissance period, it would ignite during the Enlightenment period. This period of learning was fueled by wealth especially in Italy with the Medici family and the papacy. Art flourished during this time creating artistic legends known by single names: Da Vinci, Michaelangelo, Titian, and Raphael, to name a few.

The Enlightenment period, also known as the Age of Reason, occurred in the seventeenth and eighteenth centuries following the Renaissance period. A shift to reason-based thinking or rationale humanity focused on knowledge, freedom, and happiness. Although Aristotle and other philosophers led the roots of enlightenment, the birth of Christianity interrupted philosophical attempts to discover and explain the natural world beyond faith-based explanations. The Renaissance renewed classical learning, the Reformation severed the Christian church in western Europe, and the scientific revolution was led by Francis Bacon, René Descartes, Nicolaus Copernicus, Johannes Kepler, Galileo Galilei, Gottfried Wilhelm Leibniz, and Isaac

Newton. Their pursuit of science paved the way for understanding the capacity of human learning of the world. With this basic knowledge, let's embark on the origins of civilizations.

Civilizations through Time

Before discussing civilizations throughout time, differentiating between civilization and empire is a good beginning. According to National Geographic, *a civilization is a complex human society that may have certain characteristics of cultural and technological development.*[36] The field is wide open to all the civilizations that have existed since the beginning of time. Narrowing down the field, I look to an encyclopedia expert Britannica for the definition:

major political unit in which the metropolis, or single sovereign authority, exercises control over a territory of great extent or a number of territories or peoples through formal annexations or various forms of informal domination.[37]

The tables below depict a list of empires in world history constructed by James A. Paul of the Global Policy Forum in October 2005. He cites that the dates are interpretative and meant to be suggestive of the information largely taken from the Times Atlas of World History. Some of these civilizations built extraordinary structures noteworthy to be a Wonder of the World or designated a UNESCO World Heritage Site. To name just a few: Great Pyramids during the Egyptian Empire,

Parthenon during the Athenian Empire, Colosseum during the Roman Empire, Angkor Wat during the Kymer Empire, Chichén Itzá during the Maya Empire, and Machu Picchu during the Inca Empire. Exceptional construction was not limited to just large empires, the Nabataean Kingdom carved from rock the city of Petra in Jordan eventually to fall under the Roman Empire in 106 AD.

Again, this section is not meant to provide in-depth information on each of the empires mentioned below but just to make the reader aware that these empires existed and have made an impact on the world of today. Through my travels, I expect to discover structures, artifacts, and remnants left by civilizations that shed light on their culture and way of life. I recommend to readers through exploration and adventure learning more about the history of these empires.

Ancient Empire Period	Timeline
Egyptian Empire	3100 BC to 30 BC
Norte Chico Empire	3000 BC to 1800 BC
Indus Valley Empires: Harappa and Mohenjo-Darro	2550 BC to 1550 BC
Akkadian Empire (2500-2000 BC)	2500 BC to 2000 BC
Babylonian Empire (1792-1595 BC)	1792 BC to 1595 BC
Ancient Chinese Empires: Shang Chou	 1751 BC to 1111 BC 1000 BC to 800 BC
Hittite Empire	1500 B to 1200 BC
Assyrian Empire	1244 BC to 612 BC
Persian Empires: Achaemenid Empire Sassanian Empire	550 BC to 637 AD 550 BC to 330 BC 224 BC to 651 AD
Carthaginian Empire	ca 475 BC to 146 BC
Athenian Empire	461 BC to 440 BC 362 BC to 355 BC
Macedonian Empire	359 BC to 323 BC
Roman Empire	264 BC to 476 AD
Parthian Empire	247 BC to 224 AD

List of Empires
(https://archive.globalpolicy.org/component/content/article/155-
history/25992-empires-in-world-history.html)

Pre-Modern Period Empires-to 1500 AD	Timeline
African Empires:	
Ethiopian Empire	Ca. 50 to 1974
Mali Empire	Ca. 1210 to 1490
Songhai Empire	Ca. 1468 to 1590
Fulani Empire	1800 to 1903
Mesoamerican Empires:	
Mayan Empire	Ca. 300 to 900
Teotihuacan Empire	Ca. 500 to 750
Aztec Empire	1325 to ca. 1500
Byzantine Empire	330 to 1453
Andean Empires:	
Huari Empire	600 to 800
Inca Empire	1438 to 1525
Chinese Pre-Modern Empires:	
T'ang Dynasty	618 to 906
Sung Dynasty	906 to 1278
Islamic Empires:	
Umayyid/Abbasid	661 to 1258
Almohad	1140 to 1250
Almoravid	1050 to 1140

Carolingian Empire	Ca. 700 to 810
Bulgarian Empire	802 to 827 1197 to 1241
Southeast Asian Empires: Khmer Empire Burnese Empire	 877 to 1431 1057 to 1287
Novogorod Empire	882 to 1054
Medieval German Empire	962 to 1250
Danish Empire	1014 to 1035
Indian Empires: Chola Empire Empire of Mahmud of Gharzni Mughal Empire	 11th century 998 to 1039 1526 to 1805
Mongol Empire	1206 to 1405
Manluk Empire	1250 to 1517
Holy Roman Empire	1254 to 1835
Habsburg Empire	1452 to 1806
Ottoman Empire	1453 to 1923

List of Pre-Modern Period Empires
(https://archive.globalpolicy.org/component/content/article/155-history/25992-empires-in-world-history.html)

Modern Period – Empires (after 1500 AD)	Timeline
Portuguese	ca. 1450 to 1975
Spanish Empire	1492 to 1898
Russian Empire/USSR	1552 to 1991
Swedish Empire	1560 to 1660
Dutch Empire	1660 to 1962
British Empire	1607 to ca. 1980
French Empire	ca. 1611 to ca. 1980
Modern Chinese Empire: Ch'ing Dynasty	 1644 to 1911
Austrian/Austro-Hungarian Empire (see also Habsburg Empire)	ca. 1700 to 1918
US Empire (1776-present)	1776 to present
Brazilian Empire	1822 to 1889
German Empire	1871 to 1918 1939 to 1945
Japanese Empire	1871 to 1945
Italian Empire	1889 to 1942

List of Modern Period Empires

(https://archive.globalpolicy.org/component/content/article/155-history/25992-empires-in-world-history.html)

One can draw some conclusions from the table; empires come and go and have existed around the world including on five of the seven continents, all but Australia and Antarctica. Most scholars believe that the earliest civilizations first emerged in modern-day Iraq, Egypt, India, China, Peru, and Mexico beginning approximately between 4000 BC and 3000 BC. Civilizations started on the continents of Asia (Iraq, India, and China), Africa (Egypt), South America (Peru), and North America (Mexico), all but Europe, Australia, and Antarctica.

With respect to the origins of human history, one theory is it began approximately 7 million years ago in central Africa spreading sequentially to Europe, Asia, throughout southern Asian islands to Australia, across the land bridge connecting Asia and North America, down through North America to South America, and from North America to Greenland as depicted in Jared Diamond's book, *Guns, Germs, and Steel: The Fates of Human Societies*.[38]

Groups of humans increased their population into larger communities through farming versus the hunter-gatherers that tended to stay smaller in numbers. Civilizations, as complex societies, developed some means of governing themselves through the creation of political systems.

Description of Political Systems

Through antiquity, the concept of politics was developed. Where it first started and who first created it is a debate for scholars, but historic thinkers influenced where we are today in world politics and international relations: Confucius in China, Kautilya in India, Ibn Khaldūn in North Africa, the

Greek philosophers of Socrates, Plato, and Aristotle, and then there's Niccolo Machiavelli's *The Prince*, a practical guide for ruling during the Renaissance period. These and many more have shaped the governing of the past, present, and future. One could fill multiple books discussing the political ideas of historic figures, so instead, I will provide general information on the major types of political systems: democracies, monarchies, oligarchies, and authoritarian and totalitarian regimes or some combination.

American philosophy characterizes that the best political system is a democracy as depicted through its national security strategy to establish democracies wherever it treads in conflict. We can thank the Greeks for the concept of democracy: *democracy, literally, rule by the people. The term is derived from the Greek dēmokratia, which was coined from dēmos ("people") and kratos ("rule") in the middle of the fifth century BCE to denote the political systems then existing in some Greek city-states, notably Athens.*[39] A democracy does not guarantee good leadership; it just guarantees that the people have an influence in their governance. Of course, the more competent the voting population, the greater the probability that those selected can handle the highly complex job of governance.

Democracies are hard to establish and maintain. When inappropriately managed, less than stellar government leaders can be voted out by the people; therefore, the greatest benefit of a democracy is the ability of people to rid the government leadership of poor performers and keep good performers if only for a limited timeframe. Democracies require the population to put affairs of the nation above their own; focus service to the nation first for the specified period of governance; and to make hard, what can be unfavorable decisions for the best interest of the nation in the long run. Democracies have facilitated great leaders such as John F. Kennedy, whose famous quotes reflect his leadership style of service. From his 1961 Inaugural Address:

let every nation know, whether it wishes us well or ill, we shall pay any price, bear any burden, meet any hardship, support any friend, oppose any foe to assure the survival and success of liberty.... And so, my fellow Americans-ask not what your country can do for you--ask what you can do for your country.[40]

I never grow tired reading those words for they encapsulated the American persona for so many years.

What other recent political leaders have expressed this same demand of their citizens to be part of their government's solutions through actions? Reflect on President Abraham Lincoln and his struggle to keep the nation together when it was being torn apart over the issue of slavery which had been percolating for decades. Amazing, he wrote the speech himself while on the train to Gettysburg; do leaders today instill this personal commitment of writing?

The words are immortal delivered on November 19, 1863:

four score and seven years ago brought forth on this continent, a new nation, conceived in Liberty, and dedicated to the proposition all men are created equal...government of the people, by the people, for the people shall not perish from the earth.[41]

Only a great leader of democracy could articulate those words, solemnly walking a perilous line not to display triumphant zeal over the northern success at the Battle of Gettysburg, but the somber Father of a Nation subdued by the fighting of his children. This was the American culture, instituted by the founding fathers who risked treason to ensure that citizens of America had the right to select their leadership. Is this still the American culture of today?

The downside of democracy is that when long-term change is required, the system falters through turnover and an inability to define, plan, and implement long-term strategies in a short-term governing window. Long-term planning can result in short-term pain when changes mean the temporary loss of jobs shifting to new, different skilled workers. Too much of humankind avoids change and if long-term success means short-term change, it will be unpopular, even embattled. Democracies become fragile under these conditions. As Lincoln added in his famous speech, *now we are engaged in a great civil war, testing whether that nation, or any nation so conceived, and so dedicated, can long endure.*

When political parties provide the underlying long-term

planning, the change in leadership does not affect the planning and progress if the same party stays in power and if the people see value in the party's goals and objectives. This diminishes the role of the democratic leader away from a popularity contest which many democratic political campaigns have become. The democratic political system alone does not yield favorable results for a nation; much more is needed to achieve progress.

Maybe Winston Churchill got it right when he expressed his reservations in 1947:

Many forms of government have been tried and will be tried in this world of sin and woe. No one pretends that democracy is perfect or all-wise. Indeed, it has been said that democracy is the worst form of government except for all those other forms that have been tried from time to time.[42]

Churchill governed under a system entwined with a monarchy. Monarchies tend to provide long-term stability attained through the ruling class staying in power until one's death or close to it. There are legendary monarchs of old and new: Queen Elizabeth I ruled from 1558 to her death in 1603, considered a long era of stability and domestic peace for England. Some monarchs and monarchies have been very effective throughout history, but others have not. The problem with monarchies is that you can't vote out a bad monarch and sometimes the heir apparent is not *the brightest light bulb on the shelf.* Without an ejection plan, monarchies can be destructive to a nation.

What about those rulers that have attained the word *Great* after their name: Alexander the *Great* of Macedonia, Cyrus the *Great* of Achaemenian, Akbar the *Great* of Mughal Empire, Peter the *Great* of Russia, Catherine the *Great* of Russia, and Frederick the *Great* of Prussia, to name a few? In many cases, the connotation of Great related to their motive and actions to expand their empire and not necessarily their concern or best interests of their people.

What is an oligarchy? An oligarchy is defined as a governing system by a few which tend to be a few very powerful people. Looking at countries that have recently been considered oligarchies, Russia tops the list. When Vladimir Putin took control of Russia, he faced well-connected, influential wealthy Russian business leaders who embraced capitalism and had control over most of the country's economy. He gave them the option of prison or loyalty to him; those who chose him gained lucrative government contracts. Former Soviet regimes are susceptible to becoming oligarchies. As cited in a *USA Today* article in 2023, *Ukrainian President Volodymyr Zelenskyy signed a "deoligarchization" law in 2021 that cracks down on monopolies and places limits on the political influence of the elite.*[43] The majority of the population may not benefit from an oligarchy focused on wealth of the few at the top. On the other hand, those wealthy at the top probably would not be content with change and policies that spread wealth around.

Although China defines itself as communist, the political system is a hybrid of centralized power with capitalistic elements, which results with power held by a few for a very long period. The expression, *power tends to corrupt and absolute power corrupts absolutely*, by Lord Acton comes to mind. This hybrid approach allows a long-term plan and implementation with capitalistic incentives for a large population to drive economic gain, an element lacking in the Soviet Union form of communism. Robert Kaplan in his book *The Revenge of Geography* states

While the rulers of China in the second decade of the twenty-first century may not be so heartless as Mao, China's history can, however, never be far from their minds. Though China's current borders encompass Manchuria, Inner Mongolia, East Turkestan, and Tibet-all the surrounding plateaus and grasslands, that is-the very economic and diplomatic strategies of China's rulers today demonstrate an idea of China that reaches beyond territorial extent of even the China of the eighth century Tang and the eighteenth-century High Qing. China, a demographic behemoth with the world's most energetic economy for the past three decades, is, unlike Russia, extending its territorial influence much more through commerce than coercion.[44]

Iran has been called a theocracy and a clerical oligarchy because of the power held by the clerics. A Supreme Leader is chosen by the Assembly of Experts who controls the country with 2,000 clerical field operatives. Under the 1979 constitution, all judges must base decisions on sharia law or Islamic law adding further aggressive control over its citizens.

An outlier as an oligarchy is the Philippines. When President Rodrigo Duterte threatened to dismantle the country's oligarchy, he came under criticism from those opposed or had different views, also questioning his own involvement. However, the most surprising is that of a *USA Today* article's claim that the United States has been acting as an oligarchy for the last few decades with the American economic elite representing the business interests and too much influence on United States policy over the general population. The comment was made by Vermont Senator Bernie Sanders who also claimed that Europe, United Kingdom, and all over the world a small number of wealthy people are influencing the actions of government in their favor.[45] No nation will claim their political system to be an oligarchy, since it has acquired a rather negative connotation.

Although there are similarities between authoritarian and totalitarian regimes, such as discouraging individual freedom of thought and action, there are differences that create the distinction. Totalitarians actively assert control over citizens' lives whereas authoritarians focus on the submission of the citizens to political authority. Totalitarian governments tend to have a guiding, unifying objective at the expense of all others.

Examples of totalitarian governments are Nazi Germany under Adolf Hitler, Fascist Italy under Benito Mussolini, the

Soviet Union under Joseph Stalin, the People's Republic of China under Mao Zedong, and North Korea under the Kim Dynasty. According to *Wikipedia*, perceived examples of authoritarian capitalist governments, which are highly centralized but allow capitalistic elements, are China since economic reforms, Hungary under Viktor Orbán, Russia under Valdimir Putin, Chile under Augusto Pinchot, Singapore under Lee Kuan Yew, and Türkiye under Recep Tayyip Erdoğan.[46]

Margaret Thatcher recognized Singapore's Yew as *one of the twentieth century's most accomplished practitioners of statecraft.*[47] He served as Singapore's first Prime Minister from 1959 to 1990. Yew took the country of Singapore out of colonialism, past rejection to be part of Malaysia, and survived independence in a part of the world full of aggressive neighbors to be one of the most successful economies on earth. As Henry Kissinger summarized in his book, *Leadership*, on Yew: *Lee's statesmanship illustrates that the best determinants of a society's fate are neither its material wealth nor other conventional measures of power but rather the quality of its people and the vision of its leaders.* He cites Yew's words: *if you are realistic, you become pedestrian, plebeian, you will fail. Therefore, you must be able to soar above the reality and say, "This is also possible".*[48] Prime Minister Yew was not only a visionary but also had the ability to implement his vision.

I'll add one more point clarifying this premise. Leaders

must have a vision of where to go but also must understand how to get there. Vision without good planning to attain results is just spending money and falling far short of successful goals. One cannot plan without the vision of where to go first. The lack of the two elements leaves nations initially in status quo and long-term decline. Is this why great empires have declined?

Bill Gates uses the analogy of a runner to describe the personal computer race, *as long as the leader keeps running fast or faster than the others, he stays in the lead and competitors will have to keep trying to catch up. If, however, he slacks off or stops pushing himself, the rest will pass him by.*[49] In the corporate competitive world, this is true. Does it also reflect the mechanics of international politics and power?

Eventually, inadequate leadership develops less capable people, and the empire never recovers with new empires of great leadership setting goals and obtaining performance. Part of Yew's success is the result of his long-term commitment during his service to the country. Thirty-one years of implementation of a vision allowed him to measure and adjust accordingly to maintain the exceptional performance of the nation over the long haul.

Unfortunately, democracies usually do not provide this kind of stability to attain national performance, especially under dramatic change, when leadership becomes a revolving door every few years. Totalitarian and authoritarian governments can achieve results through long-term governance; unfortunately, in most cases, the results are at the expense of morality and the welfare of the nation.

Many countries are a combination of political systems, for example, a constitutional monarchy. It is one answer to move away from a monarchy system without full-scale upheaval and erasure of the royal line as in the case of France and Russia. A monarch shares power with a constitutionally organized government. In some cases, the monarch is the de facto head of state or merely a ceremonial role. The constitution assigns the remainder of government responsibilities to the legislature and judiciary.

The United Kingdom is one of several constitutional monarchies in the world. The British monarch is also the head of state for Antigua and Barbuda; Australia; Bahamas; Belize; Canada; Grenada; Jamaica; New Zealand; Papua New Guinea; Saint Kitts and Nevis; Saint Lucia; Saint Vincent and the Grenadines; Solomon Islands; and Tuvalu. Other countries with a constitutional monarchy system are Belgium, Cambodia, Jordan, Netherlands, Norway, Spain, Sweden, and Thailand.

A parliamentary system is a form of democratic government. The party or a coalition of parties with the greatest representation in parliament manages the government with their leader known as the prime minister or chancellor. Below is a map of the countries by government system created by the Visual Capitalist organization.

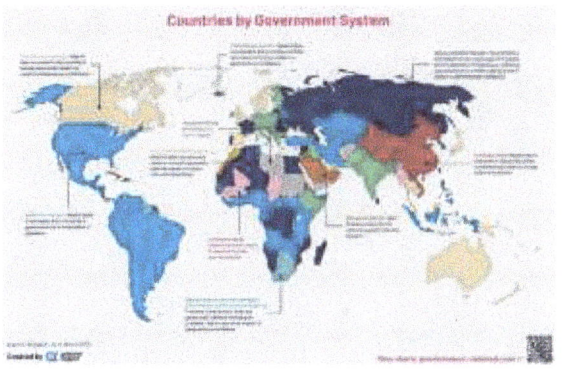

countries by government system
https://www.visualcapitalist.com/cp/mapped-worlds-government-systems/

Description of Religious Systems

Although many religions exist in the world, I will focus on the five most prevalent because they are largely encountered through one's travels: Christianity, Islam, Hinduism, Buddhism, and Judaism, in order of population. These summaries may appear over-simplified because religious practices can be quite complex, but my intent is to provide a general overview on similarities and differences. Before embarking on this knowledge adventure, let's first differentiate between polytheistic and monotheistic religions.

Polytheistic religions are associated with ancient times. Paganism, a term developed by Christians, denotes those religions that do not worship a single God such as the God of Abraham, central to Christianity, Judaism, and Islam. Ancient worshipers built elaborate structures to gain favor from the Gods. Using the broad definition of paganism as a religion that worships multiple deities, most religions that existed before Abraham fell into this bucket: Sumerian, Egyptian, ancient Greek and Roman, Viking, Slavic, and South American tribes, to name just a few.

However, Hinduism and Buddhism may also be considered polytheistic with temples that date back to ancient times. Most Hindus believe in one supreme god, The Brahman. Everything is a manifestation of the Brahman; however, the Brahman's powers may be represented by a great diversity of gods or deities that emanate from The Brahman. Buddhists do not believe in a deity or God but do believe that supernatural figures can help or hinder one on the path of enlightenment.

Monotheistic religions comprise Christianity, Islam, and Judaism with Judaism being the oldest. All denote religions that worship the God of Abraham. Ironically, with this foundational beginning, the turmoil created between the religions is mindboggling. Although believed to be facilitated by God, all are traced to writings by man: for Christianity, Jesus and his disciples; for Islam, Muhammad; and for Judaism, I look to the Institute for Advanced Study for the answer:

Who wrote the Torah? In light of more than two hundred years of scholarship and of the ongoing disputes on that question, the most precise answer to this question still is: We don't know. The tradition claims it was Moses, but the Torah itself says otherwise. Only small portions within the Torah are traced back to him, but not nearly the whole Torah: Exodus 17:14 (Battle against Amalek); 24:4 (Covenant Code); 34:28 (Ten Commandments); Numbers 33:2 (Wandering Stations); Deuteronomy 31:9 (Deuteronomic Law); and 31:22 (Song of Moses).[50]

For a brief description of each, we'll start with the oldest. Hinduism originated on the Indian subcontinent. If the Indus Valley civilization of the third to second millennium BCE was the earliest source of traditions and practices, then Hinduism is the oldest living religion on Earth. Through writings in Sanskrit, Hinduism spread to other parts of the world. The Brahman's various manifestations created different branches of philosophy and beliefs. The Hindu concept of time has no beginning nor end. Albert Einstein and Stephen Hawking would be interested in learning more about the physics of that concept. Einstein with his theory of relativity and that time is relative and Hawking on his pursuit of the interconnected theory to explain everything.

Previous universes were preceded by an infinite number of universes and future universes will be by an infinite number too, time is an infinitesimal continuum. I'm not sure I can visually wrap my brain around that concept other than a circular shape. Whereas the Western tendency to think of religion as a system of beliefs, Hinduism is considered a frame of mind or a way of life with a tangle of customs, obligations, traditions, and ideals embracing every aspect of one's life. Framing a way to live, Hinduism became a dominant presence in Southeast Asia by the fourth century CE.

Buddhism originated in Southern Asia around the fifth century BCE eventually spread around the world. Buddhists believe that human life is a cycle of suffering and rebirth. Through the state of enlightenment or nirvana, one can escape this cycle. Siddhartha Gautama was the first person to attain this enlightenment state and became known as the Buddha. Gautama was born in Nepal as an Indian prince. He became disenchanted with his royal state after seeing poor people sick and dying. He concluded that human life is suffering and renounced his wealth adopting the life of a poor beggar spending his time meditating and traveling. Still remaining unsatisfied with his life, he realized that the path to enlightenment meant neither poverty nor wealth but rather a life between the two extremes. Gautama would achieve enlightenment underneath a Bodhi tree, known as the Tree of Awakening. The Mahabodhi Temple in Bihar, India is the site of his enlightenment becoming a major Buddhist pilgrimage site.

There are Four Noble Truths in Buddhism. The first truth (dukkha) is that suffering is part of life. The second truth (samudāya) relates to the origin of suffering rooted in desire. The third truth (nirodha) is the cessation of suffering, the possibility to stop suffering and achieve enlightenment. The fourth truth (magga) is the path to cessation of suffering, the steps to achieve enlightenment. Buddhists believe in rebirth into different bodies based on actions, good or bad, of one's past or present life impacting their future. The practice of Buddhism places a high value on ethical conduct and compassion through service.

The monotheistic religion of Judaism was practiced by the Israelites and considered the original religion of the Abrahamic faith. The Jewish sacred text, the Tanakh or Hebrew Bible, includes the same books as the Old Testament in the Christian Bible, however, arranged in a slightly different order. The Torah, also referred to as the Pentateuch, the first five books of the Tanakh, outlines the laws of the Jewish religion. God's message was conveyed through prophets such as Abraham, Isaac, Moses, Solomon, and others. Worldwide there are approximately 14 million Jewish followers who worship in religious centers known as synagogues.

Christianity diverts in the Bible from Judaism in the New Testament and the belief that Jesus is the son of God sent to teach God's words and absolve the sins of mankind through his birth (Christmas) and death and resurrection (Easter). Judaism acknowledges that Jesus existed but does not believe he is God's messiah. Islam also acknowledges that Jesus existed as a prophet and miracle worker but not as the Son of God. Although there is an abundance of Christian religions, Christianity historically separated into three major branches: Roman Catholic, Eastern Orthodox, and Protestant.

The pope, as the bishop of Rome and the Holy See, forms the Catholic church's central government making decisions on issues of faith and morality for the followers. The first pope, Saint Peter, who reigned from 33 to 67 was the longest running of the first ten popes from 33 to 154 with Hyginus (pope nine) lasting only four years from 136 to 140. Saint Peter, the Apostle, was one of the 12 disciples of Jesus Christ.

It was Emperor Constantine who erected the basilica on Vatican Hill in 326 over what he believed to be the tomb of Peter. According to an article in *America* magazine: *While scholars are certain St. Peter's ancient tomb was located on Vatican Hill where he had died a martyr and where Constantine ordered a basilica be built, his remains have been a source of much controversy and mystery.*[51] Although several excavations have been conducted in search of Saint Peter's bones, none have conclusively satisfied the scholars. Until the mid-nineteenth century, the pope's governance expanded over neighboring regions. Between 1309-1377, the papal residence moved to Avignon in France eventually returning to Rome. Pope Pius IX experienced the end of the pope's role in a governing power and shifted the focus to spiritual. In 1506 the cornerstone of Saint Peter's Basilica was laid, although it was not finished until 1626. In 1512, Michaelangelo completed his famous painting on the ceiling of the Sistine Chapel. The site is considered synonymous with the Renaissance period with papal leadership financially facilitating the eruption of creativity of the art world, largely expressed through religious artwork.

Historic Catholic churches are concealed art galleries, displaying masterpieces. The expression *a picture is worth a thousand words* describes their purpose but also that the population was largely illiterate and therefore the pictures illustrated the message of the Catholic leadership.

How did the pope finally acquire a permanent home? The Lateran Pact was an agreement signed between Prime Minister Benito Mussolini on behalf of King Victor Emmanuel III of Italy and Cardinal Secretary of State Pietro Gasparri on behalf of Pope Pius XI on February 11, 1929, establishing Vatican City as an independent territory, giving the pope a permanent home outside of any superior governance.

The creation of the Eastern Orthodox Church occurred from the Schism of 1054 between Rome and Constantinople. With the center in Constantinople, its geographic congregation encompassed the Middle East, the Balkans, and Russia with missionary expansion into Asia. A significant strife resulted when Western Catholicism of Rome introduced the Nicene Creed, the doctrine that the Holy Spirit proceeds not from the Father alone, as the church had taught, but from the Father and the Son. There were additional disputes over authority and differences in religious practices, such as the ability for clergy to marry in the Eastern Church versus celibacy for Roman Catholic clergy.

The Church of the Holy Wisdom, or Hagia Sophia, was built by Emperor Justian in the sixth century to become the center of religious life for the Eastern Orthodox world. As cited previously as one of the finalists for the Seven Wonders of the Modern World, Hagia Sophia became a museum in 1935 under President Ataturk, a UNESCO World Heritage site in 1985, and then repurposed as a mosque under President Erdogan in 2020. This action created quite a stir within the country and internationally with the historic significance of the church.

Thought-provoking questions: Has the Turkish government embraced the concept that a place of worship is merely a material structure with no connection to religion, beliefs, or historic purpose; any structure can be used as a place of worship? Should the repurpose of existing underused buildings be the first choice for establishing new places to worship before diverting funds for the expense of new buildings? Is it the responsibility of a nation's leadership to ensure that historic relics are available in their historic state to the largest proportion of the world population? Hagia Sophia is an architectural icon of the period but also the symbol of the birth of the Eastern Orthodox Church. The impacts of this change were elaborated by UNESCO's leadership.

The Director-General of UNESCO deeply regrets the decision of the Turkish authorities, made without prior discussion, to change the status of Hagia Sophia. This evening, she shared her serious concerns with the Ambassador of Turkey to UNESCO. Hagia Sophia is part of the Historic Areas of Istanbul, a property inscribed on UNESCO's World Heritage List. "Hagia Sophia is an architectural masterpiece and a unique testimony to interactions between Europe and Asia over the centuries. Its status as a museum reflects the universal nature of its heritage, and makes it a powerful symbol for dialogue," said Director-General Audrey Azoulay.[52]

Great Camlica Mosque, Türkiye's largest mosque started construction on August 6, 2013, and opened for worship on March 7, 2019. It can be seen from every point in Istanbul. The mosque can hold 63,000 people for prayer. Does Istanbul really need Hagia Sophia as a mosque or is it better purposed as a museum where all can view its historically derived birth of the Eastern Orthodox Church? Former President Ataturk was a world visionary to understand the church's role in history and formerly designate it as a museum.

Another Christian religious schism occurred during the Reformation and the creation of Protestantism during the sixteenth century. Considered one the most important events in Western history, concluding the Thirty Years' War. What initiated the movement was the corruption of the Catholic church. There's nothing more magnificent than walking into a Catholic church built during the Medieval and Renaissance period. The architecture, the frescoes, and the flying buttresses ignite one's emotions of awe at what the labors of mere man accomplished back then, but possibly at the expense of the welfare of the population.

Whether it is the religious elite, monarchical elite, or capitalistic elite, the *have nots* will resent what the *haves* acquired especially when the disadvantaged population is footing the bill. The populous in many cases funded and built these religious icons of man's capability largely to impress the divinity. The expense of wars to expand the rulers' empires or resolve disagreements with those in power are added to the cost. Was the leadership held accountable?

Yes, the populous may become disagreeable with the decisions of religious leadership.

The Protestant Reformation completely changed the European cultural, religious, social, and political landscape and is often referred to as the birth of the modern age as it coincided with and was encouraged by the Renaissance of the 15th-16th centuries. Although there were earlier movements in response to the corruption of the Church, modern technology in the form of the printing press allowed for the dissemination of protestant literature and the publication of the Bible in the vernacular, resulting in widespread support for the cause and the end of the monolithic religious, cultural, and political authority of the Church.[53]

Unfortunately, under papal governance, the system lacked the checks and balances needed to ensure that church decisions were in the best interest of everyone. Corruption of the church led to the Thirty Years' War and the schism that created the many denominations of Protestant religions: Anglicanism, Baptist, Calvinism, Lutheranism, Methodist, and Presbyterian, to name a few.

The last of the five major religions to summarize is Islam, born by Mohammed through the belief that the archangel Gabriel expressed to him the revelations of God collected and codified as the Qur'an, the Muslim Holy Book. Muhammed was born in Mecca, a prosperous city on the trade route and a pilgrimage site for pagan deities worshipped at the time. Mohammed's message initially was unpopular in Mecca; he was forced to emigrate north to Medina in 622 where he attracted followers, and his teachings spread. Although he died in 632, his followers, led by a series of four caliphs continued to spread the message of Islam.

Under their command, the Arab armies carried the new faith and leadership from the Arabian Peninsula to the shores of the Mediterranean and to the eastern reaches of Iran. The Arabs conquered Syria, Palestine, and Egypt from the Byzantine empire, while Iraq and Iran, the heart of the Sasanian empire, succumbed to their forces. Here in these lands, Islam fostered the development of a religious, political, and cultural commonwealth and the creation of a global empire.[54]

Upon the Prophet Muhammad's death, a political disagreement caused a split between Sunni and Shia followers on succession. He died without a male heir or succession plan, creating the Islamic schism of whether the successor should be chosen or inherited through Muhammad's family. The majority leaned toward selection and became known as Sunni with Muhammad's close friend Abu Bakr becoming the first caliph. Shia supported inherited succession selecting the cousin and son-in-law Ali. Ali would become the fourth caliph but would be assassinated during his reign. This conflict pushed the Shia minority into Iraq, Lebanon, and Iran where a significant number still reside today. Sunni Muslims comprise approximately 85 percent while Shia are 15 percent and have remained a *bone of contention* between the two Islamic groups.

Religious actions seem to be rooted in some major premises: an evolution from paganism to a one God belief with faith derived from Abraham; the desire to help those less fortunate; there is only one right religion and practices with all others being considered wrong; and the desire to spread the faith through conflict, coercion, or conciliation. Is this what the creator of the universe envisioned?

This paragraph will probably raise angst with some religious advocates, but its purpose is to initiate thought-provoking dialogue. Although religions are by some treated as a birthright, they are not part of our gene makeup. One is not born of a religion, but some religions treat the practice as if it is a heritage. This tends to create nationalities that are rooted in a particular religion. Again, one's chosen belief is not part of one's DNA, whether chosen by parents when born or facilitated by parents later in childhood. One's nationality may be rooted in DNA born to parents whose heritage developed in some parts of the world. Hereditary tools can estimate where your ancestors originated in the world based on your DNA.

An underlying theme of all religions is living a charitable life aiding the disadvantaged. In ancient times when these religions were created, life was extremely harsh, especially under severe environmental conditions in many parts of the world, like the Middle East or Asia. A sense of community and helping each other would make the difference between getting through another harsh day or not. It is reasonable that faith and belief would have this element of benevolence. It's also reasonable that it would take on a greater role in one's life, being the anchor to hope for a better way of life. As you create your bucket list and travel to exotic places around the world, socialize with this general knowledge and ponder over the questions that I have raised. Explore places that might be outside of your general interest or comfort zone for more personal growth.

Fund for Peace Index

To understand the stability of a nation, a means to measure and compare performance to other nations is required. For my doctoral dissertation on *Defense Institutional Building-Integrating the Work*, I reviewed several nation indices and selected the Fund for Peace Fragile State Index. The index tracked all nations, it was comprehensive with data collected on the elements of power: political, social, economic, and military; and it covered a reasonable timeframe since 2006.

The Fragile State Index generated from the Fund for Peace's propriety Conflict Assessment System Tool (CAST), is a mixed methods approach using quantitative and qualitative techniques. Twelve primary social, economic, and political indicators are further divided into sub-indicators. Applying content analysis approach, CAST uses sophisticated search parameters and algorithms to search millions of documents. A big data analytics method searches and compiles the data into measurable indices. The sub-indicators are assessed and compiled into the primary indicators for each of the twelve areas.

The composite fragile state index is a cumulative total of each of the primary indicators, with all sub-indicators weighted equally. Through both integration and triangulation techniques, CAST separates the relevant information from irrelevant using a propriety algorithm. Scores are compared with a comprehensive set of vital statistics, as well as human analysis, to ensure that the software does not misinterpret the raw data. A team of experts reviewed the final score to ensure validity of results. Since the assessment has remained the same over the period of collection, a comparison of a nation over time can be accomplished as well as a comparison between nations.

The sub-indicators are divided into four categories with three factors in each category. Cohesion indicators include security apparatus, factionalized elites, and group grievance. Economic indicators include economic decline, uneven economic development, and human flight and brain drain. Political indicators include state legitimacy, public services, and human rights and rule of law. Social tend to be cross-cutting indicators that include demographic pressures, refugees and internally displaced persons (IDP), and external intervention. Each sub-indicator is scored from 0 to 10. Cumulatively the score of the sub-indicators is compiled to achieve the total index score, which is from 0 to 120. The higher the score, the more fragile the nation. The lower the score, the more stable the nation.

The Fund for Peace provides this information to the public for betterment of nations as a public resource for credible nation stability assessments through the composite index. The Fund for Peace publishes the results of the index every year with articles on specific regions or countries that have improved or degraded over the year. Since the index is generated at the beginning of one year, it actually represents the national activity over the previous year. Fund for Peace is a Washington, DC headquartered non-governmental organization (NGO).

To have meaningful early warning and effective policy responses, assessments must go beyond specialized areas of knowledge, narrative case studies, and anecdotal evidence to identify and grasp broad social trends. An interdisciplinary combination of qualitative research and quantitative methodologies is needed to establish patterns and acquire predictive value. Without the right data, it is impossible to identify problems that may be festering below the radar. Decision makers need access to this kind of information to implement effective policies...the social science framework and software applications upon which it is built makes political risk assessment and early warning of conflict accessible to policy- makers and the public.[55]

For each of the countries that I visit, I will provide the Fragile State Index and provide a short trend assessment. Although tourism organizations closely watch the environment of social, political, and economic factors, one should also stay abreast of concerns when visiting countries. This doesn't mean that one should only visit the most problem-free, stable countries because many are managing through internal issues that can be a diamond in the rough. In addition, tourism fuels improvements in social, political, and economic elements of the country. One's receptiveness to take a chance can mean a lot for improving future stability.

Fund for Peace has added a parallel assessment of a country's resilience. Resilience can reflect individuals, but it can also reflect nations. This new index reflects the country's ability to recover from a crisis, relative to the severity of the crisis, through preparation and management. The COVID-19 pandemic shocked the foundation of countries to handle the crisis from a political, economic, and social perspective. More resilient nations will successfully ride out the crisis with marginal long-term impacts. The Resilience State Index comprises ratings on inclusion, social cohesion, state capacities, individual capabilities, environment and ecology, economy, and civic space.

I will discuss both the Fragile State Index and the Resilience State Index for the countries that I have visited. For some, I will explore trends, whether improving or declining in stability. Collectively, this information reflects how well the world is developing.

Chapter 5

Portugal

The triumph of culture is to overpower nationality. -
Ralph Waldo Emerson
(http://www.notable-quotes.com/c/culture_quotes.html)

Background: History, Culture, and Environment

Olá, meu amigo.

A trip to Portugal will transport one back in time to constructing medieval castles and beautiful, ornate churches. Some have fared well during the hardships of centuries and others have not. Portugal was founded in 1143 based on the Zamora Treaty, an agreement between D. Afonso Henriques, the first King of Portugal, and Alphonse the VII of Leon and Castile which recognized Portugal as an independent kingdom. In 1179, Pope Alexander III confirmed this independence. Through the twelfth and thirteenth centuries, Portugal would expand its border close to what exists today. At the end of the thirteenth century (1290), King D. Dinis founded the prestigious University of Coimbra, one of the oldest in Europe.

In 1385, a new reign of King D. Jao I and his sons would focus the country's development on social progress in education and governing skills. Portugal also represents discovery and exploration. It was Infant D. Henrique, also known as Henri the Navigator, that led Portugal's exploration of the seas. During the next several centuries, Portugal navigated to Africa, the Far East, and South America competing for land and wealth expansion with other European countries such as England, France, and Spain.

Expansion consisted of maritime discovery of the routes to India by Vasco da Gama (1498), Brazil (1500), Malaysia (1511), Timor (1512), China (1513), and Japan (1543). It was Ferdinand Magellan who circumnavigated the globe between 1519 and 1522. The next chapter in this book documents my travels to Patagonia and cruising Tierra del Fuego through the Straits of Magellan, named for the Portuguese navigator.

With the wealth accrued through maritime discovery and expansion, rulers constructed magnificent buildings such as the Jeronimos Monastery in Lisbon by King D. Manuel. After the tragic death of young King D. Sebastiao in a battle in Northern Africa, the throne was held by Spanish kings for 60 years. In 1640, Portugal regained their independence under the Portuguese King D. Joao IV. In 1755 a devastating earthquake hit Portugal practically destroying Lisbon. It was King Joseph I's Prime Minister, the Marque de Pombal, who rebuilt Lisbon to endure future acts of nature.

During the nineteenth century, Napoleon invaded Portugal, and the monarchy moved to Brazil. Napoleon's name has surfaced frequently during my travels, especially in

Europe. In 1821, the monarchy returned home under King Joao VI. However, the Portuguese people's desire changed from an absolute monarchy to a transformation of the political system. The first Constitution was drafted, changing the King's power to no longer be absolute. After King D. Joao VI's death created a power vacuum, civil war broke out between his two sons who were on opposite sides of support for the Constitution:

D. Miguel (opposed) and D. Pedro (defended). The conflict was settled in 1834 when the Convention of Evora Monte was signed, ending military operations and the return to a liberal and constitutional version of the monarchy.

This did not end the country's desire for political change. After King Carlos I's assassination in 1908 and a revolution in 1910, Portugal finally became a republic. D. Manuel II was the last King of Portugal and Teofilo Braga, the first Republic's Head of State. Manuel de Arriaga was the first elected President of the Portuguese Republic. It was after World War I when a military coup occurred resulting in the authoritarian rule of Antonio Oliveira Salazar, who governed the country for 50 years. Finally, on April 25, 1974, the Carnation Revolution returned Portugal to a democracy and reversed its position on colonization recognizing independence for former African colonies.

The post-revolutionary constitution was adopted in 1976 but modified several times. It established a semi-presidential system with the executive power divided between a president and a prime minister. In 1982 the constitution was revised to minimize ideological elements and in 1989 to pave the way for privatization and a transition to a free-market economy.

Portugal joined the European Union in 1986 and was one of the first countries to adopt the euro on 1 January 1999. Portugal is a country of magnificent historical construction, whether castles or churches; stunning beaches; delicious food; and an abundance of fresh fruits and vegetables. A trip to Portugal should be on everyone's bucket list. There are several UNESCO World Heritage Sites that are part of a standard 10- to 12- day country tour.

Portugal falls number 28 on the list of 201 countries for average life expectancy of 82.4 years in 2023, a significant increase from 58.5 years in 1950. The median age in the country is 45.8 years old, therefore an older population. Countries with an older population are more open to immigration policies to increase youth numbers.

Portugal has a public healthcare system called the National Healthcare Service (SNS), established in 1979, which provides the most essential services at no cost to citizens and legal residents. The SNS covers a network of facilities, private institutions, and independent professionals with administration through the Ministry of Health. Education is administered through the Ministry of Education and is free for public schools through secondary education. Private institutions do charge a fee. Public and private universities charge tuition fees.

Using the Fund for Peace Fragility State Index, Portugal is at a comfortable 164th place out of 179 nations with a score of 25.9. In fact, a much more stable country than the United States at 141st and a score of 44.5, imagine that. Through my travels around the country, I did feel safe even when spending time on my own or walking with my travel mate. Adding time on the beginning and the end of the trip, we did spend quite a bit of time on our own. No surprise that Portugal scored 7.3 out of 10 on its State Resilience Index. In all seven sub-indicators, the country scored well above average.

If that isn't enough to convince one to visit the country, Madonna chose Portugal to live buying an eighteenth-century Moorish revival mansion, Quinta do Relogio, in Sintra in June 2017. The homestead with over 16,000 square feet (22.144 square m) should provide sufficient space for the *Material Girl's* family and probably a few other families too. It is nestled in the beautiful countryside of Sintra, which is included in the UNESCO World Heritage Site designation for the Cultural Landscape of Sintra.

Travel Itinerary

The trip started in Porto (five nights); then to Tomar (one night); then to Evora (one night); and finally, Lisbon (four nights) with stops in Guimaraes, Braga, Coimbra, Fatima, Castelo de Vide, Sintra, Obidos, Alcobaca, and Nazare. Since I arrived two days early in Porto before the tour began, I partook a separate one-day trip to Santiago de Compostela in Spain. I finished the trip staying one extra day in Lisbon.

https://free-map.org/

Travel Journal

On October 31, 2022, I boarded a flight to Porto, Portugal via Madrid, Spain at 8:38 pm from John F Kennedy (JFK) Airport after taking the New Jersey Transit (NJT) train from Trenton Station to Penn Station, New York, and then a Long Island Railroad (LIRR) train to Jamaica station connecting to the Air Train to JFK. I've come to refer to this multi-transportation feat as the reverse of planes, trains, and automobiles. With overnight flights, one runs the risk of arriving too early to check into the hotel. If you can catch a few hours of sleep on the airplane, seeing some sights before checking in is beneficial. If you don't get any sleep, then those couple of hours waiting to check-in can be brutal. By the time we had lunch and returned to the hotel, we were able to settle into the room. Although general travel guidance is to stay awake for that first day, I've found that getting a few hours of sleep helps me acclimate without affecting my sleep that night. But everyone's biorhythms are different. Taking melatonin can also help to recover from time zone adjustment.

The next morning, we were up early for an independent trip to Santiago de Compostela. The drive was about two hours each way. Heading north out of Porto, we saw nothing but vineyards everywhere: backyards, land strips between roads, and any plot of land no matter how small. It was pretty comical to see how resourceful people could be in growing a few vines for their vino. Northern Portugal is wine country. As we drove north, we passed beautiful lakes with small towns nestled around the shoreline.

Arriving at Santiago de Compostela, we had several hours to tour the town, and the famous church made popular by the movie *The Way* with actor Martin Sheen and directed by son Emilio Estevez. The movie depicts the pilgrimage (Camino de Santiago) from France across northern Spain to Santiago de Compostela, the burial site of the apostle Saint James. Actress Shirley MacLaine undertook the journey in her sixties and then wrote the New York Times Best Seller, *The Camino: A Journey of the Spirit*. If one wants to read a book on the Camino journey written along the style of a day-by-day journal, *The Only Way Is West: A Once In a Lifetime Adventure Walking 500 Miles On Spain's Camino de Santiago* by Bradley Chermside depicts his journey. Other Camino pilgrimages include traversing from Porto northward to the cathedral. If I ever hike to Santiago de Compostela, I will probably start with the Porto route first since it is shorter, closer to 150 miles (241 km) versus 500 miles (805 km).

Although Saint James died in Jerusalem, it is believed that his bones were taken to Spain. These bones were discovered in a tomb in 813 CE instilling a rallying point for Christian Spain, confined to a narrow strip of the northern Iberian Peninsula, against the Moors, occupying most of the remaining territory. Alfonso II of Asturias built a church over the tomb. Alfonso III then replaced that structure with a larger structure. Through the Middle Ages, a town grew around the church creating the city; however, in 997 CE the whole town was destroyed except the tomb by Abu Amir al-Mansur, a military commander of the Moorish caliphate of Cordoba.

In 1078, Alfonso VI of Leon and Castile began the church structure of today. Over centuries, the structure has continued to expand, as well as the buildings around the cathedral. For Christians, Santiago de Compostela is the most important pilgrimage after Jerusalem and the Vatican. In 1985, the city was designated a UNESCO World Heritage Site. In 1993, the route of Santiago de Compostela was also designated a UNESCO World Heritage Site. On July 24, 2013, a train carrying pilgrims to the site for the festival of Saint James derailed just outside the city killing at least 77 people and injuring more than 140 people in one of the worst rail disasters in Spanish history.

The Cathedral of Santiago de Compostela is as magnificent as the movie depicts. I also saw pilgrims outside the side entrance with large backpacks gaily conversing with each other. Quite a remarkable feat for those who started the trip in Saint-Jean-Pied-de-Port, France over the Pyrenees Mountain range, and registering at all 24 towns along the 500-mile (805-km) trail to acquire the stamp for one's pamphlet for certification. I can only imagine that those who met fellow travelers along the way might become lifetime friends. The Cathedral, built and rebuilt over centuries, reflects Romanesque architecture with other styles incorporated. The interior is a French-influenced floor plan shaped in a traditional Latin cross with three aisles in the nave and transepts. From east to west, the main nave is about 308 feet (94 m) long. The transept is 206 feet (63 m) from north to south, making the Cathedral the largest Romanesque church in Spain.

The tomb of Saint James the Apostle rests below the Main Chapel, resulting in little change in this area. The baldachin and the Baroque silverwork surround the stone statue of a seated Saint James sculpted by Master Mateo. The Apostolic Crypt is below the Main Chapel, consists of a Roman mausoleum where the sepulcher containing the remains of Saint James and his disciples was discovered in the nineth century. The renowned Botafumeiro, the expeller of smoke, seen in the movie *The Way* is the sixteenth century pulley system and rope suspended from the octagonal dome over the transept in front of the altar. As depicted in the movie, the Botafumeiro swings back and forth dispelling incense throughout the cathedral.

Although it was worth the trip to see this beautiful place, we did not have sufficient time to see everything. Plan for several hours especially if wanting to visit the museum. For those looking for a virtual tour of the Cathedral of Santiago de Compostela, the link below provides a visual tour both outside and inside.

https://artsandculture.google.com/story/a-virtual-visit-to-the-cathedral-of-santiago-de-compostela-cathedral-of-santiago-de-compostela/IQVBcpdeUMCMqw?hl=en-US

I left two days ahead of the tour to spend a day in Santiago de Compostela and now I had an extra day in Porto. A friend's daughter had visited the bookstore, Livraria Lello, which inspired JK Rowling for the Harry Potter books. So, we ventured out to find the bookstore, opting to walk and see the city. My suggestion is to walk whenever possible, especially with organized tours. One will eat far more on a group tour than at home and the extra exercise helps to compensate for or work off those extra calories. Livraria Lello was everything described but also the word is out; we spent about 45 minutes in line to get tickets. Either buy tickets ahead of time or get there just when it opens. Near Livraria Lello are several interesting churches to explore, some have a small fee to enter as a visitor. I don't mind the fee; I'd do anything to help sustain these irreplaceable treasures.

On the first day of the organized tour, a local guide showed us the historic Porto Center which has been a UNESCO World Heritage Site since 1996. Of significance is the Church of Sao Francisco, with a gothic exterior and baroque

146

decorated interior, and the Stock Exchange building known for its neoclassical façade and ornate gilded Arabian Hall. Porto would not be complete without a cruise on the Douro River. We also visited the Burmester Cave Cellars to learn about making Port wine. It is located on the opposite side of the Douro River requiring us to walk across the Ponte da Arrábida and take in the picturesque river views below. There are riverboat multi-day cruises that leave from Porto and cruise the Douro River through the Douro Valley stopping at the many vineyards, wineries, and restaurants along the way. I have added that to my bucket list after enjoying the delicious Portuguese wines on this trip.

On the waterfront, we experienced the social scene of many city waterfronts. Lots of outdoor cafes with street musicians playing and demonstrating their artistic skills.

On the following day, I participated in the optional morning Medieval Portugal tour which included a stop in the town of Guimaraes. The historic town center has been a UNESCO World Heritage Site since 2001. Well-preserved medieval buildings such as the tenth-century Guimaraes Castle and restored Dukes of Braganca Palace have a museum with furniture, tapestries, and weapons of the period. Between these two structures lies the Romanesque Sao Miguel do Castelo Church built in the thirteenth century.

From there we headed to Braga, founded by the Romans then known as Bracara Augusta. We had lunch at Restaurante Cruz Sobral, at the time of my visit a Michelin star restaurant; the meal served family style was delicious. The group splitting into tables of 6-8 people made it more receptive to communication and the ability to get to know each other. Passing the dish also encourages dialogue for the earlier part of group tours. The Sanctuary of Bom Jesus do Monte in Braga rests on a 1,300-foot-high hill, Mount Espinho, with a neoclassical church positioned atop an elaborate 17-flight staircase known as the Holy Way staircase which overlooks Braga city. Fortunately, we drove to the top and walked down the staircase. However, many visitors were walking it roundtrip. The views from the top of the hill were splendid and I thoroughly enjoyed the walk down admiring the fountains, sculptures, and gardens. I think UNESCO said it best with their description:

The Bom Jesus ensemble is centred on a Via Crucis that leads up the western slope of the mount. It includes a series of chapels that house sculptures evoking the Passion of Christ, as well as fountains, allegorical sculptures and formal gardens. The Via Crucis culminates at the church, which was built between 1784 and 1811. The granite buildings have whitewashed plaster façades, framed by exposed stonework. The celebrated Stairway of the Five Senses, with its walls, steps, fountains, statues and other ornamental elements, is the most emblematic Baroque work within the property. They are framed by lush woodland and embraced by a picturesque park that, masterfully set on the rugged hill, highly contributes to the landscape value of the ensemble.[56]

My suggestion is to pace yourself on the walk down; there is much to see and a leisurely walk to the bottom browsing the many relics is the way to do it.

The next morning, we started the drive to Tomar, but first passing through Buçaco National Park. The park was a beautiful stop, but we had a unique experience with a vintage road race occurring during our visit; quite interesting standing at the corner of a 90-degree turn to watch the racers make the bend. Of course, I kept my distance from the corner should centrifugal force overtake the car.

It was then on to Coimbra. Coimbra is the third largest city and home to the University of Coimbra, one of the oldest universities in Europe. The university was added to the UNESCO World Heritage Site list in 2013, as cited in its description.

Situated on a hill overlooking the city, the University of Coimbra with its colleges grew and evolved over more than seven centuries within the old town. Notable university buildings include the 12th century Cathedral of Santa Cruz and a number of 16th century colleges, the Royal Palace of Alcáçova, which has housed the University since 1537, the Joanine Library with its rich baroque decor, the 18th century Botanical Garden and University Press, as well as the large "University City" created during the 1940s. The University's edifices became a reference in the development of other institutions of higher education in the Portuguese-speaking world where it also exerted a major influence on learning and literature. Coimbra offers an outstanding example of an integrated university city with a specific urban typology as well as its own ceremonial and cultural traditions that have been kept alive through the ages.[57]

Another possible Portuguese inspiration for Harry Potter is the uniforms worn by Coimbra students, complete with a long cape. In addition, the Biblioteca Joanina, the library at the University of Coimbra, is breathtaking. If you've seen the movie version of *Beauty and the Beast*, then you have seen the library, used as the Beast's library in the movie. Although JK Rowlings resided in Scotland of the United Kingdom, Portugal was an inspiration for her while living in Porto during the first three chapters of her first book, *Harry Potter and the Sorcerer's Stone*.

Then onto Fatima, one of the most important Catholic shrines in the world dedicated to the Virgin Mary. During World War I, Pope Benedict XV made numerous pleas for peace. In May of 1917, three shepherd children (Francisco, Jacinta, and Lucia Marto) saw the Apparitions of Our Lady of the Rosary. Between May 13 and October 13, 1917, the apparition appeared six times to the children. The children told their parents and word spread of the event; by August, people were traveling to Fatima for the day of the apparition.

Although the children were temporarily jailed, they never relinquished their testimony. There were three secrets conveyed by the apparition to the children: (1) a vision of hell, (2) World War I would end but another war would start, and

(3) the persecution of the church and the assassination of *a bishop dressed in white*. The apparition had told two of the children that they would have short lives; both died within two years from the Spanish flu. The Basilica of Our Lady of the Rosary of Fatima is built on the location where the children stood for the first apparition's visit. In 2017, Pope Francis canonized two (Francisco and Jacinta) of the three children. In adulthood, Lucia became a nun passing in 2005 but has yet to attain sainthood.

We arrived in Tomar just in time for a late dinner at the hotel. From our hotel window, we had a beautiful view of the Convent of Christ complex lit at night. However, it was the next morning when we visited the convent to see the famous Manueline window.

There's possibly no finest example of the Manueline style than the Window of the Chapter House at the Convent of Christ in Tomar. This window in Portuguese is known as Janela do Capítulo and it shows most of the motifs related to the maritime discoveries of the Portuguese, centuries ago. The Chapter Window is an amazing, elaborated masterwork of the Manueline architecture with themes like corals of the beaches the navigators landed, ropes from their caravels, and the vegetation they found in distant strange lands.[58]

The Convent is surrounded by the Castle of Tomar walls and belonged to the Order of the Templars founded by the Grand Master of the Knights Templar, Gualdim Pais, in 1160. Being built over five centuries, the architecture is a combination of Romanesque, Gothic, Manueline, Renaissance, Mannerist, and Baroque styles. The Convent's centerpiece is the twelfth-century rotunda, Oratory of the Templars, influenced by Jerusalem's Holy Sepulcher rotunda. This fortress reminded me of the Palace of the Grand Master of the Knights of Rhodes, another Knights of Templar castle built on the Greek island of Rhodes, also a UNESCO World Heritage site.

We were off again heading for Evora but not before stopping at the small medieval town Castelo de Vide positioned on top of a hill. The town had a small Jewish quarter with a single-room synagogue remaining, one of the oldest in the country. After the Inquisition in 1497, an expulsion decree banned Judaism in the Iberian Peninsula. Jews either converted to Catholicism, practiced in secret, or left. It was not until the eighteenth century that the Inquisition's discrimination and persecution ended, and Jewish communities re-emerged in Portugal.

The town as well as most of Portugal is very hilly with some stretches being steep. I know why everyone looked in great physical shape, walking anywhere means a rigorous workout. As I looked out the coach window leaving Castelo de Vide, I could see another similar-looking medieval town just on the next hillside. I wondered just how many are scattered around Portugal's countryside. After we left Castelo de Vide, we crossed the Tagus River, the longest in the Iberian Peninsula, and stopped at a cork factory.

Who would have thought that cork could be so fascinating. Yes, the object plugged into wine bottles is a cork and there is a very interesting story on how and where it is produced. We learned all about it at the cork factory. Learning about cork was actually very interesting; cork is the only material when compressed on one side that does not increase its volume on the other side. It therefore can adapt to variations in temperature and pressure, warranting its usage as a stopper.

We got to the hotel just in time for dinner. Although there are long days with driving and sightseeing stops, it's the best way to see more aspects of a country than merely focusing on one or two cities. Most tour coaches have Wi-Fi available although there may be areas where access is limited or non-existent. The historic center of Evora has been a UNESCO World Heritage Site since 1986. The town depicts fortified walls, the Roman Temple, and the famous Sao Francisco Church, which houses the Ossuary Chapel or Chapel of Bones (Capela dos Ossos in Portuguese).

What is unique about this chapel? The walls are decorated with over 5,000 human bones and skulls. Seeing is believing, the entire room is filled with human bones. With very little light entering the chapel, it is a very creepy place. Three Franciscan friars built the chapel in the seventeenth century with the purpose of conveying the message that life is temporary and fragile. The translation of the words over the chapel entrance is *"We bones that are here, for yours we wait"*. I think the friars had a sense of humor. It is refreshing to know that even under the hardship life of the seventeenth-century Europe, people had a sense of humor to manage their life challenges. A glass case displays the complete skeleton of one inhabitant. The rest of the bones were exhumed from local cemeteries and catacombs. There is much artistic creativity in their patterns on the walls and columns.

The chapel decoration wasn't just a philosophical statement. In the sixteenth century, there were almost 42 monastic cemeteries in the city. Perceived as a better utilization of land space, the bones were exhumed and used for a more practical approach of decorating the interior of the chapel in the seventeenth century. Besides the bones, there are a few religious statues and paintings of the Renaissance and Baroque styles. I've decided that one of the pictures for Portugal to include in this book will be for this chapel. No description can do justice to the emotional feeling of standing in the chapel; hopefully, a picture is worth a thousand words.

Bone decoration is not just a Portuguese art. Sedlec Ossuary in Kutná Hora, Czech Republic is a bone church ornately decorated with the remains of 40,000 to 70,000 people that died in the fourteenth and fifteenth century. It is one of the most visited tourist sites in the Czech Republic. Why not? Something as unique as a *chandelier of bones, which contains at least one of every bone in the human body, hangs from the center of the nave with garlands of skulls draping the vault*, is worth a detour in one's travel plans to view.[59]

Then onto the vibrant city of Lisbon. As cited in the section on the Seven Modern Wonders of the World, the Jesus statue, Christ the King or Cristo Rei, stands on the banks of the Tagus River on the Almada side of the 25 de Abril Bridge connecting Almada to Lisbon. As we crossed the bridge, the statue has shone in all its glory since its inauguration on May 17, 1959. The bridge does have a San Francisco Golden Gate Bridge vibe to it.

The first evening we had an optional Fado dinner. For many international trips, there will be planned or optional cultural dinners with local music and dance. These are well worth the experience. If they are not part of the tour package, check travel websites for dinner packages. Fado is a type of Portuguese singing associated with pubs and cafes providing an expressive and melancholic style, maybe a Portuguese version of the blues.

The next morning, we started the driving tour with a stop at Edward VII's park to take in the view over the hills of Lisbon and the Tagus River. We then ventured down to the river to see Portugal's monument to discovery which is also an UNESCO World Heritage Site since 1983, the sixteenth-century Belem Tower. A short distance away is Jeronimos Monastery, also known as the Monastery of the Hieronymites and also included as a UNESCO World Heritage Site. King Manuel I built the large monastery near the location of a church built by Prince Infante D. Henrique, better known as Henry the Navigator, in the mid-fifteenth century by the invocation of Saint Mary of Belem.

To immortalize the memory of Henry and recognize his intense devotion to Our Lady and faith in Saint Jerome, King Manuel I founded the Monastery of Saint Mary of Belem near the Tagus River in 1496. In the nineteenth century, the church became a sepulcher for heroes and poets and the final resting place for explorer Vasco de Gama. Today, it is known as Jeronimos Monastery. This site is routine for tourists, so expect long delays to enter both the monastery and church. Although often tour groups can bypass the general admission line, not in this case. We spent about 45 minutes in the entrance line, but it was worth the wait.

While we were waiting in line, our tour manager departed for a quick trip to a local bakery and the purchase of the famous and delicious Portuguese dessert, pastéis de nata. It is a creamy custard tart that caramelizes while baking in a flaky pastry crust in the oven.

Flaky is right; it makes the tart very light which means one can gobble several quickly. It's impossible to eat just one. The famous tart was created at the Jerónimos Monastery in Belém, so what better place to try one than right outside the doors of the monastery. Pastéis de Belém is widely acclaimed as the patisserie to sample for an authentic dessert in Lisbon.

The legend goes that the monks created the secret recipe for the custard tarts and sold them to raise money after the Liberal Revolution of 1820 and the closure of many convents and monasteries. When the monastery closed in 1834, one monk joined a sugar refinery and continued to make the desserts. By 1837, the owners of the refinery opened the Fábrica de Pastéis de Belém and sold the tarts using the monk's recipe. The recipe remains a secret with only a few master confectioners employed to create the pastries today. Pastéis de Belém does have a large window which allows visitors the ability to watch part of the baking process. For a slightly different taste, dust with cinnamon or powdered sugar.

For the afternoon, I signed up for the optional trip to Sintra, considered by Lord Byron as the *Glorious Eden* and the summer retreat for the royal court. Although we took the coach, the town is accessible by train from Lisbon. En route to Sintra, we stopped at Cascais, also accessible by train, the summer retreat of the Portuguese nobility, in other words, the Portuguese Riviera. King Luis I proclaimed Cascais as the preferred location for his royal summer retreat bringing an influx of wealth and power to the town. Although the beaches north of the town are known for surfing, the town boasts museums, art galleries, fine restaurants, hiking trails, and boating. The proximity to Lisbon makes both Cascais and Sintra convenient day trips for tourists or longer timeframes.

Quaint describes the town surrounding the Sintra Royal Palace, the fifteenth-century royal residence, containing one of the largest tile collections in Portugal. Sintra has been designated as a UNESCO World Heritage Site since 1995.

A summary of the cultural landscape is provided below:

In the 19th century Sintra became the first centre of European Romantic architecture. Ferdinand II turned a ruined monastery into a castle where this new sensitivity was displayed in the use of Gothic, Egyptian, Moorish and Renaissance elements and in the creation of a park blending local and exotic species of trees. Other fine dwellings, built along the same lines in the surrounding serra, created a unique combination of parks and gardens which influenced the development of landscape architecture throughout Europe.[60]

Although we did not have time to visit, the National Place of Pena is perched above the city and quite ornate to view. It is considered a renowned jewel in the Sintra Hills. The surrounding park affords a beautiful walking space.

For the last organized day in Lisbon, we explored the countryside around Lisbon. Heading north, we made a short stop in medieval Obidos, the gift from King Denis of Portugal to his queen on their wedding day in 1282. The town has a UNESCO Creative City of Literature designation. This honor acknowledges the city's quantity, quality, and diversity of literary accomplishments. Buildings have been repurposed as bookstores, such as a former church and wine cellar. The town has the traditional stone-walled castle on a hill built in the Moorish period.

Our journey continued to Alcobaca to visit the Monastery of Santa Maria d'Alcobaça, the first building in Portugal built with a Gothic style and the largest church in the country. The church has a romantic connection, a love story, with the tombs of King Pedro I and his lover Ines de Castro. Infante Pedro, the son of King Afonso IV, was married but initiated a relationship with Ines de Castro, his wife Constance's maid. When Constance died in 1345, Peter and Ines lived as a married couple with their children.

King Afonso IV disapproved of the relationship and in 1355 ordered the murder of Ines de Castro to break the union. Pedro never forgave his father and when he took the crown in 1357, he ordered the arrest and execution of Ines' murderers by ripping their hearts out. King Pedro I declared that Ines be recognized as his wife and Queen of Portugal, posthumously. In April 1360, he ordered her body to be moved from Coimbra to the Royal Monastery of Alcobaca, where their tombs eternalize their forbidden love.

The perfect Medieval love story, their intricately detailed tombs lie on each side of the church. This storyline sounds like a perfect plot for a Medieval-based movie about monarchies, outrageous and violent behavior, amorous relationships including incestuous or maybe the plot would be better as a television show.

The final stop was the charming fishing town of Nazare, with its gorgeous half-moon-shaped beach and crystal blue waters. Nazare is known to surfers, as is most of the Portuguese coastline, and there were a few out during our visit. The waves were breaking with vengeance. I couldn't resist dipping my toes into the water but was surprised by a wave breaking farther on the beach than normal and got a little more wet than expected. It seems like an area where a strong undertow could be dangerous to the inexperienced swimmer.

Extending the trip to Lisbon an extra day, we explored the local art museum, Calouste Gulbenkian Museum. From there, we walked downtown to the Carmo Convent in the Chiado neighborhood, the remaining evidence of nature's destruction in Lisbon. On November 1, 1755, during an All-Saints Day crowded church service, the stone roof of the church collapsed on the congregation. The Great Lisbon Earthquake registered a magnitude of 8.7 on the rector scale killing possibly 40,000-70,000 people in the city.

Although the earthquake caused significant destruction, the second-order effects of it escalated the problem. Across the city, fires broke out from candles, stoves, and oil lamps falling and igniting. The fires drove people to the banks of the Tagus River and the city's harbor. Then, a 16.5-to-33-feet (5-to-10-meter) tall tsunami entered the Tagus River from the Atlantic Ocean smashing ships against each other and washing many away who sought safety by the river. The church walls, with no roof, still stand as a reminder of the loss of the city.

Practically next to the church is the Santa Justa Lift or Elevador de Santa Justa which stands 147 feet (45 m) tall and is built in the same style as the famous architecture of the Eiffel Tower in Paris. Raoul Mesnier de Ponsard was an admirer of Gustave Eiffel and therefore applied the same architectural techniques so famous in the Eiffel Tower to the elevator. The elevator or lift has an observation deck with spectacular views over Baixa. I even got some pictures of Lisbon all the way to the Tagus River.

Lisbon has a high-end shopping hub on Avenida Liberdade; you will find all the expensive stores found in other major cities of the world. The question is whether your credit card can handle it? The street is lined with elegant cafes too. Maybe sit and have a cappuccino taking in the street of luxury and save the shopping for the mall at home. Most trips have allowed only one suitcase, so making purchases has become managing your suitcase's space and weight. How badly do I need that item? Save the space for the truly Portuguese souvenirs that you can't get anywhere else. Keep this in mind when picking the suitcase of choice. I now pack only half to three-quarters full to allow space for mementos of the trip.

Our trip came to an end, and we flew back to the United States. Although there were 44 people in our tour group, the group never felt that large. During the farewell dinner, travelers jotted down their contact information on a sheet of paper and passed it around for everyone to take a picture with their smartphone. Over the following year, continuous email dialogue had transpired. Some ask questions about future trip interests while others provide information on current trips. There were holiday wishes being exchanged before the end of the year. One last point, although our trip did not allow enough time to visit the Portugal Tile Museum in Lisbon, I would be remiss in not mentioning that this is considered a *must do* by many tours and travelers. I guess I'll visit it on my next trip to Portugal.

I'd also like to mention that I found Portugal English language-friendly. Most people that I encountered on the street or when purchasing merchandise or meals were very familiar with English. For those times that I was on my own, three days between Porto and Lisbon, I did not feel angst at being able to communicate with others. Also, I found everyone extremely friendly and helpful. My travel mate and I on our return to the hotel in Lisbon became a bit disoriented and had trouble finding the hotel. When asking strangers, they were very helpful in providing directions. We were also a bit off course in Porto and asked locals who got us back on track. I wouldn't think twice about returning to Portugal and experiencing more of the beautiful country's landscape as well as its history, culture, and people.

There are also the enjoyable wines of the country. Two types to single out are Port and Vinho Verde. Port wine or Port is produced in the Douro Valley of northern Portugal. Although typically sweet red wine or dessert wine, it also comes in dry, semi-dry, and white varieties. Vinho Verde translates to green wine for the lush green environment of the area, not the color of the wine. The wine is also released within three to six months after the grapes are harvested, therefore a young wine. It is usually bottled with a boost of carbon dioxide to create a light fizzy experience in the mouth.

For the food enthusiasts especially the seafood enthusiast, there are several Portuguese dishes that were recommended, for example, Bacalhau à Brás is a seafood lovers' specialty. It consists of shredded salted cod (bacalhau) mixed with finely chopped onions and crispy fried potatoes all bound together with scrambled eggs. Yes, I said scrambled eggs. Another must-try is Francesinha which is a Portuguese sandwich from Porto with layers of toasted bread and assorted hot meats such as roast, steak, wet-cured ham, linguica or chipolta with sliced cheese melted by ladling near-boiling tomato-and-beer sauce called molho de francesinha over it.

Yes, it is a rather heavy sandwich and is typically served with French fries. For those of us who like more petite meals, share it with a friend. The story behind the dish is that Daniel David de Silva returned to Portugal from visiting France and Belgium and tried to adapt the croque-monsieur to the Portuguese palette. In 1953 he introduced the sandwich at A Regaleira, a restaurant in the section of Rua do Bonjardim in Porto. The sandwich became a hit and is now served all over Portugal.

Another dish is Carne de Porco à Alentejana made from tender cubes of pork, crispy fried potatoes and littleneck clams simmered in a white wine. The dish is topped with black olives, fresh cilantro and jardineira, which is a medley of pickled carrots, red peppers, and cauliflower. The last dish I'll mention is Cataplana, a savory Portuguese fish stew made with mussels, fish, potatoes, sausage, saffron and smoked paprika. For those who like savory stews that combine fish and meat, I was told this is a mouthwatering treat. I'll mention again the dessert, pastéis de nata, is an absolute must-try.

According to the *Bucket List: 1000 Adventures Big and Small*, chomp churros in Lisbon is a bucket list type activity.

It's thought that the Portuguese brought churros to Europe from China, and the capital city is still arguably the best place to eat them. Wander through Lisbon's handsome streets with a light, hot, sugarcoated, doughy treat preferably dipped in chocolate-to enjoy a decadent start to any day.[61]

I did wander through Lisbon's streets but did not try one of the churros. I guess that will be on my next visit to the beautiful country.

The following UNESCO World Heritage Sites were part of my tour in Portugal: Convent of Christ in Tomar (1983); Monastery of the Hieronymites and Tower of Belém in Lisbon (1983); Historic Centre of Évora (1986); The Monastery of Alcobaca (1989); Cultural Landscape of Sintra (1995); Historic Centre of Oporto, Luiz I Bridge and Monastery of Serra do Pilar (1996); Historic Centre of Guimarães and Couros Zone (2001); University of Coimbra – Alta and Sofia (2013); and Sanctuary of Bom Jesus do Monte in Braga (2019).

In addition, my one-day trip north to Spain added the Routes of Santiago de Compostela: Camino Francés and

Routes of Northern Spain (1993). Unfortunately, we did not have time in Sintra to visit Pena Palace located in São Pedro de Penaferrim, a municipality of Sintra. As previously mentioned, the palace sits atop a hill within the Sintra Mountains overlooking the city. I could see the colorful palace from below, but it would take a full day to venture up the hill for touring.

Cathedral of Santiago de Compostela

Santiago market   Tower of Belem, Lisbon

Church of Saint Francis, Porto   University of Coimbra

mode of transportation   Casais Beach

Convent of Christ in Tomar   Carmo Convent Ruins

Fatima   Livraria Lello

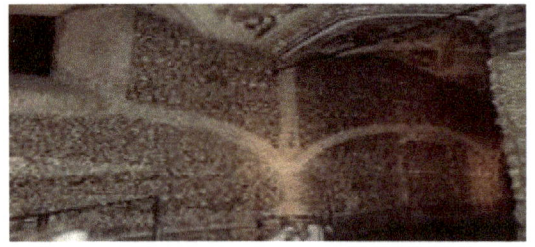

Chapel of Bones (Ossuary)

Sintra, Portugal   Santa Maria d'Alcobaça

Chapter 6

Patagonia (Argentina and Chile)

Carve your own path
Go slow
Channel your strengths
Smooth the path for others
Keep moving forward
Avoid meltdowns
Be cool!

Advice for Life Greeting Card (myadviceforlife.com)

Background: History, Culture, and Environment

Hola mi amiga y amigo.

Patagonia is the area of southern South America comprised of deserts, mountains, rainforests, glaciers, and fjords governed by both Argentina and Chile. The Andes Mountains traverse through this area stretching into the ocean. The combination of environment and climate produces bird and sea life more plentiful than other areas of the world. Although Wonders of the World are tracked by the number of seven, animals seem to be tracked by the number of five. The Big Five animals of Patagonia are the Andean condor, the guanaco, the Southern Right Whale, the puma, and the Magellanic penguin.[62] Well, that's one list but I've also found a separate list: Andean Condor, guanaco, puma, huemul or south Andean deer, and ñandú or Darwin's rhea.[63]

Well, the best way to solve that dilemma is to put both lists on your bucket list. We saw three out of the five; Mother Nature was kind to us for this trip. We saw condors at Petitio Moreno Glacier outside of Calafate, Argentina and guanaco and puma at Las Torres del Paine, Chile.

Patagonia is home to five penguin species: Magellenic, Humboldt, Gentoo, Southern Rockhopper, and King. Antarctica is home to Adelies, Kings, Chinstraps, Emperors, Gentoos, Macaroni, and Rockhoppers. In fact, penguins are found in the following ten places of the world: Antarctica, Australia, Argentina, Falkland Islands, Galapagos Islands, Tristan da Cunha (south Atlantic Ocean), New Zealand, and South Africa. Another unique find in Patagonia is the Chilean flamingo, normally found in much warmer weather. We saw several flamingos near the shores of Lake Argentina in Calafate, Argentina.

Had we been able to land the zodiacs at Tucker Island, I'd be adding penguins to my list. Well, I have trips to Seattle and Alaska in 2023, so maybe I'll still check whales off my list. A trip to South Africa in January 2024 should bring luck seeing the African black-footed penguin. I'll need a trip to Antarctica to view the King, Emperor, or Gentoos or return to Patagonia for another chance to see the Magellanic, King, and Gentoo. I don't think anyone gets tired watching those tuxedo-dressed wobblers interact.

Charles Darwin's book, *On the Origin of Species*, referenced research around the world but South America with Patagonia and Galapagos Islands are locations where he physically led expeditions to characterize flora and fauna; however, he is most known for the Galapagos Islands. There are 460 species of birds in Patagonia, enough to keep Darwin and his crew busy for more than two years. His boat HMS Beagle and crew of 80 spent more than half of the five years in Patagonia. He also visited the Cape of Good Hope for nineteen days towards the end of his five-year circumnavigation of the world. The term Patagonia was devised by the sixteenth-century Spanish explorers to describe the region's indigenous people, the Tehuelche. Although most historians conclude that it was the explorer Ferdinand Magellan that coined the name from Patagones, the controversy is over where the term existed and what it meant. The name stuck and is still used today. Explorers and settlers inadvertently harmed the indigenous people while trying to help. Their attempts to aid the Tehuelche are an example of how good intentions can lead to bad consequences.

Pictured at the Ushuaia Airport are a few painted naked Tehuelche men; this was how they lived. Without the means to produce clothing material, the people would cover themselves with seal oil creating a barrier between the exterior environment and their skin. This barrier protected them from rain and cold effects on their bodies. Naïve explorers provided clothing to the Tehuelche people, thus eliminating the need to cover their bodies with seal oil. When the clothing became wet, it did not readily dry out thus they became more vulnerable to the harsh elements; the Tehuelche population had no natural immunity to European diseases, and their numbers plummeted.

The islands south of the Strait of Magellan to Cape Horn are known as Tierra del Fuego, Land of Fires, inhabited by the Fueguians. When Magellan discovered the namesake strait, he saw fires along the coastline from the indigenous people and created the name Land of Fires. The major economic activities of the region include fishing, petroleum and gas exploration, ecotourism, and sheep farming; the area did not become as industrialized as the northern part of South America.

With both Argentina and Chile formed under Spanish colonization, a modified Spanish cuisine accompanies both countries. Asado is considered not just a dish but a ritual and a social event with different cuts of beef, pork, ribs, sausages, and sweetbread cooked slowly over an open flame to ensure tenderness and seasoned with pepper and salt to make the perfect entre for a meal. A favorite meal of the gaucho or cowboy. Empanadas are also available for both cuisines. The empanada was introduced to Spain by the Moors who then introduced it to South America. These are deep-fried or baked pastries that can be filled with savory meat and vegetable stuffing or sweet filling. Carbonada, a hearty stew with beef and vegetables in a thick broth with additional ingredients of sweet potatoes, pumpkin, potatoes, bacon, green beans, corn on the cob, carrots, and peppers can be acquired in both countries.

Chimichurri is Argentina's go-to condiment made with finely chopped parsley, oregano, onion, garlic, chili pepper flakes, olive oil and just a touch of lemon or vinegar for acidity. It is often used as a marinade for meat. Another dessert choice is dulce de leche or milk jam, condensed milk and sugar are slowly reduced until it is sweet and sticky like caramel. It can be drizzled over cookies, such as alfajores, or dessert empanadas, or over ice cream. In Argentina, October 11 has been declared National Dulce de Leche Day.

During our travels through Chile, Chilean hake, a member of the cod family, is a white-fleshed fish of mild flavor and firm, flaky texture often served to those desiring a fish choice. It has a sweet taste and is low in fat and calories, a good choice to complement a three-meal-a-day eating regiment. Empanadas are also a staple in Chilean cuisine. Pataska is an Andean stew from the mountains made with a potato base and boiled maize combined with charqui, dried horse or llama and flavored with various herbs and spices. Chorillana is a favorite sharing food, French fries topped with chorizo sausage, sliced steak, diced onions, and a fried egg.

Pastel de choclo is a corn pie native to the Andean's regions. It is layered with ingredients such as minced beef or chicken, onions, olives, raisins, and hard-boiled eggs. The chupe de centola is a traditional Chilean dish of a seafood stew with Patagonian King Crab, breadcrumbs, and a thick, creamy chowder base. Of course, filete de guanaco is also on the menu made with tender and lean guanaco meat. They all sound like a couple of spoonsful of the dish will eliminate anyone's hunger quickly.

Catholicism is most prevalent religion in both countries; therefore, the celebration of the birth of Jesus is an important holiday. Christmas is celebrated similar to the United States with activities such as house decorating, Christmas tree, and Christmas lights when affordable. Advent is celebrated among the Chilean Catholics with special church service for nine days before Christmas known as Novena. Christmas Eve is the most important day with dinner served at 9:00 pm or 10:00 pm with family and friends. The more common dishes served are asado (barbecue) and chicken, turkey, or pork. The Chilean Christmas cake is Pan de Pascua like Panettone. A popular Christmas drink is Cola de Mono or Monkey Tail made from coffee, milk, liquor, cinnamon, and sugar. A late-night church service follows the meal and then presents are opened. Santa is called Viejito Pascuero (Old Man Christmas) or Papa Noel (Father Christmas).

Argentina is the second-largest country in South America by size after Brazil and the eighth largest in the world with a population of over 40 million. Argentina is a republic that gained its independence in 1816 from Spain through the Argentine War of Independence. Like the United States, its government comprises three branches: executive, legislative, and judicial. There are 23 provinces and one autonomous district, the Federal Capital.

Chile's geography constitutes a long, narrow country stretching along the Pacific Ocean and separated from Argentina by the Andes Mountain range. It also has a similar government structure to Argentina with three branches: executive, legislative, and judicial with the head of state also being the head of government. The country is much smaller in landmass and population size, with almost 17 million people. The country declared itself an independent state within the Spanish monarchy on September 18, 1810; however, it did not acquire full independence until February 12, 1818.

For one to gain insight into the stability of Argentina and Chile in 2024, Argentina ranked 142nd just above the United States (141st at 41.1) with a score of 44.2 in the Fund for Peace Fragility State Index. Chile ranked slightly better at 146th with a score of 41.1. Both countries have come a long way from their previous conflict environment. Although this trip focused on Patagonia, which I found to be a very safe environment in the small towns, the big cities have their share of crime, as do most large cities of the world.

With respect to the State Resilience Index, Argentina at 6.2 falls on the average or slightly above for all the indicators representing a minimal place to be but there's always room for improvement. Chile's score of 6.9 reflects better but more impressive is that the country scored above average for all the indicators expect social cohesion in which it matched.

Travel Itinerary

The tour started in Buenos Aires, Argentina (two nights) then a flight to El Calafate, Argentina (two nights), drive to Torres del Paine, Chile (two nights), drive to Puerto Natales, Chile (one night), then board the expedition cruise (four nights), disembarking in Ushuaia, Argentina to fly back to Buenos Aires (one night) and then onto Miami International Airport for a connecting flight home.

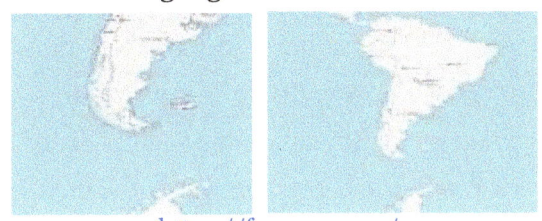

https://free-map.org/

Travel Journal

For those seeking an active vacation, a Patagonia expedition is a must, and I would recommend a combination of land and cruise. Since the tour arrangements were leaving from Miami to fly to Buenos Aires, I headed to Miami a day early to do some touring on my own. My travel mate and I arrived in the morning and had a combination of Miami city and boat tour arranged. The tour is a combination of driving around Miami Beach and includes a stop in Little Havana. The boat portion cruises past the waterfront homes of the rich and famous with the guide pointing out who owns or previously owned pertinent houses. If one is going to connect to Miami for a trip to Central or South America, then leverage the flight and spend some time there. On the second day, we did an airboat ride in the Everglades. Although the temperature was unseasonably cold in the sixties and I was freezing on the ride, I always wanted to do an airboat ride and got my chance. I checked this activity off my bucket list. The event occurred at an alligator refuge center, combining the ride with learning about alligators. It was an enjoyable way to spend the day before leaving for Argentina.

This was one trip where temperature ranges could be significant resulting in multiple wardrobes to accommodate very hot to very cold. Buenos Aires was predicted to be in the 90 degrees F with the other extreme of the most southern tip of South America in the 40 degrees F. I very much overpacked to make sure that I was covered for whatever weather. A very large suitcase, a large carryon, and a giant backpack as my personal item for the airplane. The lesson learned from this trip was that whatever one brings, they must haul it around the entire time. I won't overpack again. The large backpack stays home.

The flight from Miami was an overnight flight scheduled to land in Buenos Aires at 7:30 am the next morning. However, fate did not work in our favor that day. The pilot notified us that fog conditions warranted us to circle for a while to see if the skies cleared. Unfortunately, that didn't happen, and we were diverted to Santiago, Chile to land. American Airlines had the unplanned hotel expense for the entire airplane passengers for one night at a four-to-five-star hotel with lunch and dinner included. We then flew from Santiago, Chile to Buenos Aires, Argentina the next day. My passport is stamped going in and out of Chile, but I really didn't feel that I warranted the stamp merely spending a night in the hotel.

Lesson learned: always bring a change of clothes in your carry-on luggage. This is a lesson I had learned long ago when traveling for my job but with so many times there being no problem, I became complacent. Although one can take a shower, it just doesn't feel the same putting on the same clothes. We had a very early 2:15 am departure for the airport for a 7:00 am flight. Some fellow travelers took advantage of the opportunity to stop in Santiago and went out to see the city. However, my travel mate and I were exhausted, so we spent the time sleeping in the room after we spent two hours in line for hotel registration. The other shortcoming of an entire airplane trying to check into three hotels at the same time. We were able to work the free lunch and dinner around our nap time. We also notified the emergency number for the tour office of our diversion to Chile and a one-day delay in arriving.

Upon completing the flight to Buenos Aires, we caught up with our tour group and finished the morning's events. The tour manager had restructured the morning's itinerary to schedule open time in the afternoon for those who arrived on time. During that time, he took us on a separate tour retracing the steps that we missed in the morning. The tour manager's flexibility enabled the five of us, who were delayed, not to miss anything, nor were the other tour guests adversely impacted.

We toured the city of Buenos Aires viewing the Pink Palace, the location of the President's office. The tour manager pointed out the balcony where Eva Peron stood addressing the Argentinian citizens replicated by the actress Madonna when filming the 1996 movie *Evita*. Once returning to our hotel, we walked to the Recoleta Cemetery for the grave of Eva Peron in the Duarte family crypt. Although I had seen the movie, I even rented it again to watch before the trip. The story was originally documented in the Broadway musical *Evita* in 1978 by Andrew Lloyd Webber and Tim Rice.

The tour manager summarized her life on the walk; a woman who came from poverty to marry the eventual ruler of Argentina and use her influence to make a better life for lower class citizens. Watching a news release on the Argentinian monetary crisis in 2023, the Argentinian President's explanation of the problem was that it was generated during Juan Peron's timeframe and has merely grown worse. Ironically, from 1880 to 1930, Argentina was one of the world's ten wealthiest nations, a result from the rapid expansion of agriculture and foreign investment into the infrastructure.

Evita died at a very early age, only 33 years old from cervical cancer. According to a British Broadcasting Corporation (BBC) article, new evidence depicts that Evita had received a lobotomy prior to her death. Yale University Medical School neurosurgeon Daniel Nijensohn obtained and reviewed x-ray scans of her skull after her death depicting drilled holes. Although very sick from the cancer, she eventually stopped eating and died. Could the operation have led to the loss of her appetite? The article describes multiple possible reasons for the operation, severe attempt at pain management but also to subdue feelings and quiet a revolutionary Evita to change conditions of the working class before her demise. This new conspiracy theory adds more controversary to an already very controversial woman.[64]

We drove to the colorful neighborhood of La Boca, a popular destination for tourists visiting Buenos Aires. Caminito is a pedestrian street museum with colorful houses where one can watch tango dancers perform the dance. San Telmo is the oldest neighborhood in Buenos Aires with colonial-style homes, museums, and trendy cafes. Both areas allow one to get in touch with their artistic side.

That evening an optional activity was attending a tango show at Café de Los Angelitos but beforehand we were given tango lessons to not only watch the dance but embrace it. My partner was my travel mate, so we weren't gazing into each other's eyes during our lesson; however, we did learn the mechanics of the dance. Tango is a partner dance of passion that originated along the Rio de la Plata, the natural border between Argentina and Uruguay. Combining a couple of other dance moves, the Argentine Milonga, Spanish Cuban Habanera, and the Uruguayan Candombe, the dance was practiced in the brothels and bars of the ports. Business owners employed bands to provide entertainment to the patrons and the erotic dance spread around the world. Argentina and Uruguay submitted a joint proposal for the dance to make the UNESCO Intangible Cultural Heritage List and on August 31, 2009, UNESCO approved it. The list started in 2008 and is evaluated every year for new additions.

The next day we left for the town of Calafate in the southern portion of Argentina. The word calafate is a type of berry. A small airport and small town, it was alive with youth. With Argentina Lake, mountains, and glaciers, this is a perfect spot for trekking, fishing, kayaking and other outdoor activities. We stayed at a four-star hotel with a very nice pool, hot tub, and spa facilities. However, there was no air conditioning; this is common in areas that do not see high temperatures for very long. The solution is easy, open a window. In the morning, we traveled to Los Glaciares National Park, the location of the Perito Moreno Glacier. Argentina is home to 35 national parks, with Los Glaciares being one of its most popular.

There are seven panoramic boardwalks ranging from 460 feet to 2,100 feet (140 m to 640 m) depending on how far and long one wants to walk. They are constructed in front of the glacier providing an incredible view. We ate a bag lunch across from the glacier watching and listening for the calving sound, that intense sound when the glacier cracks and a piece breaks away from the massive structure. This happened numerous times during our viewing since January is South America's summer and the weather is at its warmest. It is impossible to snap a picture while calving; there's no warning before it occurs, and it happens so quickly it's impossible to get one's camera up and ready before it happens. Numerous times I felt I was close but missed most of the action. The icebergs make their way down to Lake Argentina. This was one of those surreal moments enjoying my bag lunch, even though I'm not a fan of bag lunches, as I waited for the sound of the glacier's calving on a beautiful sunny day. My thoughts were *life just doesn't get any better than this.*

The tour company brochure nailed it:

An unforgettable day filled with astonishing scenery as you travel to the Perito Moreno Glacier at Los Glaciares National Park, declared a World Heritage Site by UNESCO. This park, established in 1937, is the largest ice cap outside of Antarctica and Greenland with an ice field that controls the world's third largest reserve of fresh water. You'll observe the glacier's massive ice wall, almost 3 miles wide and over 240 feet high above the lake's surface, from a cliffside promenade that overlooks the constantly shifting ice. The easy access to this site has crowned Perito Moreno as one of the most visited glaciers in the world.[65]

I guess I need to add both Antarctica and Greenland to my bucket list. During our time walking the boardwalk, we also saw the Andean condor, several of them. Although I took pictures, I'm not sure anyone could identify the bird so high in the air. We saw a total of five Andean condors which is amazing when our Californian travelers had never seen a California condor, and they spent a lot of time hiking in California. This is one of the five big animals for Patagonia, so I had a big check for that box.

A boat ride is available to take passengers up close to the glacier and a kayaking trip that parallels the boat to get a closer look. Unfortunately, we did not have the time to sign up for either. Both seemed as if they were pre-planned, so there were no available spaces. One can also walk on a glacier, but this should be accomplished through an organized tour where experts can guide one on where to walk and where not to walk. Horseback riding is another activity available.

As we headed back, we passed the flamingoes huddled along the shoreline in the Argentina Lake. It was amazing to see them in their natural habitat and not just in a zoo. There are six species of flamingoes: four found in the Americas and two are native to Africa, Asia, and Europe. The Chilean, Andean, and James or puna flamingos are found in South America. The American or Caribbean flamingo is native to Mexico, the Caribbean, and the northernmost tip of South America. The greater flamingoes are found in the Middle East and Asia. The greater and lesser flamingos live in Africa.

Almost everyone has wondered why the flamingo has that stunning pink or reddish body. That distinctive color is the result of their diet, the beta-carotene pigments found in shrimp and plankton. The color is dependent on the quantity of carotenoid pigments consumed. The brightest of the species are the American or Caribbean flamingo. Once the flamingos shed their feathers, the feathers quickly lose their color. Their long-stilt-like legs allow them to wade in deep water for food. Besides color, flamingoes are also noted for standing on one leg. This has befuddled scientists for years since there is no way to confirm with the birds on why they do this. Their long, S-shaped necks and strong, hooked bills, facilitate more easily catching their prey.

Similar to other animals these beautiful birds are studied to ensure their species do not disappear.

Adult flamingoes have few natural predators, as their habitat is not suitable for most animals. However, flamingo chicks may be preyed on by larger birds like eagles. The largest threat to flamingo populations is habitat loss due to human activity and expansion. Flamingoes have been used for food and medicine over the years, which created another threat. Currently, none of the flamingo species are considered endangered. However, some flamingo species have battled population declines.

In 1924, the puna or James's flamingo was thought to be extinct but was rediscovered in 1957. In 1989, about 100 Caribbean flamingos died from lead poisoning in Mexico's Yucatan Peninsula after the ingestion of lead shot. This incident led to the prohibition of lead in the region. The rarest flamingo species is the Andean, which can be found in the high mountains of South America. Their eggs are collected by native populations. Humans have expanded into their habitats with farms and infrastructure.[66]

To ensure preservation, Chile established a national flamingo reserve around one of the lakes used by the birds for breeding colonies, expanding this effort is a goal of the country. The small town of Calafate has a very friendly vibe. If English is your first or second language, you'll not have a problem conversing. The town attracts the international community; so, don't be surprised to hear more languages than Spanish and English being spoken. Calafate is a place that I would like to return with my children and explore further on my own.

From Calafate, we drove to Torres del Paine in Chile but not before our tour manager pointed out in the distance the famous Monte Fitz Roy. Also known by other names such as Cerro Chaltén, Cerro Fitz Roy, and Mount Fitz Roy; the mountain lies on the border of Argentina and Chile located near the village of El Chaltén. Located in the Southern Patagonian Ice Fields at 49°17′S 73°05′W, it stands at 11,171 feet (3,405 m) high. On some future return trip with my children, I would split my time between Calafate and El Chaltén not to climb the famous mountain but get a little closer view of its majestic grandeur. After all, it is the logo for the brand *Patagonia*.

French climbers Lionel Terray and Guido Magnone first scaled the mountain in 1952. So why wasn't it named after them? Perito Moreno first saw the mountain on March 2, 1877, and decided to name it in honor of Captain Robert Fitz Roy of HMS Beagle exploration with Charles Darwin.

It is one of the most difficult mountains to climb in the world; therefore, Yvon Chouinard and fellow climbers scaled the mountain in 1968 and then made a movie, *Mountain of Storms*, of his adventure or one can read about it in the book, *Climbing Fitz Roy 1968*. The mountain climate is very unstable; therefore, climbers have a short window to traverse in the summer months. The clothing label *Patagonia* used Mount Fitz Roy for its logo. Cerro is the Spanish word for hill while Chaltén is a Tehuelche word meaning smoking mountain. The local people mistook the mountain for a volcano because the peak usually is covered with clouds. Mistaking clouds for smoke is a reasonable error if one has not climbed to the top to investigate the source.

After an uneventful border crossing with immigration and customs, we were in Chile. All tour managers prepare their tours for the dreaded border crossing which can be smooth or not. Fortunately, ours was smooth with minimal wait. Torres del Paine National Park, a 700-square mile World Biosphere Reserve designated by UNESCO and considered the Eighth Natural Wonder of the World, is a trekking hub with small camps around the base of the mountains. Chile has 42 national parks, but Torres del Paine National Park is one of the most popular.

We stayed at an all-inclusive four-star hotel, but again no

air conditioning. In areas where high temperatures only occur for a short timeframe, the cost of air conditioning is not cost effective. Leaving the windows open, the night air cooled the room, but moths congregated in the bathroom. That was a manage your expectations moment; not everywhere will have all the conveniences of home even for four-star hotels. The hotel being at the base of Paine Massiff's, we had gorgeous views from the backside of the hotel of the three granite peaks.

This trip was my first organized introduction to observing wildlife. As we drove around the park, we were searching for flora and fauna, and we saw it. Fields were plentiful with an assortment of animals: guanacos, like llamas; rheas, the South American version of an African ostrich and an Australian emu; and the grey fox. Well, I see grey fox in my backyard in Maryland. The puma is the most sought after with puma trekkers driving around the park looking for pumas to snap a few pictures. We spotted the puma trekkers first and then the puma they were watching.

On another day, we spotted two pumas along the shoreline of a pond. Since our tour was a small group of twenty-two, we had ample space on the coach to spread out. Picture in your mind that every time we saw something, one side of the coach rushed to join the other side of the coach for that photographic moment. Fortunately, coaches are more stable than boats, so all travelers pressed against the windows on one side didn't tip the coach over. Much excitement is generated in searching for and finding wildlife. Of course, we exchanged pictures afterwards since some members of our group were avid photographers equipped with more than their smartphone.

On the second day in Torres del Paine, we walked along Lago Grey Beach to view Grey Glacier, an enormous wall of ice over three miles wide with the electric blue icebergs that broke off into the water. That day and probably most days, the wind was incredible when clearing the protected area of the shoreline. A family was playing along the water, and I feared the small child would be blown into the water. At times, I felt like I was standing still while trying to walk with the winds obstructing any movement. In the opposite direction, I was assisted in traversing the stretch in a fraction of the time. I felt like a real trekker exploring the land under nature's terms and conditions.

In 2019 at Grey Glacier, the alarm was sounded when two huge icebergs broke off from the glacier. One was the size of 12 soccer fields. The second occurred 15 days later. The previous large detachment occurred in 2017 and before those dates to the 1990s, so the increased frequency of these massive chunks warrants the alarm.

The next morning, the group split into two groups: one for a four-mile hike and the other to learn about native people and customs. Although I enjoy learning about native customs, I still didn't get enough hiking in this incredible country and chose the hike. A women's group of hikers passed us on the trail; they were backpacking to stay overnight at one of the campsites around the base of the mountain. Hikers must register to stay overnight to ensure space is available within camping locations. We walked along the shore of Laguna Inges, viewing Monte Almirante rising to the north and Lake Nordenksjold to the south.

After lunch, we gathered our belongings and headed for the coach and our next destination. Unfortunately, we had one small snafu. The winds kicked up just as we were leaving causing our tour manager to have his prescription sunglasses blown from his face. Twenty-two people searched on the ground for close to 30 minutes and couldn't find them. It's amazing that they were blown that far away to be hidden from our view. It does get very windy there and it can kick up quickly too. The hotel crew gave us an extraordinary send-off by four horsemen riding along the coach, two on each side, waving flags to enhance our departure. I felt like desert royalty.

We drove to Puerto Natales, formerly the hub of the ranching industry in the twentieth century, located in the Senoret Channel of Patagonia; it's very windy there too. After checking in, I went for a not-so-pleasant walk as the winds off the water channeled through the streets. This area is known for the discovery of a well-preserved, giant sloth-like creature that lived more than 10,000 years ago in the Mylodon Cave located just 30 minutes from Puerto Natales. For people traveling directly to Torres del Paine, Puerto Natales is the closest airport.

The next morning, we headed for Punto Arenas and boarded the Australis for our expedition cruise but first, we spent time in the town. Punto Arenas is located on the Strait of Magellan, named for the famous explorer who discovered the strait looking for a better path around South America to navigate from the Atlantic Ocean to the Pacific Ocean. We stopped at Museo Nao Victoria which opened October 1, 2011, before entering the town. The museum provides information on the sailing history of the area and incorporates replicas of noteworthy boats on the grounds. The Nao Victoria of Ferdinand Magellan was the first ship to navigate the globe. Captain Fitz Roy and Charles Darwin's HMS Beagle allows one to climb aboard for an imagery experience. The La Goleta Ancud schooner commemorates the sailing on May 22, 1843, to colonize the Strait of Magellan under Chilean control. Even one of Sir Ernest Shackleton's ice boats, the James Caird, is represented at the museum. The wreck of a Chilean Navy ship also sits on the waters of the museum.

Punta Arenas is a city near the tip of Chile's southernmost Patagonia region. Due to the town's strategic location, it is often used as a base for excursions to the surrounding wilderness and Antarctica. The Plaza Muñoz Gamero has a memorial to explorer Ferdinand Magellan. We had a few hours in the town intended for shopping and lunch. Concerned that I might not have appropriate waterproof clothing, I sought outdoor shops and found the most reasonable and practical waterman's gear in a hardware store.

Although not very fashionable, the pants and jacket are completely waterproof; the set was a deal at $25.00. As we left the store, we encountered other group members and pointed them to the same store. My guess, the store sold out of this inelegant but practical apparel shortly after my visit.

Fed and shopped, we boarded the boat and sailed. The ship navigated through the Amirantazgo Sound, arriving at Ainsworth Bay within the Alberto Agostini National Park. The Marinelli Glacier descends from the Darwin Mountain range, a spectacular view. Obviously, the mountain range is named after Charles Darwin. Although his fame as a naturalist is more associated with his work in the Galapagos Islands, he was part of the second hydrographic survey expedition on the HMS Beagle in Patagonia. Darwin's South American journey covered leaving Plymouth, United Kingdom in December 1831. From February 1832 to September 1835, he sailed between the cities of San Salvador, Brazil to Lima, Peru. Captain FitzRoy and his team led the first passage during their voyage from 1826 to 1830.

Darwin's famous and controversial natural selection theory supposes that nature inherently works to produce superior products with inferior eliminated through extinction. Where gaps exist in evolutionary evidence, the gap-filler has not yet been uncovered by archaeologists from the vast space of the earth is one theory.

It may be said that natural selection is daily and hourly, scrutinizing throughout the world, every variation, even the slightest; rejecting that which is bad, preserving and adding up all that is good; silently and insensibly working, whenever and wherever opportunity offers, at the improvement of each organic being in relation to its organic and inorganic conditions of life. We see nothing of these slow changes in progress, until the hand of time has marked the long lapse of ages, and then so imperfect is our view into long past geological ages, that we only see that the forms of life are now different from what they formerly were.[67]

Although not a naturalist like Darwin, my college courses in biological principles enabled me to feel connected to the mission of the great nature explorer. Traveling and experiencing first-hand what one reads in books is a connection not otherwise accomplished. The combination of researching through reading and the actual exploration through traveling not only enhances one's ability to learn but synthesizes one's ability to integrate the knowledge between the two and draw one's own conclusions.

Our first zodiac launch took us for a walk through the rainforest in the Magellan Forest. We split into a couple of groups, with an earlier group canceled because of winds. There was significant guidance on entering the zodiac, especially in rough waters. The emphasis was to sit, as quickly as possible, and slide around the edge of the boat versus walking in the large rubber raft. Several people had to be reminded over the next couple of days to immediately *sit and slide*. To fully embrace the experience of the rainforest, mother nature brought on the rain but fortunately only a drizzle. For my bucket list, I can add and immediately check off walking through a rain forest in the rain.

The second zodiac excursion, Tucker Inlet, was canceled again due to winds. We were all distraught; this is the island of Magellanic penguins. Winds and rough seas are the biggest obstacles for Patagonia sailing. We also watched two BBC documentaries on Patagonia and a three-part story on Shackleton's incredible journey of endurance in Antarctica. Although I was aware of his journey, I had not read the book, *Endurance: Shackleton's Incredible Voyage* by Alfred Lansing, before my trip but soon ordered it after my return.

Lansing's research includes reviewing the journals of the crew in addition to first-hand interviewing them. The book documents the mission and tribulations of Captain Ernest Shackleton and his crew in what is considered the most successful failure ever encountered, describing how the captain and crew survived the 22-month ordeal stranded in Antarctica. As cited by a New York Times Book Review, *one of the great adventure stories of our time,* is written on the front cover of the book. Although Shackleton had not succeeded in his 1914-1915 quest to cross the continent of Antarctica, he succeeded in the safe return of all 27 crew members under extremely harsh conditions and at great risk. With every fork in the road of survival decision-making, his choices led to their eventual return. Most choices were unthinkable under any other circumstances.

We quite frequently scoured the water and air for sea life and bird life. The sighting of an albatross brought the clamor of people from one side of the boat to the other. Why did the albatross get so much attention?

They have the largest wingspan of any bird;
they can go years without touching the ground;
they can live and raise chicks over the ripe old age of 60;
similar to other birds, they mate for life;
they have an elaborate courting dance; and
they can smell food in the water from 12 miles away.[68]

That is one amazing bird. Mother Nature is just remarkable as to what she can invent. The main threat to the albatross is long-line tuna fishing. The vessels lay out up to 50 miles of line and hooks, baited with bits of squid just below the surface. The birds go for the squid and get caught by the hook. Hundreds of thousands of albatrosses are killed each year; a bird that only lands on the water to feed. Conservationists from Aves Argentinas have been working with fishermen operating out of Mar del Plata.

Buoyant-colored tags are fitted to the lines of hooks that are hidden beneath the water's surface. The tags scare the birds away from the trawler cables. First, it takes the knowledge of a problem and then special expertise to obtain solutions and choose the best solution for a specific situation. Tracking animal numbers allows wildlife protectors to know if mankind has imposed its unforgiving will on nature, changing our world forever, usually for the worse.

The third excursion occurred after navigating the Beagle Channel and disembarking at Pia Fjord to see Pia Glacier. The zodiac landing positioned us right next to the glacier.

The views and pictures were awesome. We then hiked up to a higher location for even better pictures. A rope side rail allows one to partially climb (more like a diagonal rope climb) and partially walk up the steep trail. A bit challenging but very doable, just take your time. Afterward, we continued along the Beagle Channel through the majestic Glacier Alley.

The ship's crew did an outstanding job entertaining us while we passed through the alley of glaciers. Each glacier is named for a country and the crew served drinks and appetizers to culturally align cuisine with the country. Germany was beer and tiny wieners; France was champagne and pastries; Italy was wine and pizza bites; and the Netherlands was pale lager and fried dough balls. The room was alive with conversation and laughter. Every time we passed a new glacier, half the group would run out the door, including myself for pictures. The cold temperatures didn't bother us. Wearing a miniskirt, my brief time outside was exhilarating. I had packed for summer in South America, not necessarily summer at locations 500 miles from Antarctica.

Our next excursion was Cape Horn National Park via the ship navigating through the Murray Channel and Nassau Bay. Cape Horn was discovered in 1616 with a sheer 1,394 foot-high (425 m) rocky cliff; it was declared a World Biosphere Reserve by UNESCO in 2005. Often considered the end of the earth, to me it seemed like the loneliest place on earth.

Captain Joshua Slocum, during his famous sailing around the world in 1895, accounts in his book, *Sailing Alone Around the World*, it was perilous rounding Cape Horn fighting the Milky Way of the sea, located northwest of the Cape with white breakers over sunken rocks. He reiterates Darwin's words about the experience in the Beagle: *Any landsman seeing the Milky Way would have nightmare for a week.*[69]

The ship's crew warned us that previous expeditions since the beginning of the year had to abandon landing due to the winds and rough seas. We waited with great anticipation for the captain's call on the sea conditions and were ecstatic when he decided to launch the watercrafts. It was rough seas, and so extra time was given for debarking and embarking. There was an extremely long staircase to get to the top of the rock island named Cape Horn. Once on top, the winds were unbelievable. There's a small lighthouse manned by a father with two daughters. Besides the lighthouse, the island has a chapel, swing set, and a striking monument, a sculpture to honor those sailors who perished making the treacherous journey, and that's about it. Not a tree anywhere on the grassy rock.

As I stood in line on the steps waiting my turn to catch a zodiac back to the ship, I noticed one of our zodiacs bringing passengers from another boat to our landing area. As they disembarked, the three adventurers explained the reason they had an exceptionally large camera was to film a documentary on climate change; they were there for research. Well, that was exciting. I warned them that the winds were brutal once they cleared the top of the staircase. They really needed a tight grip on everything.

The last excursion took us to an island in historic Wulaia Bay or Bahia Wulaia. Why is Wulaia Bay considered historic? It is the site of one of the region's largest Yamana aboriginal settlements. It is also where Darwin landed in 1833 during his famous voyage. We had a long hike ascending at times a steep incline. Again, there were ropes along the path to assist in pulling yourself along the way. It was a sunny, sweltering day and a few of us stripped off our extra clothes.

I was down to a T-shirt and jeans. As another group member reduced clothes, he unveiled a t-shirt with the expression, *MATH the only subject that counts*. Sometimes it's just one moment or action that truly conveys one's persona and sometimes one just needs the right one-line for a chuckle. Near the top of the forested hill, we had spectacular views over the bay.

On the beach was a self-guided museum, a former Chilean Navy communication building. There was a box of letters; one would either leave or deliver a letter. There was also a plaque commemorating Charles Darwin's exploration in Patagonia from 1832-1835 and dated disembarking in Wulaia Bay on January 23, 1833, as the center of Yámana territory. In the nineteenth century, the Yámana tribe numbered 2,500 to 3,000 people. They were a hunter/gatherer society with a diet comprised of shellfish, seals, whales, and birds with a few berries and several varieties of fungi rounding out their diet. An archeological dig was occurring close to the building. Looking back to the description of Shackleton's diet while stranded in Antarctica, it was largely seal. Fresh seal meat, especially the organs, contains vitamin C or ascorbic acid needed to protect against scurvy.

At one point on the expedition, we had a group meeting, and the tour manager discussed the relationship between Argentina and Chile. Border disagreements occur between many countries, Argentina and Chile are no different. In 1978, Chile and Argentina were on the brink of war over the possession of the Picton, Lenox, and New Islands along the Beagle Channel. Both countries at the time were under military rule. Pope John Paul II intervened and through mediation, the area was confirmed as Chilean territory. Our tour manager worded it that the Pope told both rulers to work it out or he would kick them out of the church; that's a pretty powerful threat considering both countries' religious majority is Catholicism.

As recently as August 2023, Argentina claimed that Chile had incorrectly claimed jurisdiction over a section of Argentina's territorial waters. Within twenty-four hours of the publication, Gabriel Fuks, Argentina's Under-Secretary for Latin American Affairs at the Foreign Ministry submitted a protest to Chile's Ambassador Barbara Figueroa objecting to the new maps marking of the region south of Tierra del Fuego.

Argentina's other high-profile conflict occurred with the British over an area in the Atlantic Ocean off the coast of Argentina. The dispute was over the sovereignty of the Falkland Islands, also known as Islas Malvinas in Argentina, South Georgia, and the South Sandwich Islands. In 1982, Argentinian President Leopoldo Galtieri decided to take control of the Falkland Islands from Great Britain. The conflict lasted 74 days at a cost of over 900 lives, 649 Argentinian, 255 British, and three Falkland Islanders. On June 14, 1982, Argentinian forces surrendered. My suggestion to Argentina is not to pick a fight with one of the greatest naval forces in history unless you really stand to benefit from the venture. Prime Minister Margaret Thatcher led the United Kingdom to victory through this conflict. Proving that royalty does not mean exception to military service, Prince Andrew sailed into the Falkland Islands War. His nephew Prince Harry served in the Afghanistan War decades later.

On the final day of the expedition, we arrived in Ushuaia, Argentina. As I walked out on the deck to get one last view, a very large National Geographic ship was docked next to our sportier expedition ship. National Geographic recognized Ushuaia's Les Eclaireurs in its *Destinations of a Lifetime* book, recognized as the *Lighthouse at the End of the World* guiding shipping through the treacherous Beagle Channel.

We had some time before needing to be at the airport, so we had a tour of the Museum of the Prison of Ushuaia.

Historically, prisons were built in remote areas to isolate the convicts from civilization. Built between 1902 and 1920, it operated until its closure in 1947 when the complex was transferred to the Marine Ministry with a naval base established in 1950. The museum also includes information on the Ushuaia area.

The mountains around Ushuaia are beautiful. Although we didn't have time to enjoy them, it looked like a perfect location for hiking. Our meeting spot to rendezvous for departure to the airport was in front of the Hard Rock Café Ushuaia. Well, for the city to have a Hard Rock Café it must be a chic town. In fact, there are three ski resorts located in the mountains around Ushuaia; so, the city affords boat tours to islands in Tierra del Fuego in the summer and skiing in the other seasons.

We flew back to Buenos Aires to spend a day on our own before flying back to Miami. We visited the Museum of Latin American Art of Buenos Aires (MALBA) within walking distance of the hotel. It holds more than 400 pieces exhibiting significant works by Frida Kahlo, Diego Rivera, and Antonio Berni. Landing in Miami, we were informed that an earlier flight to Washington, DC was available, and the check-in attendant put us on it. It did mean running through the airport to make the flight. It was worth it to be home sooner than sitting waiting for our original flight, a couple of hours later.

As mentioned previously, somewhere in the future will be

a return to Patagonia. I might not be scaling Mount Fitz Roy but attempt a tamer trekking adventure. This trip also intrigued my interest in a trip to Antarctica. Crossing the 600-mile Drake Passage is a rite of passage with concerns of rough seas, high winds, and tremendous swells. Having a history of seasickness, I can't imagine persevering through 24-48 hours of *wanting to die* physical duress, even if the outcome is a few glorious days transcending the ultimate continent with playful penguins. Oh, and remember that the only way back is through the Drake Passage again. I think I would have to be sedated to make a return trip if I had experienced Satan's inferno swells on the first crossing. If flying is an option, I might be enticed to take that means of transportation even at a premium price.

For those interested in reading a book on South American rustic adventure travel, I would recommend *The Condor's Feather: Traveling Wild in South America* by Michael Webster. A middle-aged couple from the United Kingdom decided to modify their Toyota Hilux truck with a small camper and travel to South America in search of nature. Combining their experience as photographers and filmmakers with their love of birds, their adventure was to observe and document the feathered wildlife in this part of the world that has about a third of all bird species on earth. They start their adventure in Argentina and the exploration of Patagonia moving northward over a four-year period. Their exploits provide a phenomenal overview of South America from an outback perspective versus guidance on city living and the vibrant nightlife. They soon embrace a quest to find the hooded grebe in the area around Perito Moreno and produce the film *Tango in the Wild* on the unusual courting dance of the birds. The dance can be found on the youtube video: (https://www.youtube.com/watch?v=1hoL93tEkrM).

Finding and filming this video was no easy feat since the birds' habitat is near isolated lakes in the most remote areas of Patagonia.

I enjoy reading books on other people's adventures exploring new countries. The more athletic travelers' choices for exploration by other means than driving is accomplished by two British women who decided to bicycle 5,500 miles through South America to experience cycling the Andes Mountains. *LlamaDrama* by Anna McNuff described their journey from La Paz, Bolivia heading south to embrace the mountain range, scorching heat, high crosswinds, snows, glaciers, and possible threat of meeting unsavory characters along the way through Patagonia. Having done this trip before I read the book, I could picture in my mind and recollect on the environmental conditions and the beautiful landscapes that they described. I'm blown away with their bravery and capability to have accomplished such an amazing feat.

The UNESCO World Heritage Site visited for this trip was in Argentina, Los Glaciares National Park designated in 1981. Other recognitions include Argentine's Tango as a UNESCO Intangible Cultural Heritage List (2009) and Las Torres del Paine National Park in Chile designated as a UNESCO World

Biosphere and the Eighth Wonder of the World (2013). *The Bucket List: 1000 Adventures Big and Small* lists tango dance lessons as one activity in Buenos Aires. Fortunately, my organized tour included tango lessons for the group before the evening's tango show. I did get to experience the mechanics of the dance but not the passion with my dance partner being my travel mate. Romantic couples had a more emotionally connected experience.

Everglades

Perito Moreno

Glacier Grey Glacier

Las Torres del Paine

rainbow in Las Torres

zodiac excursions

Pia Glacier

Cape Horn National Park

Bahia Wulaia

Pia Fjords

Magellan Forest

Nao Victoria Museum

Part 2 – My Big Year

Chapter 7

Italy

Let food be thy medicine and medicine be thy food. – recognized to Hippocrates

(https://pubmed.ncbi.nlm.nih.gov/29936236/)

Background: History, Culture, and Environment

Ciao amico mio.

Italy is the birthplace of the Renaissance and Catholicism channeling human spiritual emotions through art, architecture, and food. With 60 UNESCO World Heritage Sites, one visit cannot do the country justice; Italy is a significant part of world history. The country shaped like a boot, has the Italian Alps in the north, long coasts on the Tyrrhenian and Adriatic Seas, and with the southern part in the Mediterranean Sea lie the islands of Sicily and Sardinia. The country hosts such famous cities as Florence, Rome, Milan, Naples, and Venice. The extensive coastline into the sparkling waters makes it the aquatic playground for the world's jetsetters.

Archaeological records stretch back tens of thousands of years. Italian history largely begins with the Etruscan civilization between the Arno and Tiber rivers. It was the Roman Empire that succeeded the Etruscans in the third century BCE and expanded their ruling power ultimately from India to Scotland by the second century CE. Through warring factions over the years, the Roman Empire fell in the fifth century CE after invasions by the Huns, Lombards, Ostrogoths, and Franks.

The political change became one of city-states, independent sovereign cities ruled as the center of political, economic, and cultural life. Many of the city-states flourished during the Renaissance period, a time marked by intellectual, artistic, and technological advances. City-states were governed as republics or by a single person or family. This was also a time of warfare between states loyal to the pope or to their own independence. The Renaissance was rooted in Italy through the artistic advances of DaVinci, Michaelangelo, Raphael, Donatello, Botticelli, Brunelleschi, Caravaggio, and Titian creating the euphoria that spread across all of Europe leaving the world the treasure of paintings and sculptures that exist today. During the Renaissance period, both popes and family heads commissioned paintings and sculptures. Leonardo da Vinci would eventually leave Italy and move to France at the request of King Francois I staying at the royal Chateau d'Amboise; he is believed to be buried in the chapel there. The Medici family, also known as the House of Medici, attained their wealth through banking and commerce in the Florence region. In 1434 Cosimo de Medici or Cosimo the Elder established the family's patronage using wealth to fuel the arts and humanities, making Florence the birth of the

Renaissance. The Medici family, while acquiring wealth, also acquired power and influence ensuring four family members resided as popes: Leo X, Clement VII, Pius IV, and Leo XI. His grandson, Lorenzo de Medici, also known as Lorenzo the Magnificent, continued to support the artistic talents of Florentines. As depicted in books during the Renaissance period, such as *The Agony and the Ecstasy*, scientific exploration also included the dissection of cadavers to better understand the human body. Although illegal at the time, both Da Vinci and Michaelangelo experimented with cadavers and applied this knowledge to their painting and sculpting, advancing a realism in vein-popping muscles not previously illustrated in artwork.

After Lorenzo's death on April 8, 1492, at the age of 43 years old, his eldest son Piero succeeded him but was not favorable among the public due to accepting a peace treaty with France. After only two years in power, he fled the city in 1494 and died in exile. Catherine de Medici, daughter of Piero's son Lorenzo, became Queen of France from 1547 to 1559 by her marriage to King Henry II and the mother of French kings Francis II, Charles IX, and Henry III. European history reflects noble bloodlines crisscrossing empires through marriage to avoid warfare and protect wealth. This inbreeding created genetic deficiencies in offspring and eventually led to the risk of serious impacts for future generations, such as hemophilia and the fall of the Russian Empire.

How does one end a dynasty? The answer is producing no heirs. The last Medici ruler died without a male heir in 1737, Grand Duke Gian Gastone, ending the family dynasty after almost three centuries. The marriage of Francis of Lorraine to Habsburg heiress Maria Theresa of Austria forged the long European reign of the Habsburg-Lorraine family. The unification of Italy is marked as March 17, 1861, when the parliament assembled in Turin officially proclaimed the Kingdom of Italy with King Victor Emmanuel II of Sardinia. Economically, Italy became split between the industrialized north, such as the rise of the car industry, and the agricultural south.

Post-World War I brought the rise of significant economic problems to Italy: the overprinting of money to pay for wartime arms created inflation, savings became worthless, industries created for war went bankrupt, and unemployment skyrocketed. The political environment was ripe for a significant change, ushering in the Fascist party with Benito Mussolini, as an alternative to Socialism. World War II brought the fall of Mussolini, the Fascist party, the end of the Kingdom of Italy, and a separate papal city. In May 1946, King Victor Emanuel III abdicated. Although his son initially became King Umberto II, he was forced to leave the country a month later when a referendum chose a republic political system.

In 1929, the Lateran Treaty established between the Kingdom of Italy and the Holy See founded the recognition of

Vatican City as an independent city-state, guaranteeing papal independence from Italian secular rule. It was signed by Benito Mussolini for the Italian government and by Cardinal Secretary of State Pietro Gasparri for the papacy. It was confirmed by the Italian constitution of 1948.

Through my European trips and acquiring knowledge on the history of countries, one disconcerting theme appears to be hatred against Jewish people traced back to even the Black Plague timeframe. In 1938, Italy imposed similar anti-Semitic laws signed by the Italian King as did Germany through the National Socialism (Nazi) regime. Jews were defined as unpatriotic, excluded from government jobs and the military, banned from entering Italy, and banned from attending or teaching school. Of course, many Jews fled the country like the exodus found in Germany. It appears that in times of unrest, there is no more effective way of uniting people than around a mutual scapegoat.

Italy is a parliamentary republic with a prime minister as the head of government and a president who is the head of state and appointed by the prime minister. Parliament consists of two houses: the Chamber of Deputies and the Senate of the Republic. A rather unusual circumstance occurred in Italy's political history. On March 16, 1978, the former five-time prime minister of Italy, Aldo Moro, was kidnapped by the Red Brigade. He was held until May 9 when he was found in the back of a car in the center of historic Rome with multiple gunshot wounds. The Italian government had refused to negotiate with the terrorist group. Moro was the centrist leader of the Christian Democratic Party and a probable Presidential candidate for the then-upcoming election in December. The Red Brigade was established in 1970 by Italian Renato Curcio to employ terrorist activities such as bombings, assassinations, kidnappings, and bank robberies to promote radical communist revolution within Italy. Curcio and 12 other Red Brigade members were on trial in Turin when Moro's kidnapping transpired. Italy's Communist Party condemned the terrorist actions.

No discussion on Italy would be complete without a few words on food. Cuisine is artistic creativity applied to cooking; Italian cuisine is artistic creativity applied with a Mediterranean flair. Our organized tour included Naples, the home of the Margherita pizza; I had my share of this memorable fare. The tomato sauce is unbelievable, and the fresh mozzarella accents the taste; I've never had pizza that delicious anywhere else. I wonder if the volcanic soil enriches the taste of the tomato because it is bursting with rich flavor. One can't go to Naples without doing a cooking class; so, try to work that into any Italian trip. Also, don't even think about dieting on a trip to Italy.

For savory soup with ingredients known to boost a healthy immune system, butternut squash, sweet potato, and ginger soup warms the tummy. A combination of ingredients of the soup's name: butternut squash, sweet potato, and fresh ginger is combined with onions, garlic, and turmeric. The soup uses only a little olive oil with no heavy cream. For a hearty soup try the creamy sausage, kale, & white bean soup. Again, the main ingredients are in the name: sausage, kale, white beans with chicken broth and heavy cream to achieve the creamy consistency. The choice of sausage, whether mild or spicy, adds a different taste to the soup. It can be garnished with cracked black pepper or Romano cheese. So maybe Italian cuisine names are more about description than creativity.

The national dish of Italy is a pasta dish, Ragu alla Bolognese, a meat and tomato sauce with tagliatelle pasta or maybe just the people of the city of Bologna believe that. Let's check the history and origin of the dish.

While the meal has been enjoyed in Italy for more than a century, the earliest written record of Bolognese was a recipe dating back to the 18th century, which was found in Imola, a town near the city of Bologna. Pellegrino Artusi, renowned 19th-century Italian chef, is credited with writing a recipe for the meat sauce in his 1891 publication. Artusi named the meat sauce *Maccheroni alla bolognese*, which is believed to have signified the origin of the sauce in Bologna. In his book, Artusi states that the key ingredients in the preparation of Bolognese were lean veal fillet, butter, carrot, onion, and pancetta. These ingredients were cooked with butter and later with broth.[70]

But of course, any pasta dish speaks Italy. Other cuisine favorites are lasagna, risotto, ravioli, spaghetti, and the list continues.

For desserts, my favorite is tiramisu; the delectable delight comes from the Italian region of Veneto. The combination of espresso-soaked ladyfingers surrounded by lightly sweetened whipped cream and a rich mascarpone, an Italian cream cheese. Alcohol can also be added: dark rum, marsala wine, amaretto, or coffee liquor.

Italy tied with Chile at 146th ranking in the Fund for Peace Fragile State Index for 2024 at a score of 41.1. Italy has erratically been improving over the last decade from a score of 45.8 in 2012 to its new low.[71] The problem years were 2006 through 2010; hopefully, the country will continue to trend in the right direction. With respect to its State Resilience Index, Italy scored above average on all the indicators except social cohesion in which it matched the average with a total score of 7.0.

Travel Itinerary

The tour starts with a flight to Milan and then I stayed in Como (two nights), Venice (two nights), Florence (two nights), Rome (three nights), and Sorrento (five nights). En route to locations, there were stops in Verona, Pisa, Assisi City, Pompeii, Capri Island, and the Amalfi Coast. From north to south, this was a well-rounded travel adventure.

https://free-map.org/

Travel Journal

My journey started on the drive to Philadelphia to meet up with my travel mate and the train ride to John F. Kennedy International Airport (JFK). We experienced the reverse planes-trains-and-automobiles journey again. It was an evening departure with an overnight flight arriving mid-morning into Milan, Italy. Our transport took us to our hotel in the city of Como on Lake Como. Como is on the edge of the Italian and Swiss Alps. We had the traditional welcome group meeting and dinner to go over the itinerary.

This type of tour allowed participants to opt in or out of the front-end and back-end locations. My first trip to Italy; I wanted to experience the full two weeks and added two extra days on the back-end in Naples. On our first full day, we sailed on Lake Como to Bellagio. On the ride, the tour manager pointed out Sophia Loren's and George Clooney's homes, the building used for filming *Casino Royale*, and Richard Branson's home leasable for special events. Bellagio is an old-world charm, nestled on a land point within Lake Como. I noticed quite a few stores selling leather goods, wallets,

215

purses, belts, etc.

Once back in Como, the afternoon was on our own and I took the funicular up the steep slope to the town of Bramante above Como. The main tourist activity is a walk to the lighthouse which is two to three miles uphill. You'll get quite a workout but will feel all the better for it on the way down. Near the funicular, there are several restaurants, but they don't open until 7:00 pm. Rather than wait, I opted to stand in line for the return trip on the funicular and have dinner in Como.

Since it was the Saturday night before Easter, I asked my Catholic travel mate, if she wanted to attend Easter Mass at the beautiful church behind the hotel. She jumped at the offer, and we were off to the church. A bonfire was ablaze outside the front door, and she described the practice. The celebration of light (Lucernarium) is represented by the bonfire flame in front of the church doors blessed by the priest. When the Paschal candle is lit, the community ceremoniously enters the dark church chanting. Fire is the symbol of light and glory of the Resurrection of Jesus Christ. We stayed about 45 minutes; the Italian-spoken mass created the problem that neither one of us understood most of what was said but it sounded beautiful.

We awoke to Easter morning and a journey to Venice but first a pitstop in Verona, the town most known for William Shakespeare's *Romeo and Juliet*. Although a fictional story there is a house within Verona that resembles that described in the story and reflects the period. In the movie *Letters to*

Juliet, the heroine finds a lost letter hidden in the wall from a young woman left decades before and writes to her to ease her pain and answer her question. This practice depicted in the movie does happen at the courtyard wall in Verona. Unfortunately, Easter Day is a bad day to visit the house; the line was much too long. It's probably a bad day anywhere in Italy to visit. Ironically, I was so excited to be visiting Italy during Easter that I didn't even consider the crowds that had the same idea.

Verona is a medieval and partially fortified town on the Adige River. The Verona Arena is a first-century Roman amphitheater now used to host concerts and large-scale opera performances. We did a short walking tour of the town and then had lunch before heading off to Venice. Originally used for gladiator games, it also was used for jousts and tournaments during the Middle Ages. Spain is not the only country to have bullfighting, the Arena provided the venue for this activity. However, it eventually became home for theater performances first used as an opera theater in 1913. As with several other Roman or Greek historic gems, music concerts have become a standard. Even rock and roll legends such as Bruce Springsteen and Roger Waters have played at the Arena.

Venice is a beautiful city with canals versus roads. By the time we checked into the hotel and finished dinner, it was bedtime, but the next day we were afforded a boat ride to Murano and the famous Murano glass factory tour. We watched the glass-blown process and then it was time for shopping. Several rooms of beautiful glass; I purchased a stunning green vase, necklace, and earrings and my travel mate purchased a red wine decanter set. A short boat ride took us to a location for the walk to Saint Mark's Square and a visit to Saint Mark's Basilica.

Being the largest expanse of dry land in the otherwise water-bound city, St. Mark's Square Venice has always been a favorite among those seeking to experience the real Venice. This piazza has been the hub of activity since the days of the early Republic, when it served as a marketplace and focal point for civic, religious, and political life...Since 829, when some of St. Mark's bones were transferred here from Alexandria; this old chapel of the Doges has served as a religious center for the city. St. Mark's Basilica became immeasurably wealthy when Venetian crusaders returned with ships laden with Byzantine art treasures following the fall of Constantinople.[72]

Venice and its lagoons have been a UNESCO World Heritage Site since 1987; therefore, there are restrictions for renovations to buildings. All the buildings are brick with plaster on the walls. The roofline cannot change; in some cases, roof balconies were added years ago. No new ones can be added now, nor can any current ones be destroyed. Maintaining homes must be very expensive in the city. The city was founded in the fifth century and spread out over 118 small islands. Venice became a major maritime hub in the tenth century with its convenient access to the Adriatic Sea.

The only romantic experience more than being in Venice is a serenaded gondola ride in Venice. For couples on the trip, this was probably the highlight, several mentioned it. Our gondola had four single women, maybe not romantic but still a memorable experience. We were on our own for the rest of the day to explore Venice: shop, dine, and drink. Venice should be on everyone's bucket list; the use of boating to transit from one place to another is a unique activity.

The next day brought a drive through Tuscany to Florence (Firenze) but first, a stop to see the Leaning Tower of Pisa. Yes, the Pisa Tower does visibly lean, but it was started in 1173 and finished two hundred years later. It has survived four earthquakes, so maybe it isn't as fragile as it looks. The tower is only one of four buildings that comprise the cathedral complex, known as Campo dei Miracoli meaning field of miracles, in the town of Pisa. It is built with white marble, one of the best examples of Romanesque architecture in Italy. The top of the tower is about 17 feet from vertical, yes feet not inches. In the 1920s, the foundation of the tower was injected with cement grout which largely stabilized it. Piazza del Duomo is the cathedral within the complex and a UNESCO World Heritage Site since 1987. The complex also includes the Baptistery and the Monumental Cemetery.

We arrived in Florence, home of Renaissance art and architecture, just in time to look for dinner options. I don't think it's possible to have a bad meal in Italy. The next morning was the walking tour of Florence. We walked past the Medici Palace, which contains the garden where Michaelangelo worked. Every street contains points of interest, making for a very slow walk. The Cathedral of Saint Mary of the Flower now just called Florence Cathedral is magnificent with a terracotta-tiled dome engineered by Filippo Brunelleschi and bell tower by Giotto di Bondone.

The dome of the Florence Cathedral is significant because it was the largest dome of its time and is still the largest brick dome in the world. I am forever enamored when viewing the architectural wonders of the world. Acquiring a doctorate in civil engineering with a major in project management, I am flabbergasted by those who ventured to accomplish what would be considered impossible during their time centuries ago. Failure wouldn't have just been losing money but imprisonment or worse. For those funding the venture, was it a case of ignorance is bliss; they really didn't appreciate what it would take to accomplish the construction?

The afternoon was designated as on our own, so my travel mate and I bought tickets for the Uffizi Gallery online through a third-party seller. I wasn't sure that someone would meet us with tickets, especially when the person was a couple of minutes late for our time slot. After the angst over whether we would gain entry, the visit was memorable. The gallery exhibits such masterpieces as Sandro Botticelli's *The Birth of Venus* and *La Primavera*, Leonardo Da Vinci's *Annunciation,* Michaelangelo di Lodovico Buonarroti Simoni's *Doni Tondo*,

Raffaello Sanzio da Urbino or Raphael's *Madonna of the Goldfinch*, Tiziano Vecellio or Titian's *Venus of Urbano*, and Michelangelo Merisi da Caravaggio's *Bacchus*. A regular who's who of the Renaissance art world where one is legendary to be known by only their first or last name, like the singing star Madonna Louise Ciccone or just Madonna.

Others of the group went to the Galleria dell' Accademia which displays Michaelangelo's *David* sculpture. I'll state again, Florence is the birthplace of the Renaissance period, walking down every street and past every building that has lasted centuries, one appreciates how religion was integrated into the population's lives. Well explained in Irving Stone's book, *The Agony and the Ecstasy*, upward mobility was only acquired through a connection with the church. The priceless relics of today whether architectural or artistic masterpieces are the result of the Catholic church's monetary investment in building and designing structures and artwork to last for eternity. Good or bad, it is why these treasures exist today at the expense of the subservient population living in poverty. Italy's remarkable period correlates to the Catholic church's rise in power and financial affluence and its desires of popes to further create a society of resurgence. Is there a similarity of this period to the French monarchy's period for building chateaus? Their efforts resulted in architecturally striking, but hopefully timeless structures. The resurgence period holds a two-fold requirement: one who has the vision for the extraordinary and then those that have the capability to create it. The Pope, without an implementer like Michelangelo, Da Vinci, or Filippo Brunelleschi, had only an idea but not the means to employ it.

Taken from the book, *The Agony and the Ecstasy*, I leave the reader with the advice given by Father Bechiellini to Michaelangelo, *"Try to think of your whole life as a unity, rather than a series of unrelated fragments."*[73] I interpret this as one shouldn't be focused on any specific events but on how the events weave together to produce a trend or life story. There is too much to see and do in only one afternoon in Florence. I would also advise reading *The Agony and the Ecstasy* or one of the books on Leonardo da Vinci, such as *Leonardo da Vinci* by Walter Isaacson, or other Renaissance artists before a trip to Florence. Learning details of their quests facilitates embracing this emotional, creative period and will enhance your experience.

Leaving the Uffizi Gallery, we had trouble hailing a taxi and just made it back to the hotel in time to leave for the drive to a winery for dinner. Leaving Florence, we stopped on the hill near Piti Palace overlooking the city with its breathtakingly beautiful view: the cathedral rising high above the other structures, the Arno River with the enclosed bridges, and red roof-tiled houses.

Dinner at the winery was a real treat; the Italian buffet was delicious, and the wine was flowing. I discovered that wineries in Italy can ship wine to the states; other countries in Europe are not as accommodating. I can see returning to

Florence to visit all the other museums and historic sights missed this first trip.

It was off to Rome the following day after a late return to the hotel. En route, we stopped at the medieval town of Assisi perched atop a hill in the Umbria region. The town is best known as the birthplace of Saint Francis of Assisi, the patron saint of Italy. The thirteenth-century Basilica di San Francisco contains the sacred relics of Saint Francis, and Giotto di Bondone or just Giotto's remarkable frescoes.

There is a routine practice for walking tours with lunch stops in notable towns between overnight locations. Again, Italy has so much culture and history to offer that traveling from north to south in two weeks is a lot to absorb in so short a time, a real whirlwind experience.

This is probably a good time to provide a brief description of the Franciscan order, one of the four great mendicant orders of the Roman Catholic church. Founded in 1209 by Saint Francis of Assisi, its members strive to live a life with the ideals of poverty, chastity, and obedience. The other religious orders one might stumble across on visits to monasteries and Catholic churches are Benedictine, Carmelites, Carthusians, Dominican, and Jesuit. Saint Benedict founded this Western monasticism ca. 525 AD, the first monks to live in community versus living as hermits. The eleventh-century abbey and a fortified medieval village of Mont Saint Michel is an example of the Benedictine order.

The Order of Carmelites originated on Mount Carmel in then-Palestine time. As cited in the Book of Kings, the great prophet Elijah defended faith in the God of Israel against the priests of Baal. At the western edge of Mount Carmel is Stella Maris Monastery, the world headquarters of the Carmelites.

The Carthusian order was founded by Saint Bruno of Cologne in 1084 in the valley of Chartreuse just north of Grenoble, France. The Dominican order, also known as the Order of Preachers, was founded by Saint Dominic in 1216. The Jesuit order was founded by Saint Ignatius of Loyola in 1534 and officially attained papal approval in 1540. The order is recognized as the principal agent of the Counter-Reformation of the sixteenth and seventh centuries, later leading the modernizing of the Catholic church. In 2013, Pope Francis, formerly Cardinal Jorge Bergoglio of Buenos Aires, became the first Jesuit to serve as pope.

We reached Rome by late afternoon with time for an early dinner and then a walk around Saint Peter's Square. Our hotel was merely a couple blocks from the Vatican maximizing on the ability to stroll the streets to many locations. Our tour manager suggested this short visit to Saint Peter's Square in the late evening to view the square without the crowds. He was right, the visit the next day was much different when besieged with tourists waiting to enter the Vatican. Saint Peter's Basilica was initially planned in the fifteenth century by Pope Nicholas V to replace the previous structure built in the fourth century by Constantine the Great. Pope Julius II started construction on April 18, 1506, with completion on November 18, 1626.

UNESCO summarized the core of the Holy See: *The Vatican City, one of the most sacred places in Christendom, attests to a great history and a formidable spiritual venture. A unique collection of artistic and architectural masterpieces lie within the boundaries of this small state. At its centre is St Peter's Basilica, with its double colonnade and a circular piazza in front and bordered by palaces and gardens. The basilica, erected over the tomb of St Peter the Apostle, is the largest religious building in the world, the fruit of the combined genius of Bramante, Raphael, Michelangelo, Bernini and Maderno.*[74]

The visit to the Vatican was crowded but memorable. We strolled through the section of the Gallery of Tapestries and Geographical Maps with a description of each from our guide. At the end of this section lies the entrance to the Sistine Chapel, with Michaelangelo's remarkable ceiling fresco painted from 1508-1512 described in *The Agony and the Ecstasy*. One cannot appreciate the long hours for which he laid on his back on scaffolding painting until one is in the actual space. This quest has been on my bucket list for decades. Saint Peter's Basilica rests on the recognized burial site of Saint Peter within the square.

The ceiling illustrates nine scenes from the Book of Genesis: Separation of Light from Darkness; Creation of the Sun, Moon, and Plants; Separation of the Earth from the

Waters; Creation of Adam; Creation of Eve; The Fall and Expulsion from the Garden of Eden; Sacrifice of Noah; The Deluge; and Drunkenness of Noah. The most famous being the Creation of Adam. Michaelangelo demonstrates his keen understanding of the male body, acquired through the illegal dissection of cadavers to gain knowledge of muscle structure. Leonardo da Vinci also risked imprisonment to better understand the physiology of the human body and enhance realism of his artwork. The painting illustrates God reaching out to Adam who appears to be leisurely resting and limply reaching back. There are many interpretations for this scene but only Michaelangelo knows the message that he was conveying.

Extracted from the book *The Agony and the Ecstasy*, Michaelangelo understood how creativity works in one's mind: *Where do ideas come from, Tamao? Sebastiano asked that same question when he was young. I can only give the answer I gave him, for I am no wiser at eighty-two than I was at thirty-nine; ideas are a natural function of the mind, as breathing is of the lungs.* [75]

This perspective of Michaelangelo aligns with what is commonly heard from musicians, that the words just came to them. My conclusion is that creativity cannot be taught but must be groomed within those who have naturally acquired an innovative ability. Speaking of creativity, I again borrow from the book *The Agony and the Ecstasy* on Michaelangelo's perspective on sculpting multiple statues at one time. When criticized by Sebastiano for carving three blocks at one time and the ability to get mixed up or remember what to do with each of them when he would move from figure to figure. Michaelangelo's response: *I wish I could have all twenty-five blocks standing around in a great circle. I would move from one to the other so fast that in five years I'd have all of them completed. Have you any concept of how thoroughly you can hollow out blocks of marble by thinking about them for eight years. Ideas are sharper than chisels.*[76]

In other words, Michaelangelo conveys that there is much perspective to be acquired from the integration of multiple works by doing them in parallel versus sequential, which is how most work is usually planned and implemented. That level of understanding back in the sixteenth century is astonishing when there are few government leaders that would take that perspective today. A question to ask of the most successful entrepreneurs is whether they prefer to do work in parallel or sequential. In parallel applies being a multitasker which has gotten a lot of negative criticism lately, but studies have shown that people who are capable of multitasking do not experience the anxiety associated with people who are not adept at multitasking but put in a situation to accomplish it.

In other words, anxiety is created in people when they do activities that they don't do well. Since polymaths acquire knowledge and skills across many disciplines, is this the natural trait of a polymath to integrate work versus differentiate?

Besides painting, sculpting, drawing, architecture, and the ability to physically extract marble from a quarry, he managed his financial affairs very well even providing for his father's living expenses and lifestyle under the conditions of uncertainty in payment, even the hesitation or uncertainty of payment from popes. Michaelangelo demonstrated the characteristics of a polymath. DaVinci has long been labeled a polymath with his variety of accomplishments across several disciplines. A polymath is also referred to as a Renaissance Man.

Fortunately, tour groups have a timed entrance which eliminates a long line for tickets. When we were leaving, the line for tickets looked to be about a three-hour wait. That much downtime can spoil the best of experiences. Unfortunately, picture taking is not allowed in the Sistine Chapel; one will have to go online and view those memorable paintings and the ceiling as a reminder of one's visit.

Rome can be considered one of the most successful empires in history, at least right up to its fall. *Rome grew from a small town on the Tiber River in central Italy into a vast empire that ultimately embraced England, all of continental Europe west of the Rhine and south of the Danube, most of Asia west of the Euphrates, northern Africa, and the islands of the Mediterranean.*[77]

This vast area was ruled by one leader. Rome's foundation

is derived from legend, the legend of Romulus and Remus, two twin brothers in 753 BC. The twins, believed to be the children of the god Mars, were abandoned in a basket on the Tiber River by the King of Alba. The boys survived being nursed by a she-wolf and responded by avenging the king. The brothers eventually quarreled with Romulus killing Remus and solely controlling Rome.

Romans largely achieved their success through military, political, and social institutions. Rome was more willing to acclimate conquered people into their social and political systems than the Greeks. The Greeks excelled in intellectual and artistic ventures; however, the Greek city-states excluded foreigners in political participation. The fall of Rome began in 410 AD when the Visigoths attacked Rome and ended in 476 AD when the German leader Odoacer overthrew the last Roman emperor, Romulus Augustulus. Ancient Rome made a lasting mark; the romantic languages of Italian, French, Spanish, and Romanian are derived from the Roman Latin language. In addition, many of Rome's ancient sites were constructed during the Roman Empire.

In the afternoon, I opted for the optional walking tour of the grand piazzas to include the Spanish steps, the renowned Trevi Fountain, a view of the Pantheon, and the baroque Piazza Navona. Whether depicted in the classic movie *Roman Holiday* or the more recent *Book Club: The Next Chapter*, these are legendary tourist sights. Yes, I did the classic performance of throwing a coin over my shoulder into the Trevi Fountain; however, the number of other tourists at the sight made picture taking of the act rather challenged.

The next day was a driving tour of Rome, first past the triumphal Arch of Constantine, erected by the Roman Senate to commemorate Constantine's tenth year of leadership over the customary name Eternal City. It was then a walking tour of the archeological sites of the Roman Forum; this area was used as a marketplace and amply provided for socialization as a public meeting area.

Today, there still lie some of the ancient government buildings in ruins, a reminder of the Great Roman Empire. From here is a short walk to the Colosseum, the largest amphitheater built in the Roman Empire to seat over 50,000 spectators. The Colosseum's construction was started by Roman Emperor Vespasian between 70-72 CE and completed by his son, Emperor Titus in 80 CE. The Colosseum brings mixed emotions; on the one hand, it is an architectural wonder as one of the Seven Modern Wonders of the World. On the other hand, it represents the brutal abuse of people and animals. Unfortunately, history has a dark side.

Although we have all read about these in books, there is so much more emotional impact when one stands among these historical relics which can represent the beast side of human behavior. In the picture section of this chapter, there is a snapshot of a seagull at the Colosseum. It looks like it made a tourist stop to acquire a better view; yes, even seagulls are impressed with the structure. National Geographic recognized the Colosseum as one of the 225 World's Most Amazing Places and destinations of a lifetime.[78]

Rome was a walled city. Portions of the original sixth-century BC Servian Wall are left near the 1930s Termini Train Station. The Aurelian Walls were created by Emperor Aurelian in the third century AD with the population increasing to over 1.2 million. In the ninth century BC, Pope Leo built the Leonine Wall as reinforcement around Vatican Hill. Initially, the Basilicas of Saint Peter and Saint Paul were located outside the wall but their attack by Aghlabids' Islamic raiders from northern Africa, currently the area of Tunisia and Algeria, in 845 necessitated new reinforcements. In 1643, Pope Urban VIII built a stretch of fortified wall along the Tiber River designated the Janiculum Wall.

Besides the city walls, there are seven iconic bridges of Rome, each with its own unique history and recognition. The oldest bridge is the Fabrician Bridge dating back to 62 BC and is also the best-preserved bridge. The Milvian Bridge dates to 109 BC and was used with the surrounding area for battle engagement over the centuries. Constantine was crowned as the sole ruler of the Western Empire in 312 AD.

Saint-Angelo Bridge connects Hadrian's Mausoleum with the Vatican. This bridge has a sordid past. In 1450, an accident involving Pope Nicholas V caused hundreds of people to fall into the river and drown. The bridge was also used for executions with the most famous executioner, Giovanni Battista Bugatti's ghost paying penitence walking the bridge at night.

Aemilius Bridge has changed its name many times over the centuries but is now known as Broken Bridge. This bridge is known for its routine destruction due to the violent waters of the Tiber River in that area. Even Michaelangelo led a reconstruction project in 1552 but his endeavors only lasted five years.

The Sixtus Bridge is deemed the most romantic with the backdrop of Saint Peter's Dome, especially in the evenings with the array of pink, purple, and orange hues of a setting sun. It was built for the Jubilee of 1475 to facilitate pilgrims stroll to the Vatican and other parts of the city.

The Duke of Aosta Bridge is deemed the most scenic with its location among the stylish palaces, immense villas, and impressive rowing clubs. The marble statues on the four corners depict scenes of battles led by the Third Army commanded by Duke Emanuele Filiberto of Savoy-Aosta. The seventh bridge, the Music Bridge, is the youngest bridge and used for pedestrians and cycling and is the only modern steel bridge crossing the Tiber River.

With our hotel so close to Vatican City, Catholicism's history was on my mind. It is strange to think that the Pope at one time was not only the religious head of the Catholic faith but also political head of Rome. While proponents for the unification of Italy were making plans, they included turning Rome into a republic with a constitution and assembly selected by male suffrage.

Pope Pius IX would escape Rome on November 24, 1848, under disguise and spend over a year in southern Italy in Gaeta under the hospitality of King Frederick and Queen Maria Theresa of Naples. Rome would be attacked and occupied by the French to restore papal control. At this time, Rome had a population of 170,000 and 400 churches.[79]

Although Rome's republic government lost to the French and papal control was restored to Rome, Pope Pius IX selected Cardinal Gabrielle Della Gringa, Cardinal Luigi Vannicelli, and Cardinal Prince Lodovico Alteri to be the governing commission, allowing no representation of the people in governing Rome.[80] It became a witch hunt for anyone perceived connected to the Republic. The Eternal City and the birth of the Renaissance experienced one of its darkest days in history during this birth of enlightenment and the need for the population to want representation of its governing leadership.

One can only wonder what a Christian God's role and message was to the papal leadership. Under ironic circumstances, the French would vacate Rome to fight a war with Prussia. The unified Italy would fight the papal forces and win control of Rome and Italy for King Victor Emmanuel, reducing the Pope's role to just spiritual leader and confined to the Vatican. Rome became Italy's capital and a constitutional monarchy. King Emmanuel died in January 1878, and Pope Pius IX would die four weeks later. The separation of church and state became the standard for Europe.[81]

Although we had three nights in Rome, that wasn't nearly long enough. I was packing up my clothes and embarking on the coach to head south for Naples and Sorrento to finish the trip. A few people headed to Rome's Airport choosing a shorter timeframe trip. Before checking into the hotel in Sorrento, we stopped at the infamous Pompeii, the Roman city in 79 A.D. buried by 19 feet of volcanic ash and debris from Mount Vesuvius. It is estimated that over 2000 people perished. On the day of our tour, a light drizzle darkened the walk leaving slippery stoned streets, like the occupants during that period.

Walking among the ruins strikes a multitude of emotions: despair, admiration, and repulsion. So how can so many emotions come to heart? For its time, Pompeii was an upscale Roman town. Walking through the ruins, one can see the stone formations of previous homes with even courtyards. The admiration for the construction during that time. The despair comes with the surprise volcano attack of Mount Vesuvius and the death of most of the town. If one happened to be out of town like across Naples Bay fishing, then they were spared the tragedy. As we walked around the site, we entered a room with drawings on the wall depicting certain acts of lust. Our tour manager explained that prostitution was legal in Roman times, and the drawings depict optional services. It was a man's world back then. Repulsion reflects the world's oldest profession.

Mount Vesuvius is considered a stratovolcano. The volcano's current shape is the result of explosive eruptions over the last 25,000 years; the volcano is still dangerous and unpredictable today.

As the African tectonic plate is pushed under the Eurasian plate, a portion of the lower plate has detached from the upper part, creating what is known as a "slab window." This promotes melting of a different type of rock underneath Vesuvius than what is around it, and this winds up favoring violent eruptions. This rock is known as andesite, a volcanic rock that has around 50-60% silica content. This relatively high amount of silica creates "sticky" magma that traps gases and water to create explosive eruptions, making Vesuvius especially dangerous and unpredictable.[82]

The last eruption of Mount Vesuvius was March 17, 1944, and since then the city of Naples has grown around the base and up the mountainsides. Herculaneum is the other town buried in volcanic ash. What dictates the fine balance for decision factors between progress and unnecessarily putting people and their assets at risk? Nature has and will continue to unleash catastrophic events onto the earth; to what extent does protection of these catastrophes become the responsibility of the government and the people?

Buildings still exposing half their height depict the ruins

of the Pompeii; many show the footprint of large, wealthy families of the time. If possible, tour the site with a guide to better understand the purpose of the buildings and the layout of the city.

Once through the archeological site, the museum displays the ash frames of people caught in the volcano's blast. There's a feeling of eeriness seeing the preserved outlined bodies of men, women, and children in sleeping positions forged in ash. It is a chilling feeling to imagine what the city dwellers experienced.

After this sobering excursion, we checked into our hotel in Naples Bay in Sorrento.

The hotel is a summer resort and had only opened for the season earlier in the month. The next morning, we embarked on an optional excursion to Capri Island on the Tyrrhenian Sea, a boat ride included. There are two towns on the island, and we made our way to both: Capri and Anacapri. Capri has the Piazzetta at its center and Anacapri is at a higher elevation on the slopes of Mount Solaro. We took the chair ride to the top of the mountain. An essential quest, the view is spectacular. Capri is known for its grottos which are better seen from the water. We took a boat ride around the island and saw many picture-perfect grottos with sparkling turquoise water. The only problem is that everyone else wants to see them too. So often other boats were at the same site, and we had to maneuver or wait our turn to get a closer look.

Capri was discovered by Emperor Caesar Augustus in 29 BC, being the first to build a villa there. However, before he ventured there, excavations depict Greek civilization on the island earlier in the eighth-century BC. It is believed that during the Paleolithic era, the island was joined to the mainland. During World War II, Capri became a strategic spot for Allied invasions into southern Italy after successful campaigns in Sicily. During the war, the current Hotel Punta Tragara was appropriated and used as a rest camp for United States Air Force officials. General Dwight Eisenhower, General Mark Clark, and Prime Minister Winston Churchill met there to form Allied plans for Italy. In 1943, General Mark Clark was the Commanding General of the 5th Army in Italy, and in 1944, he assumed command of the 15th Army Group, consisting of all the Allied Forces in Italy.

The next morning, we were off to the famous Amalfi Coast; I now know why it is recommended not to drive yourself. It was particularly concerning in a large touring coach. The road is extremely curvy with many spots that the coach had to maneuver on both sides. One cannot drive and take in the spectacular views, so pay someone to do the driving. We spent lunch in the town of Amalfi and of course with time for shopping. It was Margherita pizza for me again, probably my fifth time on the trip. Yes, it is that good; also, one must try the limoncello. It is an Italian lemon liqueur produced in southern Italy, especially around Naples, the Amalfi Coast, and Sicily. It is traditionally served chilled as an after-dinner drink but can also be served as a spritzer.

A word for managing one's expectations, the view is exceptional but there is very little beach area. Boating is the prevalent water activity in the area. The town is absolutely charming with tiny walking streets but expect high-end prices. We took the road back over the mountain which provided a different terrain perspective of southern Italy.

For most of our group, they flew back home the next day; however, my travel mate and I planned two extra days. So, we signed up for cooking classes in Sorrento. After some confusion in finding the meeting spot to be picked up for the class, we were off to the combination winery and restaurant. My mate and I were the only two people doing the eggplant parmigiana, so we received special attention. We watched how mozzarella is made and then onto making ravioli using the mozzarella and the eggplant parmigiana. We ate our results or at least half of it; there was too much for one meal. The remainder of lunch came back with us for dinner that night. Again, the tomato sauce is just phenomenal, bursting with flavor.

The following day was a rest day, hanging around the hotel. This hotel was in Naples Bay, so an incredible view but not very close for walking to stores. That evening, a former military co-worker stationed in Naples took me and my mate out for dinner. We ate at a seafood restaurant in a small town near the marina. The seafood had to be fresh, right from the boat to the kitchen. The next morning, we were up at 3:00 am for our ride to Naples International Airport. The very early morning departures are rough, but the back end of the early start is getting home earlier. When we arrived at JFK airport, we had a 90-minute wait in passport control/customs; a very long time when one has just flown for hours. I'm not sure why the long delay; it is possible that it was still the fallout from Coronavirus (COVID-19) with reduced manning. It was multiple transportation means from New York City to my home in Maryland again.

This trip had a bit of a delayed reaction impact when the following two days I experienced lumps on my chest, neck, and face. Although I thought I had gotten a couple of mosquito bites during the trip, I assumed the number of lumps, about the size of quarters, must have been an allergic reaction. By Sunday night, two days after my return, I visibly had a big problem and went to the emergency room at the hospital. After a five-hour wait, I was seen by the doctor, who confirmed what I already suspected, bed bug bites.

I've heard about bed bugs and knew that they are possible even at the most expensive hotels but did not expect it. I've traveled extensively in the United States and some abroad and fortunately this is the first time that I encountered a bed bug problem. I also as a precaution left my luggage open in my bedroom with the clothes spread out and bombed the room with insect spray. If one brings bed bugs back, they can be difficult to purge from your house. The doctor prescribed prednisone and once I started taking the medication, the itching subsided. How to check for bed bugs? Look for red blood stains on sheets, small black dots as excrement, and white or yellow eggs about the size of an apple seed. Lift the mattress and shine a flashlight on it to detect any bugs embedded in it. Also, there can be a sweet, musty smell.

Although tour groups have adopted procedures for making people aware of group participants who have tested positive for COVID-19, I believe there should be procedures for other issues such as bed bugs. In general, what are the conditions and the methods for notification to all group travelers? Even with this calamity at the end of my tour, it will not lessen my desire to return to Italy including the southern part.

I loved everything about the country: the people, the culture, the history, the landscape, and the food, especially the tomato sauce. One really needs to traverse the entire country to appreciate the difference from north to south and east to west. I found little difficulty conversing in English; most people seemed to know enough for me to get by, other than attending mass in Como which was in Italian.

As I was reviewing the final edits for the book in 2025, the tragic occurrence of Pope Francis saddened the world, particularly for the Ponitff's Catholic flock. He served since 2013 known as Jorge Mario Bergoglio before his selection as the head of the Catholic Church through the conclave. He chose the name Francis to honor Saint Francis of Assisi, admired for his dedication to the poor, peace, and humility.

I remembered my stop in Assisi while en route to Rome on the trip. Coincidently, the movie *Conclave* starring Ralph Fiennes, Stanley Tucci, Isabelli Rossellini, and John Lithgow released in movie theaters in 2024 depicted the political procedure for selection of a new pope. As I read media coverage leading up to the start of the papal conclave and then throughout the few days, I remembered my time back in Rome and inside Vatican City.

Although a number of popes have been selected during my lifetime, I connected more with this particular one because of my trip and the ability to visualize the locations discussed by the media. The benefit of travel allows one to emotionally connect to current events around the world. The uniqueness of the plot to depict a priest from Kabul particularly tweaked my memory with my experience attending mass at the only Christian church in Afghanistan located within protected walls. The conclave, held in the Sistine Chapel on May 7, selected a new pope by day two. American-born Cardinal Robert Francis Prevost chose the name Pope Leo XIV; he is also the first American pope.

Although not a Catholic worshiper, I was married in a Catholic Church and have attended mass numerous times with my then-husband. The announcement of the new pope is merely the designation of white smoke from the Sistine Chapel chimney versus black smoke indicating no decision. Curious to know the status, I tracked the media attention daily. On the second day, a video was posted of the white smoke results with a precocious pigeon also interested in knowing the results. I've come to believe that the pigeons of Rome are intimately involved in the activities of the Eternal City. Such as the ones hoovering around the Colosseum and every square and statue I saw in the city. As the crowds waiting for the results in Saint Peter's Square cheered for the announcement, the little fellow bathed in white smoke flew off to convey the message to other pigeon friends.

There were several UNESCO World Heritage Sites visited during the trip: Historic Centre of Rome, the Properties of the Holy See in that City Enjoying Extraterritorial Rights and San Paolo Fuori le Mura (1980); Vatican City (1984); Historic Centre of Florence (1982); Piazza del Duomo, Pisa (1987); Venice and its Lagoon (1987); Archaeological Areas of Pompei, Herculaneum and Torre Annunziata (1997); Costiera Amalfitana (1997); Assisi, the Basilica of San Francesco and Other Franciscan Sites (2000); and the City of Verona (2000). As of 2025, Italy has 60 UNESCO World Heritage Sites, so my eight locations that I have visited leaves quite a few left to venture on future trips.

I also can check the bucket list for one of the Seven Wonders of the Modern World, the Colosseum. With respect to churches, temples, and synagogues, I can check the following locations of worship: Saint Peter's Basilica in Rome, on Wikipedia's list and Road Affair blog; Saint Mark's Basilica in Venice, also Wikipedia's list and Road Affair blog; and Saint Maria del Fiore in Florence, on Road Affair blog.

Unfortunately, I did not have time to venture to Saint Maria Maggiore in Rome so that visit will have to occur on another trip to Italy. I can check the box for the Vatican Museum too.

Lake Como

Florence

Venice

Vatican

seagull at Colosseum

white smoke   Medusa   Leaning Tower of Pisa

Trevi Fountain   Amalfi Coast

Pompeii ruins   ashen formations

245

Chapter 8

Seattle, Washington, United States

In every walk with nature, one receives far more than he
seeks. – John Muir

(https://www.brainyquote.com/quotes/john_muir_108391)

Background: History, Culture, and Environment

Hello, my friend.

Seattle, Washington is known for many icons: the Space
Needle, the *Frazer* television show, the movie *Sleepless in
Seattle*, Microsoft Corporation and one of its founders Bill
Gates, and Boeing Corporation's commercial airline
manufacturing to name a few. However, the history of Seattle
reflects five different boom periods. The first was the lumber-
industry boom in 1848 aligned with the California Gold Rush.
The Great Northern Railway linked the transportation of
freight in and out of Seattle in 1884; however, it was 1906
before a major rail passenger terminal was in the city. The
Klondike Gold Rush started in Alaska in 1896 but did not
spread to Seattle until July 1897. Prospectors would sail from
Seattle to Skagway or Dyea in Alaska. I learned more about the
Alaskan Gold Rush during my trip to Alaska later in the year.

Shipbuilding became the next boom for Seattle which
peaked in World War I and then typical of war-fueled

industries crashed afterward. World War II brought the greater need for a United States Air Force and Boeing fulfilled that need. Using fixed-fee type contracts, the company produced 8,200 planes including 6,981 B-17 bombers and more than 1,000 B-29 bombers. Boeing was the largest employer in Seattle during this time. Airplane manufacturing wasn't the only wartime industry for the Seattle area. Shipyards sprung up in Puget Sound and the greater Seattle area producing many war vessels to meet the United States maritime mission against a competent Japanese Navy.

After the war, Boeing turned their focus to commercial airlines. Since Boeing's start, the company had only 13 Presidents including the previous David L. Calhoun. As of August 8, 2024, Robert "Kelly" Ortberg replaced Calhoun as President and CEO. The company has seen many highs and lows since its start. William E. Boeing founded the company in 1916 and was its President from July 1916 to May 1922 and from January 1925 to February 1926; during the time from 1916-1926 he was also the Chief Executive Officer. From May 1922 to January 1925, for this short period, Edgar N. Gott held the position of President. William Boeing exemplified the entrepreneurial spirit, leaving Yale University in 1903 to venture to Washington and the Northwest timber industry. A true entrepreneur, he took advantage of the need for aircraft as industry shifts occurred.

A trip to Seattle will probably mean indulging in seafood: salmon, halibut, rockfish, lingcod, Dungeness crab, oysters, mussels, scallops, and clams to name a few. Alaska King Crab and Alaskan Snow Crab can also be found. Washington is one of the 50 states of the United States; Seattle has its tourism cruising connection with the popular Alaska cruise destination.

Although considered a superpower of the world, the United States shockingly did not fall in the top 10 percent or even the top 20 percent based on the Fund for Peace Fragile State Index for 2024 ranking with a place of 141st and score of 44.5. The two sub- indicators that drove the results are social factors: factionalized elites (7.4) and group grievance (6.2). Seattle became one of the cities to defund its police budget after several cities saw surges in social unrest. Based on an article from the National Police Association, the purpose of defunding the police was for police reform and police accountability. This crisis started in Minneapolis when George Floyd's life was taken by a police officer with three other officers involved. This event fueled riotous behaviors and protests across several cities.

In 2021, Seattle defunded its police budget by nearly 17 percent. As possibly the result of that defunding, the number of homicides increased by 24 percent. The year after the budget cuts, the police department lost 130 officers in the same year resulting in a record number of shootings or shots fired. For 2023, the police department had shrunk 23 more positions, the result of its inability to find qualified personnel to fill the positions. The last sentence of the Straight Arrow

News article says it all: *The data reflects a current trend that less police equals more crime. It's another concern for a city struggling to retain its image as a safe tourist destination.*[83]

I would enjoy seeing a mapping of how defunding the police equates to lower crimes. A cause-and-effect analysis seems to be required here. Fortunately, our trip to Seattle was uneventful with respect to not experiencing any of the crime surge found in the city. However, I would caution anyone traveling to Seattle or any other major city in the United States to take routine precautions for your safety. That advice is not merely relevant today but dates back decades for crime in major cities of the United States. As someone who had their battery stolen from their car sitting next to the curb on the street outside the engineering building at Temple University in Philadelphia, Pennsylvania in the 1980s, crime has been an enduring problem.

Most of Europe scored better than the United States but the nation did score better than the tiny island of Barbados which claimed the spot of 140th. Well, there's a national accomplishment to be more stable than the small island of Barbados. In 2008, the United States ranked 161st at a score of 32.8 just squeaking past the United Kingdom at 160th with a score of 32.9. Over the past sixteen years, the United States has significantly lost ranking among world nations for stability.

So how did the world superpower perform for the State

Resilience Index? With a score of 7.4, the United States scored well above average on all the indicators but two: environment and ecology and social cohesion. I think the United States leadership has some homework to do to identify problems' root causes and solutions before developing a plan for implementation with metrics to track status. That sounds like the basics for a course in problem solving.

Travel Itinerary

We stayed for seven nights just outside of Seattle, Washington, renting a car for travel around the area.

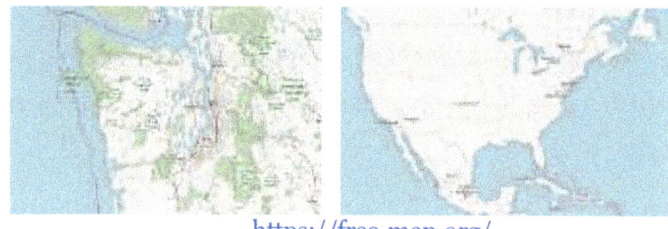

https://free-map.org/

Travel Journal

This was a pseudo-family trip with my two sons, one daughter-in-law, and a granddaughter accompanying me. Besides having my family with me, the best part of the trip was staying in one hotel and venturing out within a one-day locale and returning. This was still on the early side of my marathon travel sprint for the year, but with the number of trips that required moving from one location to another, it was so nice having a *ground zero* to operate for a week. We flew out of Dulles International Airport using long-term parking and all fitting the crowd and luggage into my Honda Pilot. We arrived at a reasonable two hours before domestic travel but did not anticipate more than an hour's wait in the security line.

Yes, we spent about an hour and a half in line and by that point, I was getting a bit concerned. When I finally cleared security, my daughter-in-law got hung up with something in her luggage, so the rest of us persevered to the gate promising to hold the airplane until she arrived. It's not easy to have a five- year-old continue without her mom with promises that she will catch up. She was also exceptionally patient, waiting in the security line in a stroller and with a notebook to be comfortable and entertained.

Once at the gate, my son circled back for some airplane exhibit pictures and my daughter-in-law caught up. My other son was considering going for a milkshake and I warned him that we were boarding in less than five minutes; so, based on my strong recommendation, no one left the gate. Fortunately, we had a direct flight from Dulles, Virginia to Seattle, Washington. Remember that domestic flights no longer provide meals free for travel; although you may buy one on the plane, they don't always stock enough for everyone. I usually purchase something at the airport or en route to the airport. Fortunately, I had purchased our sandwiches before the airport because we didn't really have any time at the airport. My daughter-in-law always prepares snacks for the family on road trips, so they had provisions.

We landed in Seattle in the late evening and then headed to the rental car service. After several minutes of negotiating for the best deal with three potential drivers, a smart toll box, and a suggested upgrade to a larger SUV because we were going to national parks which still had snow, we left the airport bound for our Fun Center hotel, a hotel located next door to a Fun Center.

On our first full day, we kept our itinerary a bit easy and ventured to the Museum of Flight at Boeing Corporation. My son and daughter-in-law were doctoral students in aerospace engineering, and I've spent a good portion of my career in the aerospace engineering field of naval aviation, so we spent most of the day there. The museum boasts of being the largest non-profit, air and space museum in the world. *With over 175 aircraft and spacecraft, tens of thousands of artifacts, millions of rare photographs, dozens of exhibits and experiences and a world-class library, the museum and its people bring mankind's incredible history of flight to life.*[84]

By day two, we ventured to downtown Seattle and purchased the combination ticket for two trips up to the Space Needle in 24 hours, as well as a trip to the Seattle Aquarium, and three other locations. If you have a couple of days, this is the best bargain. We maximized the first day by doing morning and evening Space Needle trips, the Glass and Garden Museum, and a harbor cruise with transcending locks.

Atop the Space Needle, my granddaughter was spread out over the Plexiglas floor high above the city coloring a picture; she was not bothered by the virtually hanging in the air at that height. Fear of height must be a learned problem because I was gripping the stationary wall as the floor rotated around for a 360-degree view.

The Chihuly Garden and Glass Museum displays the stunning work of Dale Chihuly, the most famous glass artist in the world. Chihuly transcended the use of glass for functional applications to the level of artistic creativity attained in fine art. The designs are exquisite and the color beyond vibrant. From a tour through his art pieces, one appreciates the passion that some people have for artistic perfection and creativity and will settle for nothing less.

The Harbor Cruise was a real treat, besides passing the house that was used to film *Sleepless in Seattle* with Tom Hanks and Meg Ryan, we saw harbor seals at the end of the inlet. At the end of the cruise, we asked our boat guide for restaurant suggestions, and he recommended one of his favorites, *Chinooks*, a seafood restaurant in the marina. So, it was off to Chinooks and a very filling seafood dinner for everyone but me because I'm not a diner of seafood. Love the sea environment but not the food that comes from it. The next morning it was motoring to Olympic National Park which has been a UNESCO World Heritage Site since 1981.

Located in the north-west of Washington State, Olympic National Park is renowned for the diversity of its ecosystems. Glacier-clad peaks interspersed with extensive alpine meadows are surrounded by an extensive old growth forest, among which is the best example of intact and protected temperate rainforest in the Pacific Northwest. Eleven major river systems drain the Olympic mountains, offering some of the best habitat for anadromous fish species in the country. The park also includes 100 km of wilderness coastline, the longest undeveloped coast in the contiguous United States, and is rich in native and endemic animal and plant species, including critical populations of the endangered northern spotted owl, marbled murrelet and bull trout.[85]

Although it was early May, this time of year can be on the questionable side for some national parks to be fully opened. Snowfall over the winter can accumulate and require further into the summer for snow to melt and no longer be a driving hazard. We found an additional problem with a road closure based on a fire earlier in the week at a lodge being renovated. So, we hiked what we could. We did a short hike in the Olympic National Forest close by and then went to the trail along the Elwha River passing a former ranger station, closed because the road had previously washed out and was never fixed. At the end of the trail is the location where a dam existed but since it has been removed.

The Elwha and Glines Canyon Dams were built in the early 1900s, generating hydropower to supply electricity for the emerging town of Port Angeles and promoting growth on the Peninsula. Man's progress can have adverse effects on nature; in this case, the construction of the dam blocked the migration of salmon upstream, disrupted the flow of sediment downstream, and flooded the historic homelands and cultural sites of the Lower Elwha Kallam Tribe.

In 1992, Congress passed the Elwha River Ecosystem and Fisheries Restoration Act, authorizing dam removal to restore the altered ecosystem and the native anadromous fisheries. It took two decades of planning before the largest dam removal in history started on September 17, 2011. Six months later the dam was gone, and the Glines Canyon Dam was removed in 2014. The hike is about five miles roundtrip, and my five-year-old granddaughter was getting tired near the two-mile point, so I headed back with her as the rest of the group had to double-time it to the removed dam location and return before the park closed.

After a day of hiking, we used the other combination pass to visit the Seattle Aquarium. All children love aquariums and so do parents, especially watching the otters. Otters just represent playfulness. A couple of river otters with some floating toys in their water home and everyone was mesmerized. The aquarium had daily activities on harbor seals, marine mammal feeding, sea otters and feeding, Northern Fur Seals, and information specially for Washington state waters.

Then onto Pike's Market for lunch, a must-see for any Seattle visitor. I don't think the fish gets any fresher, especially at Pike Place Fish Market where it is known for the tradition of fishmongers throwing the fish purchased by customers prior to wrapping it. The eateries at the market were rather busy with a small seating area. As we were walking around, we stumbled across Starbucks. Why the mob in front of Starbucks at lunchtime? Yes, that's right it was the first Starbucks, and the masses were waiting to check the bucket list item: *had a coffee at first Starbucks.*

The story of Starbucks begins in 1971 along the cobblestone streets of Seattle's historic Pike Place Market. It was here where Starbucks opened its first store, offering fresh-roasted coffee beans, tea and spices from around the world for its customers to take home. Their name was inspired by the classic tale Moby-Dick, evoking the seafaring tradition of the early coffee traders. Over the next 50 years, they would grow to open stores globally and welcome millions of customers each week, becoming a part of the fabric of tens of thousands of neighborhoods all around the world.[86]

Somehow, waiting in a long line with a five-year-old just for a coffee didn't seem to be the smartest idea, so we reluctantly moved on. We headed back to the hotel late afternoon to take advantage of the Fun Center next door.

The next day's journey was a trip to Mount Rainer National Park. My daughter-in-law had read recent reviews that some paths were still snowy and required snowshoes. We opted for a path that appeared to be cleared or mostly cleared. It started out fine but about halfway it became very snowy and then icy. With a waterfall at the top, we ventured on very slowly. When one stepped off the path, you were in knee-high snow. I saw my daughter-in-law fall backward a few times landing on her derriere. My granddaughter gave up on the way back and her father had to carry her. I grabbed a stick for walking which did help a lot with balance on the icy parts. This was one of the better trails that opened in early May. After we returned to the car, we drove to the lodge towards the top of the mountain which was closed but what a beautiful view of the snow-covered top of Mount Rainer. There were a few people hiking with appropriate gear there.

One always enjoys seeing wildlife in hikes through national parks. Mount Rainer is home to a variety of mammals such as bears, bobcats and mountain lions, coyote and cascade red fox, racoons, and in the weasel and skunk family: fisher, American marten, American mink, striped skunk, Western spotted skunk, long-tailed weasel, short-tailed weasel, and wolverine. I have seen the racoon and the striped skunk in my backyard in Maryland.

For our last day in Seattle, we went to the Woodland Park Zoo; children and parents all love zoos too. My granddaughter loved the goat petting zoo the most; we had trouble getting her to leave the pen, as did most of the other parents with their children. It was advantageous visiting the zoo because it happened to be the only place that we had animal sightings besides the aquarium. The animals were still not stirring very much in the national parks at that time of year.

For those who enjoy penguins, the zoo has a Humboldt

Penguin exhibition. It is estimated that there are only 30,000 Humboldt penguins left on our planet. These birds are only found in the Pacific coastal areas of Peru and Chile. Humboldt penguins dig through guano, accumulated seabird droppings, to build their nests and raise their chicks. Believe it or not, there is another use of guano, as an agricultural fertilizer. This purpose is now competing with the penguins for sufficient material to make nests. In addition, these penguins are having more problems finding the food they like such as anchovies and sardines which prefer colder water. As tidal water changes occur, fish and plant life change to accommodate. As the waters closer to Peru and Chile become warmer, the penguins must move farther out to sea to find the seafood that they like. They compete with other more capable wildlife making it harder to find sufficient food. Is this another example of impacts of climate change?

Humboldt penguins are one of only four banded penguin types named for the horseshoe black band or stripe around the front of their bodies and across their chest. The other three types also prefer a more temperate climate than those found in Antarctica: the African penguin, the Magellanic penguin, and the Galápagos penguin. Humboldt penguins are currently listed as a threatened species, vulnerable to extinction unless there is improvement to the circumstances threatening their survival.

North Cascades National Park is located about three hours north of Seattle. Most of the roads were closed so we didn't even think about driving for the three-hour one-way to visit. It is better to stay closer to this park or camp during the summer months. The park is home to 75 mammal species in 21 families with three species, gray wolf, grizzly bear, and Canada lynx, being listed as threatened or endangered under the Endangered Species Act.

It was time to fly home in the morning but not without an hour-long queue at security in the Seattle International Airport. Like Washington Dulles International Airport for our departure, this delay was probably the result of an increase in passengers flying and the airports still ramping up from the COVID-19 pandemic reduction in air travel during 2023.

On my trip to Seattle, Washington, I visited one UNESCO World Heritage Site, Olympic National Park (1981). Many of the United States' UNESCO sites are national parks. As President Theodore Roosevelt stated: *the establishment of the National Park Service is justified by considerations of good administration, of the value of natural beauty as a National asset, and of the effectiveness of outdoor life and recreation in the production of good citizenship.*[87] His famous distant cousin, President Franklin Roosevelt continued this admirable opinion further connecting nature and Americanism: *there is nothing so American as our national parks...The fundamental idea behind the parks. Is that the country belongs to the people, that it is in process of making for the enrichment of the lives of all of us.*[88]

Seattle skyline with Space Needle

Mount Rainer National Park

Humboldt Penguins

Chihuly Glass

stellar jay

Mount Rainer hike

Olympic National Park

Sleepless in Seattle house   line at Starbucks

waterfall in Mount Rainer   otters at play

Chapter 9

Switzerland

The Mountains are Calling, and I Must Go – John Muir

(https://www.brainyquote.com/quotes/john_muir_380220)

Background: History, Culture, and Environment

Bonjour mon ami. Hallo mein Freund. Ciao amico mio.

When one hears the country name Switzerland, one pictures majestic mountains, grassy valleys, and sparkling lakes as pictured in multiple movie versions of *Heidi* since 1937, played by child star Shirley Temple. This is the story of a little orphan girl who is sent to live with her grumpy grandfather in the remote Swiss Alps, from the book written by Johanna Spryi in 1881. The stunning scenery is genuine, but Switzerland has become more metropolitan than the movie depicts.

Switzerland borders on Germany, France, Italy, and Austria therefore creating a multi-lingual pot of German, French, and Italian with the addition of Romansh as national languages. English is also spoken widely. Our trip took us near the borders of each of these countries and languages. This melting pot of culture within one country yields differences in some ways (language, food, customs) but similarities in others. The country is about half the size of Scotland, measuring 135 miles (220 km) from north to south and 220 miles (350 km) from west to east. Traveling 135 miles (220 km) usually takes a couple of hours but not when one must navigate the Swiss Alps Mountain range.

Switzerland is also considered the hydrographic center of Europe providing the source of many major rivers including the Rhône which flows to the Mediterranean Sea and the Rhine which flows to the North S e a. Swiss citizens share strong individual rights balanced with community and national interests. These similarities forge the Swiss culture. The Swiss Confederation dates to 1848 as a federal republic of relatively autonomous cantons. Currently, there are 26 cantons, similar to states. Berne is the administrative capital, Lausanne is the judicial center, and Zurich is the most important economic center of the country. Geneva hosts the highest number of international organizations in the world, also known as the location of the signing of the Geneva Convention reflecting the treatment of wartime non-combatants and prisoners of war.

The physical barriers of the Swiss Alps create a sense of isolation or self-sufficiency. Neutrality is one of the main principles of foreign policy and external agreements. Switzerland is not part of the European Union nor the NATO; however, they have participated in NATO's Partnership for Peace (PfP) program since 1996.

- Based on a commitment to democratic principles, the

purpose of the Partnership for Peace is to increase stability, diminish threats to peace and build strengthened security relationships between NATO and non-member countries in the Euro-Atlantic area.

- The PfP was established in 1994 to enable participants to develop an individual relationship with NATO, choosing their own priorities for cooperation, and the level and pace of progress.

- Activities on offer under the PfP programme touch on virtually every field of NATO activity.

- Since April 2011, all PfP activities and exercises are in principle open to all NATO partners, be they from the Euro-Atlantic region, the Mediterranean Dialogue, the Istanbul Cooperation Initiative or global partners.[89]

Switzerland has not participated in a foreign war since it's neutrality was established by the Treaty of Paris in 1815, making it the oldest military neutrality policy in the world. Although not part of the European Union, Switzerland is a participant in the Schengen Area.

What does that mean? If one has a visa issued by a Schengen member state, then an additional tourist visa is not required. One can pass between Schengen Areas without typical border crossing procedures or at least a modified procedure.

If anyone has ever seen the abbreviation for Switzerland

it's CH, ever wonder why? Switzerland was founded in 1291 by an alliance of cantons, similar to states, against the Habsburg dynasty called the Confoederatio Helvetica (CH) or Swiss Confederation. In 1848, Switzerland adopted a new constitution forming the present nation. Although before 1848, conflict was common; it's been peaceful since the mid-nineteenth century. It is a union of 3,000 communes or municipalities located in 26 cantons, with six of these considered demi cantons or half cantons but functioning as full cantons. What does that mean? Ordinary citizens have much control in deciding and exercising political actions. What is the result of this political responsibility? Swiss citizens have greater voting power on a broad range of expenditures creating lower taxes than other European nations. It also results in slow political decision-making with individuals allowed to express opinions at every level. Referendums are one means of political decision-making.

When one thinks of Switzerland, the Alps come to mind, but they are largely used for beauty, hiking, and winter sports. Raw materials, food, vegetable oils, and fuel account for about one-quarter of total imports. Limited raw materials such as gravel, sand, limestone, and clay are mined and used in construction. The major exports are machinery and equipment, chemical-pharmaceuticals products, watches, and textiles and apparel.

One can get to know a country by its traditions and what better way than through holiday traditions. The Swiss celebrate Christmas with Samichlaus, a Swiss Santa Claus, who delivers presents not on December 24 but on December 6, this tradition dates to the fourteenth century. The traditional Christmas meal is fondue and Filet im Teig, pork or veal fillet wrapped in pastry. Gluhwein is a warm drink popular in the Christmas season. It can be found served at holiday markets, public town areas, and even the ski slopes. Nothing like a glass of warm gluhwein to add to a winter wonderland or festive occasion.

Switzerland is one of the least fragile countries in the world ranked at 174th with a score of 16.2 in 2024 for the Fragile State Index, only Denmark, New Zealand, Iceland, Finland, and Norway scored better. Four of the five countries lie in northern Europe with New Zealand in southern Asia. Does this mean that people that live in colder climates create less fragile nations? I need to add these countries to my bucket list to possibly discover the reason. For Switzerland, living in mountainous seclusion seems to appeal to its people; they take a very independent, neutral perspective on the rest of the world.

Switzerland equally performs well for the State Resilience Index at a score of 8.3; all indicators were well above the average. The citizens of Switzerland pride themselves on independence and therefore there's no surprise that this independence may manifest into resilience. The remoteness of the mountains would certainly result in an attitude of self-sufficiency.

Travel Itinerary

My tour started with a flight to Geneva and then a transfer to Lausanne (two nights), Zermatt (two nights), Lugano (one night), St. Moritz (one night), Interlaken (two nights), and Lucerne (two nights). Stops along the way in Switzerland were the villages of Broc; Gruyere; Simplon Pass; Brienz; and Stresa, Italy.

https://free-map.org/

Travel Journal

My trip to Switzerland had a little bumpy start; while driving up to Pennsylvania the night before for an automobile, trains, and plane transit again, I had to detour around Philadelphia because of closures on highway Interstate-95 at Aramingo exit from an accident and fire damaging the road. My driving app had me bypass Philadelphia via Valley Forge, adding an extra hour on the trip.

The journey to John F Kennedy International Airport (JFK) was uneventful, always nice; however, there was an hour delay in leaving due to the pilot's oxygen tank needing to be replaced. Yes, in a cockpit decompression emergency, the pilot needs supplemental oxygen, so the wait is worth it. Having spent over a decade designing oxygen systems for Naval aircraft, I appreciated the urgency and accepted the wait.

Although the flight was to Geneva, our stay was in the French area of Lausanne for two nights. Once we checked into the hotel, my travel mate and I crashed for a few hours, waking in time to dress for the welcome dinner. The general guidance is not to sleep when arriving, but instead power through it to let your body catch up to the time change. I've found that at times a couple of hours nap works better for me. I'm not a zombie at the welcome dinner and still fall asleep quickly the first night. Regardless of guidance, do what works for you.

The first full day we went to the Maison Cailler chocolate factory in Broc, had cheese fondue in Gruyere, and then toured a local winery. Fondue is Switzerland's culinary claim to fame; small pieces of bread dipped in cheese eaten in a social setting. It was a means to get to know our group mates, at least pairs, with four per table for sharing. The experience sparked conversation while dipping and eating. I live in the Chesapeake Bay area of Maryland where eating Maryland blue-claw crabs is more a social event than a dining experience or a meal sufficiency. I think that eating fondue falls in the same social gathering objective. After the fondue-sharing experience, I was on a quest to purchase an appropriate size fondue set.

Rosti is the national dish, thinly sliced potatoes fried in

oil. The classic style is only potatoes, but it also can be found combined with eggs, bacon, apple, and cheese. I noticed that food specialties were also aligned with the neighboring country: Germany, Austria, Italy, and France. Also, I didn't really know that Switzerland made wine, but all its neighboring countries do; so, it is reasonable it would too. A vineyard positioned along the shores of Lake Geneva is just stunning.

The next day, we traveled along Lake Geneva with a short stop in Montreux en route to our destination of Chillon Castle built by the House of Savoy. Montreux is a beautiful lakeside resort hosting the Montreux Jazz Festival every July and home to the Freddie Mercury statue commemorating his performance at the festival in 1978. He retained an apartment in the city until his death in 1991. Yes, we walked along the boardwalk with pictures taken at the statue. Other noted festival performers are Elton John, David Bowie, Prince, Aretha Franklin, and Lady Gaga, to name a few.

Only a short distance drive and we were at Chillon Castle, a castle sitting on a rock island with only access to land from a drawbridge. Although it's a fairytale-charmed structure on Lake Geneva, it is the writings of Lord Byron that made the castle famous. While sailing on Lake Geneva, he ventured a visit and was inspired to write *The Prisoner of Chillon* poem in 1816, chronicling the imprisonment of Francois Bonnivard, a Genevois monk, from 1532 to 1536. Many political and religious prisoners were held in the dungeon, but Byron sympathized with Bonnivard's story of being shackled to a pillar with only a three-foot-long chain from whence to pace in the dark. How the monk didn't go mad one can only question. During the fourteenth century, Jews were blamed for the spread of the plague across Europe. Jews were wrongfully accused of poisoning drinking water and imprisoned in the dungeon. It is so unfortunate that such a beautiful, romanticized castle can have such a dark history, but then again, the medieval times are a time of sizable construction concurrently with human destruction. Most medieval castles share a dark history.

Our ultimate destination that day was Zermatt, the embodiment of a Swiss chalet town. We took a train from the town of Tasch because no roads lead into Zermatt. Whether by car or train, travel through the Alps is spectacular. Zermatt is at the base of the Matterhorn; this giant standing at 14,691 feet (4,478 meters) is the symbol of Switzerland. Each morning, I walked to the location in the center of town where the mountain was most visible and took a few pictures. That night I enjoyed the pool and hot sauna at the hotel which turned out to be a nightly event. The next day, I took a cogwheel train ride to Gornergrat which hosts a hotel, restaurant, and simulated paragliding experience. While on the top of the mountain, the weather would change frequently: sunny, cloudy, windy, and calm but never rained. The ski slope across the other mountainside had an active chair lift for skiing.

After snapping several pictures at the top, I took the cogwheel down a couple of stops to Riffelsee Lake, known for the reflection of the Matterhorn on a clear day. Walking down to the lake was easy but walking back up to the train was much harder. I remember reading in the book, *Einstein: His Life and Universe* that Albert Einstein liked to hike in the Swiss Alps and even shared the trail with another Nobel Laureate, Madam Marie Curie.

A couple more stops, and I walked to Alphitta restaurant with great views of the Matterhorn. Other travelers walked down from the lake to our lunch spot with the path continuing all the way down to the town, although they opted to ride the train after the lunch stop. On their way to the restaurant, they spotted Valais Blacknose sheep with spiraled horns, black face and ears, and a woolly white coat. Once back in town, I spent another night at the pool with the soothing blue light and hot sauna; the word tranquility comes to mind.

I hated leaving Zermatt with its relaxed environment, charming chalet-style construction, and stunning views of the Swiss Alps from every direction. We needed to continue with the Swiss experience and were not disappointed. We left Zermatt and traveled through the Simplon Pass to Lake Maggiore, on the Italian border of Switzerland, stopping for lunch and shopping in Stresa, Italy. That evening we checked into our hotel in Lugano and then took a boat ride to a lakefront family-run restaurant. The wine flowed as we ate homemade Italian food; the boat ride back after dark displayed a sparkling-lit coastline.

The next day it was on to St. Moritz, a former Winter Olympic-hosting town in 1928 and 1948. The climb up the mountain to the town was daunting as we traveled on switchbacks climbing steeper. At the top, we stopped for that picture-taking moment. A line of vehicles behind us proved this was the main road ascending from the valley to the mountain area. Once in St. Moritz, I took a walk around the two-mile lake. It was cooler in the mountains but when the sun was out there was quite a difference in temperature. What is more fitting for a mountain retreat than a horse-drawn carriage ride? Bundled in our blankets, we clip-clopped down the path taking in the stunning views of the mountains.

Unfortunately, we had only one night in St. Moritz and then climbed aboard the Glacier Express in St. Moritz for our five-hour train ride to Andermatt through the Alps via Albula Pass, Landwasser Viaduct (pictured in Harry Potter movies), and Oberlap Pass. The Glacier Express is considered one of the top ten scenic rails in the world. In certain compartments of the train, the window can be opened for pictures, otherwise camera shots are taken through the window. Many of our group stayed close to the open windows for continuous picture-taking. Yes, for about five hours of picture-taking, there's never a bad view. From the train station in Andermatt, we had about a two-hour drive to Interlaken. That evening, we had a group dinner in our hotel and discussions for the next day of adventure.

The morning started with a short drive to Lauterbrunnen, the town with 72 waterfalls, and a hike through Tremmelbach Falls, with ten glacial waterfalls inside the Black Monk Mountain. Trummelbach is nature's solution to draining the glacial walls of three surrounding mountains: Eiger, Monch, and Jungfrau with a dramatic volume of 20,000 liters of water per second. This is a UNESCO World Natural Heritage Site designated in 2001.

The extension of the natural world Heritage property of Jungfrau - Aletsch – Bietschhorn (first inscribed in 2001), expands the site to the east and west, bringing its surface area up to 82,400 ha., up from 53,900. The site provides an outstanding example of the formation of the High Alps, including the most glaciated part of the mountain range and the largest glacier in Eurasia. It features a wide diversity of ecosystems, including successional stages due particularly to the retreat of glaciers resulting from climate change. The site is of outstanding universal value both for its beauty and for the wealth of information it contains about the formation of mountains and glaciers, as well as ongoing climate change. It is also invaluable in terms of the ecological and biological processes it illustrates, notably through plan succession. Its impressive landscape has played an important role in European art, literature, mountaineering and alpine tourism.[90]

Then onto Staubbach Falls and a climb of 984 feet (300 m), considered one of the highest free-falling waterfalls in

Europe. Lauterbrunnen is a charming town nestled amongst the cogwheel railway and cable cars for access to the surrounding mountains. For those wanting a more remote feel to their stay, this is a good option.

At this point, the group split with a few venturing off on their own to discover Schilthorn-Piz Gloria, the famous 360-degree revolving restaurant used in the 1969 James Bond film, *On Her Majesty's Secret Service*. Later when we met up with these adventurers, they really liked the restaurant but warned that it would take all day to get there and back with multiple cog trains and cable cars. There's no easy way to get around or over mountains.

The basic group took a cog train to Wengen and then a cable car to the top with a restaurant and folklore festivities entertaining the patrons outside among the stunning mountain views, including the view of Jungfrau, which translates to virgin. What is so special about Jungfrau? It is the top of Europe and has the world-famous centennial railway which was inaugurated in 1912 to take people to the top at an astonishing 11,332 feet (3,454 m) high at Jungfraujoch station. One will never get tired of looking at these breathtaking mountains and views. Jungfraujoch has snow and ice all year long on its glacier platform. Aletsch Glacier is the largest glacier in the Alps with 11 billion tons of ice and a thickness to 2,953 feet (900 m). Also, atop the mountain are the Jungfraujoch Ice Palace; an ice tunnel with walkways and halls created by mountain guides in the 1930s; the Sphinx observation building; the plateau for walks in the snow; and Europe's highest permanently manned research and weather station.

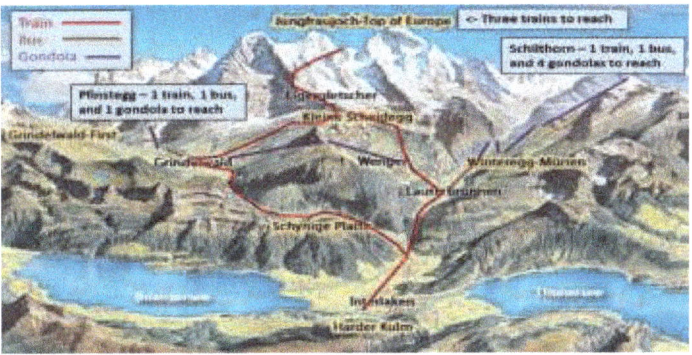

Jungfrau Top of Europe
(https://www.balmers.com/visit-the-jungfrau/)

In the valley, I could see the charming village of Grindelwald in the Bernese Oberland. The village looked like a perfect place to find a boutique bed and breakfast or Swiss-style chalet. Grindelwald was first discovered by the English explorers and mountaineers in the Alps in the eighteenth century. Nature enthusiasts can combine skiing, hiking, and mountain biking to fully appreciate what the Alps have to offer. Besides Jungfraujoch, there is the Alpine Museum and Glacier Gorge. I also see it as a perfect place to curl up with a good book around a crackling fire and just soak up the majestic scenery.

I had to pull myself away from the beauty to make it back down to Wengen and meet our tour group before the designated departure time. That evening we took the funicular to the top of the hill above Interlaken for dinner. Although the view was great for dining, there was a long line to use the funicular creating some angst among the waiting patrons. Once back down the hill to town, we had a very enjoyable walk to the hotel. Hang gliding is a popular activity with participants landing in a small field just around the corner from our hotel. Interlaken is a town that attracts a high-activity group. I'm not going to say younger or older age group because some people on the tours are in their seventies and eighties and are still active. So, I'll differentiate between more active and less active people.

Our last city to visit in Switzerland was Lucerne but, on the way, we stopped in Briez, a charming town of eighteenth-century wooden chalets, to visit a woodcarving museum. Incredible workmanship and details in the carvings are displayed. Once in Lucerne, we took a casual walk around the city to get the lay-of-the-land for where and what to do in our free time. Another stunning city with mountains, a lake, and medieval architecture. Highlights are strolling across the Spreuer Bridge with the macabre paintings depicting the *Dance of Death*, Chapel Bridge considered Europe's oldest covered bridge, and the Monument of Lion, a rock sculpture by Bertel Thorvaldsen Lukas Ahorn in 1820-1821 to commemorate the Swiss Guards that were massacred in 1792 during the French Revolution and the storming of the Tuileries Palace in Paris.

Upon checking in we learned that we were staying at one of the oldest hotels in Europe, the Hotel Wilden Mann Lucerne. The building dates back 500 years and has been a hotel since 1860. I had a room on the top floor which had a living room area and a separate bedroom. One can stay in a modern hotel anywhere, so take advantage of the opportunity to stay in a historic hotel or bed and breakfast for the real experience of a city or town. The website states

Welcome to one of Lucerne's most tradition-steeped hotels. Guests have been well looked after here for 500 years. It was originally a bar, later a tavern. We have been a hotel since 1860. Yes, the Wilden Mann certainly has seen an eventful history. You will sense this when you hear the floor and woodwork creaking as you walk along the winding passageways. Come in and be enchanted.[91]

Yes, the building has an aged mood but that is what makes it charming and enchanting.

The finale of the fantastic trip was visiting Mount Pilatus, at an altitude of 7,000 feet. It was very foggy when we reached the top after our cog train ride. The train climb is steep at an angle of up to 48 degrees. We spent about an hour on the top with a cafeteria, hotel and restaurant. There is an area where the path traverses inside and outside the mountain. With limited time, I was not able to make it to the end. The fog obstructed most of the view; however, on a clear day, it would be spectacular. Unfortunately, weather plays into the full experience of every location.

Accept that not every day will be the perfect weather day. Heading down we stopped at a location that had a toboggan run, and the group couldn't resist convincing the tour manager to allow time to fit it in. There was a long line, and it took over an hour in the queue. However, the experience was worth it. If there wasn't a line, I would have gone again no matter what the cost. At 4,429 feet (1,350 m), Frakigaudi on the Frakmuntegg is the longest summer toboggan run in Switzerland. You zoom through steep curves, dragon dens, and over jumps fully managing your own speed. I rode the brake a lot in the beginning until I got the hang of it.

After we returned to the hotel, we turned the television on only to hear about the Wagner Group, a Russian government-funded private military company, staging a coup causing a 24-hour period of tensions between the Russian Ministry of Defense and Wagner's leader Yevgeny Prigozhin. Ultimately, Prigozhin ended the political conflict exiled to Belarus. On August 23, 2023, while I was on a trip to Australia, the news was reported that a plane had crashed with three leaders of the Wagner Company including Prigozhin. It is very interesting watching or hearing about international news outside of the United States and the reactions of people from other countries. Are those circumstances a little too coincidental?

The following day we had a flight from Zurich with a connection in Amsterdam, and then onto JFK. Arriving at JFK rather late, we found out that our luggage hadn't arrived. We were not the only people in this situation; several of us were waiting at the baggage carousel for a long time. We all queued up to fill out the paperwork for lost luggage. It was after 11:00 pm when we started the trip back to Trenton Station via JFK train, Long Island Railroad (LIRR), and New Jersey Transit. It was around 2:30 am when we got to my travel mate's apartment outside Philadelphia. The next couple of days were phone calls to first Delta and then to KLM who operated the flights.

I only had five days between returning from Switzerland and leaving for Northern France and needed my large suitcase. By the time I left for France, my bag still wasn't located. Fortunately, I had a backup suitcase to use. I did have to buy travel electrical adapters though. At least the luggage was lost on the return and not on the way there or I'd have had to buy a whole new wardrobe. Always keep a change of clothes or two in your carry-on luggage just in case. Didn't I already learn that lesson from Patagonia?

Switzerland was an amazing trip, and I look forward to spending more time in the country taking advantage of the great hiking. I don't know how many ways there are to say stunning, spectacular, amazing, remarkable, but that describes the grandeur and beauty of the Swiss Alps. This is one destination where tour groups arrange a walking or hiking tour for people looking for more outdoor experience. I can see myself either arranging a tour myself or utilizing an organized tour group focused on hiking for a return trip.

I found most Swiss people to be comfortable with conversing in English, most are multi-lingual with being centrally located surrounded with German, French, and Italian languages. As I described in the section on background, history, and environment, they are very independent and self-sufficient. This is not surprising living amongst the grandeur and isolation of the mountains, I think anyone would develop self-sufficiency skills and an independent personality in the same situation.

As I was shopping for souvenirs for friends and family, I noticed a Saint Bernard stuffed keychain. I then realized that Saint Bernard dogs are somehow connected to Switzerland. Intrigued, I had to research using google. It all began in the eleventh century in the Great Saint Bernard pass, a mountain route between Italy and Switzerland. It was a treacherous route with many pilgrims attacked by Alpine bandits. Bernard de Menthon (also known as Bernard du Mont-Joux), the Archdeacon of Aosta decided he needed to make the pass a safer place. He founded the Great Saint Bernard hospice, which was placed under the jurisdiction of the Bishop of Sion. The hospice provided travelers shelter and worship.

The hospice acquired its first dogs as far back as 1660-1670. It is believed that the Saint Bernard dog descended from the dogs originally bred to protect the hospice residents. The dogs displayed incredible capabilities for rescuing travelers lost in the mountains and buried under the snow. Legend also has it that it was Napoleon Bonaparte's soldiers in 1800 that spread the reputation of the remarkable canines.

During the trip, the tour visited the UNESCO World Heritage Site of the Swiss Alps region of Jungfrau-Aletsch (2001) visually seen from my visit to Wengen and the scenic train ride on the Glacier Express which passed through the Rhaetian Railway in the Albula Bernina Landscapes (2008). With 13 sites for Switzerland, I will need to return at least once to check a few more off my list.

As I was finalizing this book, an unfortunate natural catastrophe occurred in the central part of Switzerland on May 28, 2025. A huge mass of rock and ice from a glacier roared down the Swiss mountainside burying 90 percent of the village of Blattan. Three hundred people of the town were evacuated earlier for precautions.

Swiss glaciologists have repeatedly expressed concerns about a thaw in recent years, attributed in large part to global warming, that has accelerated the retreat of glaciers in Switzerland. The landlocked Alpine country has the most glaciers of any country in Europe and saw 4% of its total glacier volume disappear in 2023. That was the second-biggest decline in a single year after a 6% drop in 2022.[92]

In 2023, the village of Brienz experienced a near-calamity when a huge mass of rock slid down the mountainside, stopping just short of the town. The village was evacuated in 2024 for fear of another rockslide. I've now traveled throughout Switzerland and experienced these charming small villages where life transcends the hustle and bustle of city urgency. In merely minutes, these people, who are synonymous with punctuality, hard work, quality of product and services, strong sense of responsibility, and value in privacy, lost their most prized possessions, their homes and their personal and historic belongings.

the Matterhorn above Zermatt

St. Moritz

Jungfrau

Freddie Mercury

Chillon Castle

Lucerne

Lauterbrunnen Valley

Frakigaudi on Frakmuntegg   cable car to Mount Pilatus

Lake Geneva   Gornergrat, Zermatt

Chapter 10

Northern France

I love the man that can smile in trouble, that can gather strength in distress and grow brave by reflections. –

Thomas Paine

(https://www.brainyquote.com/quotes/thomas_paine_1630_18)

Background: History, Culture, and Environment

Bonjour mon ami.

This trip takes one on a journey through French history and architecture and its connections to the rest of the world. It included a tour of the Louvre Museum, the former palace begun by King Francois I in 1546 on the site of the twelfth-century fortress built by King Philip II. During the French Revolution in 1791, it was decreed that the Louvre should become a museum of the arts with its inauguration in 1793. The finale of the trip was the Palace of Versailles, the residence of King Louis XVI and Queen Marie Antoinette. On October 5, 1789, a mob descended on Versailles and demanded that the royal family return to Paris. The royal family transferred to the Tuileries Palace where they escaped the night of June 20, 1791, possibly with the assistance of the Queen's lover. They were caught in the small town of Varennes-en-Argonne. The flight sealed the King's fate with his execution in 1793. Marie Antoinette was born in Vienna, Austria as an archduchess on November 2, 1755, to Emperor Francis I and Empress Maria Theresa of Austria. Marie and Louis XVI were married on May 16, 1770; Marie was only fourteen years old. They had four children together but only a daughter survived past the French Revolution. Marie was executed on October 16, 1793, buried at the Basilica Cathedral of Saint Denis, in the northern suburb of Paris.

The Palace of Versailles has American connections with visits by Benjamin Franklin during the American Revolution to request of King Louis XVI financial and military support for the American fight against the British. The famous Treaty of Versailles, the peace document signed at the end of World War I between the Allied and associated powers and Germany occurred in the Hall of Mirrors in the Palace of Versailles on June 28, 1919, and became effective on January 10, 1920. American Revolutionist and former President Thomas Jefferson spent from 1784 to 1789 in Paris as Franklin's political replacement. Although Jefferson stayed in four locations, he resided in the Hôtel de Landron in the Cul-de-sac Taitbout and then Hôtel de Langeacon the Champs-Elysées most of the time. Both buildings no longer exist and have been replaced with more modern structures. I guess there won't be a sign that states Thomas Jefferson slept here.

The historic architectural design of France is best depicted in chateaus and churches. A bit of a lesson in architectural styles affords one to better appreciate what one is looking at when entering these mammoth houses of worship. The major styles of the Medieval period include pre-Romanesque, Romanesque, and Gothic. Pre-Romanesque featured thick rubble walls, small windows, vault-less roofs, and rhythmic ornamental arches. The Romanesque style featured round arched columns, thick walls, and small windows. The Gothic style featured pointed arches, gargoyles, stained glass windows, and flying buttresses that allowed for the construction of grander, taller, and more elaborate buildings by diverting the weight of the roof off the walls. This allowed thinner walls and more windows permitting more light into the building. The Renaissance style followed this period and focused on beauty based on the geometry of proportion and symmetry.

French historic architecture provides exquisite examples of these designs with many having elements of more than one due to construction occurring over centuries or destruction through fires or war and the need to rebuild parts of the structure. Loire Valley is home to 300 chateaus in the 175-mile (282 km) stretch of the Loire River, therefore the densest collection of French castles. Every town has a church; France is home to some of the most magnificent structures found in the French countryside.

Like other democracies, France's political system has three branches: executive, legislative, and judicial. The executive power is exercised by the president as the elected head of state. The prime minister who is appointed by the president, is the head of government.

Northern France holds memories of historic battles fought, won, and lost. The World War II Normandy Invasion occurred on June 6, 1944, under the mission codename Operation Overlord. Britain, Canada, and the United States ground forces landed on five separate beachheads of Normandy with airborne operations recognized as the largest seaborne invasion in history. The Allies launched the invasion with over 5,000 ships and landing crafts and more than 150,000 troops on the five beaches. Ground troops then landed across five assault beaches – Utah, Omaha, Gold, Juno, and Sword. The United States landed at Utah and Omaha, Canada at Juno, and the British at Gold and Sword.

By the end of August 1944, Northern France was liberated. The Allied forces then turned toward Germany eventually meeting the Soviet forces advancing from the east to end the Nazi Reich. Separate cemeteries exist today in Normandy for the burial of the allied soldiers. We visited the American cemetery during our trip.

Tour managers are a wealth of information, but it sometimes feels like a fire hose of information even though it is extremely worthwhile to gain an understanding of the history, culture, and environment of the country. Our tour manager was originally from Belgium and dismissed a common American myth that French fries originated in France. They were culinarily introduced by Belgium, but American soldiers stationed in the northern part of France who found themselves on Belgian soil mistakenly called them French fries, not Belgium fries. This is the story that we got, but if you google "who invented French fries", you'll get a plethora of answers, even one claiming that Thomas Jefferson or his slave James Hemings brought French fries to America from Paris. Who knew that the origin of French fries is such a controversial topic. The good news is that on my world travels they seem to be found just about everywhere.

The French motto: Liberty, Equality, and Fraternity reflects the values of the French people. One will find that the French citizens outside of Paris to be very warm and welcoming. Parisians have their own characteristics which may come from living in shoeboxes in one of the most expensive cities in the world. In my observations, Parisians do love spending time outdoors, the banks of the Seine River were crowded with people just enjoying the day whether alone or in groups. Eating is a social function more than a biological function. Cafes with pastries are as plentiful as a pizza/hoagie shop is on every street corner in the American city of brotherly love- Philadelphia, Pennsylvania.

I'm not sure that I would describe any large city to have the warmest people including those in large cities of the United States. I was in Los Angeles once asking where the La Brea Tarpits were and getting brushed off, even with two small children and a teenager.

This was before the maps app. After several attempts at questioning people on the street and in stores, someone provided directions to the location which was only a couple of streets away. Maybe people in Los Angeles just don't know historic spots in their own city. If I was a foreigner, I think I would have left with a rather unfavorable opinion. Go to any small town in the United States and ask a similar question, the responder will not only tell you where but probably walk you to the location.

Of course, when one is part of an organized tour group, the tour manager will be well-versed in your language, especially English but I found that in many countries, a large part of the population does speak English fairly well. This was the case in France, especially when traveling around northern France.

So how did France fair with the Fund for Peace Fragile State Index? Well, much better than the United States with a ranking of 162nd and a score of 28.3. I'll just say, bien joué! There's no surprise that France scored rather well for the State Resilience Index at a score of 7.5. Again, the country scored well above average for all the indicators except social cohesion.

Travel Itinerary

The trip started in Paris (three nights), Normandy (two nights), St. Malo (one night), Loire Valley (two nights), and Versailles (two nights).

https://free-map.org/

Travel Journal

Is there no better way to start a trip than with the City of Lights, Paris? But let me regress, the trip started from Trenton Station on the New Jersey Transit to Penn Station in New York City and connecting to the Long Island Railroad to Jamaica Station and connecting to the JFK air train. Yes, the usual triple transportation mode to New York City and return. Our travel time from Trenton to JFK was two and a half hours. After I checked in at the airport, I went to baggage claim to see if they had my missing bag from the Switzerland trip. There were a lot of bags sitting in one area roped off. One of the bags in the middle of the pile looked like mine, so I slid around the rope to get a closer look. Of course, the baggage security person caught me and conveyed that I couldn't be there. After communicating my baggage problem, he maneuvered to the bag and brought it over for me to check; it wasn't mine. Now his supervisor noticed me and questioned what I wanted. She looked up the baggage number in the database and stated that it was not there. Her assumption was that the bags had not made it to JFK yet.

Not finding my bag today; so, I headed to the gate for a three-hour wait for departure. However, I was impressed with the attention given by the misplaced baggage department at JFK airport. Taking the train to JFK is far better than driving if one lives a reasonable distance from mass transportation, but it does mean allowing more than sufficient time in case there are delays making connections. On the other hand, there is no more comfortable feeling than sitting at the gate waiting for the flight or grabbing a drink at the airport bar right down from the gate. One is not then stranded in traffic or delayed somewhere stressing over catching the flight. The line for security at JFK is a *roll the dice* prospect. This time it took about 45 minutes. The flight had about a two-hour delay due to air traffic. Of well, that is why one always carries a book. You aren't flustered waiting; you are blessed with more time to read.

We arrived in Paris an hour late due to the delayed takeoff. It was about an hour's drive to the hotel, which still meant that we were too early to check in. My travel mate and I were too tired to walk around, so we found two comfy sofas out of the way and nodded off. Hotel management didn't like that and woke us up, stating that they would try to have our rooms ready before noon. I really can't blame them for our arousal; the hotel lobby is not a hostel. If you are arriving in the morning, then you might want to book the hotel room for the night before so you can check in right away and sleep. We had a welcome dinner at a local restaurant, that was very good; an appetizing meal is a nice way to start the trip. We also discovered that the tour had only eight people so it would be a very intimate group.

The next morning, we did the driving tour of Paris: Champs Elysees, Arc de Triomphe, Concorde Square, Eiffel Tower, along the Seine River, and Rive Gauche area. The city was preparing for the Bastille Day festivities. Bastille Day is the nation's holiday for celebrating the fall of the Bastille in Paris on July 14, 1789. The combination of previous and the then-current French monarchies' extravagant spending and assistance to the American colonies for their independence left the French government on the brink of economic disaster. Extensive crop failures in 1788 caused famine across the country. *Bread prices rose so high that, at their peak, the average worker spent about 88 percent of his wages on just that one staple.*[93]

Bread was and still is a primary staple of French cuisine. With high unemployment and a harsh winter, these were the ingredients for civil unrest. Although turmoil had been growing, it was on July 14 when an unruly mob acquired muskets and set for the Bastille to acquire gunpowder. Built in the 1300s during the Hundred Years' War against the

British, the Bastille was designed to protect the eastern entrance to Paris. Used as a prison, it held political dissidents, such as the writer and philosopher Voltaire, who was an advocate of freedom of speech, freedom of religion, and separation of church and state.

A group of men scaled the wall, lowered the drawbridge, and the angry mob attempted to claim the fortress. Guards opened fire on the mob and temporarily quelched the conflict. Later that day, when a mutinous French guard detachment arrived, Bernard René de Launay, the governor of the Bastille surrendered. De Launay was beheaded with his head paraded around the city; the guillotine appears to be the murderess act of the time with both King Louis XVI and Queen Marie Antoinette falling victim to a similar fate. We then went to the Louvre. Although I had been there in 2009, it's always a thrill to visit. Being that it was July, it was also very crowded. The tour group allocated a couple of hours to spend in the museum and then we went back to the hotel for an open period in the afternoon. With respect to space, the Louvre is the largest museum in the world.

The structure was originally built in the late twelfth to thirteenth century under King Philip II. In the basement, remnants of the Medieval fortress are still visible. As the city expanded, the fortress lost its defensive purpose and under King Francis I, it became the royal primary residence in 1546. King Louis XIV would move the residence to Versailles in 1682 leaving the Louvre for an exhibition of the royal collection. During the French Revolution, the National Assembly decreed that the Louvre should be a Museum. Under Napoleon's reign, he not only increased the collection of art but changed the name to Musée Napoléon, only temporarily.

Our tour manager led us to three masterpieces to ensure that we left with no regrets in our limited time: the *Mona Lisa*, *Venus de Milo*, and *Winged Victory*. Leonardo da Vinci's *Mona Lisa* is considered the most popular work of art in the world and therefore probably the most expensive at $660 million. When I was there in 2009, the museum had no restriction on pictures and so I took pictures from the left-side, middle, and right-side of the room. Why? Supposedly, *Mona Lisa* appears to be looking at you no matter where you stand. I'm not sure if it's just wishful thinking or an actual illusion but it did appear so. Times change and museum rules also change.

Now, one must stand in line to take a picture at one specific spot. So, one cannot do today what I did in 2009. There was also a considerable line and with limited time, I decided not to queue and snapped a quick shot as I walked past the painting heading for the room exit. Yes, the queue attendant caught me and reminded me of the rule of no pictures unless I stood in the line. *Venus de Milo* was sculpted by Alexandros of Antioch around 150 BCE, thought to be the ancient Greek Goddess Aphrodite. It was found in pieces on the Aegean Island of Melos on April 8, 1820 and given to Louis

XVIII who donated it to the Louvre Museum. The *Winged Victory* statue hails from Samothrace, another island in the Aegean Sea, but the sculptor is unknown.

If I had to do it again, I would have stayed longer at the Louvre and either walked back to the hotel or took a taxi. I really felt like I needed at least another hour. After grabbing lunch near the hotel, I walked to the Opera House for a tour. It was very crowded, and a little confusing as to where to enter the building. The architecture is beautiful, but the crowds made it difficult to walk around and appreciate. On the way to the hotel, I did some shopping because I had not expected cooler weather in July and forgot a jacket. I didn't expect it to be in the low 60s degrees F in the evenings and early morning in July. We were heading further north for the rest of the trip, which meant even colder weather. Check the temperatures online before packing; so, you know what clothing choices are best for the trip. Fortunately, I got a nice jacket on sale.

After breakfast, we drove to the champagne region in Epernay. It was fascinating seeing how champagne is made, not at all like wine production. Champagne ages in each bottle, not in a barrel like wine, with the sludge or settlement eventually removed. Although I thought about buying some to take home, I'm not sure how it would travel in my luggage staying corked under aircraft storage pressure changes. Only products from the champaign region of France can be called champagne; so, anything sparkling in Italy is called sparkling wine or another descriptive label.

En route for lunch at Brasserie de la Banque in Epernay, we drove down the elegant Avenue de Champagne. A very quaint town, the tour group of eight made a very intimate lunch in a restaurant that was formerly a bank. I always enjoy eating at restaurants in which the building is converted or re-purposed from a former business. I've eaten at the Vault Brewing Company in Yardley, Pennsylvania in the United States, housed in a bank from the 1800s specializing in non-traditional brewpub reminiscent of old Philadelphia speakeasies.

The Church Brew Works in Pittsburgh, Pennsylvania is a former church converted to a microbrewery. The Church Brew Works opened in 1996 as the first and only brewpub in the country to be formerly located in a historic church. As business industries or religious structures experience a sinusoidal wave trend of peaks and valleys, I hope innovative entrepreneurs continue to find alternative business applications for historic sights protecting the architectural design of past structures for future generations.

We drove to Reims to visit the magnificent Gothic Reims Cathedral, a UNESCO World Heritage Site since 1991. The complex encompasses the Notre-Dame Cathedral, the Palais du Tau, and the former Abbey of Saint Remi, now the Saint Remi Basilica and museum. The historic path to the current church occurred over centuries. In the middle of the third century, Bishop Saint Sixtus decided to build the Church of the Holy Apostles, located to the east of the current building.

In the fifth century, Bishop Nicaise built the cathedral on the current site dedicating it to the Virgin Mary. King Clovis was baptized in 498-499 in the baptistery in front of the church by Bishop Saint Remi, who instituted the Holy Anointing of the Kings. The former abbey still has its beautiful ninth- century nave, where lies the remains of Archbishop St Rémi (440– 533). In the 780s, Pope Adrian I conferred on the bishop of Reims the rank of archbishop.

In 1027, the Archbishop of Reims established the Cathedral of Reims as the cathedral for coronations; all but two kings were crowned there with King Louis VI the Fat and Henry IV crowned in Chartres Cathedral. The church was consecrated by Pope Leo IX in 1049. Although Archbishop Samson had enlarged the cathedral in the twelfth century, a fire destroyed it on May 6, 1210. The first stone for the foundation was laid a year later by Archbishop Aubry de Humbert for the current cathedral. By the end of the thirteenth century, the nave and the roof were finished with only part of the façade. Then in 1481, a fire destroyed part of the roof. The roof and towers were rebuilt but the spires planned on the towers and the crossing of the transept were never built due to the costly restoration. The cathedral is truly magnificent and worthy of hosting the coronation of kings. In 1996, Pope John Paul II attended the 1500-year celebration of the conversion of the Frankish King Clovis to Catholicism, called the Baptism of France, at the Abbey.

After our visit to Reims, we drove back to our hotel in Paris.

In the evening, my travel mate and I used public transportation to venture to the Eiffel Tower area for a boat ride on the Seine River. This is essential for anyone visiting Paris. Many of Paris' famous buildings are seen differently from the river, such as Notre Dame. I visited Paris in 2009 before the fire. From the river, I was able to get a fairly good view of the construction of rebuilding the magnificent structure. Also, the boat moved along slower than the traffic, so I was able to get more stable pictures with my smartphone.

People were picnicking along the water confirming how much Paris is a social city. Whether it was just two or groups of several, the riverside was comfortably crowded with people just enjoying the night. In a couple of spots, there is a small, paved area where people were dancing. Afterwards, we stopped at a nearby restaurant before heading back to the hotel. Paris is a beautiful city, day or night.

As we left Paris for Normandy, we drove down the Champs Elysees where preparations were starting for Bastille Day, July 14. Fortunately, the town of Giverny lies between Paris and Normandy. Giverny is the home of the famous impressionist painter Oscar Claude Monet, in fact, his house and gardens are the inspiration for many of his paintings including the waterlilies pond. Like many painters, his life experienced many tragedies from birth to death (November 14, 1840-December 5, 1926); he enjoyed being alone with nature, probably even therapeutic. During his life, Europe saw conflicts in the Franco-Prussian War and World War I.

He left France during the Franco-Prussian War traveling to other areas of Europe and gaining an awareness of impressionistic painters of the same period. After losing his first wife in 1880, he was left with two sons still living with friend Alica Hoschede and her large family of six children after her husband had abandoned her. In 1892, Alice became his second wife when her husband Ernest Hoschede passed away. In 1883 he rented the house in Giverny and eventually purchased it in 1890 for his large family of eight children. It's during this time that his paintings started to sell, especially in the United States. Following the events of the death of his wife Alice in 1911, later the death of his son Jean, turmoil during World War I, and cataracts forming over his eyes, he stopped painting living out the rest of his life in the house and garden so inspirationally portrayed in many of his paintings.

After a memorable encounter walking through Monet's house and gardens, including taking many pictures of the lily pond, we traveled to an eighteenth-century water mill restaurant for lunch on their patio. It was a French meal with foie gras and French wine. For those that have never heard of foie gras, it is the liver of a duck or goose that has been fattened by force-feeding. This cooking practice dates to 2500 BC and the Egyptians who would force-feed birds. Many of our travelers were thrilled with the option; I've not really been a fan of foie gras and opted for a salad. Every culture has some food choices that are loved by some and not so loved by others.

I have a trip to Scotland in the spring of 2024. I'm sure haggis, a pudding containing sheep's heart, liver, and lungs; minced with onion, oatmeal, spices, and salt; mixed with stock; and cooked encased in the animal's stomach, will be on the menu. I was surprised to learn that Mallorca has its own version of a haggis-like dish. Frit Mallorqui is a combination of chopped heart, liver, and lungs of sheep mixed with potatoes, onions, and peppers. I don't think I will be a fan of either dish. To be fair, I'm from the Philadelphia area in the United States and have friends who love scrapple, a combination of ground organs including lungs, buckwheat, cornmeal, and spices; but I'm not a fan of scrapple either. At a time when food was scarce, the cooks used all parts of the animal. I guess that's how some very unique cuisine has been created.

We stayed in Cabourg for two nights, an upscale, quaint seaside town with a racetrack and casino. Unfortunately, we had no spare time to partake in the racetrack or the casino. From my hotel window, I could get glimpses of the horse race the first night. This first night we had a historian meet us at the dinner restaurant and provided a brief on the D-Day invasion. The next day we made several stops:

(1) St. Mere Eglise on the Cotentin Peninsula where on June 5, 1944, during an American airborne landing, paratrooper John Steele landed on the church steeple. Unable to untangle himself, he faked death to avoid German capture. A mannequin with a parachute still

hangs from the church to commemorate his courage. We were able to enter the church and visit the Airborne Museum providing insight into the airborne tactics for the Overlord Mission.

(2) The Ranger Memorial at Pointe du Hoc is a monument erected by the French to honor the American Second Ranger Battalion's scaling the 100-foot cliff to seize the German artillery pieces from firing on the American troops landing at Omaha Beach. The monument consists of a simple granite pylon positioned atop a German concrete bunker with tablets at the base inscribed in English and French.

(3) A cemetery was established for each country; we visited the American Cemetery at Omaha Beach. The expansive field of tombstones leaves one distraught by the human waste of war; there are 9,387 graves in the 172.5-acre burial ground. With respect to World War II, the American involvement was unavoidable with the attack on Pearl Harbor. Part of the field was roped off, I asked one of the caretakers why. Although the land is American, the French are responsible for maintaining the grounds. They rotate closed sections to do routine maintenance, something to consider if visiting to see a specific grave. Although I would like to believe that if requested to see a grave in the closed area, you would be escorted to the sight. The ground crew were very personable and diligent. From the cemetery, we then headed down to the beach.

Omaha Beach today is a quaint seashore community that seems to have retained its original simplicity. It hasn't turned into a tee-shirt tourist trap like some American battlefields, for example, Gettysburg, Pennsylvania, and its connection to the American Civil War.

(4) Arromanches-les-Bains lies on the English Channel six miles (10 km) northeast of Bayeux. During the Normandy invasion, it was part of the Gold Beach landing area taken by the British 50th Division on D-Day. The town became one of two assembly points for the Mulberry artificial harbors, temporary jetties of prefabricated concrete supports, steel spans, and floating piers that were towed across the channel in sections and aligned perpendicularly to the beach. The other artificial harbor at Saint-Laurent-sur-Mer on Omaha Beach was destroyed during the harsh storms of June 19-22. The remains of the Mulberry can still be seen from the shoreline.

(5) Then we traveled to the colorful, waterfront town of Honfleur, which was an inspiration for impressionist painters such as Claude Monet. I'm probably overusing the word quaint but in this area of France, no other term describes these picturesque towns. We returned to the hotel emotionally somber from walking on the soil that our American soldiers fought on almost 80 years ago to ensure American and European citizens continued to be free to govern. I was more than awed that almost 80 years later French citizens in the area still feel tremendous

gratitude to Americans for liberating France from Nazi control. For all retired military, a trip to Normandy is a pilgrimage to connect with what military service is all about. For non-military, it is a pilgrimage to appreciate the role of the military in our quest to continue to live the American dream of freedom.

The next day we checked out of the hotel en route to Mont St. Michel, but didn't immediately leave the Normandy area. We detoured to Caen and the Caen Memorial Museum, believed by many to be the most comprehensive museum on World War II in France. The museum covers from World War I to the Fall of the Berlin Wall. Although we were given two and half hours to stroll through the large building with three floors and almost 3.5 acres (14,000 square meters) of exhibition space, I could have spent another hour at least. I sprinted through the post-World War II section to not be late for the coach departure. I'm not sure anyone made it through the whole building amply studying the exhibits. A common theme with group tours; for some activities, one wishes they had more time while others may have wanted less. An oh-by-the-way, the town of Caen is not only known for its location in the Normandy area and World War II, but William the Conqueror, King of England was buried in the Abbey of Saint-Etienne after his death in Normandy in 1087.

Leaving the Caen Memorial Museum, we were now in transit to Mont Saint Michel, a UNESCO World Heritage Site designated in 1979. As I was staring out the window of the coach, I could see a structure in the very far distance. There's no mistaking it. I said to the tour manager, "*is that Mont Saint Michel off there in the distance along the seacoast line*". He just smiled and said "*Yes*".

As we approached Mont Saint Michel, the complex just got bigger and bigger with the flat land and sea surrounding it. I found myself mulling over this question in my mind, *why would someone undertake such a monumental endeavor to build a monastery on top of a rock island?* But that is the underlying theme with manmade wonders and UNESCO World Heritage Sites, the vision beyond typical or routine. It takes not only that vision, but persistence and the ability to know how to accomplish. A bridge now allows access to the rock-island medieval town. Picture a walled fortress sitting on an island rock. Although not built as a king's castle, the structure inadvertently provides the kind of protection of a fortress.

Perched on a rocky islet in the midst of vast sandbanks exposed to powerful tides between Normandy and Brittany stand the 'Wonder of the West', a Gothic-style Benedictine abbey dedicated to the archangel St Michael, and the village that grew up in the shadow of its great walls. Built between the 11th and 16th centuries, the abbey is a technical and artistic tour de force, having had to adapt to the problems posed by this unique natural site.[94]

The story of the Monastery and Abbey date back to 708 when the Archangel Michael appeared to Bishop Aubert three times in a dream. Archangel Michael asked to have a sanctuary built in his honor on Mont-Tombe Island. This was not the first time for a request from the Archangel Micheal to a bishop accomplished by appearing three times for the purpose of worship.

According to the legend, around the year 490 AD, the Archangel Michael appeared three times to the Bishop of Sipontum near a cave in the mountains of Puglia province in Italy requesting that the cave be dedicated to Christian worship and promising protection of the nearby town of Sipontum from pagan invaders. The Sanctuary of the Archangel Michael is a Roman Catholic Shrine on Mount Gargano, Italy; it is the oldest shrine in western Europe dedicated to the Archangel Michael and an important pilgrimage since the Middle Ages. On May 8, 663 AD the Sipontans and Beneventans led by Grimoald I, Lombard Duke of Benevento, were victorious against invading Greeks. Pope Gelasius I directed that a basilica be erected, the Basilica di San Giovanni in Tumba, holds the tomb of the Lombard King Rothari, who died in 652 AD.

In 966 Duke Richard I of Normandy established the site of Mont Saint Michel for the worship of Benedictine monks; however, it was not until 1023 that construction started for the Abbey's structure known today. During the year 1421 of the Hundred Years' War, England laid siege to the Romanesque architecture Abbey. Over the next century, it was rebuilt but with a Gothic style; the common result of war on land and structures can transcend centuries yielding a combination of architectural designs for the structures.

The main, cobble-stoned, narrow street is a tourist center for shopping and restaurants leading the way to a set of steep stairs to the Abbey entrance. Anyone willing to take the challenge will not regret the beauty of the grand room and ability to view the sacred relics on display as well as the stunning water views outside. Navigating the Abbey takes one through many rooms and many steps, both up and down.

On our way back to the coach, we passed another touring coach that broke down, and its passengers set up a camp next to their coach sharing food and drinks, probably waiting for another coach. Sometimes, you just have to make the most of it whatever the situation. We boarded our coach happy that it was working fine and drove to Saint Malo, the pirate town on the Atlantic Ocean. French kings allowed pirates to live and work out of Saint Malo to antagonize France's enemies such as England and Spain's ships with robbing their valuables and provisions. The Saint Malo Cathedral is a combination of Romanesque and Gothic style featuring stained-glass windows that depict the city's history, located in the center of town. Tall granite walls surround the charming old town, with a couple of sailing ships in the harbor used for tourism. The town still resembles a pirate town. Our hotel had a delightful indoor pool which I browsed before dinner. At dinner, it had become the topic of conversation, and several group members joined me after for a swim.

We only spent one night there and were on our way the next morning, or so we thought. Only about a mile from the hotel, the coach's transmission would not shift out of second gear. We pulled over and the driver investigated a few options before calling for assistance. The assistance suggestions didn't work. Our tour manager had been a previous coach driver, and he provided his expertise, but to no avail. It was decided that a road assistance mechanic be dispatched to the coach. So, the tour manager walked us a short distance to the public bus stop; we took the public bus back to the town. He improvised with a little walking tour and then we stopped for coffee. Most group members also did a little more shopping staying close to the café. The delay was only a couple of hours; the tour manager was able to call and arrange for our afternoon activities to be extended so nothing was canceled. I am very impressed with the caliber of tour managers and the ability to deal with out-of-the-ordinary situations. I was also remembering the coach stuck at Mont St. Michel. Ironically, I had verbalized at the time, *"I'm glad that isn't us stranded"*.

Our first stop was Château d'Angers and the fourteenth-century Apocalypse Tapestry. Duke Louis I of Anjou commissioned Nicolas Bataille, the famous fourteenth-century tapestry merchant, to produce the 90 scenes in the 328-feet (100m) tapestry using 35 weavers. It consists of six sections with each divided into seven tableaux. It took seven years to complete, an inspiration of the Book of Revelations.

This last book of the bible was written by Saint John the Divine, who was banished to the Aegean Island of Patmos by the Romans. The tapestry depicts the battle between good and evil through John's eyes, who is present in almost all the panels. Benches are provided opposite the tapestry to contemplate the story depicted in each section. The timing of the tapestry occurred during the Hundred Years' War and not long after the Black Plague, a time fueling the devastation and doomsday prophecy. There's no surprise that the tapestry reflected an Armageddon theme.

In this area of Northern France, there exist cave systems that have been commercially purposed. Our next visit was to a cave winery for wine tasting. Caves maintain a cooler temperature required for wine storage. There are also cave restaurants and cave hotels. Our next two nights were at Chateau du Rochecotte in the Loire Valley located near the town of Saint Patrice. Loire Valley was the summer retreat of French royalty; the Valley has the densest collection of 300 chateaus in a 175-mile (282 km) stretch of the river. The chateau lived up to the description of old-world charm. Staying in a French chateau is a truly unique experience. Instead of taking the small elevator, I used the stairs to explore each hall and passageway. While walking through the fashionable living room, a young boy staying at the hotel was playing the piano, it was the perfect mood setting. Could he be a budding Mozart?

The Comte de Rochecotte was the original owner;

however, he became one of the leaders of the second Chouannerie in Maine and was executed. The chateau is best known for its connection with World War II when the Ministry of Foreign Affairs kept diplomatic documents there for safekeeping. These documents included the original Treaty of Versailles signed by Georges Clemenceau in the Hall of Mirrors at Versailles in 1919, the Treaty of Saint Germain-en-Lave in 1919, the Treaty of Westphalia which ended the Thirty Years' War, and others. Early in the war, the Germans became interested in diplomatic archives investigating the Quai d'Orsay. Based on accounts from Karl Epting, a collaborator with the German ambassador Otto Abetz, at the end of June 1940, the Germans visited the chateau.

At the beginning of August 1940, the Germans claimed that shots were fired from the town Saint-Patrice resulting in the tightening of surveillance around the chateau. This action was probably a ruse to acquire access to the chateau. The Germans investigated further the treaty room. The French officials believed that only the German ratification copy of the treaty, bound in brown leather, was at the chateau and the original bound in white leather was kept in Bordeaux. However, upon opening the wooden box containing the document, it was the white-bound copy, therefore the original Treaty of Versailles. The Germans confiscated the document around August 11 or 12, 1940, taking it to Berlin to present to Adolf Hitler. However, it was recovered by the Soviet Army in Czechoslovakia but was not included in the documents

312

returned to the French government in 1993-1994 and remains missing. Will an estate auction someday uncover this priceless document, or will it inadvertently be tossed out?

Leaving the beautiful chateau, we drove to Chateau de Chenonceau with its Renaissance architecture over the Cher River. Catherine Medici, the wife of King Henry II, stayed there; however, the King's mistress, Diane de Poiters, also stayed there and added the beautiful gardens. Probably not the first time that a king had a mistress or that there was friction between the Queen and the mistress. If the Medici family name sounds familiar, Catherine was born in Florence, Italy to Lorenzo de' Medici, Duke of Urbino, and his wife, Madeleine de La Tour d'Auvergne. In 1533, Catherine at the age of 14 years old married Henry, King Francois I and Queen Claude of France's second son. Onward to La Cave aux Fouees, a cave restaurant, for wine tasting and lunch.

We had a traditional French dish, pork cassoulet with nonbread. After lunch, we drove to the Royal Chateau d'Ambroise of King Francois I, who brought Leonardo DaVinci to his court in 1516. There is a small chapel in the corner of the courtyard; it is believed that when DaVinci died on May 2, 1519, he was buried there. The chapel was under construction at the time of our visit; so, we could not enter. During King Francois I employment, DaVinci stayed at nearby Chateau of Clos Luce. An underground passage between the two chateaus allowed easy access for DaVinci's visits to the King.

The next day, it was off to the Royal Chateau of Blois, the residence of King Francois I with six other kings and 10 queens eventually residing. This chateau was built during multiple timeframes and styles. There are four wings that represent the French architecture from the thirteenth century to the seventeenth century. Although the area was used as a medieval fortress dating back to the ninth century, the only structures remaining date to the thirteenth century. Starting in 1498, King Louis XII transformed the fortress into a Gothic-style residence, now known as the Louis XII wing and used as a Fine Arts Museum. Then in 1515 after ascending to the throne, Francois I expanded the structure adding an Italian Renaissance style. By 1634, Gaston d'Orleans, the brother of Louis XIII and heir to the throne, decided to build a new Classical-style castle. Before it was finished, some of the previous dwellings were destroyed. Work stopped in 1638 when the birth of Louis XIV removed d'Orleans from succession and financing was halted.

While strolling through the chateau, one will encounter an unusual painting with an unusual story behind it in the Queen's chamber. The portrait is of Antonietta Gonsalvus painted by Lavinia Fontana in 1595. The girl could be mistaken for a werewolf suffering from a genetic disorder called hypertrichosis or werewolf syndrome. Her father, Pedro Gonsalvus, also acquired this genetic disorder and was brought to France from the Canary Islands. At the time, unusual people were considered rare and regarded with fascination by royals; so, Antonietta was invited to the European courts. This malady inspired the novel *Beauty and the Beast*, originally written by Gabrielle-Suzanne Barbot de Villeneuve in eighteenth-century France. Walt Disney Productions adapted their own version of the story for their original movie in 1991.

Continuing to stroll around the room, one learns that Catherine de Medici died in this room in 1589. The life of a Queen was probably rather routine.

The walls are decorated with the monogram of the queen, which consisted of two C's intertwined with the H of Henri II. This room provides an occasion to describe a day in the life of the queen. First thing in the morning, she went to Mass, after which she received visitors. Once the midday meal was over, she received ambassadors and distinguished guests. During the afternoon, the women witnessed the sporting achievements of the men and could themselves ride a horse, shoot their bows or follow the hunters, but most of the time they would prefer conversation, music and needlework. Last but not least, supper in public was often followed by a concert or a ball.[95]

Our next stop was Chateau de Chambord, the largest residence in Loire Valley built in the sixteenth century by King Francois I. It is believed that DaVinci influenced the use of the French Renaissance design, which is very unusual for the timeframe. The building is very non-symmetrical. Since King Francois I had the two royal residences of Chateau Blois and

Chateau d'Ambroise already, Chateau de Chambord was to be his hunting lodge. Its construction occurred from 1519 to 1547, a 28-year span, with the king spending less than seven weeks total there before his death in 1547. The huge structure is not located near a town and therefore lacked the means to provide supplies locally other than hunted game. Supplies would have been brought with the entourage to the castle, making visits impractical. The chateau sat empty for almost a century when in 1639 King Louis XIII gave it to his brother, Gaston d'Orleans, who carried out significant restoration work. King Louis XIV had additional restorations made and added the 1,200-horse stable to use the structure as a hunting lodge and a place to entertain; however, he would eventually abandon it in 1685. From 1725 to 1733, Stanislas Leszczynski (Stanislas I), the deposed King of Poland who was also the father- in-law of King Louis XV, lived at Chambord.

In 1745, the king gave the chateau to Maurice de Saxe, Marshall of France, as a reward for his valor, but with his death five years later the chateau sat empty again. After the French Revolution, furniture, wall paneling, and floors were removed by the government. Emperor Napoleon Bonaparte gave the chateau to one of his subordinates, Louis Alexandre Berthier. When he died his widow sold it to the Duke of Bordeaux, Henri Charles Dieudonne, who took the title of Comte de Chambord. Although the grandfather, King Charles X, started to restore the chateau, both were exiled in 1830. During the Franco-Prussian War (1870-1871) the chateau was used as a field hospital. After the Comte de Chambord died in 1883, the chateau was left to his sister's heirs, first to Robert, Duke of Parma and then Elias, Prince of Parma. World War I and II left the chateau in stagnation with the French state owning the chateau and surrounding ground (13,400 acres) since 1930. Does the expression money pit come to mind? It is believed that in 1939 the art collections of the Louvre and Compiegne were moved to Chateau de Chambord.

Then on June 22, 1944, an American B-24 Liberator bomber crashed onto the expansive chateau grounds. The chateau features 440 rooms, 282 fireplaces, and 84 staircases with four rectangular vaulted hallways on each floor forming a cross and is now one of the most visited chateaus in France. I guess that makes up for the years that it sat vacant.

Then it was off to Chartres Cathedral, the greatest Gothic church in France and the crowning for two French kings, King Louis VI and Henry IV, not coronated at St. Remis Cathedral. It was partially built in 1145 but reconstructed after a fire in 1194. It is also known for its 176 stunning stained-glass windows; based on the surface area, the cathedral is the greatest in the world to have preserved this much original stained glass from the Romantic and Gothic periods. Another significant point of the cathedral is that it holds the Sacred Veil of Mary. This is an oblong piece of silk worn during the Annunciation of Jesus' birth by the angel Gabriel. King Charles the Bald gave the veil to the Chartres Cathedral in 876; his grandfather, Charlemagne had received it as a gift from the Byzantine Empress Irene. However, during the French Revolution, the veil was cut into pieces; some were later returned to the cathedral. Two of the pieces are on display. The cloth was tested in the twentieth century and found to contain pollen from the first–century period in Palestine.

The cathedral is also unique in that it contains a great number of intricate statues ranging from large columns to miniatures for the purpose of preaching and teaching scenes and figures of the Old and New Testaments of the Bible.

Our final stop was the finale of the trip, the Palace of Versailles, built in the town of Versailles. What started as a modest hunting lodge by King Louis XIII in 1624 became the royal residence of France from 1682 until the French Revolution in 1789. King Louis XIV, known as the Sun King, moved the royal residence from Paris to Versailles, located about 10 miles from Paris, to gain more control of the government from the nobility and distance himself from the Paris population.

The palace was significantly expanded by tripling its size and adding the stunning features of the Hall of Mirrors, the Royal Opera, and the Grand Apartments. There are 2,300 rooms covering 721,206 square feet (67,002 sq m) with the Hall of Mirrors being 8,256 square feet (767 sq m). The gardens alone are almost 2,000 acres with cascading fountains. On our visit, all the fountains were turned off but one to save water. The sole operating fountain danced to music from speakers around the area; I spent about 30 minutes sitting and enjoying the entertainment.

The palace is an impressive display of Baroque architecture in French grandeur style. The Palace of Versailles is a UNESCO World Heritage Site and essential to anyone's bucket list for France. Our hotel was only a block away from the palace, making an exceptional walking commute. The restaurant area is also within a few blocks of the palace. For those staying in Paris, it is just a short train ride. After a guided tour, we were free to spend the rest of the day viewing the interior and the gardens returning to the hotel at our leisure.

That evening we had the typical farewell dinner at a nearby restaurant and talked about the amazing places that we had visited. The following day was Bastille Day, July 14. I found the Palace of Versailles to be rather crowded with holiday visitors, especially inside the palace. On the next day while en route to the airport, we watched the French Air Force flying their aircraft low over our heads as they headed to the center of Paris for the Bastille Day festivities. This trip provided a very historic perspective. Between the battles fought in France and the monarchy's architectural extravagances, many of the architectural works of art have been rebuilt using a combination of styles: Romanesque, Gothic, and Renaissance providing a unique appearance with each erection or renovation.

A few days into my trip, I received an email about my misplaced luggage and where to send it. Although the airline was willing to send it to France, I did not want my bag chasing me around the country nor did I want to deal with two large suitcases on my way home if it caught me. I had the airline deliver it to my home. Unfortunately, the suitcase was sitting in the driveway when I got home, a little wet from the rain earlier in the week.

I'd like to add to all my comments and suggestions that Paris is a city where one can spend a week with plenty to do and the city has a good public transportation system to get around. I emphasized that just walking or picnicking along the Seine River is a very enjoyable experience. Having been there twice now, I still haven't scratched the surface of seeing the city; so, added to my bucket list is to spend a week in Paris and just enjoy what the city has to offer.

I've also noticed a trend of Europe. Coffee provided in the room, when available, is instant powdered coffee made with an electric pitcher to heat the water. As long as I can have coffee in the morning to get me going, I can adapt to instant coffee. The UNESCO World Heritage Sites with their designation year that I visited during this trip through France include Chartres Cathedral (1979); Mont-Saint-Michel and its Bay (1979); Palace and Park of Versailles (1979); Cathedral of Notre-Dame, former Abbey of Saint-Rémi and Palace of Tau, Reims (1991); Paris, Banks of the Seine (1991); the Loire Valley between Sully-sur-Loire and Chalonnes (2000); and Champagne Hillsides, Houses and Cellars (2015).

I can add the Chapel of Saint-Michel d"Aiguilhe on

Architectural Digest list and Road Affair blog to my church list and a second visit to the Louvre for my museum list. For castles, I can check Mont Saint-Michel off my list cross-referencing Travel Pirate list and savingcastles blog; Château de Chambord off the savingcastles list; and Château de Chenonceau off the famous castles list. Quite a bit of checking occurring during this trip. Château de Chenonceau was also recognized by National Geographic in their *Destinations of a Lifetime: 225 of the World's Most Amazing Places* under the section for Fairyland Castles. I'm not sure how they narrowed down the list because there are hundreds of amazing castles around the world.

view of Paris

Notre-Dame in Paris

Notre-Dame of Reims

Claude Monet lily pond

St. Mere Eglise

Omaha Beach

Arromanches-les-Bains   Tapestry

Mont Saint Michel

Apocalypse   Antonietta Gonsalvus

Chateau de Chambord   Chartres Cathedral

Part 2 – My Big Year

Chapter 11

Australia

The sea, once it casts its spell, holds one in its net of wonder forever. –

Jacques Yves Cousteau

(https://www.brainyquote.com/quotes/jacques_yves_cousteau_204406?src=t_nature)

Background: History, Culture, and Environment

G'day mate.

The movie Australia, with Nicole Kidman and Hugh Jackman as heroine and hero, portrays the British colonialization of the country. Australia was born from the age of exploration of the seas. The British under Captain James Cook explored the ocean around Australia at first using the HMS Endeavor in 1768. Landing at Botany Bay and Possession Island on August 23, 1768, he claimed the land, naming it New South Wales. Colonization of South Wales occurred in 1788 under Arthur Phillips through the first convict settlement in 1788 in Sydney. One theory on the colonization of Australia was to transfer prisoners from British prisons to Australia since the American colonies could no longer be used after the American Revolution. Another was to establish British sea power in the eastern seas; even possibly introducing settlements for the economic exploitation of the area. It is possible the British government saw benefits in all three objectives.

A penal settlement, port Arthur, was developed on the Tasmania Peninsula. Prisoners received one-way transport from Britain to Port Arthur. Once their prison sentence was completed, few had the funds to pay for the return voyage to Britain and settled in Tasmania or moved to mainland Australia. So settled Australia was born from the isolation and abandonment of British convicts.

The famous story of *Mutiny on the Bounty* written by Charles Nordhoff and James Norman Hall illustrated in the films of 1935, 1962, and most recent 1984 with Anthony Hopkins as William Bligh, Mel Gibson as Fletcher Christian, and Liam Neeson as Charles Churchill depict the Bounty's Voyage from England to Tahiti. On December 23, 1787, the Bounty sailed from Spithead, England for Tahiti by way of Cape Horn, South America. However, arriving at the tip of South America in late March, the ship encountered severe sea conditions, forcing Bligh to change course for a 10,000-mile detour around Africa's Cape of Good Hope. By May 24, 1788, the Bounty reached Cape Town and stayed for 38 days replenishing. Seven weeks after leaving Cape Town, the Bounty anchored off Adventure Bay in Tasmania; here signs of unrest appeared between the captain and crew. The ship reached Tahiti on October 24, 1788, but problems grew worse when crew and supplies went missing causing Bligh to become more authoritarian. The climax occurred on April 28, 1789, when Fletcher Christian bound Bligh with ropes and set him assail with a few crew members in a boat. Eleven months later and through a 3,618-mile voyage, Bligh returned to England, a phenomenal feat. An out-of-the-way museum on Bruny Island off Tasmania holds artifacts from both Cook's and Bligh's sailing career. Amazing, original journals from their voyages are displayed.

As had occurred in other areas of the world such as North and South Americas, indigenous populations didn't fare well when colonizers arrived in Australia. The number of Aboriginal and Torres Strait Islanders have fallen from the initial landing in 1788 of around 750,000 to 93,000 in 1900. People were either driven from the land or died from diseases such as measles, smallpox, and tuberculosis. In fact, the term *first nation people* is becoming popular to refer to the indigenous people living on the land at the time that European settlers arrived to tame the land and the native people. Australia is sensitive to their plight, and we experienced numerous examples of repairing past exploitations on our travels throughout the country.

On January 1, 1901, Australia became a nation when the six British colonies of New South Wales, Victoria, Queensland, South Australia, Tasmania, and Western Australia united and became the Commonwealth of Australia. During our 16-day trip in August during their winter, we gained an excellent overview of the country having visited five of the six states.

When one hears the term Australian cuisine, what comes to mind? After visiting the country down under I would conclude an international cuisine filled with meats, especially beef and lamb, and seafood. Australia is one of the top beef producers in the world. One can also try kangaroo meat which can be bought in the supermarket as steaks or ground for burgers. For those who are vegetarian or vegan or just prefer a less meaty diet, there are good options according to Australia's tourism website.

Australia has a tradition of eating meat going back some 60,000 years, but the nation's population of plant-based foodies is rapidly increasing in line with the number of vegetarian and vegan dining options available. From "heat-and-eat" meals available in supermarkets to health-focused cafés and vegan or vegetarian restaurants, along with omnivore eateries who can accommodate vegans and vegetarians with some notice. Even pubs, famous for their meaty menus, now typically have at least one plant-based dish on the menu.[96]

For parents and grandparents, the tourism website has a very enjoyable film on Australia that will have your little ones clamoring to go. The website address is (https://www.australia.com/en-us/gday-the-short-film.html). Be ready to make the arrangements and start packing.

Australia ranked in 2024 at 169th with a score of 19.6 for the Fragile State Index, not shabby at all for the nation down under. In fact, in 2008 Australia also ranked 169th but then a score of 24.6. I'd conclude that the land of kangaroos and koalas is a pretty stable country. Australia's score of 7.8 for the State Resilience Index reflects a well above average score for each indicator. The country is stable and resilient.

Travel Itinerary

My trip started in Cairns (two nights) then traversed Australia with flights to Ayers Rock (one night), Sydney (two nights), Adelaide (two nights), Tasmania (three nights), and ending in Melbourne (two nights).

https://free-map.org/

Travel Journal

Travel to Australia means flying halfway around the world for those people living in the Americas and Western Europe. So, if one is going to take the trip, then make the most of the flight and go for at least two weeks. My tour was 16 days, and I loved every minute of it. I flew from Washington, DC to Los

Angeles Airport (LAX) and then the entire tour group flew from Los Angeles to Cairns (pronounced "cans"), Australia on the same flight. But the impacts of my adventure started two days before leaving when I was stung by a yellow jacket bee on the back of my right hand while pulling weeds around the house. It hurt and swelled, what a way to start a trip. So, for the next few days, doing anything with my right hand was challenging. To include getting to the airport with luggage, checking in, and getting to the gate for the first five-hour flight and then followed by a fourteen-hour flight. Note to self: limit activities just prior to trip departures to ensure not getting hurt before leaving.

We had a connecting flight in Charlotte, North Carolina and when navigating to our connecting gate, we hit a section of the terminal that was impassable. It was too narrow for the number of people trying to go each way. If one did not push through the bottleneck, then one would have been there for quite a while. Those complying with etiquette to form an orderly line were merely being forced further in the back with those coming from higher number gates dominating the terminal space. I was traveling in the middle of August, so I'm not sure if the surge in airport pedestrian traffic was due to vacations or what, but it was a serious problem for the movement of people through the terminal.

When we reached Los Angeles, we got our checked luggage and then went to the international terminal. Amazingly, there was no line in security, and we breezed through with the time being around 7:00 pm. Yes, I said Los Angeles airport. The fourteen-hour flight was uneventful, just how one would like it to be. Between napping, reading, and watching movies, the time passed amply. Since Australia is about the size of the United States, our tour was different than the tour coach approach to visiting a country. We flew from destination to destination. I was a little concerned about how well that would play out, but not enough to avoid the trip.

We arrived in Brisbane and then had a connecting flight to Cairns. When flying in this direction, you lose a day crossing the international dateline. Cairns is a small town on the northeast coast of Australia known for the Great Barrier Reef and rainforest mountains surrounding the city. After checking into the hotel, I walked along the water on the esplanade (boardwalk). Warning, there is no swimming in the waters around Cairns. The sand is more like quicksand and inhabited with crocodiles. It's not your typical beach community. There is a public swimming pool, and hotel pools also provide a swimming environment, just don't go to the beach.

On the second day, we hit the ground running by heading to the Great Barrier Reef but first stopped at Green Island after an hour's boat ride. We had two hours on the island on our own to explore. My travel mate and I decided to go to the Marineland Crocodile Park, a short walk from the boat landing. It's the home of Cassius, the largest crocodile living in captivating. Cassius measures nearly 18 feet (5.5 m). The park has over 60 other crocodiles, sea turtles and other sea life to keep him company. Why are the crocodiles there? Naughty or injured crocodiles come to the marine park. What is naughty crocodile behavior? Eating outboard motors on boats for one. Cassius was captured in 1984 and noted in the *2011 Guinness Book of World Records* as the largest crocodile in captivating. His offense was causing trouble at a cattle farm and eating outboard motors. Cassius is estimated to be about 120 years old. Although he didn't move around much while we were there, he is intimidating and I'm glad that a barrier separated us. If you stop at Green Island, check out the marine park.

We were then onto the Great Barrier Reef after another hour's boat ride. The Great Barrier Reef is the largest collection of coral reefs, with 400 types of coral, 1,500 species of fish, and 4,000 types of mollusks in the world. Scientists studying the area gain more insight into the habitat of species such as the dugong (sea cow) and the large green turtle both threatened with extinction.

Platforms are set up alongside the reef for adventure companies to have a structure from which to operate. Fortunately, I was close to the front leaving the boat and headed straight for the semi-submersible, a partially submerged submarine that allows viewing of the reef from underwater. The semi-submersible moves alongside the reef. Just like the submarine voyage ride at Disneyland but in the real environment. After lunch on the platform, I was ready for snorkeling. Light-weight suits and snorkeling gear are provided. Once in the water, I was hooked. I was mesmerized by the beautiful coral and fish swimming through the coral reef. In some areas, the reef is close to the surface, and one needs to stay within gaps between the reefs to swim without touching the coral. As I swam through the canyons, I looked up and found myself in one location but couldn't swim directly to another location without maneuvering back through the canyon. Also, fish are protected so no touching them, but they may want to touch you. One large grouper liked hanging near the back of the platform around the crowd staying close to the launch and recovery section. He brushed up against me on one pass, a rather friendly fellow.

I spent about an hour and a half in the water loving every minute of it. The coral was iridescent blue and purple in some areas. At times, I swam through schools of brightly colored fish, or they swam past me. A small floating platform allowed swimmers further from the boat platform a place to rest for a few minutes. I circled back to it several times. The area is roped off, but I noticed that while in the water it is difficult to see the limitations of the enclosed area. Basically, my advice is to keep swimming until you run into the rope in every direction. The areas where the reef is close to the surface make it difficult to reach all the bounded areas, access is through the canyons. The deep areas are a dark blue, the shallow areas turn to turquoise, and areas in between are a combination. Near Green Island, the waters were very turquoise.

On our way back, the group chatted about the experience. Some already were remiss for not spending longer in the water after hearing about the beauty of the reef in areas further from the boat platform. Before making this trip, one should investigate getting an underwater camera. I look at my trip pictures now and would love to see the coral and fish colors that are not viewable from the surface or in the semi-submersible. I think this will be a place that I will return to someday, especially to enjoy with my children and their families.

So, the next day we were off to the airport heading for Ayers Rock or Uluru located in the center of Australia and more remote than Alice Springs. Since we didn't leave the hotel until 10:35 am, I took a long walk on the esplanade which reflected 4,200 steps on my phone's health app. I've said this many times before and will say it many more times, take advantage of every opportunity to walk. The tours have significant coach or airplane sedimentary time and therefore one needs to actively compensate for that by walking, whenever possible. The 4,200 steps were a nice start to the day.

The flight was about three hours with a ten-minute ride to the hotel, no traffic in the desert. Yes, it looks like a desert with some trees and reddish soil from high iron content. I immediately thought of the movie *Crocodile Dundee* and its sequel of Mick's adventures in the Australian outback. Although the movies were filmed at Kakadu National Park in the Northern Territory of Australia, Ayers Rock/Uluru is located in the southwest part of the Northern Territory. From my memory, there appeared to be some similarities in the landscapes. Paul Hogan as Mick Dundee surely exemplified Australian sexy; I think it's time to watch both movies again.

The evening was truly memorable, dinner in the desert and stargazing. Wow, within a two-day period, I swam in the Great Barrier Reef and dined in the desert while staring at one of the most spectacular night displays in the world. The sunset was beautiful, but it was afterwards that the magic started with an astrophysicist describing the astronomy of the sky, to include the southern cross only visible in this part of the world. Although I enjoy visiting planetariums, this experience surpasses any simulation confined to a building. The stars sparkle brighter than I have ever seen them. After the scientist's presentation, he offered to the group a view of Saturn with rings from his telescope set up off the path.

The food was great and the experience phenomenal. The only downside, and it is more a manage your expectations comment, is that you are picnicking in the desert with tables set up in the desert, buffet food brought to the spot, and an outhouse used as a bathroom facility. There is no good way of saying this; hold your nose while doing your business. Once sufficient distance away, inhale all the desert air you can.

The memorable night was followed by a memorable morning. We met around 5:00 am to venture into the desert to a lighted field called *Field of Light Uluru*. The display was created by artist Bruce Munro as a temporary exhibition in 2016; it was so successful it was extended indefinitely.

In 1992, journeying to Uluru through the Red Desert in central Australia, Munro felt a compelling connection to the energy, heat and brightness of the desert landscape, which he recorded in his ever-present sketchbooks. Field of Light is the embodiment of this experience. Munro recalls "I wanted to create an illuminated field of stems that, like the dormant seed in a dry desert, would burst into bloom at dusk with gentle rhythms of light under a blazing blanket of stars". Having developed the idea for over a decade, the first Field of Light was created in the field behind his family home in Wiltshire. Munro returned to the very space that inspired him, to Uluru in 2016 for the installation of Field of Light.[97]

The light field is four football fields large with paths allowing one to meander through the field of light. With pure darkness surrounding the lighted path, it is mystical, magical, and a little spooky when walking by yourself. You hear voices off in the distance from fellow group members but can't see anyone nor is there a direct path to any spot through the lighted field. As the sun starts to rise, you finally get an idea of the terrain encompassing the lighted field. Ayers Rock or Uluru as the indigenous people have called it comes into view. The sun rising over the desert is beautiful and the sunlight shaping the Uluru makes the rock even more mystical.

Although it appears as a single rock formation, millions of years ago the rock was part of a mountain range that has since

336

eroded, leaving what geologists refer to as an inselberg, or island mountain today. The huge rock formation sitting isolated within a desert suggests a similar mysticism found with Stonehenge or Easter Island. However, in Uluru, it's nature that created the isolated rock formation. We had a short hike around the base with a guide that explained its significance to the indigenous people. While driving around the foundation, there is a section with etchings where photography is not allowed. From Uluru, we headed straight to the airport and flew to Sydney.

Typical group travelers aren't the only visitors. In a 2017 article on celebrities energetically describing their visit to Uluru: Prince William and Catherine Duchess of Cambridge watched the sunset in 2014 while actress Nicole Kidman's visit provided the cover for *Vogue Australia* describing the place, *"It's just a very, very magical, special place."* It was noted that Chris Hemsworth took his family and described in an email, *"awesome...fascinating and inspiring"*. Russell Crowe's view on Twitter was *"every kid should visit Uluru."*[98]

Besides Australian actors, what other prominent visitors were attracted to the rock? The Dalia Lama on June 15, 2015, enthused locals with his visit. His Holiness' comments were focused on the indigenous people of the area:

I always express my respect for indigenous peoples whenever I have the opportunity to meet them. I have great admiration for the way they preserve their culture and language. When we Tibetans had to break our isolation, it

337

gave us the opportunity to meet and learn from other people. Now, we try to preserve traditions without that protection...

On an earlier occasion when I met an indigenous Australian, I remember telling him that I think it's important for indigenous people to retain and use their own original names. Then when you introduce yourself, it presents your identity. I also want to tell you that the colonial dominance that characterized the 18th and 19th centuries is over. Now, the world supports you and your right to keep your culture and identity alive...

For many years I've had an interest in the indigenous people of different continents, the indigenous Australians and this famous sacred rock. Now, today, I've had the opportunity to see it close up for myself and even to touch it. And I've heard the stories you tell about it, all of which makes me very happy...

I've met many indigenous peoples in different places, all of them trying to preserve the language and traditions. To succeed, I think you have to be realistic. Some of them like those in South America prefer to maintain their isolation. Others like the Sami of Lapland, your neighbours the Maoris in New Zealand and people of Canada's First Nation, try to combine their efforts to preserve their heritage with modern knowledge. I think that education is important and that it is necessary to accept some modern facilities and to learn English.[99]

National Geographic was also enamored with Uluru-Kata Tjuta National Park, citing it in their book of *Destination of a Lifetime: 225 of the World's Most Amazing Places.* Bicycle rentals are available at the Cultural Center. The Anangu people request that visitors refrain from climbing on the rock out of respect for the rock's sacredness. This is a common request amongst areas of the world that are natural wonders, but indigenous people have adopted a spiritual protection over the natural wonder.

Although actors or Very-Important-People (VIP) from the United States have visited or worked in Australia, few seem to venture to the center of the country to visit Uluru. However, celebrities do visit Sydney partaking in the Sydney Bridge Climb. On March 29, 2023, the Obamas ascended the 1,332 steps along the arch of the Sydney Harbor Bridge taking in the breathtaking 360-degree view of the harbor. Although I have been to Sydney twice, I have not had this exhilarating experience. Besides the Obamas, the list is impressive: Prince Harry, Crown Prince Frederik and Crown Princess Mary of Denmark, Oprah Winfrey, Will Smith, Matt Damon, Nicole Kidman, Kylie Minogue, Justin Timberlake, Cameron Diaz, Robert DeNiro, and Pierce Brosnan.

This list is not all-inclusive because I think I remember seeing a picture of Bruce Springsteen with his sons when I stood waiting at the exit for friends doing the climb in 2009. I'm feeling like a wimp. If I ever get back to Sydney, I'm going to have to overcome my fear of heights and go where so many have gone before, the top of the Sydney Harbor Bridge.

Landing at Sydney Kingsford Smith Airport, we were out of the airport and off to the hotel in a short time. That evening we had a buffet dinner at SkyFeast at the Sydney Tower, an all-you-can-eat restaurant with abundant options. The restaurant rotates so when you go back to one of the stations, it will have moved. The restaurant boasts 30 international dishes including seafood and desserts. As I departed, I had to be rolled to the elevator I ate so much. The next morning, we had a tour of Sydney traveling to the major sightseeing areas. The tour started in historic and fashionable Paddington with unique terrace houses.

From there we continued with a stop at Mrs. Macquarie's Chair (yes chair), an exposed sandstone rock hand-carved by convicts in 1810 for Elizabeth Macquarie, the wife of Major-General Lachlan Macquarie, Governor of New South Wales. The bench resides on the peninsula of Sydney Harbor. This spot provided excellent views and smartphone shots of the harbor and the Sydney Opera House. We continued the drive past historic buildings such as Parliament House, Saint Mary's Cathedral, and the Queen Victoria Building.

We also had a stop at the famous Bondi Beach. The beach is 0.62 miles (1.0 km) long and produces world-class waves drawing the most competent surfers. It is also the only beach open all year round. The word Bondi comes from the aboriginal word boondi meaning *water breaking over rocks*. The beach is known for the tragedy on Sunday, February 6,

1938, when a backwash swept swimmers away from a sandbank, carrying more than 200 people into the deep water. Five people died and the others were saved through a mass rescue.

After our fun in the sun, we headed to The Rocks, for a short walking tour and then lunch. Today, The Rocks is a cultural and social hub at the center of Australia's largest city. But ten thousand years ago, The Rocks was a pristine coastline inhabited by the Gadigal people. Fast forward to January 26, 1788, with the first colonial fleet sailing into the western side of Sydney cove calling the area, The Rocks. The name stuck. Like colonization in other lands, the indigenous people or First Nation People did not fare well, losing most of their land and 80 percent of the population wiped out by the introduction of new diseases. This area is the first settled in Australia, still retaining cobblestones from the past. First Fleet Park was the first marketplace established.

Although I did not do the Bridge Climb, one couple in our tour group did during our leisure time. I did a tour of the Opera House on a previous visit over ten years ago but enjoyed it so much I wanted to do it again. The building had some renovation since my previous visit, but all the grandeur is still there. I didn't remember it being that different.

The Sydney Opera House is a UNESCO World Heritage Site inducted in 2007, an iconic symbol of Sydney and Australia. I can't say it any better than the UNESCO description for outstanding universal value:

The Sydney Opera House constitutes a masterpiece of 20th century architecture. Its significance is based on its unparalleled design and construction, its exceptional engineering achievements and technological innovation and its position as a world-famous icon of architecture. It is a daring and visionary experiment that has had an enduring influence on the emergent architecture of the late 20th century. Utzon's original design concept and his unique approach to building gave impetus to a collective creativity of architects, engineers and builders. Ove Arup's engineering achievements helped make Utzon's vision a reality. The design represents an extraordinary interpretation and response to the setting in Sydney Harbour. The Sydney Opera House is also of outstanding universal value for its achievements in structural engineering and building technology. The building is a great artistic monument and an icon, accessible to society at large.[100]

John Utzon designed the building with a series of white roofs shaped like sails of boats to reflect his love of sailing and a fitting theme within the harbor. Although construction commenced in 1959, the building wasn't finished until 1973 causing much angst within the Australian government. Although Utzon finally resolved the shell construction problems, he left the project in 1966 after disagreements with government officials related to cost overruns and design. Australian architect Peter Hall finished the project. Utzon never returned to Sydney to see his masterpiece finished.

Although the initial estimate for the project was $7 million, it finished at $102 million. This raises the problem of cost estimation when one is operating at the forefront of innovation. Inflation increases over the fourteen years would account for some of the cost overruns but resolving groundbreaking engineering problems where there are no predecessor examples are high-risk ventures. There inherently was risk in the cost estimate accuracy. The iconic building represents the city of Sydney and the country of Australia, how does one put a price on that?

Sydney was a quick turnaround city, two nights for such a vibrant city but the desire to stay longer is a common dilemma. Since I hadn't had enough of the city yet, I got up at 5:45 am and took a walk around the harbor area. I can't quell my passion for the Opera House. I tried to walk through the Botanical Gardens, but they were still closed so I took the sidewalk beside it. On a previous visit in 2009, I spent much free time walking through the gardens which are home to white macaws and very large, scary bats. There wasn't a better way to start the day than a morning walk around the harbor.

A cruise ship had come in overnight, adding a new look to the harbor scenery. One last comment on Sydney deals with the hotel. It was unusual that the lobby wasn't on the first floor but the second floor from the top. The elevators were *smart* elevators which by scanning your room key determined which elevator would arrive first and you entered. The more mature members in the group, which were most of the group, had a difficult time with this new technology. It did seem cumbersome when checking in getting the group to the almost-top floor to register. The bar/restaurant was on the top floor with a happy hour special going on at the time causing elevator space competition with the bar. Just another *roll with it* moment.

Again, the airport transfer was smooth, and we were on our way to Adelaide. Arriving in the afternoon, I went for a walk through the Botanical Gardens after registering at the hotel. I can't get enough of the gardens wherever I go. Along the gardens resides the National Wine Center, I stopped in for a visit. They have a small museum describing wine making with some interactive displays. I tried a wine flight with a bowl of pumpkin soup, one of the best that I've had. Pumpkin soup is a common theme on my travels; if it's an option as an appetizer, then I will be choosing it. We had a late dinner in the hotel, and most people were ready to retire afterwards.

The next morning, I left early and walked to the Central Market where the group was headed later. I enjoy watching the vendors set up their space. I like watching the day start through the commerce lens. Whether it's sitting at a café and watching people traveling to their jobs or vendors getting their stores ready to open. The Central Market had the same vibe. As I headed down the sidewalk, I passed a dog washing machine. Dog lovers must be clean conscious to give their dog a bath after a walk. Unfortunately, no one was using the device while I passed because it would have been interesting to watch. A cooking show was being filmed in one location of the market, and I found a spare chair across the aisle. My guess is that they decided to film early before the aisles were packed and noisy. What a fun experience I had being the audience for a cooking show. When they wrapped it up, I continued my stroll and found a second-hand bookstore. Perusing the books, I found two I couldn't resist: *Beneath the Southern Cross* by Judy Nunn describing the birth of Sydney and *True at First Light* by Ernest Hemingway describing his Kenya safari experiences in 1952. Since I have a trip to South Africa, Botswana, Zimbabwe, and eSwatini in January 2024, a Hemingway book on any African country is a nice way to get acquainted with safari. Learning about the roots of Sydney needs no further explanation.

One glitch in my early morning solo walk to the Central Market occurred when I was waiting at one entrance and the tour group was waiting at another entrance for me. Two entrances on opposite sides of the building. They had taken one path walking there and I had taken a different route thus putting us at different locations. Someone realized that maybe I was waiting at the other entrance and came and found me after a few minutes. Only a small snafu and then we were guided around the market tasting samples of some products. Lunch was at the market and then we drove to Cleland Wildlife Park outside the city of Adelaide.

There aren't words to describe how great this day was at the wildlife park. We walked among kangaroos, wallabies, wombats, bettongs, potoroos, and emus feeding some by hand a crafted mix resembling rabbit pellets. As we approached, many of the creatures were leisurely laying in the grass having a siesta; but they quickly jumped up and became quite sociable. We learned that kangaroos aren't as aggressive as one might think; they were quite docile and delightful. Twenty-two people reconnected with their inner child excitedly wandering from animal-to-animal handfeeding them screaming to get the picture. The more aggressive animals were in cages such as the Tasmanian devil and dingo. The finale was a picture with a koala. Although one cannot hold the adorable, cuddly animal, one can stroke them on their back.

Australia is home to the majority of the world's marsupials with the remainder being in Papua New Guinea, Eastern Indonesia, and the Americas. What constitutes a marsupial? Well, they are pouched mammals, most people's understanding. However, they also have live births but do not have long gestation periods like placenta mammals. Most development occurs after birth. Placenta mammals nourish the developing embryo using the mother's blood supply through the placenta. Marsupials have a yolk-type placenta which provides minimal embryo support thus needing to further develop after birth. Marsupials in Australia are koalas, kangaroos, wallabies, wombats, bettongs, and potoroos. Marsupials in the United States are opossums.

In the evening, we walked to a local restaurant; I had a

very large beef schnitzel with potato mash and pavlova for dessert. I've said this before and will say it again, one challenge of tour-managed trips is not overeating and gaining weight through the week or two. Manage your diet by not making every meal a *"I'm on vacation so what the heck"*, particularly the more mature traveler with a slower metabolism. Remember the expression: *a moment on the lips, a lifetime on the hips.* Adelaide is a walking town where most hotels are located near activities and restaurants, allowing one to maximize on the exercise of walking to counter all the eating. Traveling at the frequency of one trip a month, I really need to manage food intake and exercise. The walk back to the hotel after dinner was very enjoyable, really a blessing.

The next day we ventured again out of Adelaide to Barossa Valley and a day of wine tasting at three different wineries. The valley is hilly and very green; the grapevines were in their winter state in August. Southern Australia is known for shiraz, cabernet, and grenache. We had lunch at the second winery; I really like the combination of wine tasting and lunch. The first winery was Jacob Creek a distributor in the United States and six wine tastings, but I bought two bottles of wine that aren't distributed outside Australia. Onto Lambert Winery with five different tastings served with a family-style lunch of tender roast beef, chicken in pesto sauce, mashed sweet potatoes, and French fries. The finale was chocolate port for dessert. Being well-fed, we moved on to the third winery, Pindarie Winery, but had to make a stop at a chocolate factory for more desserts. At Pindarie we had five more tastings; we were one happy group on the drive back to the hotel, but no one was even close to being drunk.

Dinner was at a local hotel with family-style sharing and we walked to and from the restaurant complementing some exercise after another gastro delight. The next morning, we again headed for the airport but not before having a very thick French toast with berries for breakfast. I hoped Tasmania would be as active as the mainland to help counter all those calories.

We arrived late in the afternoon after a connecting flight in Melbourne with dinner at the hotel in Hobart. Hobart Airport has limited gates with direct access from the airplane to the terminal. In our case, we had to depart the plane down steps and then walk into the terminal. Not a problem on our day because it was clear but on a rainy day, not so enjoyable. Also, if one has heavy carryon luggage, it can be cumbersome holding the rail with one hand and holding the suitcase with the other.

We started the Tasmanian adventure the next day with breakfast as usual at the hotel. We drove to Port Arthur located on the other end of the island from Hobart. Port Arthur is a historic nineteenth-century penal settlement with a huge penitentiary, solitary confinement building, asylum, Convict Church, and leadership housing co-located on the complex. We were given a guided tour with details on the activities that transpired. Britain's approach to criminals was to remove them from the mother country and relocate them in penal complexes in several colonies. They leveraged the remote site of Tasmania to send what was considered their most hardened convicts whether man, woman, or child. UNESCO has deemed the Australian convict sites, Port Arthur being one, as World Heritage Sites:

Around 166,000 men, women and children were sent to Australia over 80 years between 1787 and 1868, condemned by British justice to transportation to the convict colonies. Each of the sites had a specific purpose, in terms both of punitive imprisonment and of rehabilitation through forced labour to help build the colony. The Australian Convict Sites presents the best surviving examples of large-scale convict transportation and colonial expansion of European powers through the presence and labour of convicts.[101]

Although convict age could start at seven-years-old, a plaque provides the story of a nine-year-old sent from England for stealing; offenders could be from England, Scotland, or Ireland. I'm not sure how a repeated offender for stealing at the age of nine-years-old could be considered hardened criminal activity but maybe in the eighteenth and nineteenth centuries. I can't even fathom separating a child from the family, transporting the child on a ship for many weeks, and isolating the child in a remote country at only nine-years-old.

My granddaughter, at five years old, would only be four years younger than that child. It is shocking to think how she could have dealt with that situation. Those that served their time were then released but very few could afford transportation costs back to Britain; so, they ultimately settled in Tasmania or made their way to Australia's mainland. We cruised Port Arthur harbor passing Isle of the Dead, the island used as the prisoner cemetery. Without a doubt, it was a solemn visit.

When I asked my question about ghosts, the guide responded that ghost sightings have been reported. In fact, an article written by ABC news on September 11, 2000, entitled *Ghosts Draw Tourists to Australian Ruins* describes the practice of ghost tours at Port Arthur until April 1996 when the gunman Martin Bryant went on a shooting rampage killing 35 people. The tours stopped for several weeks but then restarted emphasizing the reported ghost sightings with connections to the history of the place. I didn't see any ghosts that day, although when I entered one house, there was no electricity. I used my smartphone flashlight to walk through the house but decided that it was a little too creepy by myself and quickly left.

Australia is not the only country with a history of British penal settlements. Between 1718 and 1775 over 52,000 convicts were transported from the British Isles to America, mainly to Maryland and Virginia, sold as slaves. It is believed that a quarter of the British immigrants to colonial America in the eighteenth century were convicts. Britain's Transportation Act of 1718 allowed convicts to be transported out of the country as a means of punishment.

The British penal system was not intended for long-term incarceration. Prior to the act, many criminals were punished by whipping or branding and then released back onto the streets; for others, it was hanging. The act changed the solution to criminal punishment.

From 1700 to March 1718, only one percent of convicts was transported for punishment. From May 1718 to 1775, that changed to over 70 percent. So, for those Marylanders and Virginians that have roots going back to the eighteenth century, your British ancestor may have been convicted of a crime and received a one-way free trip to colonial America to start a new life. I'm not sure how we ever 'right all the wrongs that have occurred for centuries, maybe millennia, to probably every ethnic group that ever existed around the world. Colonization was a double-edge sword situation. Lands and people benefited from development initiatives from the mother country, but the mother country also exploited their young colonies.

I wouldn't want readers to walk away with the idea that Tasmania is only about penal colonies, quite the contrary. Tasmania is all about wildlife and spectacular outdoors. Port Arthur Historic Site happens to be the starting point for the Three Capes Track, a 30-mile (48 km) track designed for a wide variety of ranges and abilities. Hikers will then board the Pennicott Wilderness Journeys vessel for a cruise exploring coves and the tallest sea cliffs in the southern hemisphere. The hikers then start their four-day walk at Denmans Cove traversing a path that takes them through tall eucalypt forests, coastal heath, and Australia's highest sea cliffs. Cabins are available in Surveyors, Munro, and Retakunna for overnight accommodations. As we sat having a box lunch in the visitor center, hikers were registering and preparing for their four-day journey. I so much would love to add this to my bucket list, but I'm not sure that I have the physical condition to handle it.

Did you know that Tasmania was the home of the World Flyfishing Championship in 2019? Fishing in Tasmania is exceptional, advertised as *our wilderness fishing is unique with thousands of lakes and tarns offering fishing like nowhere else.*[102] Just another reason to explore the wilderness in Tasmania.

The next day, I was able to check a bucket list item, riding a vehicle ferry. We took the ferry to Bruny Island seated on the coach. This may not seem like a big accomplishment, but bucket lists aren't only about visiting epic sites or experiencing once-in-a-lifetime events. Sometimes it's a simple thing that is not part of your routine life that you need to take extra steps to make happen.

Once on Bruny Island, it was a series of stops to understand living on a more isolated island off another more isolated island. The first stop was a cheese, bread, and beer maker. In the United States, this would probably be three different businesses, but practicality forces one to diversify. The next stop was next to the beach and the climb of 287 steps to view the beaches on both sides of the causeway. Most of the group made it to the top, including 70+ and one 80+ age group member for stunning views. I've said this before and will say it many more times, I'm so impressed with the physical condition of many of the more mature travelers on these trips. Kudos to you!

On the way to the seaside restaurant, we had a hike through the rainforest to search for white wallabies. We didn't find any during the hike but did find one not too far from the restaurant in a small field next to a house. Wallabies here are like rabbits back home, plentiful. I had my favorite pumpkin soup for lunch with a sandwich. The next stop was to the Bligh Museum of Pacific Exploration. Although a small building, it is stocked with artifacts from Pacific Ocean exploration from 1642 to 2000.

The museum was established in 1954 by Dr. J. Bruce Hamilton to display historic maps, documents, paintings, and other artifacts related to landing at Adventure Bay, some related to James Cook, William Bligh, and Abel Tasman. If the names sound familiar, Captain James Cook sailed the Pacific Ocean between 1768-1779 charting land masses; Vice-Admiral William Bligh, former Governor of South Wales in Australia and captain of the USS Bounty during the mutiny; and Abel Tasman, Dutch explorer serving the Dutch East India Company. This museum is an absolute gem with journals from some of their travels. It is worth the trip to Tasmania and then the ferry ride to Bruny Island to see it if you are one captivated with maritime history.

Heading back to the ferry, we stopped at a chocolate shop, walked through a garden, and finished at a honey and ice cream store. Since my sandwich at lunch was too large to finish, it was my meal for dinner.

Tasmania wilderness has been a UNESCO World Heritage Site since 1982 and meets seven of the ten criteria. The region has been subjected to severe glaciation, creating steep gorges in a rainforest environment, perfect for parks and reserves. Based on remains found in limestone within caves, it is believed human occupation of the area dates back 20,000 years.

Tasmanian Aboriginal people adapted to a changing climate and natural environment through a full glacial-interglacial climatic cycle and were the southernmost people in the world during the last ice age. Evidence of their culture remains in the property today, with significant Pleistocene cave occupation sites, and later Holocene sites, demonstrating a richness and variability rarely seen in comparable global contexts. The rock markings in caves represent an extraordinary connection to their ideas and beliefs.[103]

The next morning, we were onward to Hobart Airport and flying to Melbourne. After checking into the hotel, we were on our own for the day. I walked to Cathedral Church and Minor Basilica of Saint Patrick or Saint Patrick's Cathedral, the largest cathedral in Australia. In 1974 Pope Paul VI conferred the title of minor basilica on the church. In 1986, Pope John Paul II visited the cathedral. A plague commemorates this visit to the cathedral stating: *His Holiness Pope John Paul II successor of Saint Peter confirms the faith of his brothers and sisters by his prayerful visit to Saint Patrick's Cathedral on 28 November 1986.*

The architectural style is specifically Geometric Decorated Gothic, exhibiting this style in its most complexity is the large west window of the nave. This style was borrowed from medieval Gothic churches in England in the late thirteenth century. Saint Patrick's of Melbourne shares the honor with Saint Patrick's of New York City to be the two largest churches substantially completed in the nineteenth century. With most of the Catholic community in Melbourne at the time Irish, the cathedral was dedicated to Saint Patrick, the patron saint of Ireland.

From there I walked to the tram heading for the harbor. As my travel mate and I were passing Marvel Stadium, I noticed several patrons entering, so questioned them on the sport, Australian football. We bought tickets in the rafter section, the only area still available, but really enjoyed watching. The gentlemen sitting behind us were helpful with the rules of play.

The sport has several names: Australian football, Australian rules football, Aussie rules, or just footy. I'll let Wikipedia describe the play and rules of game:

During general play, players may position themselves anywhere on the field and use any part of their bodies to move the ball. The primary methods are kicking, handballing and running with the ball. There are rules on how the ball can be handled; for example, players running with the ball must intermittently bounce or touch it on the ground. Throwing the ball is not allowed, and players must not get caught holding the ball. A distinctive feature of the game is the mark, where players anywhere on the field who catch the ball from a kick (with specific conditions) are awarded unimpeded possession. Possession of the ball is in dispute at all times except when a free kick or mark is paid. Players can tackle using their hands or use their whole body to obstruct opponents.[104]

Being familiar with American football, the rule of no throwing the ball makes a significant difference. It didn't take long for me to turn to the two gentlemen behind us and ask why aren't they throwing the ball? For those unfamiliar with the term handballing, the player holds the ball in one hand and punches it with the other. I'd call that movement ball bouncing or hand ball bouncing. There are time limits on certain plays. The game was fast-paced, and I thoroughly enjoyed watching this Australian version. For travelers on organized tours, try to partake in some local activities outside the prescribed itinerary; encourage your tour manager to provide information on these local activities. We luckily stumbled across the football game, but others in our group would have enjoyed the event had they known.

Although it was a previous late night, I was up and ready for our three-hour walking tour of Melbourne the next morning, tasting samples along the way. During our walk, group members received notice from the airline that the return flight was canceled, and we were rebooked for a flight leaving a day later. After informing our tour manager, she worked with the tour group and rescheduled us to a morning flight the same day. The much earlier arrival at Los Angeles meant changing the connecting flight, which had a considerable increase in cost. Keep in mind, anything can happen when traveling. Crisis averted; I then spent the afternoon at the aquarium. The penguin exhibit, both king and gentoo penguins, was fantastic. The penguin area had stones; the pairs would move the stones from one place to the nest. One penguin would stay by the nest while the other one walked the stones and then they switched roles. It was so much fun to watch; the exhibit drew the largest crowd. Within the penguin habitat, there was also a slide and a water tank too.

I made a short stop into Saint Paul's Cathedral. I can't get enough of looking at the architecture of these magnificent structures. From there, I retraced my steps back to a Gaming Center and stopped in for a drink. Outside street musicians were entertaining the sidewalk crowds. A nice relaxing way to end the evening; especially when faced with a 4:00 am departure for Melbourne airport the next morning. The flight from Melbourne to Sydney left at 6:30 am. At Sydney Airport, our connecting flight was delayed two hours due to an airplane tire sensor problem. Once that was repaired, we had a problem that two passengers had checked in and checked luggage but did not show up at the gate.

After numerous announcements for them, the luggage had to be removed from the airplane. Just imagine how many bags had to be checked to find theirs and be removed. This extended the delay. The flight from Sydney to Los Angeles was on an Airbus A-380 with two levels. Having to change flights, I went from a reserved aisle seat to a middle seat, not the best way to fly for 14 hours, but at least I was returning home earlier and not a day later. My next trip to Alaska was only six days later; so, I needed to get home and get ready for the next adventure. It was a managing your expectations moment; there are circumstances that are out of your control. So just make the best of it.

During the trip, we visited these following UNESCO World Heritage Sites in Australia: Great Barrier Reef (1981), Tasmanian Wilderness (1982), Uluru-Kata Tjuta National Park (1987), Sydney Opera House (2007), and Australian Convict Sites (2010). The Great Barrier Reef was a double check as one of the Seven Natural Wonders of the World. Sydney Opera House was one of the 21 finalists for the Seven Wonders of the Modern World. Stargazing in the desert should be on everyone's bucket list no matter which desert one selects to do the gazing.

Great Barrier Reef

Sydney Harbor

Bondi Beach

automatic dog wash

Port Arthur Penal Site

Saint Patrick's Cathedral

Australian football

Ayers Rock or Urulu

Field of Lights

Emperor penguins

Tasmanian devils

wallaby mom and baby

Chapter 12

Alaska and Western Canada

Look deep into nature, and then you will understand
everything better. –

Albert Einstein

(https://www.brainyquote.com/quotes/albert_einstein_106912)

Background: History, Culture, and Environment

Hello, my friend.

Alaska is the 49th state of the United States; a
microbrewery is named after this fact. The United States
purchased Alaska from Russia in 1867; I bet Russia has
regretted that more than once. Then in the 1890s, the Gold
Rush brought thousands of prospectors with some becoming
settlers in their quest to find gold.

The earliest migration to Alaska occurred around 15,000
years ago during the Ice Age when a frozen land bridge,
known as Beringia, extended from Siberia to Alaska,
connecting the continents of Asia and North America. Those
first inhabitants probably followed the migration of animals'
herds searching for better food sources. Some of those first
inhabitants stayed in Beringia and others migrated down into
North and South America being the native ancestors of those

regions. The first permanent settlements date back to about 4,000 years ago, relying on hunting sea mammals along the water and caribou in land for survival.

Russians crossed the water encountering Alaskan indigenous people in the mid-1700s. The Russian explorer, Mikhail Gvozdev, mapped Alaska and the North American coastline in 1735, however, strong winds prevented him from landing. In 1741, Danish-born explorer Vitus Jonassen Bering sailed between Russia and North America under the service of the Russian Czar Peter the Great, becoming the first Europeans to explore parts of Alaska. Although not the first to sail through the area of the Bering Strait and Bering Sea, both were named for Vitus Bering. In 1784, Grigorii Shelikhov established the first Russian settlement on Kodiak Island. In 1794, Catherine the Great sent the first Russian Orthodox monks to Kodiak Island. Along with the missionary priest Ivan Veniaminov sent to the Aleutian Islands, they created a Russian Orthodox community still active today. After the British navigator Captain James Cook sailed around Alaska in 1778, the British and Americans established fur trading operations. The Russian Czar Paul I created a Russian American fur trading business from Sitka Island in 1799. Eventually, Russia established treaties with competing countries.

In 1802, the Tlingit and Haida warriors launched a surprise attack on the Russian fort at Sitka. Tensions were growing from Russian abuses to the Indigenous people who were forced to hunt sea mammals for Russian traders. The Russians were driven from the Sitka fort. In 1804, a second battle occurred with Russians attacking the fort to drive out the warrior occupants who had secretly left the previous night. The Russians then reestablished their fort. The Sitka National Historical Park was established by the National Park Service to preserve the 1804 battleground and site of the Tlingit fort, and to commemorate the events associated with Tlingit resistance to Russian colonization. There are 11 distinct Indigenous cultures in Alaska that are grouped in five regions: (1) the Iñupiat and St. Lawrence Island Yup'ik in the Arctic; (2) the Athabascan in south-central and interior Alaska; (3) the Yup'ik and Cup'ik in southwest Alaska; (4) the Unangax̂ and Sugpiaq (Alutiiq) in south-central Alaska and the Aleutian Islands; and (5) the Eyak, Haida, Tsimshian and Tlingit in the Inside Passage.

After Russia lost the Crimean War to Great Britain in 1856, the Russian government needed funds but did not want to sell the Alaska territory to Great Britain. The British wanted to add to their British territory in North America, modern-day Canada. The United States had just ended its Civil War and was initially reluctant to make such a large purchase. Applying Manifest Destiny doctrine, Secretary of State William Seward purchased the territory in 1867 for $7.2 million or two cents per acre, under President Andrew Johnson-the deal of the century. President Dwight D. Eisenhower signed a declaration naming Alaska as the 49th state on January 3, 1959.

Or was it the deal of the century? It was President Thomas Jefferson who had made the Louisiana Purchase the previous bargain of the century at $15 million in 1803 for an area larger than Great Britain, France, Germany, Italy, Spain, and Portugal combined. The purchase gave the United States nearly 828,000 square miles (2,144,510 sq km) of land west of the Mississippi River, doubling the size of the country and costing roughly four cents per acre. Well, Johnson got a better deal at two cents per acre versus Jefferson's four cents per acre but the natural resources in the Louisiana Purchase might warrant the extra two cents per acre paid.

Since I covered the Fund for Peace Fragile State Index for the United States under the chapter on Seattle, I won't cover it again here. However, since our cruise ended in Vancouver, Canada, I will cover Canada's performance. Canada ranked 162nd with a score of 18.6 tying with Ireland. Maybe the United States needs to look closer at its northern neighbor for guidance on political, social, and economic factors that affect the stability of a country, at a minimum, the two specific areas of fractionalized elites and group grievance. Since Canada's establishment as a nation, it has had two co-official languages, recognizing an English and French immigration population during a similar period as the United States. I'll just say to Canada, well done and bien joué! Canada scored equally well for the State Resilience Index at 7.8 with all indicators well above average. Again, maybe the United States government can acquire some advice from its neighbor.

Travel Itinerary

My trip started in Anchorage with two extra days (three nights); Mount McKinley Princess Lodge (one night); Denali Princess Lodge (two nights); Copper River Princess Lodge (two nights); Sapphire Princess cruise ship (7 nights) with stops in Hubbard Bay, Glacier Bay, Skagway, Juneau, and Ketchikan; and two nights in Vancouver on our own with a trip to Victoria Island.

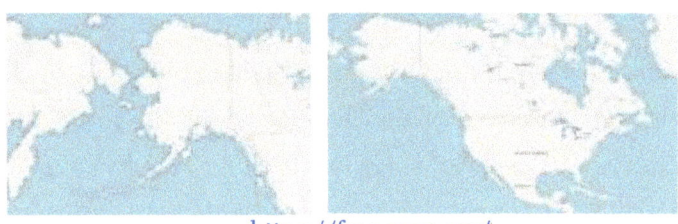

https://free-map.org/

Travel Journal

I returned from the 16-day Australia trip on August 29, 2023, and left for Anchorage on September 5, 2023; an aggressive turnaround for unpacking, repacking, and catching up on errands around the house and for myself. The flight itinerary left from Philadelphia International Airport, then to Atlanta, then to Minneapolis, and finally Anchorage. I'm always amazed when I must fly south in order to fly north.

That night my travel mate and I called it an early evening with pizza in the room for dinner.

At breakfast, I met a senior-aged woman traveling alone who setup her trip to Alaska herself. She stayed in Anchorage a few days then planned to take the train to Denali for a couple of days and then on to Fairbanks. In Fairbanks, she had planned the long van trip up to the Arctic Circle to see the northern lights. She was an inspiration for me and for those who want to travel but might not have friends or family available. What an adventure for an over eighty-year-old woman still young enough for an arctic escapade.

After breakfast, my mate and I walked to Anchorage's Federal Building, location for the National Park Service. There's an informative display and films are shown throughout the day. We walked across the street for the Anchorage City Trolley tour and took a trolley for an hour and a half around the Anchorage area. An interesting part of the trolley tour was near the airport where people keep seaplanes on the water. Alaska has 3,197 named lakes out of three million unnamed lakes, 67 named reservoirs, and 167 named dams. So, there's a lot of water-based piloting versus land-based airports. Much of the state is not accessible by road either.

We also stopped at Earthquake Park, a park located where the earthquake occurred on March 27, 1964, the largest earthquake ever recorded for North America at 9.2 magnitude occurred in Prince William Sound, destroyed this residential community. *The earthquake lasted approximately 4.5*

366

minutes and is the most powerful recorded earthquake in U.S. history. It is also the second largest earthquake ever recorded, next to themagnitude 9.5 earthquake in Chile in 1960.[105] A walking trail is near the site along the Tony Knowles Coastal Trail through the city. After the trolley, we headed back to the Federal Building and more films at the National Park Service. Dinner that night was at the 49th State Brewery.

We couldn't get enough of the National Park Service, so we went back the next day to see more films. By then it was time to check out of our hotel and check-in to Captain Cook Hotel for the Alaska land/cruise tour. It was also back to the 49th State Brewery for lunch and the yak slider special. I decided to stretch my legs and spent four miles walking the Tony Knowles Coastal Trail.

The train station located about 10 minutes from the hotel was an easy commute. The scenic train travels from Anchorage to Fairbanks; the ride takes all day. En route the hostess pointed out Denali Mountain was visible; she was quite impressed that the shy massif was showing its profile. Our destination was Talkeetna, so we were expected to be there by noon. Talkeetna is famous as the town with a cat as the honorary mayor. Mr. Stubbs governed from 1997-2017; after his passing, Denali holds the position. Yes, the cat's name is Denali. The town is small and probably meets the expression *everybody knows everybody*. From the end of the main street, we were able to see the southern side of Denali Mountain. We took a van to Mount McKinley Princess Lodge and Denali Mountain was visible there too. That's three views of the elusive mountain which shows itself only about 30 percent of the time. So, sightings are unusual and exciting. That evening, I sat around the campfire, eating popcorn, and roasting marshmallows until it started to rain.

Before our coach's departure to Denali, I walked to the infamous treehouse about a 20-minute walk from the lodge. The treehouse was built in 2017 by the Animal Planet television show Treehouse Masters and provides great views of the wilderness. It's worth the walk to see the craftsmanship in the structure. Unfortunately, it drizzled that morning, so I wasn't afforded a phenomenal view of the countryside.

The drive to Denali Princess Lodge was about two hours; we took the hotel shuttle over to Denali National Park and took the park's one-and-half-hour bus tour. The bus became excited chatter at the site of a mother moose and her young. It drizzled off and on the rest of the afternoon, so we put hiking on hold. That evening, I went to the Music of Denali Dinner Show located at the Gold Nugget Saloon located at the McKinley Chalet Resort, next to the Princess Lodge Resort. Standing with other showgoers waiting for the shuttle, we were a little confused where the show took place. Not realizing that we needed to go to another location, a few people were distressed about arriving late and missing part of the show.

The food and show were great; dinner is family-style to include roadhouse standards such as Alaskan salmon, smokehouse brisket, mashed potatoes, corn and peas, and baked apple crisps for dessert. After dinner, the comedy show depicts the legendary adventures of the first men to scale Denali Mountain at a height of 20,310 feet (6,190 m), North America's highest peak, a perfect introduction to the Alaskan wilderness. For many years, controversy has raged over the name dilemma, Denali or Mount McKinley. The mountain was unofficially named by a prospector in 1896 then officially in 1917 to commemorate William McKinley as president from 1897 to his assassination in 1901. Others believed the mountain should retain the native name given it by the Alaskan Athabaskans to mean the high one, Denali. Supported by then Secretary of Interior Sally Jewel, President Barack Obama changed the mountain's name to Denali in September 2015.

Who would have thought that naming a mountain would be so controversial? In President Trump's first few days in office in 2025, he changed the name back to Mount McKinley through an executive order. Technically, the mountain resides within a national park and therefore management falls under the federal government. The Department of Interior manages the National Park Service, and the Department of Interior is an office within the President's cabinet. So, he does have the jurisdiction, but which situation has more meaning for the United States, naming the mountain after the term used by the Indigenous people for centuries or after a President that never visited the land or mountain? Whether one believes that President William McKinley was a good president or not, naming the mountain after an avid outdoorsman would be the likely choice or one that initiated efforts to protect the area. I think this falls into the common advice that one shouldn't fight every battle; so, one should be selective in which battles they chose to fight.

The next morning, we started off with the buffet breakfast at Fannie O' Bar before heading out for the planned four-to five-hour Denali Park tour with stops throughout the park. We spotted two bull moose; hiked to Savage Cabin, utilized by National Park Service rangers during dangerous snow conditions; and then heard the story by a local native at mile marker 17 with a stunning view of Denali from the northern side. Denali is also visible between mile markers 9 to 12 on the park's main road. After our return to the hotel, we headed to a ranch for an all-terrain vehicle (ATV) ride for myself and a chuck wagon ride for my travel mate. The ATV ride comprised three men apart from myself. Partway through the ride, we stopped at a ranch house for an amazing dinner: salmon, chicken, ribs, salad (pasta, potato, and coleslaw), vegetable chili, corn on the cob, and raspberry cobbler for dessert.

The chuck wagon group was already there eating. Another group was the side-by-side utility vehicles (UTV) which showed up after us. This was a fantastic adventure and the first time that I rode through creek beds. The usual dry creek bed on the trail turned into a shallow creek from the recent two weeks of rain. Since it was a more mature group, there wasn't the mud splashing that occurs with teens or twenty-something youth. I came back fairly clean even though there were mud puddles everywhere.

Much better than the dune buggy ride in the Dominican Republic several years before with my sons; my clothes were so muddy that I got in the shower fully clothed to rinse off rather than undressing first. My sons were teenagers then and searched for every puddle to splash.

We passed an area that previously was a glacier but only dirt now. This spot is where the petrified bison named Blue Babe was found and is now in the Fairbanks Museum. If I ever get back to Alaska, I will do another ATV ride in the mountains; the scenery is just stunning. I'd also like to go to the museum in Fairbanks to see the Blue Babe.

The next day turned out to be quite a long ride to our next destination. We drove north to Fairbanks to connect with Richardson Highway and then south to Copper River, a total of five hours driving with a stop at the Santa Claus House, lunch, and a couple of bathroom breaks. Santa Claus House in North Pole, Alaska is just outside of Fairbanks and must be the largest store in the country for Christmas items, maybe the largest store in any country. It's Christmas all year long.

Cell phone service is very sporadic in mountain areas. One bathroom stop, an outhouse, was along a river where salmon are usually found making their way upstream. We were slightly off-season to sight any salmon. We arrived at Copper River

Princess Lodge in time for dinner and gathered information on activities in the area. The next morning, we started with the 30-minute dog sled ride; since there was no snow, it was a dog cart ride. Four medium dogs pulled five adults.

I then took the hotel shuttle to Wrangell-St. Elias National Park and hiked for three miles. This is a UNESCO World Heritage Site but part of the larger Kluane / Wrangell- St. Elias / Glacier Bay / Tatshenshini-Alsek. Wrangell-St. Elias is the largest park in the United States at 13.2 million acres comparable to the size of Yellowstone National Park, Yosemite National Park, and the country of Switzerland combined or another comparison six times the size of Yellowstone National Park. It rises from sea level to 18,008 feet (5,489 m). So, my three miles didn't scratch the surface of visiting this beautiful environmental haven of peaks, glaciers, rivers and streams. According to the National Park Service, it is also a recreational haven in addition to hiking the mountains, one can float the rivers, ski the glaciers, or fly over the landscape. I'm sure fishing in the rivers and streams is part of that list too.

There are also two vehicle tours: Nabesna Road, which starts at mile 60 of Glen Highway in the town of Slana and can take three hours roundtrip and the other is McCarthy Road which starts at mile 33 Edgerton Highway, in Chitina which can take four hours roundtrip. The National Park Service provides maps and audio CDs too. Camping and public-use cabins are also available. A real treat is the

Kennecott Mines National Historic Landmark, a well-preserved mine from the early 1900s to learn the processes for obtaining, concentrating, and shipping copper ore out of the Alaskan Wilderness. The mine operated from 1901-1938 and spawned a small self-sufficient town of Kennecott with a hospital, general store, school, skating rink, tennis court, recreation hall, and dairy for a labor force of 600 people.

The park service website recommends observers to *position yourself in one spot and watch sun, clouds, and storms play hide and seek with single peaks or ridges.*[106] I stood at a good overview spot to the mountain range across the valley watching the cloud cover change displaying in minutes differences in visible parts of the range. My pictures show variations in what was visible every few minutes. There's no other word to describe the park than unspoiled grandeur with four major mountain ranges meeting and nine of the 16 highest peaks in the United States. I need to revisit this park and spend a week, maybe staying in one of the cabins to get up-close and personal with the landscape and wildlife. The Wrangell's mountains have volcanic origins but only Mount Wrangell remains active with its last eruption in 1900.

National Geographic also recognized the unique flora and fauna of this mammoth landscape in their *Destinations of a Lifetime* assessment, including unique glaciers. *Roughly a quarter of the park is covered in glaciers, including several record holders. Nabesna, stretching more than 75 miles (121 km), is the world's longest interior valley glacier. The gargantuan Bagley Icefield is 127 miles (204 km) long and up to 3,000 feet (914 m) thick. The continent's largest piedmont glacier, Malaspina is more than 60 times bigger than Manhattan Island.*[107] From this description, one can appreciate the vastness of isolated landscape that Alaska provides from nature. Only about 50 people reside in the park year-round living in the small town of McCarthy.

I returned to the lodge in time for the Alaska pipeline tour. The more official term is Trans-Alaska Pipeline System (TAPS), an oil transportation system spanning Alaska that includes the pipeline, 12 pumping stations, several hundred miles of feeder pipelines, and the Valdez Marine Terminal. TAPS is the world's largest pipeline. The 48-inch diameter duct runs above and below ground depending on the ground and environmental conditions. The pipeline connects the oil fields of Prudhoe Bay in the north to the harbor at Valdez in the south, measuring 800 miles (1300 km). The concept of the pipeline goes back to President Richard Nixon signing the Trans-Alaska Pipeline Authorization Act into law on November 16, 1973. I was only thirteen years old at the time, but I still remember the controversy depicted in the media. Environmentalists saw it as doom and gloomy. Construction began on the $8 billion pipeline on March 27, 1975, and completed on May 31, 1977, with oil flowing by June 20, 1977, but didn't arrive in Valdez until July 28 due to mechanical problems.

In 1989, the Exxon Valdez tanker ran aground in Prince

William Sound spilling oil in the water; thus, validating environmentalist's concerns. Pictures of oil-slicked sea birds and otters flooded the media, alarming all the dangers imposed on the Arctic. The largest spill associated directly with the pipeline occurred in 2006 when a transit pipe at the British Petroleum Prudhoe Bay facility ruptured. Although this was much smaller than the Exxon Valdez spill, more than a quarter million gallons of oil spilled onto the tundra; production was reduced to half while engineers replaced the corroded pipe.

My combination of engineering and project management background is enticed by this topic, just fascinating. I'm sure that incident was a lesson learned for preventative maintenance and inspections to ensure the replacement of fittings before they become a problem. Engineers not only design new equipment and systems but are also responsible for the sustainment of what they design. Maintenance and logistics must be considered in the original design and not added as an afterthought.

Our guide who lives in Fairbanks informed us that every Alaska resident, including children, receives a check every year, usually a couple thousand dollars, from the profits of the pipeline. My presumption is that the payment affords TAPS management buy-in from the residential community. As we drove from Fairbanks to the Copper River area, the pipeline was visible many times, diminishing the natural beauty of the land. I don't believe that there are funds being saved from profits to pay for the removal of the pipeline once it has served its purpose and reached its end-of-life. Who will get that bill, the Alaska state taxpayers or the United States' federal taxpayers, through a Congressional allocation? Or will the antiquated pipeline merely corrode for centuries until it reunites with Mother Earth.

After the pipeline tour, which was thought-provoking, I had a great cheeseburger in the hotel bar. I then watched the northern lights symphony-panoramic show in a conference room in the hotel. I had been primed to see the northern lights but so far, they were elusive, even with the northern light's *wakeup call* established. When in Alaska and anywhere else the northern lights show their mesmerizing display, check with the reception desk if they have northern lights or aurora borealis *wake-up notification*. If the lights are visible, you will be called; it will probably be early in the morning, like 1:00-3:00 am. Unfortunately, cloud cover deterred visibility even when conditions were possible in the area. I have a specific *northern lights trip to Iceland* booked for February 2024, so 11 days in Iceland should entice the aurora borealis display for at least one or two nights. If this event is on your bucket list, then maximize your planning for a destination and timeframe that best fits conditions. It requires a little research and front-end planning.

We had an early departure, so our luggage needed to be out at 10:00 pm the previous night. We drove to Valdez port and boarded a very large catamaran to sail across Prince William

Sound to Whittier to board the cruise ship. Unfortunately, we had rain during the catamaran ride so there was not much bird activity in the sound. The boat's coordinator pointed out the location where the Exxon Valdez had come aground. I remember hearing the reports but sailing in the sound now just made everything more understandable of the severity and appreciation for the large cleanup effort. As I mentioned above, on March 24, 1989, the oil tanker Exxon Valdez ran aground in the Sound spilling 11 million gallons of oil. It was one of the largest environmental disasters in United States history. Exxon settled in 1991 with funds disbursed in three parts: criminal plea agreement was $25 million, criminal restitution was $100 million, and civil settlement was $900 million. The spill affected more than 1,300 miles of shoreline with devastating impacts on fish, wildlife, their habitats, and local industries and communities. The oil killed an estimated 250,000 seabirds, 2,800 sea otters, 300 harbor seals, 250 bald eagles, 22 killer whales, and billions of salmon and herring eggs.[108]

Based on 2020, the following species remain classified as not recovering or unknown: killer whales, kittlitz's murrelets, marbled murrelets, and pigeon guillemots. I've never heard of a murrelet or a guillemot. The settlement funds were used for multiple restoration and protection projects throughout Prince William Sound, the Gulf of Alaska, and for habitats outside of Alaska that are important for migratory species. The settlement funds and matching funds from numerous restoration, research, and monitoring programs have protected more than 600,000 acres of land. The current restoration activities are focused on long-term herring research and monitoring, long-term monitoring of marine conditions and injured resources, short-term harbor protection and restoration projects, lingering oil, habitat protection, and long-term monitoring of marine conditions and restoration effectiveness which will be an on-going effort. This negligent accident spawned a legislative response in the passage of the Oil Pollution Act of 1990, which led to the establishment of National Oceanic & Atmospheric Administration (NOAA)'s Damage Assessment, Remediation, Restoration Program (DARRP). Besides the changes to NOAA, a Regional Citizens Advisory Group was established as a watchdog to the oil industry, changes were made in tanker design for double hull, and escort tows requirements were added within the sound. Safety requirements have significantly improved since the spill.

Once at Whittier, it took about 30 minutes for the boarding process. There were a few dining restaurant options, so we decided to alternate the dining experience. That evening, it was Pacific Moon with reservations made for International Dining the next night. The ship left port at 8:00 pm so there was considerable time to settle into the cabin and wander about the ship.

The first night I went to the comedy show and settled into bed by 10:15 pm. Cruise ships are an all-you-can-eat-feast, and we also had all you can drink, so I needed to counter all the food and drink calories with exercise. I got up at 6:30 am and went to the ship's gym for a 20-minute elliptical workout. After breakfast, I attended the nature show at 9:00 am. We cruised through Hubbard Bay observing the Hubbard Glacier in the afternoon while it occasionally drizzled. In the evening, I watched the *Fisherman's Show* which showed a clip from the television show *Deadliest Catch* in which the ship was rolled by a large wave. The speaker had worked on that ship but decided to make a career change.

The next day, I thought I'd try Tai Chi at 7:15 am; it's all about the movement or slow movement I should say. Afterward, we entered Glacier Bay around 9:00 am and shortly after had a presentation by the National Park Service rangers. The most significant glacier observance occurred between 1:15 pm-3:00 pm. At the top of the bay, the ship turned around and proceeded back down. Glacier Bay National Park comprises the bay and surrounding land with the visitor center located at the mouth by the town of Gustavus. There are no roads that lead to the park.

The park covers 3.3 million acres of rugged mountains, vibrant glaciers, temperate rainforests, remote coastlines, and deep sheltered fjords. The UNESCO World Heritage Site includes 25-million acres encompassing Kluane/Wrangell-St.Elias /Glacier Bay/ Tatshenshini-Alsek, one of the largest international protected areas, of which Glacier Bay is a portion. Two rangers boarded the ship and described the passage through the bay and the sea life activity in the water.

We couldn't have had a better sailing day. Picture the scene. The temperature was about 50 degrees F but very sunny. The outside deck rails packed with passengers in awe of the beautiful surroundings. A few people soaking in the outside hot tubs, drinking and laughing. The ranger's voice booming over the public announcement system describing the landscape and taking note of the sea otters and harbor seals playing alongside the ship. We were all thinking: *life just doesn't get any better than this.*

There was a show on bears or to be more accurate *how to protect yourself from bears* in the late afternoon. Their advice was similar to the guidance depicted in the movie *A Walk in the Woods* with Robert Redford and Nick Nolte when a bear enters their campsite. Make yourself as big as you can and make a lot of noise. Wave your arms. I just hoped that I wouldn't need to use the advice on this trip. We tried the Santa Fe restaurant for dinner watching the end of a 1950-60s song trivia game for the night's entertainment.

After two days of glacier bay cruising, we docked in Skagway. One of the many films that I watched while in Alaska talked about the Gold Rush and the creation of the two towns, Skagway and Dyea. Prospectors sailed to these towns to make their way to the Yukon. Most did not find gold, and many did not survive the Chilkoot or White Pass trails to the Yukon River. The Klondike Gold Rush National Historical Park Visitor Center, the original 1898 White Pass & Yukon

Route Depot, in downtown Skagway is on Broadway Avenue, and features ranger programs, a theater, and numerous displays, including an impressive replica of the ton of supplies every miner was required to carry over the Chilkoot Pass.

Although now a ghost town, Dyea still serves as the starting point for hikes on the famous 33-mile Chilkoot Trail, one of the most popular backpacking routes in Alaska. This scenic trail takes about three to four days to complete, taking hikers along the route that gold seekers followed from Dyea to Lake Bennet, British Columbia.

We signed up for the City Tour and Summit excursion which started at 8:00 am; however, with a delay arriving in Skagway, we didn't leave the ship until 8:30 am missing the tour. The tour group upgraded our tour to include travel to Yukon for an afternoon departure. We shopped for a couple of hours and then grabbed lunch. In all three cruise ports, jewelry stores are plentiful. In Skagway, tanzanite and Alaska sapphire are the jewels of choice. Where is tanzanite found? Its name provides the answer: Tanzania. I'm not sure why the focus of Alaska jewelry stores is on a gem from Tanzania. Possibly, blue is equated with the bluish color of glaciers and Alaska's inside passage has spectacular glaciers.

We left at 12:30 pm for a three-and-a-half-hour van ride. Occasionally drizzling, we still could disembark the van and take pictures. There were lots of lakes and the summit pass. After learning the story of the gold rush prospectors, it was very interesting being in this area. Unfortunately, the desire to strike it rich motivated people to travel thousands of miles to discover extremely harsh conditions, for most acquiring nothing for their efforts. Very few ever found gold, and many died along the way. The peak of the trip was the Yukon sign, but we needed to cross the border into Canada to snap that picture. An easy border crossing, we merely showed our passports.

Sailing overnight, we arrived in Juneau the next morning. Here we were walking to a glacier, probably the most famous North American glacier, Mendenhall Glacier in the national forest. It drizzled most of the morning; Alaska in September is a rainy time. I hiked to the waterfalls next to the glacier which is a mile walk each way. The views are stunning.

Mendenhall Glacier is a blue ice sheet 12 miles (19 km) long in southeastern Alaska. It was originally named Sitaantaagu ("the Glacier Behind the Town") or Aak'wtaaksit ("the Glacier Behind the Little Lake") by the Tlingit Indians. Naturalist John Muir later called it Auke (Auk) Glacier, for the Auk Kwaan band of Tlingit Indians. In 1892 it was renamed for Thomas Corwin Mendenhall of the United States Coast and Geodetic Survey, who helped determine the boundary between Canada and Alaska.[109]

Oh no, it looks like the potential for another naming controversary. At least in this case, the glacier was named for someone who was actually connected with the site or surrounding area.

A trip to Juneau must include a drive out to the glacier; the town grew up around tourism for it. I still can't fathom how a State Capitol can only have water or air access, no roads lead to Juneau. The same is true for our next destination, Ketchikan. Usually, there are salmon in the stream near the parking lot, but it was too late in the season. After returning to the ship, I watched presentations on dog sledding and a nature show on flowers, trees, and birds. Tonight, we tried the Savoy restaurant with a special meal of steak and lobster accompanied with bearnaise sauce. I usually don't eat or like lobster, but it was smothered in bearnaise sauce and delicious. The appetizer was salmon chowder.

The next day brought our arrival in Ketchikan and a driving tour of the area to include a stop at Ketchikan Creek where ghost salmon were plentiful, another stop further along the creek where bears hang out (no bears our day), and Saxman Village known for totem pole making. Ghost salmon or zombie salmon are those close to death. The life cycle of salmon is amazing!

Set in motion at birth, the fate of Pacific salmon is like clockwork: each year a new generation returns from sea to spawn and then death. Pacific salmon spawn only once per lifetime. *As they make their final journey home, their silver sides blush as pigments that give their flesh its appetizing red hue move to their skin. The fat that mottles their tasty fillets burns up as females become vessels for plump, fatty eggs — for both sexes, fat stored in their muscles and livers is totally used up by the time they reach the spawning grounds. They grind their tails into the gravel, hoping to make deep-enough nests that withstand the scour of ice and spring floods. Males tap into their reserves to grow fearsome teeth and hooked upper jaws that they use against each other.*[110]

Nature is just amazing. I wonder how Darwin would interpret the salmon's circle of life.

All three ports reflect original fishing villages with charming wooden houses, renovated to be Alaskan tourist locations for cruise stoppage. On our cruise, we shared the ports with other companies' cruise ships. When the ships are in port, the town is packed. The local people we met were a combination of born and raised in Alaska or moved to Alaska for wilderness life. That night, we tried the Savoy Restaurant again and had beef wellington. My evening entertainment was the Fusion Club and solo dancing to the live music at the back of the room.

We had a day at sea before we arrived in Vancouver, and we disembarked. There were two informative shows presented, one on glaciers and the other on the ship's navigation. The National Geographic definition of glaciers: *Glaciers are large, thick masses of ice that form on land when fallen snow gets compressed into ice over many centuries.*[111] Most glaciers today date back to the Ice Age, ending more than 10,000 years ago. Glaciologists, those who study glaciers, closely monitor the size and shape of glaciers to determine impacts of climate change. Pictures over decades reflect whether glaciers are receding.

In January 2023, my trip to Patagonia largely dealt with observing glaciers from land and sea. For most glaciers, they have been shrinking documented through pictures. This is the case at Mendenhall Glacier in Juneau and Grey Glacier in Torres del Paine, Chile at opposite ends of the America's. One at the top of North America and the other at the bottom of South America. As cited in the chapter on Patagonia, in 2019 at Grey Glacier, the alarm was sounded when two huge icebergs broke off the glacier. One was the size of 12 soccer fields. The second occurred 15 days later. The previous large detachment occurred in 2017 and before those dates to the 1990s, so the increased frequency of these massive chunks warrants the alarm.

Although scientists believe most are shrinking around the world and within the Andes of South America even faster, Petito Moreno Glacier in Argentina is not and may be growing. An unusual phenomenon as scientists struggle to understand the impacts of climate change. I described this amazing visit in the chapter on Patagonia too.

Our gastro-dining experience featured a return to the Pacific Moon restaurant for dinner. The following morning was organized mayhem with the disembarking process in Vancouver. I felt we were at the front-end of the mass exodus, since we had a city tour of Vancouver scheduled and needed to be in the first group to disembark. The tour conveniently started by the cruise terminal and took our luggage with us on the ride. Downtown was a tour of Stanley Park and then to Grimmel Island for lunch on our own and the market for shopping. From every direction, seaplanes were landing and taking off in Vancouver harbor; what a treat to watch. I need to add a seaplane flight to my bucket list activities. At the completion of the tour, we were dropped off at our hotel in the Richmond area outside Vancouver.

The next day, we were picked up at the hotel at 8:30 am for a trip to Victoria on Vancouver Island. We were the last stop with others starting the day an hour before in the downtown section of the city. This is an all-day, 13-hour trip, so a long day. The first stop was the ferry in which our tour coach boarded the ferry too. Passengers cannot stay in their vehicles, so we disembarked and went upstairs for the stunning sights across the Strait of Georgia. Water seems to equate to tranquility; it's hard to be frazzled when looking out over the sun-glinted sea. A cafeteria is available for food, but it became very busy, very fast with those hungry for breakfast. The trip was about an hour and a half. We were then on our own to walk around Victoria and have lunch, a strikingly beautiful city with quaint English architecture and an international flair.

It was the Gold Rush that put Victoria on the map. In 1858 when gold was discovered on the Fraser River there were roughly 500 people in the town but within two months the population swelled to 30,000. The city has become home to

Canada's western naval base and a major fishing fleet. It has a successful information technology sector combined with other large industries of marine, forestry, and agricultural research.

How did Canada come under British rule to lay the foundation for a Victorian-style city? As a result of the Seven Years' War and conflict with France, France seceded Canada to Great Britain in 1763. It was 1867 when Great Britain united three of its colonies: Canada, Nova Scotia, and New Brunswick into a Dominion of Canada. On July 21, 1871, British Columbia became the sixth province of the Dominion of Canada and Victoria became its capital. As a British dominion, Canada was free to act like its own country with its own laws, parliament, and financial independence, and responsibility for defense. The American colonies did not have the same relationship and fell under full British rule, thus promoting the American Revolution for full independence.

In 1931, the Statute of Westminster gave dominions full legal freedom and equal standing with Great Britain placing Canada comparable to other Commonwealth countries. However, it was not until 1982 that Canada adopted its own constitution and became a truly independent country. It is still part of the British Commonwealth, thus a constitutional monarchy that accepts the British monarch, King Charles III. The role is merely ceremonial and does not affect Canadian self-governance.

Our next stop was Buchart Gardens, a must for a trip to

Victoria. What started as a cement business, turned into a beautiful garden by the wife of entrepreneur Robert Buchart. The Buchart family moved from Ontario to Vancouver Island to build a cement plant on a limestone quarry. As the quarry was depleted, Jennie Buchart, wife of Robert, envisioned transforming the quarry into a lovely garden. Butchart Gardens is still family-run today and is a Canadian National Historic Site. There are over 900 varieties of plants to see and smell as one wonders around the 55-acre property. We arrived back at our hotel at 9:15 pm but the other passengers were much later for their return.

It was a morning flight at 8:55 am but was delayed to 9:15 am and then changed again to 10:30 am. I was concerned about our connecting flight in Montreal, so I got in line at the gate with most of the passengers on the flight to determine the impact of the delay.

Evidently, the flight crew had arrived later than expected and still needed to rest before embarking on another flight, therefore shifting the schedule.

While waiting in line at the gate, I encountered a rather *good news human interest story*. A woman standing a couple of people behind me in the queue was trying to ask the woman in front of her why we were standing in line. Although from Romania, she spoke Hungarian and very little English. The communication wasn't going well. I offered that there are apps for translating. Both the woman trying to help and her husband had difficulty getting an internet connection in the airport. I also experienced no luck with an internet connection.

We heard the young gentlemen behind the Romanian woman speaking a foreign language and asked if they happened to know Hungarian. They were speaking Flemish and did not know Hungarian; however, they jumped in to assist. They were able to get internet and using the language translation app let the woman know that the flight was delayed. These two men in their twenties went the extra mile by calling the woman's son who she was visiting in Vancouver. The son was first concerned and then relieved to learn about the flight delay and that his mother had someone assisting her. One of the gentlemen went with the woman to the gate assistant to check if the delayed flight impacted her connecting flight, still with the son on the phone.

When I got home, I conveyed the story to my son and asked if he and his friends would have provided the same incredible assistance. I got a rather perplexed look and then he said, *I'm not sure.* I responded that I would like to believe that he would and gave him a rather determined look. The world is a better place when we reach out to help each other regardless of where we were born or currently live.

For me, there will be other trips to Alaska in the future. With a total of eight national parks, I've only visited three, so I still have five left on my bucket list. Most are not very accessible, some only by boat or airplane. Besides the national parks, there are state parks and truly unique quaint towns and villages. My bucket list wouldn't be complete without a northern lights' expedition and maybe a polar bear excursion too.

During the trip, I visited parts of the Kluane/Wrangell-St. Elias/Glacier Bay/Tatshenshini-Alsek, a UNESCO World Heritage Site in Alaska. I also visited three United States National Parks: Denali National Park, Wrangell-St. Elias National Park, and Glacier Bay National Park, some substantial bucket list checking. Although I acquired a few views of the elusive Denali Mountain, I unfortunately did not see a brown bear catching salmon, a classic vision associated with Alaska. A flight on a seaplane is also a bucket list must for the future. Dog sledding in the snow is also probably high on my bucket list too. Hopefully, another week or two in Alaska will bring a check to viewing the Northern Lights.

Anchorage

Denali Mountain

Buchart Gardens

ATV riding near Denali

Alaska menu options

moose warning sign

Site of former glacier

Alaska pipeline

Glacier Bay National Park

Mendenhall Glacier and Nugget Falls   the magic of clouds-Inner Passage

Chapter 13

Spain and France

Culture is the arts elevated to a set of beliefs –
Thomas Wolfe
(https://www.brainyquote.com/topics/culture-quotes)

Background: History, Culture, and Environment

Hola mi amiga y amigo. Bonjour mon ami.

Although I visited the northern part of France earlier in July 2023, this trip incorporated a combination of northeast Spain and southwest France generating different landscape and cultural aspects than experienced in other parts of both countries. It's also home to a couple of routes of the Camino de Santiago.

Spain is a constitutional monarchy, but it was not always that way. From 1939 to 1975, Spain was ruled by a dictator with the title Caudillo, a warlord or powerful military leader. That title was bestowed upon General Francisco Franco, probably by himself, who ruled as a dictator in every sense. Although Spain largely stayed on the sidelines during World War II, Franco had started negotiations with Germany's Adolf Hitler after the fall of France. Spain's feigned neutrality kept it shielded from the Allies purge of the Axis power throughout

Europe.

Franco's legacy is marked with controversy. Although the nature of his dictatorship improved over time, he is still responsible for the brutal repression of the Spanish people and the deaths of tens of thousands. He would bring economic prosperity to the country and gain a better relationship with Western countries when becoming more distant with the Soviet Union and the communist philosophy during the Cold War period. His leadership produced a highly centralized government and national Catholicism. In 1969, Franco selected Juan Carlos de Borbón, the grandson of King Alfonso XIII, to succeed him as head of state. When Franco died in 1975, Juan Carlos was crowned King Juan Carlos I and initiated a process for transition to democracy that within three years replaced the Francoist system with a democratic constitution.

The trip also included the wine country of France. There are six Bordeaux varietals: Cabernet Sauvignon, Merlot, Cabernet Franc, Petit Verdot, Malbec, and occasionally Carménère. A Bordeaux blend is made from combining these grapes producing unique characteristics for wine products. Knowing that both Bordeaux and Burgundy are regions within France, I was curious if there is a difference in the wines. Bordeaux is produced in a predominantly oceanic or Atlantic environment while Burgundy is a continental climate.

Bordeaux wines are distinguished by their bold textures

and powerful flavours which, while strong, don't overpower the palate. The wines of Burgundy are often the polar opposite: soft, elegant and unquestionably complex.[112]

I'll need to add a trip to the Burgundy area to complete my French wine education.

Pairing foods with wines achieves a cuisine triumph. So, what is a good dish to serve with Bordeaux wine? One source suggests steak frites or steak and duck fat fries. The boldness of the Bordeaux complements the flavor in the meat and the wine's tannins are subdued by the dish's fat content. The combination of the two produces the wine to taste sweet and fruity with the robust meat flavor, the perfect duo. Other meats that would be acceptable: black pepper steak, roast pork, filet mignon, beef brisket, buffalo burgers, chicken liver, pot roast, venison, goose, and dark turkey meat. Yes, they are all pretty savory meats.

Red Bordeaux wines should be stored below 65 degrees F and served just below room temperature around 65 degrees F. It is recommended to decant the bottle for at least 30 minutes. There is a wine museum, Cité du Vin, in Bordeaux which can answer all one's questions about wine around the world.

The Rioja region in northeast Spain is the primary wine-producing region with some 600 wineries. The Camino or Santiago del Compostela pilgrimage skirts through this area. Our tour also visited Barcelona known for Cava, Spain's most famous sparkling wine. The Catalonia region holds 90 percent of cava production comprised between Barcelona and Tarragona.

Paella is considered Spain's national dish, a saffron-flavored rice dish from Valencia. Although the traditional recipe uses rabbit and vegetables, it can be made with other variations such as vegetarian, fish and seafood, and meat and fish, or just meat. Gazpacho is a cold vegetable soup that originated in Andalucia.

It contains tomatoes, cucumbers, peppers, and olive oil. It is a perfect soup for the summer, when most hot soups are craved in the winter. Croquetas are also a popular tapas dish made from ham, chicken, and cod. Churros are fried dough pastry coated with cinnamon sugar and usually served with a dipping sauce. Don't be surprised to see churros available at any street vendor in the country.

Since I already covered France for the Fund for Peace Fragile State Index in an earlier chapter, I'll just provide comments for Spain with a ranking slightly better than the United States at 143rd with a score of 44. Its two problem areas were fractionalized elites and group grievance, the same as the United States. Although all factors can have an impact on tourism, social factors tend to be depicted in unrest and publicized by the media. With the Camino de Santiago pilgrimage traversing several areas of the northern part of Spain, the country hosts many wanderers with merely a backpack and possibly hostel reservations. These bohemians come in all walks of life, both richer and poorer. The safety of these wanderers is paramount to the hiking tourism industry. One can only hope that Spain will improve its standing because it is a beautiful country with delectable cuisine; tourism will continue to grow if tourists do not have travel concerns. With respect to its State Resilience Index, a score of 7.3 almost matches the United States' score of 7.4. The same two areas of environment and ecology and social cohesion were near average with the other indicators well above average.

Travel Itinerary

Although the tour advertised history, culture, and wine, the emphasis is on art. My trip encompassed Barcelona, Spain (five nights); Carcassonne, France (two nights); Bordeaux, France (two nights); Bilbao, Spain (two nights), and Madrid, Spain (two nights) with stops in Girona, Spain; Figueres, Spain; Toulouse, France; Biarritz, France; San Sabastian, Spain; and Rioja, Spain.

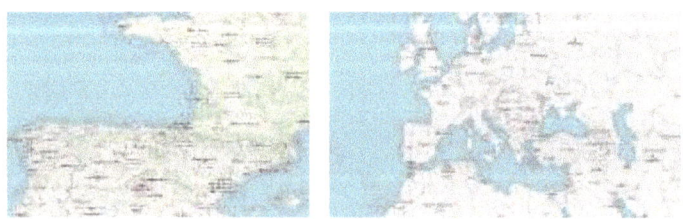

https://free-map.org/

Travel Journal

This tour was a combination of history, culture, and wine, which is typical for a visit to Spain and France, a combination of all three activities. Although I had been to Paris a decade earlier and experienced the Northern France adventure earlier in the year, this tour focused on the Bordeaux region, the southwestern part of France. Knowing that Barcelona is an essential city to visit, I arranged to arrive two days early to explore the city and surrounding areas that would not be part of the arranged tour. Montserrat was essential for my bucket list.

It was another flight from JFK Airport making the reverse planes/trains/automobiles mode of travel. The flight out of JFK left about 5:00 pm and landed in Barcelona at 6:30 am the next morning. This was the first trip arriving so early and getting to the hotel at 8:30 am even with a short drive into Barcelona in the rain and rush hour traffic. The hotel staff said they would do their best to get us a room before noon. Not having slept on the seven-hour plane ride, I arrived exhausted and ready to crash into bed to recover for a few hours.

We found a couple of sofas in the back area of the hotel and tried to catch a few winks there. The hotel staff did not appreciate our nap choice, although sympathetic to our sleep deprivation. They wanted us to move to another area and not sleep. It felt like déjà vu, didn't I have this same experience in Paris. I get it, a four-star hotel does not want to look like they are a hostel for wayward travelers. Note to self again to look at the arrival times and determine if I need to add a night before so that I can immediately get into my room. That first day can make all the difference for allowing the body to recover and make the next few days more enjoyable, not recovering from jet lag. We were able to check-in at 11:00 am after having breakfast in the hotel restaurant, slept for a few hours, and then walked locally for dinner.

On the morning of the first full day in Barcelona, I ventured to see one of Antoni Gaudí's architectural wonders. Although I had not been familiar with his work, one sight of Pedrera (Casa Mila), and I understood the artistic interest and why Barcelona is synonymous with Gaudí. Fortunately, it was only a couple blocks from the hotel. The striking exterior design had to have driven the city government crazy when built from 1906-1912. The easiest way to describe it would be a mansion for Fred Flintstone, the popular stone-age cartoon television show from the 1960's. Pedrera means stone quarry in Catalan and the house lives up to its name. Salvador Dali rented an apartment to be part of the striking architectural transformation of its time and his time. Only the apartments that were used by the Mila family on the top floor are open for public visits, but the rooftop alone is worth the view.

For that afternoon, I previously reserved an excursion to Montserrat through an independent tour group that provided hotel pickup. Although many tour groups offered trips to Montserrat, few had hotel pickups. Since I was new to Barcelona, I decided not to navigate public transportation or anticipate travel time in the city for a taxi on my first full day. The hotel pickup option meant just being in the lobby at a certain time. For future trips to Barcelona, I would be more inclined to explore public transportation options from the beginning.

The legend of the Monastery of Montserrat, *montserrat* means serrated mountain, dates to 880 AD. Shepherds were working in the mountain when they saw a light from a cave and heard music playing. When they approached, they found a sculpture of the Virgin Mary. The shepherds sought a priest and confided in their discovery. When the priest returned with the shepherds, they attempted to take the statue to the town. However, the statue had other plans; with every step, the statue became heavier causing them to abandon the endeavor. The men interpreted that the statue did not want to leave the mountain. It was eight years later that the small chapel of Santa Cova was built, and the statue placed inside. It took a century for the word to spread and interest to develop. In 1025, Abbott Oliva of Ripoll decided to establish a Benedictine monastery close to the cave.

If you've heard of the Caribbean Island called Montserrat, have you wondered if it had anything to do with the monastery? Well, yes it does. Montserrat friar Bernat de Boil sailed with Christopher Columbus on his second trip to America and gave the island the name. Pope Jules II, Guiliano della Rovere, was previously an abbot of Montserrat and sponsored the construction of the monastery cloister.

Coincidently, this Pope also commissioned Michaelangelo to paint the Sixtine Chapel.

In 1808 Napoleon invaded Spain causing the monks to flee to Mallorca taking with them their religious treasures. The Spanish Army occupied the monastery using it as a military warehouse. Napoleon would eventually take control of the monastery, only to set it on fire. Napoleon relinquished Spain in 1813 signing the peace treaty returning the crown to the Spanish King Ferdinand VII.

After the king passed away, Queen Maria Cristina became regent and her Minister of Finance Mr. Mendizabal signed the famous law of Desamortizaciones, seizing the assets of the Catholic Church which included the ruins of the abandoned Monastery of Montserrat. A group of Catalan monks returned to the monastery gradually rebuilding the holy mountain site. Even architect Antoni Gaudi participated in its renewal by decorating one of the stations of the cross on the path to the Santa Cova Chapel.

Montserrat is the second most visited pilgrimage center in Spain after Santiago de Compostela. The Camino Catalán, also known as the Catalan Way or Camí de Sant Jaume in Catalan, takes pilgrims from the Mediterranean coast in Catalonia to La Rioja, where they join the famous Camino Frances (French Way) to continue their journey to Santiago de Compostela. There are several pilgrimage paths to Santiago del Compostela or the Saint James Church, from France, Spain, and Portugal. There's even a shortened Spanish

Camino starting in Sarria for about a week's walk for those who like the concept but don't have four to six weeks to spend on the longer Camino trails. That might be a good trail for me to start with only a week walking.

We had a few people in the van for the tour. There were two couples that had flown to Barcelona for a cruise and decided to do the tour before boarding the boat. They had arrived that morning from the United States with little sleep just like me the day before. I was amazed they were able to make it through the afternoon still awake and functioning, when all were a few years older than myself. My hat goes off to those travelers because I wouldn't have been able to make it the day before. I barely made it to the 11:00 am early check-in time for the hotel. What made this flight more challenging for recovery was the total lack of sleep. Other long flights, when I had only a few hours of sleep, made a significant difference between being conscious and a walking zombie.

It took about an hour to drive to the mountain and the journey up the mountain was a bit hair-raising at times. Once there, potential activities include touring the basilica, a small but impressive art museum, hiking around the mountain area to include a path to the cross that overlooks the town below, and a funicular up to the top of the mountain, as well as one that travels down the mountain to the town below. Most arranged tours are planned for half a day, which limits activities to maybe one or two. On our day, fog embraced the top of the mountain so rather than waste time on the funicular, I toured the art museum after a short tour of the basilica. The basilica houses the famed statue of the Black Madonna.

Although a remote location, the impressive collection at the art museum contained paintings from Pablo Picasso, *The Old Fisherman* and *Altar Boy*; Claude Monet, *Failaise Porte d'Aval par gros temps*; Edgar Degas, *Unhappy Nelly*; and Salvador Dali, *Neocubist Aacademy*. This left only a few minutes to grab a sandwich and eat before heading to the meeting point to return to Barcelona. For those into hiking, arranging your own transportation for drop off and pickup for the lower funicular is most practical. There is a hotel and hostel on the mountain which are often utilized by those walking the pilgrimage route to Santiago de Compostela, Camino de Santiago.

On day three, I visited another Gaudí stunning dwelling along the Paseo de Gracia, Casa Batllo. This house has an aquatic theme and is quite a contrast with Pedrera down the street. The exterior is a mosaic of color with a dragon positioned along the rooftop. Touring the house requires climbing several levels of stairs but it is worth the exercise. There is a small elevator for those challenged with stairs. Audio sets provide a description as one travels through the home.

On the morning of day four, we took the public bus to visit Parc Guell, a park designed by Gaudí. Unfortunately, the park was sold out for the day and when checking the itinerary for our trip that night, we already had a visit to the park included later in the week. Shame on me for not checking and re-checking the itinerary. The morning wasn't a total loss in that we went shopping. We also toured Casa Vicens, Guidi's first house built conveniently on the way back to the hotel.

The highlight of Barcelona was the tour of La Sagrada Familia, Guidi's masterpiece, first started in 1882 by a previous architect but then transferred to Gaudí in 1884. Stunning is the only word to describe both the outside and inside. Tickets for the inside can be sold out six months in advance. So, if planning an independent trip to Barcelona, give yourself plenty of time to reserve tickets or if using a group tour, ensure the tour includes an interior visit. One would not want to miss seeing the inside of La Sagrada Familia on a trip to this magnificent city. Barcelona has a lot to offer tourists, and a hop-on/hop-off bus outing provides a good overview. Our tour included a coach tour of the Montjuic recreational area housing the National Palace and the central pavilion for the 1929 International Exhibition. Montjuic is home to the 1992 Summer Olympic complex.

Below is a list of the top Antoni Gaudi buildings in Barcelona[113]

- Casa Milà
- Casa Battló
- Casa Vicens
- Park Güell
- Palau Güell

- Colonia Güell

- Sagrada Familia

- Torre Bellesguard

- Casa Calvet

- Colegio Teresiano de Barcelona

At the El Born Centre de Cultura I Memoria, an archeological site in the Borne area of Barcelona, one walks around the visible ruins of the city within the enclosure where parts of the city were destroyed by war. As a nice touch to this group tour, we experienced a group cooking class with our tour mates just a short walk away. So early in the trip made this activity more of a group icebreaker. Part of the group jumped to volunteer for cooking tasks while a few appeared reluctant to pick up the chopping knife. I heard a few grumblings from people who said they don't really cook, including my travel mate. Wine and beer were served during the cooking class and a few participants remained near the refreshments, mostly men. But not all men, some were very savvy when it came to mixing ingredients and stirring pots and pans. This wasn't their first time cooking.

We all had to wear aprons which became a bonding experience, multiple photos taken will deny any doubt of their participation. The menu was Spanish Traditional Gazpacho, Spanish Potato and Onion Omelet, Seafood Paella, Bread and Tomato, and Crema Catalana for dessert. There was a vegetarian version of Paella for the non- seafood diners. This was the first time that I experienced a cooking class as part of a group tour. I arranged separately for the cooking class in Naples while in Italy, which can be an option in some cities. As mentioned previously, adding days at the beginning or end of an organized tour allows one to take advantage of separate activities like a cooking class or well-known sightseeing spots.

From Barcelona, we headed north to Carcassonne, France with a stop in Girona (about 60 miles or 96.6 km away) and Figueres. Girona is northern Catalonia's largest city and one of Spain's most historic sites. A medieval city founded by the Romans but later taken over by the Moors and Franks before falling under Barcelona rule. The city resides next to the Onyar River which has become a shallow creek. The few remaining large fish in the river were swimming on their sides to stay under water. Aside from the shallow river, the city is rather upscale. According to our guide, several spots in the city were used for filming the sixth season of *Game of Thrones*.

One can even find a *Game of Thrones* tour by checking online tour companies. A walking tour takes you to the Jewish Quarter, one of the best preserved in the world dating with Jewish inhabitants from 982 to 1492. This area is called El Call with a maze of narrow, winding, cobblestoned streets that have stood the test of time. There is a Jewish Museum for those seeking more information. The Cathedral of Saint Mary interior has the widest Gothic vane in the world with a width of 75 feet (23 m).

Although both Girona and Figueres were part of our group tour through Spain and France, independent tour groups offer these one-day trips out of Barcelona, or one can take the high-speed train from Barcelona to Girona. From Girona, we headed north in our touring coach to Figueres, located about 16 miles (26 km) from the French border in the foothills of the Pyrenees Mountains. Salvador Felipe Jacinto Dalí y Domenech or just Salvador Dali established a museum in a local theater in his birthplace of Figueres. Dali's work encompasses the revolutionary, artistic creation of that generation in the 1920-30s. If you've ever seen pictures of melting watches, then you have seen one of Dali's iconic works, *The Persistence of Memory.*

Although he tried to improve the style of modern art, impressionism, pointillism, futurism, cubism, and neo-cubism; it was establishing a surrealist perspective in art that made him famous. Other noted paintings in the museum are *Venus and Sailor, Self-Portrait Splitting into Three, Girl from Figueres, Figure Barcelona Mannequin, The Smiling Venus, Port Alguer, Soft Self-Portrait with Grilled Bacon,* and *Portrait of Pablo Picasso in the Twenty-first Century,* to name just a few.

When we left Figueres, we skirted the Mediterranean coast to the Pyrenees mountains to cross into France arriving at Carcassonne, a fortified, walled-city and a UNESCO World Heritage Site since 1997, perched on a rocky hilltop surrounded by ancient towers and turrets. If you stay in the town, the walled city is an easy walk across the Le Pont Vieux Bridge over the Aude River. Although it is free to enter the town, there is a charge to tour the twelfth-century Chateau Comtal. The exterior of the Château became the outside of Nottingham Castle, home to Alan Rickman's Sheriff of Nottingham for the filming of *Prince of Thieves* starring Kevin Costner. Another interesting tidbit provided by our tour guide had to do with the previous guests of Hotel de la Cite Carcassonne: Michael Jackson and the Queen Mother. When researching the hotel's website, the list of particularly important people yields names from the early twentieth century to the present; Winston Churchill; Walt Disney; and Grace Kelly, the Princess of Monaco; Christian Lacroix; Johnny Depp; and Sting.

Saint Nazaire Basilica reflects a stunning combination of Romanesque and Gothic architecture. The Another Beautiful Church acronym, ABC, was expressed several times usually from the male gender; I first learned this acronym in Italy. I can only conclude that the female gender has more appreciation for religious architectural design. Although I must admit after a while, all seem to translate to one of four major architectural styles for Catholic churches: Gothic, Romanesque, Renaissance, and Baroque. These magnificent structures are beautiful, and one does not want to calculate what the maintenance cost must be on these historic relics. Although some are open to public view, many have succumbed to charging a fee or utilizing space as art galleries.

I don't mind one bit paying a fee to tour these treasures because in many areas of the United States and other countries practicing a religion through weekly visits is becoming obsolete. Whether it is caused by internet attendance or just not observing religion in the traditional way, attendance is down in many locations of worship. It must be challenging to collect the funds needed to maintain them.

Onward to Bordeaux but not before a stop in Toulouse, France, the town called the pink city but known for its aerospace industry. The Cité de L'espace is the center for scientific discovery and if we had more free time I would have enjoyed visiting that museum. Instead, our stop was largely to visit the UNESCO World Heritage Site, Saint-Sernin Basilica, built between the eleventh and fourteenth centuries and a major stop on one path of the Santiago del Compostela pilgrimage. It is also one of the largest Romanesque churches in Europe. The other church of interest is the Couvent des Jacobins with construction starting in 1230; it houses the relics of Thomas Aquinas. One must purchase a ticket to enter, and it is not open on Mondays. Unfortunately, it was Monday, so we were not afforded an interior view. After leaving Toulouse, we stopped for a wine tasting in the vineyard, Chateau Lestange, before continuing our drive through wine country.

We arrived in Bordeaux just before dinner, leaving time to explore the lively waterfront area. I enjoyed the restaurants and shops decorated for Halloween. Always a nice touch when traveling around holidays; some holidays have become rather international. Bordeaux is a bustling town comprising eighteenth-century buildings. The walking tour emphasized La Fleche Saint Michel tower, one of the tallest medieval stone towers in France; the Grand Theater and the Triumphal Arch, a monument to celebrate the reign of the Roman Empire.

One should visit the relatively new Cite du Vin, better known as the wine museum. This was not part of our tour but about ten of us decided to replace the morning walking tour downtown with a visit to the wine museum. The Cité du Vin is a museum as well as a place of exhibitions, shows, movie projections and academic seminars on the theme of wine. On August 29, 2018, the Cité du Vin passed the milestone of one million visitors since its opening and in May 2022 its next milestone of two million visitors. The museum is an interactive and sensory experience on wine. One display describes how vineyards and grapevines are grown in different countries based on the soil and climate. I spent quite a bit of time at this exhibit selecting every option. One can spend several hours watching and listening to the interactive displays.

At the end, the finale is a wine tasting. I think on a return trip to Bordeaux, I want to spend more time in wineries and wine tastings.

This visit was coordinated with our tour manager prior to

acquiring tickets. So, if one is on an organized tour, you should discuss alterations with your tour manager before making any external plans. As I have said numerous times, organized tours can be a compromise of activities, but they do provide a very efficient means of visiting and experiencing what are considered the most important sites in a region.

After lunch we traveled to Chateaux Franc-Mayne for another wine tasting near the charming town of Saint Emilion, a UNESCO World Heritage Site to include one aspect that many readers may not be aware of or appreciate; it is on the Camino Frances-Santiago de Compostela. This tour had us crisscrossing the pilgrimage territory for both Camino Frances and Camino Catalán.

Viticulture was introduced to this fertile region of Aquitaine by the Romans and intensified in the Middle Ages. The Saint-Emilion area benefited from its location on the pilgrimage route to Santiago de Compostela and many churches, monasteries and hospices were built there from the 11th century onwards. It was granted the special status of a 'jurisdiction' during the period of English rule in the 12th century. It is an exceptional landscape devoted entirely to winegrowing, with many fine historic monuments in its towns and villages.[114]

The town, originally named Ascumbus, acquired its new name from the Benedictine monk Emilion, responsible for healing miracles in the area. We spent about an hour strolling through this charming medieval town before returning to

Bordeaux.

Leaving Bordeaux, we headed for Bilbao but not before stopping at Biarritz, France and San Sebastian, Spain. Although Biarritz started as a whaling and fishing town, it was transformed into a resort for royalty when Napoleon III and his Spanish wife Eugenie built their palace there. Along France's Basque coastline, it has become a major surfing destination with long sandy beaches and surf schools. A symbol of Biarritz is the Rocher de la Vierge, a rocky bluff topped with a statue of the Virgin Mary. The location is only reached by footbridge, offering panoramic views of the Bay of Biscay.

Crossing over into Spain, we traveled down the coast to San Sebastian, known as *the Pearl of Northern Spain*. The coastal town is surrounded by green mountains and sandy beaches looking out onto sparkling bays or a more detailed description.

The city is located in the north of the Basque Country, on the south-eastern coast of the Bay of Biscay. San Sebastián has three beaches, Concha, Ondarreta, and Zurriola, and is surrounded by hilly areas: Urgull (adjacent to the old part of the city), Mount Ulia (extending east to Pasaia), Mount Adarra (south of the city) and Igeldo (overlooking Concha Bay from the west).[115]

This was a nice lunch sojourn for our group to try pintxos, small finger food famous in the Basque region of Northern

Spain. One usually discovers these snacks with a toothpick inserted to keep the ingredients joined.

Items are purchased individually with a combination producing enough for lunch. The restaurant was packed with ordering being a matter of pointing to the food, voicing the snack number, and the server compiling the ordered food onto a plate. Such as *I'll have a 25, 12, 5, and 10*. One needs to review all the choices before starting the order because a line will start behind you ready to shout their orders. You don't want to be *that guy* who stands there holding up the line figuring out the order while 20 people behind express angst. Believe me, you don't want to be *that guy* in this environment.

In arriving to Bilbao, we toured the Old Quarter, Casco Viejo, with the seven original streets dating back to the early 1400s. The fourteenth-century Gothic church, Cathedral de Santiago, is located among the narrow streets. However, the highlight of the tour was to visit the Guggenheim Museum, designed by Canadian architect Frank Gehry. Considered one of the twentieth century's most influential architectural masterpieces, the structure is striking with the use of flowing canopies, ship shapes, towers and flying fins, stunning as the sun gleams off the titanium tiles.

Although the museum houses the world's most important collection of avant-garde art, the structure alone is an artistic wonder. The Bilbao city-government paid for the construction of the building with an agreement by the Solomon R. Guggenheim Foundation to manage the institution and rotate parts of its permanent collection through the museum and organize temporary exhibits. The museum has turned a deteriorating waterfront into a flourishing area since its opening by King Juan Carlos I of Spain on October 18, 1997.

The original Guggenheim Museum is located at 1071 Fifth Avenue on the Upper East Side of Manhattan in New York City. Frank Lloyd Wright designed the museum, and it is part of a collection of Twentieth-Century Architecture by Frank Lloyd Wright to make the UNESCO World Heritage Site designation in 2019. If your bucket list includes all major art or architectural museums, then you would want to add both to your list. Solomon R. Guggenheim established the namesake foundation in 1937 to foster an appreciation for modern art.

Frank Lloyd Wright was hired to design the building in June 1943. After delays and redesign, the building was finished and formally opened on October 21, 1959. Neither Solomon Guggenheim (November 3, 1949) nor Frank Lloyd Wright (April 9, 1959) lived to see the completion of their vision and labors of love.

The UNESCO designation was announced at the World Heritage Committee meeting on July 7 in Baku, Azerbaijan citing the justification that Frank Lloyd Wright...*is widely considered to be the greatest American architect of the 20th century, and the sites in the group inscription span his influential career. They are Unity Temple (constructed*

414

1906–09, Oak Park, Illinois), the Frederick C. Robie House (constructed 1910, Chicago), Taliesin (begun 1911, Spring Green, Wisconsin), Hollyhock House (constructed 1918–21, Los Angeles), Fallingwater (constructed 1936–39, Mill Run, Pennsylvania), the Herbert and Katherine Jacobs House (constructed 1936–37, Madison, Wisconsin), Taliesin West (begun 1938, Scottsdale, Arizona), and the Solomon R. Guggenheim Museum (constructed 1956– 59, New York).[116]

I just added this to my bucket list for a New York City trip to include visiting the Guggenheim Museum. I'm probably adding Frank Lloyd Wright's creations to my list too. Back to Bilboa's Guggenheim, the best-known permanent exhibit is *The Matter of Time* by Richard Serra found on the first floor.

The Matter of Time allows the viewer to perceive the evolution of the artist's sculptural forms, from the relative simplicity of a double ellipse to the complexity of a spiral. The last two pieces of this sculpture are created from sections of toruses and spheres that produce different effects on the movement and perception of the viewer. These are unexpectedly transformed as the visitor walks through and around them, creating an unforgettable, dizzying feeling of space in motion. The entire room is part of the sculptural field. As he has done in other sculptures composed of many pieces, the artist has arranged the works deliberately in order to move the viewer through them and through the space surrounding them. The layout of the works along the gallery creates corridors with different, always unexpected

proportions (wide, narrow, long, compressed, high, low).
The installation also includes a progression in time. On the
one hand, there is the chronological time that it takes to walk
through and observe it from beginning to end. On the other,
there is the time during which the viewer experiences the
fragments of visual and physical memory, which are
combined and re-experienced.[117]

A very complex intent, I'm not sure that I completely
grasped all of it while walking through the art exhibit; it was
quite dramatic.

Although it was raining when I left the Guggenheim
Museum, I walked a short distance to the Fine Arts Museum
in Bilbao, only a couple blocks away. The building was
undergoing renovations and therefore several rooms were
closed but admission was waived to compensate. A significant
contrast from the Guggenheim, it held an array of paintings to
include Paul Gauguin, *A Washerwoman in Ares*; Francisco
de Goya, *Portrait of Martin Zapater*; El Greco, *The*
Annunciation; Francis Bacon, *Lying Figure in Mirror*; and
Bartolome Esteban Murillo, *Saint Peter in Tears*. Again, I'm
just scratching the surface of listing the masterpieces.

I then walked back to Casco Viejo to visit the Cathedral de
Santiago. It was worth the trip even in the rain with a nice
audio self-guided tour providing background information. It
was difficult to take a picture and get the whole church in
view. Truly little space is allocated outside the church walls to
get a full view for taking pictures of the magnificent exterior

structure. One gets a good perspective for how densely constructed medieval towns were back then, even with large church structures centrally located. The constructors never envisioned someone taking a picture and the inability to stand far enough away to encompass the whole church.

The Cathedral Basilica of Saint James is dedicated to the apostle James the Great and is a point of transit for pilgrims following the Northern Way of the Camino de Santiago. As I said, previously we crisscrossed the Camino during our travels and became part of the UNESCO World Heritage Site for the Routes of Santiago de Compostela.

The longest stretch of the coach ride occurred on the way to Madrid from Bilbao. This five-hour drive was broken up with a stop in the wine region of Rioja, Spain. We toured the wine caves where they store the wine prior to lunch served in a charming stone house above the cave system. A very tender veal was the menu for lunch and very filling for the rest of the long drive to Madrid. Yes, a few of us snoozed.

Upon our arrival, a couple in our group received sad news of a death in the family and needed to travel back home the next day. Unfortunately, this is a risk with travel plans anywhere that death or sickness of close family members or friends can impact the trip. If someone has close family members struggling with health issues, it may be practical to buy trip insurance to cover the need to cancel or shorten the trip and be reimbursed for expenses not utilized and adjustments to flights.

On the following day, we visited the Prado Museum after a coach tour of Madrid and a walk around the Royal Palace, only used for special occasions. Although the Louvre is the largest museum based on gallery space, Prado houses the largest collection for Spanish artists. The building dates to 1785 when King Charles III ordered its construction as a National History Cabinet, but it was King Ferdinand VII who converted the building into a museum and opened it to public view in 1819. In addition to Spanish paintings, the collection is enhanced with Flemish and Italian works of art and has the most complete collection of works by artists such as Bosch, Titian, Rubens, Velázquez, Ribera, Murillo, Goya, and El Greco.

If you're seeking Goya's pieces, the museum holds more than 140 pieces and almost half of Velázquez's life works to include some of his most recognized: *Las Meninas*, *The Surrender of Breda*, *The Spinners*, and *The Drunkards*. An unusual point of *Las Meninas* is that Velázquez painted himself as a painter in the portrait on the left-side. Besides himself, the painting includes a strange cast of characters: the princess infantas Margarita, her maids of honor, a nun, a dwarf, and King Philip IV and his Queen Mariana in the mirror. Painted in 1656 during a prosperous time of the Hapsburg Empire, it's become a mystery to art historians as to the message Velázquez was conveying. Our art guide for the museum depicted these points.

Probably the most unusual painting in the museum is by the Dutch artist Hiëronymus Bosch called *Garden of Earthly*

Delights painted in the late fifteenth century. He represents the fate of humanity through what can be considered a science fiction scene with giant birds, people inside bubbles, futuristic buildings, and an unusual depiction of fantastical beasts interacting with humans. Bosch was way ahead of his time. This painting has many experts scratching their heads as to the artist's motivation and meaning. This ultra twist on unusual became an inspiration for Dali's surrealism. Another unusual fact about Bosch, he married a woman significantly his senior which proved a financial, if not romantic, successful decision. It helped to fund his endeavors.

In the afternoon, I participated in the optional Toledo Medieval Town Tour, as a UNESCO World Heritage Site since 1986. The town is located about 44 miles (70 km) south of Madrid. UNESCO summarized it explicitly:

Successively a Roman municipium, the capital of the Visigothic Kingdom, a fortress of the Emirate of Cordoba, an outpost of the Christian kingdoms fighting the Moors and, in the 16th century, the temporary seat of supreme power under Charles V, Toledo is the repository of more than 2,000 years of history. Its masterpieces are the product of heterogeneous civilizations in an environment where the existence of three major religions – Judaism, Christianity, and Islam – was a major factor.[118]

Like many medieval towns, it is located atop a hill requiring several escalators to reach unless someone is energetic and would like to walk. The streets inside the walled town are very narrow, so my recommendation is to leave the car outside and see the town on foot. We entered a synagogue built by Muslims who included some Islamic design into the construction. Later, the building was then taken over by the Catholics adding their own religious décor. Whether a serendipitous happenstance, the three primary religions of Abraham entwined in this structure.

For our farewell dinner, we had tapas; everyone knows tapas. Small Spanish appetizers served with drinks and meant for sharing to make a meal. What I didn't know was the source of this unique Spanish cultural feature that has been adopted internationally. Legend has it that King Alfonso X, known as The Wise, in the thirteenth century was prescribed to drink a large quantity of wine while recovering from an illness and chose to eat small portions of food to diminish the side effects of alcohol. He interpreted his success as the best method to prevent public drunkenness and insisted that the practice be adopted by his subjects.

Another explanation is that barkeepers covered their patrons' drinks with a slice of bread, ham, or cheese to stop flies and dust from entering the drink. I guess the patrons would then eat their covering. Tapa means lid and comes from the verb *tapear* which means to cover. There might be some validity to an explanation rooted in linguistics or semantics. A third theory is that the origin derived from the fields and workshops of the Medieval Ages. Since workers labored from dawn to dusk, they only stopped long enough for a quick inexpensive bite to avoid wasting precious daylight. Maybe the truth of the origin of tapas has a basis in all three explanations.

The next morning, we left the hotel at 7:15 am for a 10:45 am flight to New York City and JFK International Airport. Unbelievably, we arrived at 2:00 pm because of the five-hour time change. There was hardly anyone at passport control and our luggage was in the carousel in no time; this might have been a record with airport arrival processing about 20 minutes.

On my trip, I visited the UNESCO World Heritage Sites in Spain of Works of Antoni Gaudí (1984), Historic City of Toledo (1986), Routes of Santiago de Compostela: Camino Francés and Routes of Northern Spain (1993). In France, the UNESCO World Heritage Sites were Historic Fortified City of Carcassonne (1997), Bordeaux, Port of the Moon (2007), Jurisdiction of Saint-Emilion (1999). We traveled through the Pyrenees – Mont Perdu (1993) on our way from France to Spain.

I can check Museo del Prado off my museum list and La Sagrada Familia, on Wikipedia's list, Conde traveler list and Road Affair blog, for churches. I can also check Cité de Carcassonne, France off my famous castles list. A variety of checks occurred for this trip. National Geographic recognized two places in Barcelona in their *Destination of a Lifetime* assessment, Sagrada Familia and Santa Maria de Montserrat Monastery.

421

Barcelona

Born Centre de Cultura Memoria

Gaudi's Casa Batlló

Persistence of Memory

Cathedral of Saint Mary, Girona

Carcassonne, France

Montserrat Monastery and the Black Madonna

Saint-Sernin Basilica, Toulouse   Toledo, Spain

surfers at Biarritz, France   Basilica de la Sagrada Familia

Part 2 – My Big Year

Chapter 14

Danube River Cruise (Hungary, Slovakia, Austria, Germany, Czech Republic)

For me, cooking is an expression of the land where you are and the culture of that place. – Wolfgang Puck

(https://www.brainyquote.com/topics/culture-quotes)

Background: History, Culture, and Environment

Szia barátom. Ahoj priateľ môj. Servus, mein Freund. Hallo mein Freund. Ahoj, kamaráde.

Five countries situated between central and eastern Europe traversed by floating down the Danube River are the ingredients for one awesome trip, a Danube River cruise. This cruise brings a historical perspective on the vast Austro-Hungarian Empire of the political changes on monarchies to communism. The Habsburg Empire rule of Austro-Hungary dates to 1867 with its collapse in 1918 at the end of World War I; however, the Habsburg Empire rule of Austria dates to 1804 when Francis I proclaimed himself emperor of Austria.

After the fall of Napoleon, Austria became the leader of the German states; however, the Austro-Prussian War of 1866 resulted in Austria being expelled from the German Confederation. Emperor Franz Joseph of Austria focused his policy for consolidating toward the east and negotiations led to the Ausgleich Compromise on February 8, 1867, when the agreement passed as a constitutional law by the Hungarian Parliament in March 1867. Hungary received full internal autonomy and in return agreed that the empire should be a single state for the purpose of war and foreign affairs. The elements of a common monarchy consisted of the emperor and his court, the minister of foreign affairs, and the minister of war. There was no common prime minister or cabinet.

World War I and the 1918 crop failure fueled general starvation and economic crisis yielding the dissolution of the Austro-Hungary Empire. The Treaty of Saint-German, signed on September 10, 1919, established the formal dissolution, and forced the new Republic of Austria to accept that over sixty percent of its territory became independent. In Stefan Zweig's nostalgic historical book, *The World of Yesterday*, he describes the period leading to and through World War I and then leading up to World War II. He describes how propaganda fueled hatred in World War I to coerce a largely naïve population. The arts were the victim of this manipulation.

Shakespeare was exiled from German theaters, Mozart and Wagner from French and British concert halls, German professors explained that Dante had really been of Germanic birth, the French claimed Beethoven as a Belgian-in fact the cultural treasures of the enemy countries were unscrupulously plundered as if they were supplies of grain or metal ore.[119]

The lands of Bohemia, Moravia, and Slovakia became Czechoslovakia; Bohemia and Moravia, populated by Czechs, constituted its western portion, while Slovakia occupied the eastern portion. During the period between the two world wars, this area became the most prosperous and politically stable state in Eastern Europe. Nazi Germany occupied the country from 1938 to 1945 and then dominated by the Soviet Union from 1948 to 1989. With the disintegration of the Soviet Union, former Eastern European countries sought their own political structures.

Czechoslovakia did not embrace communism throughout its political existence. In January 1968, Alexander Dubcek became the leader implementing more liberal policies such as freedom of the press. Although the people of Czechoslovakia embraced liberal change, known as Prague Spring, the Soviet Union leadership did not. In August 1968, Warsaw Pact troops invaded Czechoslovakia with Soviet tanks rolling through the streets of Prague physically dissipating student protests. Soviet loyalist Gustav Husak replaced Dubcek, and the country returned to traditional authoritarian communist administration. Once the country had a taste of liberal ideas, some citizens could not return to suppression. Jan Palach, a Charles University student in Prague, climbed the steps of the National Museum near Wenceslas Square and set himself on fire in protest. Palach lived for three days in the hospital giving interviews before his death stating his acts were to awaken people against Soviet control. The resistance went underground and political dissenters such as Vaclav Havel wrote on the need to respect human rights.

This act of setting oneself on fire has become a symbol of protest against the government and used more recently in the Middle Eastern revolts of the Arab Spring. A wave of pro-democracy protests and uprisings erupted in December 2010 initiated by the self-immolation, act of setting oneself on fire, by 26-year-old street vendor Mohamed Bouazizi. This became the Jasmine Revolution in Tunisia overturning the rule of President Zine al-Abidine Ben Ali and instilling leadership through true Democratic means. Unrest spread to other countries, some with less successful results: Egypt Uprising of 2011, Yemen Uprising of 2011-2012, Libya revolt of 2011, and Syria Civil War. On November 17, 1989, students of Prague organized a peaceful protest, the Velvet Revolution.

By November 20, a half-million Czechs and Slovaks filled Prague's streets taking over Wenceslas Square. The Communists were forced out; Czechoslovakia was on its way to an elected President for the first time since 1948. On January 1, 1993, Czechoslovakia divided peacefully into two countries, the Czech Republic and Slovakia. Havel would serve as the last president of Czechoslovakia from 1989 to 1992 and then the first president of the Czech Republic from 1993 to 2003.

Prague does not reside on the mighty Danube but is positioned further inland on the Vltava River which is the lifeline of the city and provides the foundation for the city's most important historic sites, including the Charles Bridge, named after Charles IV, known as the Great Czech and Father of the Homeland.

With history overlapping in this region, it is understandable that food would also have an overlap. A common culinary description of Central and Eastern Europe yields dishes based on meats, seasonal vegetables, fresh bread, dairy products and cheeses, and fruits. Weiner schnitzel, a cutlet of veal pounded thin with a meat tenderizer; dipped in flour, egg, and breadcrumbs; and fried until golden, is a common meal throughout the region. Strudel, a layered pastry filled with a savory fruit center, became popular during the Habsburg Empire and a dessert staple in the Austrian and German cuisine. However, one associates Hungary to the famous Hungarian goulash, a soup or stew of meat and vegetables seasoned with paprika and other spices.

As described in Claudio Magris' book, *Danube: A Sentimental* Journey from the Source to the Black Sea, his literary journey focuses on the history and culture of the people for the lifeblood of Central Europe. The journey takes one from the Black Forest to the Black Sea and the experiences that have shaped the land and its people. He weaves the cultural evolution of Central Europeans throughout the book using a complex, merged lens of philosophy, psychology, history, mythology, and probably several other ologies. Although my modern journey was one of exploration and discovery, my focus is more simplistic and relevant for today.

With respect to the Fund for Peace Fragile State Index for 2024, Hungary, Slovenia, Austria, Germany, and Czech Republic scored well. Hungary ranked 138th with a score of 46.2, Slovenia at 163rd with score 26.1, Austria at 167th with score 23.1, Germany at 166th with score 24.0, and Czech Republic ranked 152nd with a score of 37.7. Hungary had a less obvious area of concern depicted in its sub-indicators. I very much enjoyed my time in Budapest and would travel back to visit the country and the lovely city. Now, let's look at the State Resilience Index score for each: Hungary (6.5), Slovenia (7.3), Austria (7.8), Germany (7.9), and Czech Republic (7.0). Hungary and Czech Republic scored slightly below average for social cohesion. As a tourist, I did not feel this issue during my trip. In fact, I left wanting to return to both countries impressed with their beautiful landscape and historic cities.

Travel Itinerary

The Danube River cruise started in Budapest, Hungary (two nights at hotel, one night on cruise) headed west to Bratislava, Slovenia; Vienna, Austria; Durnstein, Austria; Melk, Austria; Passau, Germany; and Regensburg, Germany. While some passengers headed for the Munich Airport, those that extended to Prague headed for the Czech Republic border. An optional one-day tour afforded visiting Salzburg, Austria from Passau.

https://free-map.org/

Travel Journal

A river cruise, basically a floating hotel, sounded terrific, since I've had several trips this year where travel is by coach or airplane to various cities, towns, and regions. A leisure sailing through fall foliage sends visions of vibrant orange, red, yellow merged with brown to the countryside. My adventure started leaving for Washington Dulles International Airport, about two hours from my home, on a good day and up to three hours on a bad day. To arrive at the airport for an international flight three hours before departure means leaving for the airport 5-6 hours ahead of schedule. I decided to use the parking app versus airport parking since the trip length was two weeks. When arriving at the hotel for parking, the desk attendant informed me that they no longer had an airport shuttle service. Thinking quickly, I used the Uber app to get us from the hotel to the airport. The Uber driver arrived almost before I got the car parked in the designated parking area of the hotel. Next time, I will call the hotel beforehand to ensure that they still have an airport shuttle service, the Ways app incorrectly displayed this service.

While traveling to Budapest we had a connecting flight in Amsterdam. Some people can fall asleep anywhere, like one of my travel mates, and others like me need just the right conditions or result in being exhausted. I was able to get about two to two and a half hours of sleep on the airplane which at least takes the edge off exhaustion. In Amsterdam, passport control took about five minutes, amazing! I forgot to mention that it only took 5-10 minutes for security at Dulles Airport, which was a substantial change from the trip to Seattle earlier in May which took over an hour. After checking into the hotel in Budapest, my travel mate and I slept for a couple of hours but we awoke in time for the welcome meeting that evening.

At this point, I was on my eighth trip in eight months since retiring earlier in the year. So, the desire for a floating hotel was even more appreciated needing some recuperation from the hectic land travel tours. If one is traveling a lot, ensure that collectively the travel plan is not too aggressive yielding one to feel distraught and not excited about the trip.

The next morning, we participated in a partial walking tour of the *Pest* side of Budapest: City Park, Hero's Square, and Budapest Vajdahunyad Castle, modeled after Corvin Castle, also known as Hunyadi Castle, located in Hunedoara, Romania.

The name Budapest is formed by the two sections on each side of the Danube River, Buda to the south and Pest to the north. Although the castle appears to be from centuries past, it was built in 1896 as a temporary structure for the Millennial Celebration of Hungary's conquest of the Carpathian Basic in 895 AD and then made permanent with construction from 1904-1908. The castle contains different architectural styles: Romanesque, Gothic, Renaissance, and Baroque.

What is the connection between Vaidahunyad Castle and Count Dracula? A bust of Count Dracula is mounted on one corner of the building to reflect Bela Lugosi, the Hungarian actor who played the original role when Bram Stoker's *Dracula* movie was filmed. Dracula's character was probably inspired by Vlad the Impaler, a fifteenth-century Transylvanian prince, also known as Vlad III Dracul of Wallachia. Vlad the Impaler is believed to have been imprisoned in Corvin Castle by John Hunyadi. Why did he get this name? During conflicts with the Ottomans, he impaled 23,844 Turkish prisoners and may have killed somewhere between 40,000 to 100,000 European civilians who were considered political rivals, criminals, or useless to humanity. I'll add Vlad the Impaler to my list of tyrants guilty of crimes against humanity.

However, Bran Castle, also in Transylvania, Romania is considered the castle described in Stoker's Dracula story. Vlad the Impaler never lived in Bran Castle though; he lived in Poenari Castle also in Romania, a mighty fortress perched atop a cliff like an eagle's nest at an altitude over 2,600 feet (793 m) requiring one to climb 1,480 steps to walk amongst the ruins. Literary creativity by Stoker appears to have been based on a fictional story with factual locations and people, intertwining as desired. I might need to add Bran's Castle to my bucket list. I might need to add an increased exercise routine to accomplish the 1,480 steps of Poenari Castle before the trip.

From there, we drove to the Jewish section and Dohány Street Synagogue or Great Synagogue, the largest synagogue in Europe and fourth largest in the world. At this point, travelers could choose to stay and tour the inside of the synagogue complex or return to the hotel. I stayed and visited the museum, church, and a special exhibit in the basement on the treatment of the Jewish community during World War II. The cemetery is a mass burial site, one feels grave emotional turmoil. With so many dying at that time, mass burial was the most practical means. Perusing through the gift shop, I found a t-shirt with the statement: *Technically, Moses was the first person with a tablet downloading data from the cloud.* Whoever created that expression is just brilliant. I can't believe that I didn't buy the shirt for my son, an engineering student.

I then walked to Saint Stephen's Basilica down the street but stopped for the chimney ice cream cone on the way. A Hungarian treat worth trying and enjoy watching how the cone is baked before adding the ice cream. The cone is more like a dough than the waffle-type we are accustomed to in the United States. Once at Saint Stephen's Basilica, tickets are purchased across the plaza for entrance to the largest church in Budapest and the second largest in Hungary. As with every church, the neoclassical architecture is beautiful. However, what makes this church a little different is that Hungary's sacred treasure resides there, Saint Stephen's mummified right hand, the Szent Jobb. A spiral staircase and elevator take one to the cupola and panoramic views of the city. It took five decades to build the church, a common theme amongst churches and castles in Europe, decades and even centuries to build these impressive structures.

I then walked down the street to the Opera House to take some pictures of the exterior. I took a taxi to my ultimate location, the Museum of Fine Art with a special Renoir exhibition, at Hero's Square. Backpacks must be checked in the basement before entering the gallery. The Renoir exhibit alone made the trip worthwhile. Renoir's La Grenouillère painted in 1869 was displayed. Interestingly, Renoir and Claude Monet painted this same scene of a resort on the Seine River where people went to bathe, boat, and socialize. During this time, Renoir and Monet were both poor and exchanged paintings for food with the owner of La Grenouillère. The painting depicts a pleasant scene when many painters were expressing the challenges of life. Renoir's response was, *Why shouldn't art be pretty? There are enough unpleasant things in the world.*[120] I agree with that philosophy.

As I perused the museum, I stumbled across the painting *The Garden of Delights* by Hieronymus Bosch. I had to look twice because I saw this painting at the Prada Museum in Madrid, Spain just a month before. What was it doing here now? I then looked closer and saw that it was a copy. As I mentioned in the previous chapter, it is quite striking and unusual painted between 1490 and 1500. It looks like a garden party from outer space.

After viewing every open section of the museum, the day turned into twilight, and so I decided to walk back to the museum, catching a taxi when convenient. The walk along Andrássy Avenue with beautiful, historic homes was so pleasurable that I was back at my hotel in no time, never bothering to flag down a taxi. According to my smartphone's health app, I accomplished a record number of 24,000 steps to reward my choice to walk.

My travel mate and I signed up for the optional folklore dinner and show in Budapest at a restaurant in Buda Hills outside the city. It encompassed a three-course Hungarian dinner with aperitif and wine; a folklore show, to include audience participation at one point; and the ability to get acquainted with members of our tour in a relaxed, entertaining environment. When diners were selected to join the dance show, a whole lot of raucous laughter occurred. Smartphones were snapping pictures to immortalize dancers' capability for polka-like steps. The menu included goulash soup, family-style pork and chicken, and a sponge cake with chocolate sauce for dessert.

The next morning, we checked out of the hotel but did not leave Budapest. We toured the Buda-side of the city, the Buda palace complex, home to the Hungarian kings. Buda Castle was originally built in 1265, but the massive Baroque palace existing today was built between 1749 and 1769. Nowadays, Buda Castle houses the National Széchényi Library, the Budapest History Museum, and the Hungarian National Gallery. Also located on Castle Hill are Fisherman's Bastion and Mathias Church. Normally, a funicular would take one to the top of Castle Hill, but it was closed on our day, so the tour manager used a few tuk-tuk buses to move us from below to above and reverse.

Once finished with Castle Hill, we boarded the cruise boat for one night in port before leaving the next day. Dinner was a tender roast beef and a Hungarian Operetta for entertainment. The next morning it started to drizzle, but not enough to stop the Taste of Budapest tour. This was a walking tour from the boat of the government area but first stopped at the Shoe Monument along the Danube River. Bronze shoes representing the atrocities of the Holocaust are located where men, women, and children were shot and fell into the Danube River when Budapest was under the control of Nazi Germany. Another solemn moment to reflect and question, *how could this have ever happened*? We walked past the Parliament Building and Liberty Square with the statues of former United States Presidents Ronald Reagan and George H. W. Bush. The final stop was the Central Market and tasting of some Hungarian specialties. Paprika is the Hungarian spice used in many regional dishes; I bought plenty for myself and as gifts to pack in my suitcase for home. On the walk back to the ship, my travel mate and I stopped at a pastry shop selling mulled wine to warm ourselves from the persistent drizzle. National Geographic recognized the Central Market in their *Destinations of a Lifetime* assessment.

We set sail about 5:00 pm as the evening was darkening; the riverbanks were alive with twinkling lights on both sides. Just a picture-perfect moment. Once we passed the liveliness of the city, the 94 passengers headed inside for the rest of the evening. Entertainment for this first night was bingo and a dance competition. Not the normal dance competition, where couples compete; for this competition, each person ranked the number of people that would embark on the dance floor against a list of songs. As each song was played, the entertainment director would count the number of people who *shook their booty* on the dance floor. An ingenious idea to promote competition and entice dance participation.

Our first port docking was Bratislava, Slovakia the next morning. Once disembarking, we did a walking tour of the historic area. Afterwards, we were on our own to explore the rest of the city. I ventured up the hill to Bratislava Castle. The castle houses the Slovak National Museum collection depicting its roots of Celtic inhabitants since the Stone Age, founding a fortified settlement on the hill called Oppidum.

Over centuries, the castle foundation changed from early Middle Ages design to fifteenth-century Gothic during the reign of Sigismund of Luxembourg to sixteenth-century Renaissance rebuilt by King Ferdinand.

I headed back down the hill, explored the Gothic-style Saint Martin Cathedral, and then continued through the medieval town stopping at a magic and witchcraft store. What a delight; right out of Harry Potter. The store was crowded with a combination of curiosity seekers and actual shoppers; I was more the curious seeker but liked the scented candles and incense. After all the walking to and from the castle, I was ready for quenching my thirst. I stopped at the pub advertising 20 beers on tap and had the mad scientist-strawberry and mad scientist-tropical; I've acquired a taste for fruity beers and like the association with a mad scientist. Back on the boat, I was in bed at 9:00 pm because the itinerary for the next morning looked to be aggressively active.

We started with a walking tour of Vienna. Yes, there is always a coach tour or walking tour of cities; how else can one become acquainted with the area? Usually, this is followed by *on your own* time for lunch or dinner. We walked around the government area, which is the former palace of royalty when Austria was a monarchy. The Austrian President's office resides in part of the palace. The Sisi Museum on Queen Maria Theresa also resides in one section of the square. Around the corner from the palace is Saint Stephens Church depicting

Gothic-style architecture. Around the base of the church, Christmas Markets were being constructed. A light drizzle joined us that morning, but not enough to dampen our spirits.

The cathedral's construction started in the twelfth century, with its interior changing over centuries to a Baroque appearance. The church has four towers, the tallest being the south tower at 446 feet (136 m) with 343 steps to reach the tower room at the top. The church has 13 bells with the best known, the Pummerin, hanging in the north tower. It is the second-biggest free-swinging chimed church bell in Europe.

The afternoon brought an optional excursion to Schönbrunn Palace, the summer retreat for the Habsburg dynasty. The building and furniture have stayed original due to the non-violent change from monarchy to republic, unlike the French Rebellion in France fueling the theft and destruction of most of the furniture at Palace of Versailles. The last ruler of Austria, Emperor Charles I, abdicated and exited to the Island of Madeira. Empress Maria Theresa turned the hunting lodge into a summer retreat palace during her presence.

A note for visitors, there are no pictures allowed in Schönbrunn Palace, a bit deserting when one can take unlimited pictures at the Palace of Versailles. As we were meandering back to the boat, our guide shared some general information on Austria. The tax structure is progressive with the highest tax bracket at 52 percent. Although Austria has an army, the country has taken a neutral position for international security restricting the inclusion of any security agreements such as the NATO.

Education is free and includes the university level. Hospital care is free and started in the eighteenth century with Joseph II, son of Francis I and Maria Theresa. During the combined reign of the mother and son, the monarchy focused on social reforms. The Edict of Toleration established religious equality. In addition, Joseph II granted freedom of the press, the emancipation of Jews, transferred the management of the theaters to the actors, and established the General Hospital in Vienna. His religious reforms created friction with the Roman Catholic Church and Pope Pius VI. These changes stirred the artistic creativity of the empire and specifically Vienna. Although one usually equates monarchies to the luxury of the privileged, some royal leaders have embraced initiatives for improving the lives of the citizens.

That evening, we attended a Mozart and Strauss concert by the Vienna Residence Orchestra at the Palais Auersburg. The musical group consisted of four violins, flute, piano, and two cellos with accompaniment by singers and dancers. Of course, the *Blue Danube Waltz* was a tremendous hit. We returned to the boat around 10:30 pm just in time for an 11:00 pm sail to the next port. My only gripe is that one day is not enough to spend in Vienna.

Another day would allow more time for museums, concerts, and possibly a trip to the Eagle's Nest, Adolf Hitler's hideaway located some distance away, closer to Salzburg. I've conveyed this sentiment before, these travel sprints allow one to acquire some knowledge of areas to ascertain where to return independently for in-depth travel. One way or another, I will return to Vienna.

Sailing overnight, we arrived in Durnstein, Austria. I've probably overused the adjective *quaint* for Medieval town descriptions, so I'll use the word *charming* to describe this town along the Danube River. A bonus opportunity is that Durnstein Castle ruins tower high above the town where Richard the Lionheart was held captive for ransom by King Leopold. Energetic hikers followed the cruise entertainment manager up the steep path to climb among the ruins and view Richard's sparse jail cell. The not-as-energetic others did a walking tour of Durnstein. I was among the hikers and glad that we took numerous breaks to catch our breath on the steep climb. Along the path, signs describe the history of the town and Richard the Lionheart's predicament.

After numerous pictures from the top of the hill, I ventured back down to the town stopping to purchase wine at an *honor's refrigerator* outside a house. Residents place wine in a refrigerator outside their front door for travelers to purchase by leaving money in a box on top. It's the honor system; a list of the wine prices provides the purchase information. There were only two bottles left. So, I purchased one, a very trusting culture.

Leaving Durnstein, we sailed through Wachau Valley with stunning views of vineyards nestled on the hills. This looked like a perfect location for bicycle riding along the path paralleling the river. After about two hours of sailing, we reached a spot on the river where a former castle on top of a high hill was renovated as a hostel with minimal accommodations. When one is seeking shelter, any port is welcomed in a storm. Our next stop was Melk and a tour of Melk Abbey.

The Baroque architectural style of Melk Abbey is striking. The royal family stayed in one section when visiting, including Empress Maria Theresa (Sisi) and her son Joseph II. Unfortunately, there are no pictures allowed once entering the buildings of the Abbey, bummer again. I enjoy later perusing my pictures and reminiscing but that is more difficult with no permanent illustration. When entering the church, the choir was practicing. It was an amazing moment to listen to the youth group practice for an event that evening. Once we finished the tour, one could either take the coach back to the boat or stroll through the town for the return. I walked joining up with other riverboat travelers. With narrow cobbled streets lit with twinkling lights and shops decorated for Christmas, of course, I wanted to walk through the town. A truly memorable holiday experience.

Just after the boat sailed, we entered a river lock, and the passengers clambered to the top deck to get a closer view. It doesn't take much to excite people; one would have thought that we were going through the Panama Canal. The lock system is the mechanical operation of a boat entering an enclosed area, either raising or lowering the water level, and then a door opening and allowing the boat to continue down the river. It is exciting to watch. I have seen this in Panama and in Minneapolis on the Mississippi River and I still get excited to watch the operation, probably the connection to my engineering-side. However, so did the other passengers and they aren't all engineers. The entertainment that night was *Name that Tune* with songs from the 1950's to 1990's. I was impressed with the participants; although I recognized songs, I couldn't remember the names. I suspect that a few travelers were music trivia experts.

We made a short stop in Linz, Austria. Although some passengers stayed onboard, others disembarked for a coach trip to Salzburg. There's no way I'm missing Salzburg; I've watched *The Sound of Music* probably a dozen times. It took about two hours to drive through the Austrian countryside. Salzburg means salt (salz) castle (burg). Salt is how soldiers were paid and salt mines around Salzburg generated the town's name. Salzburg is a UNESCO World Heritage Site:

Salzburg has managed to preserve an extraordinarily rich urban fabric, developed over the period from the Middle Ages to the 19th century when it was a city-state ruled by a prince-archbishop. Its Flamboyant Gothic art attracted many craftsmen and artists before the city became even better known through the work of the Italian architects Vincenzo Scamozzi and Santini Solari, to whom the centre of Salzburg owes much of its Baroque appearance. This

444

meeting-point of northern and southern Europe perhaps sparked the genius of Salzburg's most famous son, Wolfgang Amadeus Mozart, whose name has been associated with the city ever since.[121]

The walking tour of Salzburg emphasized the spots for filming *The Sound of Music*. We walked past Mirabell Palace, acknowledging areas of the garden that were used in the film; Saint Peter's Abbey; Baroque-style Salzburg Cathedral; and Saint Peter's Cemetery. The guide also pointed out the hotels occupied by Christopher Plummer and Julie Andrews during the filming, Hotel Bristol Salzburg and Hotel Sacher Salzburg, respectively. Christmas markets were being constructed in the square by the church and abbey, providing that extra holiday spirit. There is nothing like a Medieval town decorated for the holidays to entice the brain to hum *O Come All Ye Faithful* and *Silent Night* in your head.

Lunch was at the oldest restaurant in central Europe, Saint Peter Stiftskulinarium within the walls of Saint Peter's Abbey, serving patrons since 803 AD. I love the holiday allure; the restaurant was adorned for Christmas. We were served a sizable portion of Austrian cuisine, wiener schnitzel.

Salzburg is also the birthplace of Wolfgang Amadeus Mozart, the short-lived, but influential composer of classical music. He was born on January 27, 1756, to Leopold and Maria Pertl Mozart. His father was a successful composer, violinist, and assistant concertmaster at the Salzburg Court. Along with Mozart's sister, Maria Anna, Leopold provided guidance and encouragement to Mozart at an incredibly young age to develop his natural talents. Did his father's extra nurturing of musical talent create the genius of the composer? Mozart died on December 5, 1791, at only 35 years old; the cause of death has been hypothesized. Unfortunately, his grave is unknown since he was buried in a common grave at the time.

Mozart's compositions include the successful operas of *The Marriage of Figaro*, *Don Giovanni*, and *The Magic Flute*; his last completed symphony, *Jupiter Symphony* in 1788 was completed three years before his death and is possibly his most famous; although variations on *Twinkle, Twinkle Little Star* may truly be the most famous.

Scientists would be familiar with another former inhabitant, Christian Johann Doppler, the Austrian physicist known for defining how the observed frequency of light and sound waves is affected by the relativist motion of the source and detector, known as the Doppler effect. As we left Salzburg, our tour guide added some Christmas trivia with the story of *Silent Night*. The lyrics were composed by the Austrian priest, Father Joseph Mohr, and the music by teacher Franz Gruber; the song was first sung in a church in Oberndorf, a town near Salzburg.

While we ventured to Salzburg, the boat and remaining passengers continued down the Danube River to Passau, Germany; therefore, our return coach trip required border crossing into Germany and catching up with the boat. This

446

border crossing was not a breeze through the checkpoint. The coach was pulled into a holding area, and our passports were collected. This procedure restricts the illegal practice of trafficking refugees from conflict-ridden areas near European borders. A few minutes wait is worth supporting German border control and their quest to keep the country safe.

Passau is an enchanting town that lies at the confluence of the Danube, Inn, and Ilz Rivers, the Three Rivers City. Like many European cities, there is a thirteenth-century hilltop fortress, Veste Oberhaus, now used as a museum and observation tower. The old town area is Baroque architecture, including Saint Stephens Cathedral with its distinctive onion-domed towers and an organ with 17,974 pipes, one of the largest in the world.

Nightly, we received a tour briefing to summarize the events for the next day. Upon our return to the boat, we discovered a navigational problem; the rain upstream of Passau had caused the river to rise to a point where the boat couldn't safely pass underneath the bridges. Tour and boat management determined that the boat would stay at Passau, and the tour group would be coached to and from Regensburg, Germany. Regensburg was not bombed during World War II. So, it still retains several of the original structures, resulting in the designation as a UNESCO World Heritage Site. A channel was built parallel to the Danube River allowing ship traffic to bypass the downtown area. During our visit, the Danube River was raging in this location.

Regensburg Cathedral, or Saint Peter's Cathedral, was under construction.

How long does it take to build a cathedral? The answer is almost 600 years. The original church burned in 1273, and a new church was started in 1280 by an architect trained in France thus instilling the French Gothic style. Fast forward 548 years, King Ludwig of Bavaria desired to put his taste on construction with a Neo-Gothic twist in 1828-1841. With its completion in 1872, the towers and spires soar above the town. To accommodate the king's timeline, concrete was used versus stone creating structural problems today. Scaffolding encompassed one of the towers during our visit. If one wants a structure to endure centuries, then one shouldn't skimp on building materials.

With the opening of a BMW factory in 1986 in Regensburg, the town and its people benefited. Every day, up to 1,000 vehicles of the BMW1 series, BMW X1, and BMW X2 models are produced bringing jobs and income to the town. The plant produces fully electric models, plug-in hybrids, and combustible engines. Batteries for electric models are also produced on-site. Prior to COVID-19 pandemic, the factory provided tours; what a way to spend a German day watching a BMW produced. As their website entices career seekers: *the city, too, is pleasant to live in and very charming: Regensburg is not only the fourth largest city in Bavaria, but also has a beautiful historical part of town with winding alleys that will take you back to the Middle Ages.*[122] Another fact for trivia enthusiast is that Regensburg has the world's oldest boys' choir started in 975 AD.

Back at the boat, dinner was a German feast: sausage, sauerkraut, potatoes, and pretzels. Besides preparing food and serving, the crew also provided entertainment singing to the diners. For those with a birthday, the dining room engaged in the *Happy Birthday* song while the crew delivered a special dessert.

When we woke the next morning, for some members of the tour, the trip was ending with a drive to Munich to catch a flight back to their normal life. For others, we disembarked the boat and headed to the city of Prague in the Czech Republic, known less formerly as Czechia. On our drive, we were entertained by interesting facts about the area. The first fact was dealing with the high water in Passau. Over the last year, the water was too high in June 2023 and then just a couple of months later in the September-October period, the water was too low. Now in November, it's back to too-high-water, causing disruption for all boats navigating the great Danube River.

We learned more information on Germany; for instance, it is made up of 16 states. We drove through the Bavaria Forest in transit to Prague, an incredibly beautiful area of rolling forested hills alive with color in the autumn season. Picturesque just like the many jigsaw puzzle-boxes that display the Bavarian countryside.

The capital of Bavaria is Munich, known for Octoberfest, where only Munich-produced beer can be served. German beer brewers are limited to four ingredients for beer: malt, hops, yeast, and water. The original 1516 Bavarian law specified that the only ingredients allowed were malt, hops, and water constituted beer. Next year, I have a trip to Germany planned for September encompassing a large part of the country, including Munich. Munich during Octoberfest is a bucket list item and I am already thrilled with the anticipation.

Germany has the second longest highway at 7,456 miles, or 12,000 km with Spain the longest at 9,321 miles or 15,000 km in Europe. In some sections, there is no speed limit. Did you know that *volkswagon* is the German wording for *the people's car*? It was commissioned by Adolf Hitler in the 1930s and designed by Ferdinand Porsche. In the United States in the 1960s, Volkswagen's beetle or bug, as it was affectionately called, was the symbol of rebellious youth. Walt Disney filmed a movie, *The Love Bug*, where the hero is a Volkswagen beetle with personality. Volkswagen's second vehicle produced in 1950 was the Bohemian spin-off, the Volkswagen bus, creating the concept of driving cross-country and living in one's mode of transportation.

Another interesting fact about Germany, the country no longer has nuclear power plants, the last three (Isar 2, Emsland, and Neckarwestheim 2) were shut down on April 15, 2023. Since 1989, no new nuclear power plants have been built. Although renewable energy sources (wind, solar, and hydro) comprise a significant part of German's energy production, oil, coal, and natural gas still prevail as the primary base.

Henry Kissinger, a well-known Bavarian-born United States diplomat and former Secretary of State under Presidents Richard Nixon and Gerald Ford, was born as Heinz Alfred Kissinger on May 27, 1923, in Furth, Bavaria, Germany. Although his family moved to the United States in 1938 to avoid the persecution of Jewish citizens, he would later return to his birth region as a United States soldier, initially in 1944 with the 84th Infantry Division and later in 1945 with the Counter-Intelligence Corp.

Once we crossed the border into the Czech Republic, the landscape changed abruptly from picturesque countryside beauty to stores, gas stations, and casinos. Czech Republic is part of the former Czechoslovakia, dissolved in 1992, the other part being Slovakia. Parts of this area were previously known for years as Bohemia and Moravia. The first ethnic group to settle in the area occurred in the fourth century by the Celtics Boii tribe giving the country its Latin name, Boiohaemum or Bohemia.

Since 1526, the Kingdom of Bohemia was governed by Catholic Habsburg kings who tolerated the largely Protestant population. Emperor Matthias recognizing that he would die without an heir, arranged for the territory to go to the nearest male relative, Catholic Archduke Ferdinand II of Austria. Protestants of Bohemia were concerned with reversing the Peace of Augsburg which established religious tolerance and freedom. The Defenestration of Prague in May 1618 initiated Europe's Thirty-Year War when several Czech governors were thrown out of their office window from the Prague Town Hall by a rebellious Protestant group concerned for their continued religious freedom.

The Peace of Westphalia treaty laid the foundation for the formation of modern nation-states decreeing citizens of those states be governed by laws of the state and not of other institutions, secular or religious. Up until 1918 and the end of World War I, this area was governed under the Austro-Hungary Empire; it then became Czechoslovakia. The Yalta Conference of February 4-11, 1945, occurred between the Allied leaders Winston Churchill, Franklin Roosevelt, and Joseph Stalin to define the terms for post-World War II Europe.

We had a comfort stop just after crossing into the Czech Republic. As I wandered through the convenience store, my eyes caught a rather unappealing sight. Cigarette packs illustrated the result of smoking in a rather true but harsh reality. One must be numb or in denial to pick up a pack ignoring the visual premonition.

We had a short stop in the city of Pilsen for lunch; the city might be best known for the Pilsner Urquell Brewery which specializes in bottom-fermented beer since 1842. I've found the beer in many cities. The older part of the city has the nineteenth-century Great Synagogue and the Cathedral of Saint Bartholomew of the sixteenth-century with Renaissance paintings and a tall spire with a viewing gallery. In May 1945, the city of Pilsen was liberated by United States forces under the command of General Patton. A General Patton Monument and the Patton Memorial Museum Pilsen commemorate

We stayed in the historic part of the city allowing ease of walking for most activities or a short metro ride. Our first venture was to Prague Castle and a broad review of the area. We watched the changing of the guards conducted at the hour. We then drove to historically what was the Jewish section. When the Jewish community moved out of this area, it became the ghettoes until it was rejuvenated as a high-end shopping district. Paris might have Champs-Elysées, but Prague has Parizska Avenue with top designers such as Hermes, Dior, Dolce & Gabbana, Prada, and Gucci to at least start the list. The street traverses Prague from the Čechův Bridge to the Old Town Square. We ended the walk at Prague's Astronomical Clock attached to the Old Town Hall in Old Town Square. The clock dates to 1410 and provides a show with each strike on the hour.

For lunch, we ate at the Imperial Café managed by the celebrity television star Chef Zdenek Pohlreich, the Gordon Ramsey of the Czech Republic. The restaurant boasts the original art nouveau ceramic wall tiling and mosaic ceiling from 1914, and it is stunning. The optional afternoon tour was a trip to Terezin, a Gestapo prison and Jewish Ghetto. The prison largely held resisters and political prisoners with a small number of Jewish citizens. The town of Terezin was a Jewish holding place until people were moved to an extermination camp. Those who died in prison were either killed for punishment or died under abusive conditions. The museum in the town depicts the atrocities.

Gavrilo Princip, the nineteen-year-old Bosnian Serb and assassin of Archduke Franz Ferdinand, heir to the Austro-Hungarian throne, and wife Sophie, the Duchess of Hohenberg, started World War I with his two shots in Sarajevo on June 28, 1914. Just hours before his killing, the Archduke had narrowly escaped a bomb attack. Although tensions existed, the killing justified Austro-Hungary to declare war on Serbia. Based on agreements and relationships between other European countries, most of Europe became embroiled in the First World War. When Princip was captured, he was sentenced to twenty years, based on his age, and sent to Terezin. He died of tuberculosis on May 1, 1918.

The fortress Theresienstadt was created by Emperor Joseph II in the late eighteenth century and named for his mother, Empress Maria Theresa. The town Terezin is contained within the walls of the fortress, originally created as a holiday resort for the Czech nobility. The fortress was used as a prison before World War I, but the Gestapo took control during World War II. That's a new one, re-purpose a nobility holiday resort area as a prison.

This was a very somber and emotionally poignant visit, but essential to understand history so that humanity does not repeat the atrocities. More than 150,000 Jewish people, including 15,000 children were held there for months some even years deported from Germany, Austria, Netherlands, and Denmark. The town was a holding area for the eventual rail transport to their deaths in Treblinka and Auschwitz extermination camps in Poland. Although not an extermination camp, about 33,000 people died in the ghetto from harsh conditions, malnutrition, and disease. At the end of World War II, there were 17,247 survivors of Terezin with less than 150 children surviving.

Once back in Prague, we dined in the basement of the Municipal House, an accordionist played popular American tunes, and then we watched upstairs in the Smetana Concert Hall *Vivaldi's Four Seasons*. The building is the most impressive Art Nouveau style in Prague and one of the finest in Europe. It was a great show with four violinists presenting the musical equivalent to the seasons of the year. When returning to the hotel, we discovered our departure flight to Amsterdam, Netherlands had been canceled and instead, we would be routed through Reykjavik, Iceland getting into Washington Dulles International Airport almost five hours later. I'll repeat myself, be prepared for airline changes right up to the last minute.

It was breakfast in the hotel with champagne available; so,

I made a mimosa. Today was a free day to make plans on our own; so, I went to the Communist Museum, located down the street across from the Municipal House. The museum takes one through a written history of the communist era and political change in the Czech Republic accompanied with visual images and movie clips. This was a highly informative visit, and I snapped pictures of most of the information boards presented.

After incorrectly getting on the trolley in the wrong direction, we arrived at the trolley's final station and then rode it in the opposite direction to go to Prague Castle. Well, we had a slightly broader tour of the city than expected. In purchasing a combination ticket-Prague Castle Basic Circuit, we were able to tour St. Vitus Cathedral, as well as three other locations of the complex: Old Royal Palace, Saint George Basilica, and Golden Lane.

The origins of Prague Castle date back to the late nineth century during the reign of Bořivoj, the first Christian prince of Bohemia. The construction of Saint George's Basilica started in 920 with Romanesque architecture. The martyred Prince Wenceslas I of the famous Christmas carol, *Good King Wenceslas*, was interred in 932 in the Church of Saint Vitus. Saint Vitus Cathedral was started in 1344 under the direction of Charles IV, the future king of Bohemia and the Holy Roman emperor. Ironically, the Gothic cathedral was not completed until 1929. The vault secures the crown jewels of Bohemia, but they are not on public display.

Castle workers previously lived on the lane with one famous resident, Franz Kafka, residing in house number 22 from 1916 to 1917. Kafka was a German-speaking Bohemian-Jewish novelist and short-story writer regarded as a major twentieth-century literary figure. His work fuses elements of realism and fiction. His works, *The Trial* and *Metamorphosis,* depict anxiety and alienation experienced during this period in Europe. Just around the corner is the entrance to a dungeon entered through a very narrow staircase, single file only. Yes, there are implements of torture down there. There are other tours available within the Prague Castle complex, such as the permanent exhibition and tower of the cathedral.

We enjoyed a nice stroll back to our hotel from the trolley station at the base of the castle through Malá Strana, also known as Lesser Town, the hillside area with beautiful views of the Vltava River. I stopped in a gingerbread store with more shapes of the holiday delight than I have ever seen. The John Lennon Wall is also in this area with messages from fans to the late-Beatles' band member.

After crossing the conspicuous Charles Bridge, with its 30 Baroque statues of various saints, we stopped at the beautifully ornate Mirror Chapel to watch a classical music concert, but first it was time for a glass of beer to quench our thirst. While sipping at a café, a peaceful protest parade passed us by with police officers appropriately chaperoning the event. The protest focus was the treatment of Palestinians by Israel.

Prague is a city of music, and one can find a classical concert just about any night of the week somewhere in the city in one of the beautifully architected buildings. After the show, we stopped for goulash soup and a one-liter beer near our hotel with a single guitar player for entertainment; music encapsulates this city, complementing many dining experiences.

We had a bit of drama when leaving the next morning with the realization that we only had a fifty-minute window for the connecting flight in Iceland to include clearing passport control. During the flight, it seemed that most passengers around me had the same dilemma and anxiety. Many passengers not continuing stayed seated to allow connectors to scramble off the plane and jog to their next gate. Somehow, it seems that airline scheduling could be a little better than that. Fortunately, most flights were delayed so when we got to our gate, we had ample time to catch our breath before boarding. Once we landed at Washington Dulles International Airport, we took an Uber to our parking at the hotel and then the long drive to my home; fortunately, we were post-Washington DC rush hour traffic. It was an amazing trip.

The Danube River Cruise encounters several UNESCO World Heritage Sites. In Hungary, the site is Budapest, including the Banks of the Danube, the Buda Castle Quarter and Andrássy Avenue (1987). In Austria, the sites are Historic Centre of the City of Salzburg (1996), Palace and Gardens of Schönbrunn (1996), Wachau Cultural Landscape (2000), and

Historic Centre of Vienna (2001). In Germany, the site of old town of Regensburg with Stadtamhof (2006) and in Czech Republic, the site of Historic Centre of Prague (1992).

I was also able to check a couple places of worship off my bucket list: Saint Stephen's Basilica in Budapest on *Road Affair* blog; Great Synagogue, Budapest on *Conde Traveler* list; and Saint Stephen's Cathedral, Vienna and Saint Vitus Cathedral, Prague on *Road Affair* blog. For castles, my checks include Schönbrunn Palace under Travel Pirate list and Prague Castle under Travel Pirate and savingcastles blog list. The cruise encompassing several countries provided access to a variety of globally recognized sites.

Hungarian Parliament

Prague Castle

Prague Clock

Terezin Prison, Czech Republic

Shoes Monument, Budapest

La Grenouillère

Schönbrunn Palace

Regensburg Cathedral

Danube River flood

cigarette warning

Prague peaceful protest

The Garden of Delights

Part 2 – My Big Year

Chapter 15

Costa Rica and Southern Florida

The clearest way into the Universe is through a forest
wilderness. – John Muir

(https://www.brainyquote.com/quotes/john_muir_133725)

Background: History, Culture, and Environment

Hola mi amiga y amigo.

Costa Rica was originally part of the United Provinces of
Central America, which separated from Mexico in 1823. By
1839, the United Province became El Salvador, Guatemala,
Honduras, Nicaragua, and Costa Rica, which did not formally
declare its independence until August 30, 1848. The
country's first established foreign policy for trade with the
United States was the Treaty of Friendship, Commerce, and
Navigation signed in Washington, DC on July 10, 1851, and
effective on May 26, 1852.

When one thinks of Costa Rica, the rainforest comes to
mind. Yes, Costa Rica has rainforests, volcanos, cloud forests,
black-sand beaches, white-sand beaches, and everything in
between. The country is one of the global leaders in the
preservation of the environment with almost 100 percent of
its energy source as renewable. The largest source is
hydroelectricity, but other sources are geothermal, biomass,

solar power, and wind power. From 2021, close to 100 percent of the population (5.2 million as of 2023) have access to electricity.

National parks or protected areas comprise more than 25 percent of the total land. With tourism being the number one industry, people come for the natural environment and the government understands this premise. People travel to Europe to see what man has created, but people travel to Costa Rica to see what nature has created. Coffee and bananas are the second and third economic drivers for the country, both products of nature.

Costa Rica has 31 national parks which are managed by the Sistema Nacional de Areas de Conservacion (SINAC) part of the Ministry of Environment and Energy. Our tour afforded us visiting five of the parks, just a sampling of what Costa Rica has to offer.

Sandwiched between two countries with a history of military dictatorships, Costa Rica gave up its military in 1948 under the leadership of José Figueres Ferrer, who chose to focus on domestic spending for education and healthcare. That sounds like the description of a visionary leader with such a daring decision and action to relinquish a military under the circumstances of strong authoritarian neighbors. Prior to then, the military played a key role in the nation.

In 1857, pirate William Walker was defeated by the Costa Rican armed forces, which sounds like a good topic for a Pirates of Central America Hollywood movie. The country's last coup occurred in 1917 by General Brigadier Federico Tinoco Granados; however, U.S. President Woodrow Wilson refused to recognize him, creating international isolationism for the country. Tinoco's repressive policies were unpopular with all sectors of the population, including the elite. When his brother, José Joaquín Tinoco Granados, the Minister of War, was assassinated in 1919, Federico fled the country.

The Republican Party has been in power since 1932 but in the 1940's, the party initiated an alliance with the communist party and the Catholic church, a rather strange combination. The alliance through President Teodoro Picado, 1944-1948, benefited the less advantaged classes of society through social legislation for public health, the creation of the University of Costa Rica, the inclusion of social protections in the constitution, and the enactment of a labor code. However, the period became one of political and social unrest with anti-communism attitudes during post-World War II and the government proposing an income tax. The Republican Party candidate Rafael Calderon Guardia lost to the Union Party's Otilio Ulate. The Republican Party challenged the outcome which resulted in annulling the election. This caused a Civil War with exiled political figures and leader of the revolutionary movement, José Figueres Ferrer, to return to the country. Ferrer eventually took control of the country and on December 1, 1948, issued a declaration abolishing the army. Within a year, the decision was codified by the constitution.

The country has not had a military since that time; however, that doesn't mean there haven't been conflicts with its neighbors: Nicaragua and Panama. Border disputes arise with many nations around the world, and this is true of Costa Rica. Costa Rica relies on international organizations for dispute resolution and the diplomatic support of the United States. Although the 1858 Treaty of Canas-Jerez established the border between Costa Rica and Nicaragua as the San Juan River, different interpretations of the treaty have led to disputes. In 2010 Nicaragua started dredging the river which resulted in Costa Rica dispatching their police to the area. A diplomatic intervention by the Organization of American States prevented armed conflict between the two countries and the International Court of Justice peacefully resolved the dispute in 2018.

How does Costa Rica celebrate the Christmas holiday? Catholicism is the official religion of the country but the constitution grants freedom of religion with 17 percent of the population identified as Protestantism. The Christmas meal is eaten after midnight mass and consists of chicken and pork tamales wrapped in plantain leaves. For dessert, Tres Leches Cake and other pastries are served with eggnog and rum punch. El Niño Dios, the Baby Jesus, brings gifts to the children. In parts of the United States, the family turmoil over the main Christmas dish is whether to serve turkey or ham. Costa Rica adds a Central American flavor to the holidays.

Costa Rica ranked in 2024 for the Fund for Peace Fragile State Index rather high for a Central American country at 150th with a score of 39.4, ranking at nine countries ahead of the United States. In 2008, Costa Rica ranked 140th with a score of 50.9, so the country has been moving in the right direction becoming less fragile and more stable. With respect to the State Resilience Index, Costa Rica scored at 7.1 with all the indicators well above average except economy which was only slightly above average.

Travel Itinerary

I left a few days early to go to Miami to spend time there before flying to Costa Rica. Upon arriving in Costa Rica, we stayed in San Jose (one night), Tortuguero (two nights), San Jose (one night), Arenal (two nights), Monteverde (two nights), Guanacaste (two nights), Manual Antonio (two nights), and again San Jose (one night).

https://free-map.org/

Travel Journal

For most of the tour group, the trip started on December 6, 2023; for my travel mate and I, it started on December 2,

2023, four days ahead of time. On our quest to experience United States national parks, we took advantage of a flight to Miami and spent the four days visiting Everglades National Park, Biscayne National Park, and Dry Tortuga National Park, accomplished with a boat ride from Key West. The flight leaving at 5:35 am meant going to bed at 7:00 pm the night before, to rise and allow sufficient time to travel to the airport. But we landed at Miami International Airport at 8:00 am and headed to Everglades National Park about 9:00 am. Since most hotel shuttles don't start until 6:00 am, a flight at 5:30 am meant using airport parking (expensive for 18 days) or some combination of app parking and riding.

Using my parking app, I found hotel parking within a five-minute ride and once at the hotel I used Uber app to call for a ride to the airport. It worked very well, and we weren't the only Uber riders that morning from the hotel. A family was waiting for their ride app service, and a couple was dropped off using a ride app service. I'm not sure all app rides are as responsive but in a major city like Washington, DC there were several drivers at 3:00 am. We were there before Ronald Reagan National Airport opened for check-in and departures. For the return, we used the airport shuttle service which regularly made passes through the airport for pickups.

At Miami International Airport, I used a lesser-known car rental company and was not sure of its dependability. There was no rental facility at or near the airport, the company dropped off the car at an airport garage parking space and texted the location and car description to my phone. The keys were in the glove box with the rental documentation. Exiting Miami's parking garage had its challenges, but that was not the fault of the car rental company. I was pleasantly surprised; the process was exceptionally smooth and considerably less expensive, more than half of the other car rental companies. So, every now and then take a risk and try the less branded services.

We drove to the Everglades National Park Headquarters to get information and determine what to do and where to go. We never stopped for breakfast, and I was getting a little hungry and very glad that the park service had sandwiches for purchase. After a quick bite, we headed to Anhinga Trail, named after the bird, for a ranger-guided walk around the three-quarter-of-mile boardwalk. We saw several types of birds: ibis, egret, and heron but a more unusual sight was the purple gallinule which had the ranger excited. We also spotted an alligator in the freshwater swamp below the boardwalk.

After we finished the walk, we drove forty-plus miles to Flamingo, the speed limit changes from 35-55 mph along the road, so watch your speed. Although there are several hiking trails along the way, we made one stop at the Nike Missile Site of historical significance during the Kennedy Administration's concerns with Cuba. A missile is on display inside the original hanger. Continuing, we made it to Flamingo in time to sign up for the 4:00 pm Florida Bay boat ride.

While waiting at the marina, I spotted the locally famous crocodile moving through the marina area. Although it was quite large on the surface, it is estimated to be 13.5 feet (4.1 m) long, making it close to the national crocodile record of 14 feet (4.3 m). A few days before, it had a scuffle with a smaller crocodile, and the smaller one didn't win. The bloated carcass sat on the far side of the marina. The ranger told me that they do not disturb nature and therefore the remains would stay there until nature's solution prevailed, something or somethings ate it.

Our boat trip through Florida Bay lasted about two hours to observe a stunning sunset. The evening was sunny, and the water was calm. We saw many of the standard birds recently seen but added the brown pelican to my list. On the way back to the marina, we saw bottle-nosed dolphins. It was dark when we got back to the marina and headed back the 40-plus miles (64.4 km) to Homestead, Florida for a hotel night stay before heading down to Key West the next day. I had been up since 12:15 am to drive from my house to the hotel car park in Crystal City, Virginia. So, it was a very long day.

On the way to Key West, we stopped at Biscayne National Park not too far from Homestead, about 15 minutes. There is a visitor center on the Florida mainland portion, with a short 0.6-mile (1.0 km) boardwalk. The rest of the park consists of the waters and keys offshore. This area is only accessed by boat. There is a Heritage Boat Ride which lasts about three and a half hours, but we missed it by 30 minutes, so instead I signed up for the mangrove kayaking adventure. We started with an informative slow glide along the coastline spotting birds. In one spot, the guide pointed out a fish sac floating below the surface. Now knowing what to look for, I spotted several more fish sacs in the water. We paddled around the islands and then headed across the small cove against the tide; a nice workout before disembarking the kayak.

We still had the drive to Key West so left Biscayne National Park at 2:30 pm driving south on US Rt 1 through the Florida Keys. The 113-mile (182 km) drive was pleasant apart from the seven-mile (11.3 km) bridge which gets a little unnerving at about the four-mile (6.4 m) point. I was ready to be on land. For most of the key-hopping drive, there is just beautiful water scenery with a couple of areas of civilization such as Key Largo and Marathon before Key West. After checking into our hotel at about 5:15 pm, we walked to a nearby restaurant for dinner and then called it an early evening to read in bed.

The next morning, it was a continental breakfast at the hotel and then I walked to the Ernest Hemingway House and Museum. He lived in Key West from 1931-1939, drafting his earlier books there in his study above the smaller outside building. The guided tour provides details of his life in which many of his books are fictional spinoffs from his own experiences. Several books became movies in the 1940s and 1950s, such as *Old Man and the Sea, For Whom the Bell Tolls,*

The Snows of Kilimanjaro, Farewell to Arms, The Sun Also Rises, and *To Have and Have Not.*

It was a delight learning about his life, writing, and relationships having been married four times. The story of the swimming pool, the only one in Key West at that time of his residence depicts the challenges when doing something for the first time and experiencing cost overruns. Built during 1937-1938 at a cost of $20,000 (equivalent to $365,670 in 2020), it is sized at 24 feet by 60 feet (7.3 m by 18.3 m) with a depth from five feet to ten feet (1.5 m to 3.0 m). The guide's story is that Ernest said to his wife Pauline that she spent his last penny on the pool; there is a penny within the cement next to the pool.

The method of sanitizing pools wasn't available in the 1930s, so every few days the pool had to be drained, cleaned, and refilled adding more to the extravagance. In 1939 Hemingway moved to Cuba and his ex-wife Pauline lived in the house until her death in 1951. The gift shop, located by the pool, has copies of most of his books and memorabilia for Hemingway fans. I picked up a copy of *Old Man and the Sea* for which he won the Pulitzer Prize for Fiction in 1953.

One more tidbit on Hemingway, he liked to breed six-toed cats. His first was named Snow White who passed on the polydactyly gene to offspring. If one parent has the gene, then 50 percent of the offspring will acquire the unique trait. His estate has over 60 polydactyl felines and we saw quite a few of them during our visit.

Part 2-My Big Year

From the Hemingway House, we walked across the street to the Key West Lighthouse. It takes 88 steps to get to the top and a 360-degree spectacular view. The cruise ship in port could easily be seen. After hearing about Hemingway's antics at Sloppy Joe's, we ventured to the new location (the corner of Greene Street and Duval Street) for lunch. The original location (428 Greene Street) just down the street is now called Captain Tony's. The Greene Street location was the former city morgue until Sloppy Joe Russell turned it into a bar. When he moved to the corner location, the bar became Captain Tony's and advertises *the first and original Sloppy Joe's 1933-1937.*

We then stopped at Captain Tony's for pirate punch after a visit to the Little White House, a home on the United States Navy base used as a vacation home for President Harry Truman. He spent a total of 175 days there during his Administration. Presidents Eisenhower, Kennedy, Carter, and Clinton have also vacationed there. In April 2001, Secretary of State Colin Powell hosted the international peace conference between the governments of Armenia and Azerbaijan.

The house was built in 1890 as a duplex for the commandant and paymaster. Even inventor Thomas Edison lived at the house for six months in 1918 while he invented 41 new weapons to support World War I. I'm guessing these were part of the 1,093 patents Edison recorded as an inventor and savvy businessman. His most famous inventions are the phonograph, incandescent light bulb, alkaline battery, and one of the earliest motion picture cameras. He also was the first to create an industrial research laboratory in the town of Menlo Park in New Jersey.

In 1948, the house hosted the Joint Chiefs of Staff and their historic moment to launch the Key West Accord creating the Department of Defense by merging the Departments of War and Navy. There is a lot of history in that house. After Little White House, I walked to the Mel Fisher Maritime Museum and learned the story of Mel Fisher's quest to find shipwrecked treasures. On September 4, 1622, the Tierra Firma flota of 28 ships left Havana, Cuba bound for Spain, carrying silver from Peru and Mexico, gold and emeralds from Colombia, and pearls from Venezuela and Panama. A hurricane hit the next day sending seven of the ships, crew, and passengers to a watery grave between Marquesas Keys and Dry Tortuga off Florida. Mel Fisher spent 16 years searching for the treasure of the Nuestra Senora de Atocha and Santa Margarita, losing a son and daughter-in-law in this quest.

It seemed like a suitable time for dessert, so we stopped at the original bakery of Key Lime Pie; it's as good as they advertise. Our final stop that day was at the original Margaritaville Restaurant for a cheeseburger. Many restaurants in Key West offer live music while dining; this band played several Jimmy Buffet songs including *Cheeseburger in Paradise* as we were finishing our meal.

After a day of walking, I took a dip in the pool to relax before heading to bed for an early start the next morning.

We needed to be at the marina at 7:00 am for our departure to Dry Tortuga National Park on the Yankee Freedom III. The boat trip was about two and a half hours, with the last hour and a half through rather rough waters. I spent this time outside on the stern with a couple of other passengers not feeling so well. It was no consolation when our guide said that the swells were only 1-3 feet (0.3-0.9 m); usually, they are 4-6 feet (1.2 –1.8 m) for this time of year. The boat traverses the area where Mel Fisher's treasure was found; I'm so glad we stopped at the museum to learn the story before the boat ride. On some days, other treasure hunters still search the area, since it is believed not all the treasure was found.

This island, home to Dry Tortuga National Park, was discovered by Ponce de Leon in 1513. It acquired the name based on the large population of sea turtles living in the waters surrounding the island. Tortugas means turtle in Spanish; we learned this again in Costa Rica when we visited Tortuguero. It is believed that Ponce de Leon caught over 100 sea turtles during his time on the island. Maybe he liked turtle soup? The word *dry* was added to reflect that there is no fresh water on the island.

Our boat guide was our tour guide for the park and very knowledgeable about the history of the Fort Jefferson fortification. An interesting fact is during the Civil War, the

Union held the Dry Tortuga's even though Florida was confederate. The fort was built after the Louisiana Purchase to ensure open shipping lanes from New Orleans and the Mississippi River through the Gulf Stream and up the eastern coast of America into the Atlantic Ocean to Europe. The United States Army was tasked with building the fort. The artillery design required 120 guns to be fired on any area at sea around the 360-degree fort. The fort was also used as a prison with its most famous prisoner, Dr. Samuel Mudd, sentenced as a conspirator in the killing of President Abraham Lincoln by setting John Wilkes Booth's broken leg the night of the shooting. His cell is located just above the entrance to the fort.

The reverse trip back to Key West was rough at first and then the waters calmed down as we got closer. It was a beautiful evening and dinner cruises were heading out of the port. On the short drive back to the hotel from the marina, we heard about the unfortunate accident the previous morning which had closed a section of Route 1 entering Key West. A truck flipped while driving through a construction area at 4:30 am causing a fire and road closure. Since many people live outside of Key West and commute to the town, this impacted trash delivery, stores, and even schools with teachers unable to get to their classrooms. Radio announcers repeatedly cited the vulnerability of access and departure from Key West as a major issue.

We got an early start the next morning on our drive to

Miami International Airport and the start of the Costa Rica trip. Dropping the rental car at the parking garage was convenient for direct access to check-in. I just sent a text with a picture of the location. The flight was about three hours with a one-hour time change, and our hotel transfer was waiting for us. Within 20 minutes, we were at the hotel in San Jose at around 9:00 pm. The tour manager welcomed us and let us know that we would be leaving at 6:30 am for Tortuguero and breakfast would be available at 6:00 am. Later, I heard that some people didn't arrive until after 11:00 pm. We could only take a small 25 lb. (11.3 kg) bag with us but could leave the other luggage at the hotel. I missed that point in the pre-trip documents provided; fortunately, I did some repacking of my carry-on bag and made it work.

We drove for about two hours with half the drive highway and half bumpy road. With one stop for breakfast, we explored outside the restaurant to discover a two-toed sloth and a three-toed sloth in separate trees near each other. This was quite the discovery so early in the tour. Many visitors never see a sloth during their entire Costa Rica trip. Sloths are an incredible animal. Here are some interesting facts about those adorable creatures. Sloths can spend 90 percent of their lives hanging upside down. Their organs are attached to their ribcage, so they don't weigh down their lungs and impede breathing while hanging. With their slow processing, multi-compartment stomach, they can take up to 30 days to digest one leaf.

With extra vertebrae at the base of their neck, they can turn their head on a 270-degree axis. Although they are known to be very slow on land, they can move three times faster in the water. They also can hold their breath for 40 minutes, much longer than the dolphin's 10-minute duration. They sleep eight to nine hours a day like humans. The most puzzling characteristic though is that their facial structure makes them appear that they are smiling all the time. Did nature play a prank on the poor creature? A fate of perpetual smiling.

Although the modern sloth is the size of a medium dog, the ancient sloth was the size of an Asian elephant. Megatherium or giant sloth became extinct around 10,000 years ago. I remember while in Puerto Natales, Chile on the Patagonia trip hearing about a well-preserved giant sloth-like creature found in the Myloden Cave nearby.

With respect to the bumpy road, our tour manager reminded us we were getting a free massage. En route, we passed Chiquita and Delmonte banana plantations and packaging plants. Bananas are still hand-picked, put on a cable, then manually pulled to the plant.

We transferred to the boat for another two-hour ride on rivers and canals through the rainforest. I now understand why only small bags were allowed because it's a very small river boat. During our boat ride, we saw diverse types of birds but also crocodiles. As our tour manager was reeling off the names, my head was wrapped around enjoying the scenery so not too much stuck in my memory. Tortuguero is an

478

adventure; hotel rooms are cabins without air conditioning. After settling into our rooms, we had a boat ride across the canal to the village of Tortuguero.

Our tour manager took us to the beach for a discussion on the green sea turtle and nesting. From July to October, the female turtle crawls from the sea to dig a hole with her flippers and bury the eggs. Each nest will have 100-120 eggs. She then returns to the sea only to return another day and bury more eggs. Females lay eggs every four years; so, they do not return to the beach during the non-laying years. Beaches in this area are black sand.

The eggs hatch two months later during the early morning when the babies will crawl to the sea to start their aquatic life. The beach is closed during this early morning time, so no observers for when the baby turtles crawl into the ocean and disappear. However, during the nesting period, special tours are scheduled. A lottery determines where turtle observers are located within five sections of the beach which runs about five miles. The two time-slots available are 8:00 pm – 10:00 pm and 10:00 pm – 12:00 pm. Do I need to add to my bucket list: *observe sea turtles nesting*?

Although the town is only accessible by boat or airplane, most stores and eateries take major credit cards for purchases. Wow, I did not expect that for such a remote location. I had one of the best mojitos because it was made from real juice and not artificial mixer. Prices were reasonable considering the isolation of the village, everything is transported by boat.

That evening, we had an African-Caribbean dinner: shredded beef, Russian salad, with a pasta station. I think adding beets turns any dish into Russian cuisine. Also, I'm not sure how a Russian salad is part of African-Caribbean cuisine. That night, the jungle was wet and alive, and I was awake to hear most of it. Temperamental in my sleep patterns, any noise keeps me awake. The good news, the jungle noise drowned out the snoring of my travel mate. As we boarded the boat for a ride down the lagoon, I heard a few in the group mumble about trouble sleeping. The lagoon is brackish water, a combination of salt water from the Atlantic Ocean and fresh water from the mountains. We hit the jackpot with bird and animal sightings: spider and howler monkeys, a river otter, several iguanas, long-nose bats, and even a toucan. After the boat trip, we were given free time, so I went to the pool. Other group members joined me, and we spotted monkeys, iguanas, and toucans during our relaxing swim.

At lunch, the restaurant crew spotted a porcupine in the rafters of the building. I searched my Costa Rica Wildlife Guide; there are Mexican hairy porcupines in the country. That evening at dinner, the little critter was still there. After lunch, we went for a walk to observe flora and fauna by land. Again, we saw more monkeys, birds, and leaf-cutting ants. The flora on the walk included almond, mahogany, mimosa, papaya trees, and banana plants. Nestled in holes in the ground were blue and red crabs. Our tour manager also

480

discovered a very tiny creature but relished by Costa Ricans symbolizing the country, the red-eyed tree frog. He picked it off a leaf and it fit on the end of his finger. Its bright red eyes contrast with its green body creating the eye-catching allure that overcomes size. Although currently not endangered, the eventual result of continued deforestation and climate change actions will reduce the number of tree frogs in the wild.

After the walk, I took another dip in the pool before dinner. Rainforests are very humid, but my skin felt more lubricated than ever before. It rained that night too, at times hard. Oh, I forgot to mention that Costa Rica does not allow toilet paper in their toilets; the paper is placed in the trash can next to the toilet. I found this across the entire country regardless of the hotel or restaurant's star quality; it is how the country ensures less impact to the environment.

The next morning, we headed back to San Jose via the boat and coach ride checking into the hotel late afternoon. This first part of the trip had only 25 people, but the full group of 42 people met us the next morning for the trip to Arenal. We had three stops: first at a locally made craft and souvenir store, second in Sarchi at a church and park, and the third at La Fortuna at the base of Arenal Volcano for lunch. Group tours are usually pretty good about stops to stretch one's legs and use the bathroom after a one-to-two-hour drive, better known as comfort-stops.

Unfortunately, on our way to the hotel, the volcano was blocked by clouds. During this drive, our tour manager discussed the economic and social aspects of the country. The top three industries are tourism, coffee, and bananas, respectively. About 92-94 percent of children graduate from elementary school with 90 percent at the secondary level. Although public schools provide familiarization of languages, private schools teach proficiency in languages. The two most common beers in Costa Rica are Imperial and Pilsen. I remembered from my trip to the Czech Republic and a visit to the town of Pilsner that Pilsen was created there. An interesting point commented by the tour manager, the country is a big producer of fruits and vegetables, but most are exported because Costa Ricans prefer meat, rice, and bean diets than vegetables. Sugar cane is also grown in some areas.

The cabin-style hotel is situated along the mountain requiring a bit of an uphill or downhill walk to the restaurant and lobby. The walking distance was doable but for those more physically challenged, a shuttle provided pickup and delivery service to one's cabin. I suggest doing the walk; I saw an armadillo both mornings on my way to breakfast. We spent our first full day heading to Cano Negro and a boat ride on Rio Frio near the Nicaragua border.

This was a jackpot wildlife day; we saw caiman; white-faced capuchin, spider, and howler monkeys; and a vast assortment of birds. The finale occurred leaving when a three-toed sloth was crossing the road in front of our coach and our tour manager took off his belt, lifted the critter, walked him along the coach, and then placed him next to a tree to climb.

Wow, the elusive sloth, and we got a view up- close.

On the return trip, we stopped at a restaurant for lunch with chicken and rice. The next comfort stop was at a bridge that attracts iguanas, therefore known as Iguana Bridge. That evening, an optional excursion was to the Eco Termales Hot Springs, a short drive from the hotel and included a large, assorted buffet. There were several soothing pools each at a different temperature, what a splendid way to end the day.

The next morning, we hiked to the observation point for Arenal Volcano National Park; unfortunately, the clouds still covered most of it. Arenal Volcano is famous for its cone shape. We did get great views of the lake and saw two new birds: keel-billed toucan and great curassow. Traveling around the lake, it was on to Monteverde and the cloud forest at 5,000 feet (1,524 m) altitude. Our hotel comprised lodge-like buildings along the mountain, shuttle service was the more practical approach. For those choosing the optional craft Monteverde brewery tour and dinner, we had an eating-and drinking-enticed night. There is no bottling capability at the brewery; therefore, the product is provided only locally. With the ability to sample many of the varieties, I took advantage but kept the sample a tasting size. It started to rain which continued throughout the night; it is a cloud-forest.

The next day's activities included Selvatura canopy tour, better known as zip line, and hanging bridges. Those people for the canopy tour were leaving at 6:20 am and forgot that other people were still asleep. A rumble of activity passed by our door. I decided that I didn't want to zipline in the rain and just signed up for the hanging bridge walk. It drizzled all the next day; so, we had raincoats and umbrellas for the hanging bridge walk. At least it wasn't a downpour; it is a rainforest. It takes a lot of rain to have lush, dark foliage and the forest was abundant with lush, dark foliage below us.

There were eight bridges that tower above most of the vegetation. The significant finds of the walk were a hummingbird nest with eggs and a female, orange-kneed tarantula inside its hole. At the angle of the hole, one had to almost stand on their head to look up and see it. I'm left with *canopy tour in a rainforest* on my bucket list; so, I will need to check that box another time. The hanging bridge group was damp to dry but the canopy group got soaking wet, maybe I made the right choice after all.

Heading down the mountain to a coffee plantation, we warmed up with sunshine, and the group dried out. First, we had chicken, rice, beans, fruit, salad, and a cooked vegetable medley for lunch. One won't go hungry on these trips. We then had a walking tour describing the process of growing and producing coffee. That evening, I watched the sunset over the Pacific Ocean in the far distance. At the start of the trip in Key West, I watched the sunrise over the Atlantic Ocean, sunset over Florida Bay in Everglades, and now sunset over the Pacific Ocean. All my pictures are stunning.

Problems can arise while on a trip and one needs to figure out how to roll with it. The cap for my tooth had fallen off which made chewing meat more challenging. I had to cut my food into tiny pieces to eat. Fortunately, I was able to call my dentist and get an appointment for my return.

After breakfast, we started down the mountain for Guanacaste. Our next two nights would be at Tamarindo. The Liberia Guanacaste Airport provides direct access to the region rather than flying into San Jose and driving for several hours. With this access, celebrities flock to the Costa Rican Pacific coast. On the way, we stopped for lunch at a restaurant with scarlet macaws and howler monkeys in the trees. I watched the birds and monkeys move between the trees as I sipped my chocolate banana milkshake. After checking into our hotel on the beach, I relaxed by the pool, watched the sunset over the beach, and had a chicken curry dish at the restaurant. Eating next to the beach, I noticed a group of horses walking down the beach at the end of a horseback riding excursion. The horse silhouette with the sunset belonged in a painting or photograph.

With the natural beauty of Costa Rica, it is quite a draw for celebrities to vacation or own second homes. According to Costa Rica Immigration Experts, the following celebrities own or have owned properties in Costa Rica: Mel Gibson, Mark Zuckerberg, Tom Brady and Gisele Bündchen, Lady Gaga, Michelle Rodriguez, Tom Cruise, Charlotte Flair, Brad Pitt and Angelina Jolie, Chuck Norris, Danny DeVito, and Steven Seagal.[123] It makes sense, a short distance flight from the United States to a tropical paradise. According to Costa

Rica News, Keanu Reeves vacationed on the Papagayo Peninsula in Guanacaste for thirteen days in 2022.[124]

The next morning, we traveled to Flamingo Marina and a catamaran sail to a secluded cove for snorkeling. The water was smooth, making the trip very enjoyable. On the way, we passed two loggerhead turtles mating in the water; you don't see that every day. You could distinguish that there were two turtles, and they were swirling in the water; our boat crew provided an explanation for their activity. Once in the water, I snorkeled until the crew called us out to get lunch on the boat. I took a short walk on the beach and found it full of small hermit crabs.

Lunch comprised of sandwiches with salads. It was a booze cruise, so all the alcoholic drinks one wants, but pace yourself. We were back at the hotel around 2:00 pm and I spent the rest of the afternoon sitting by the pool, swimming, and reading. What a relaxing day. We had a group dinner and a beautiful view of the beach. There were three people with birthday celebrations, so lots of singing. I got back to my room just after 9:00 pm, read for about 30 minutes before drifting off into dreamy slumber.

For part of our group, the tour ended, and they headed back to San Jose while the other part continued to Manual Antonio. At a rest stop, the group split from one coach to two coaches; however, the small coach for the group going to Manual Antonio didn't accommodate all the luggage. So, we had to switch the bags, and that group took the big coach. Now I know why they wanted the smaller coach to go to Manual Antonio.

The road leading into the hotel is alongside a steep hill and very narrow. If another car was coming in the opposite direction, they had to reverse and find a spot to pull over. The hotel driveway wasn't designed to manage a coach that big, but the driver did an exceptional job. I closed my eyes at times because I didn't want to watch. After checking in, I headed for the pool and two-for-one Happy Hour drinks. The tour manager and the coach driver also deserved a drink or two. My stomach was still full of the cheeseburger that I had for lunch when we stopped in the beach town of Jaco, so I walked down the hill to check out the beach. The beachgoers were just finishing for the day with most heading back to their hotels. A beautiful spot in a small cove area, very private; the only problem is that you must walk back up the steep hill at the end.

The next morning, it was back on the coach and out on the narrow, windy road to Manual Antonio National Park. We walked the nature trail to the beach which was about half a mile, spotting white-faced capuchin monkeys and black iguanas at the beach. Once there we had beach time to swim or just stroll along the horseshoe-shaped beach. I went for a swim which was delightful. When I got out of the water to dry, I stood along the picnic area and watched the monkeys interacting with the other beachgoers. Some monkeys were going through people's backpacks.

I observed the scene of one monkey resting in a tree. He then jumped down and leaped into the middle of a blanket that a mom, dad, and toddler were sitting on. The mom was giving the toddler a piece of banana and the monkey snatched the banana out of her hand, jumped out of their circle, and climbed a tree nearby. The scene was one for the television show *America's Home Videos*, if only someone had been filming it. The mom was in shock with the expression: *what just happened*. The toddler was crying, *where's my banana*? The dad was somewhere between perplexed, *did I just see a monkey run across the blanket*, and consoling the child, *we'll get you something else to eat*.

I don't know how they got any food in the park because they check your bags for just that reason; the monkeys are vicious when it comes to food. They also don't allow plastic disposable water bottles because they would become trash in areas that are out of reach to be cleaned up. Crocodiles are found in some of the streams throughout the park. As I left the park, I spotted a street vendor with coconut water; a real coconut that they drill a hole, put a straw in, and you drink the coconut water. The coconuts were on ice, so the juice was cold, very refreshing.

When we returned to the hotel, I was back swimming in the infinity pool where the water disappears over the scenic edge only to be recycled back into the pool. It was Happy Hour again with buy-one-get-one free drinks; I love this hotel. They also had popcorn! We had a group dinner at a restaurant that had a unique grilling experience with a basic assortment of meats: beef, chicken, pork tenderloin, and ribs.

I awoke before 6:00 am and decided to have coffee on the balcony and read. As I was sipping my coffee, a monkey jumped onto the rail looking pleadingly at me for a snack. Having bought a Costa Rica animal guide, I immediately recognized it to be a squirrel monkey, the only one of the four monkeys in Costa Rica we had not seen. I quickly jumped into the room, grabbed my camera, and snapped a shot of him sitting on the back of the chair that I had just sat in. The monkey was very photogenic and posed in the most adorable way. It then ventured off to the next balcony looking for food. I went back inside, but a few minutes later decided to go back out and check if he was still around the area. After I made a few clicking sounds, I saw the trees shaking and a pack of capuchin monkeys heading my way. They travel in packs and can be quite aggressive and intimidating when large numbers approach your balcony; I scrambled back inside.

After checking out of the hotel, we drove to San Jose stopping at a craft store on the way for a comfort stop and more shopping. We were at the hotel by noon; so, I took a taxi to the Gold Museum. The museum displays artifacts in gold from the pre-Columbian period when objects were first made. Since the museum is in the same complex as the National Museum, we met up with the rest of our tour group there. This option meant that we would miss the city tour but thought the Gold Museum might be worth it.

Unfortunately for the group but fortunately for us, the coach experienced a fender bender while waiting at the hotel to leave and then a new coach had to be sent to take the tour group; therefore, we didn't miss the city tour with the delay. Our final stop was the Gran Hotel Costa Rica, where United States presidents have stayed when visiting the city. We had dinner at the restaurant on the top floor. While eating, an earthquake occurred, and everyone started checking their smartphones for information. It was 4.6 on the Richter scale. While people were checking their phones, they also discovered that Iceland had a volcano eruption. I was a bit concerned since I was going to Iceland two months later.

It was an early evening because we needed to put our luggage outside the door at 3:15 am and depart the hotel at 3:45 am for a 6:51 am flight from San Jose to Miami. When we arrived in Miami, my travel mate and I were able to get on an earlier flight and cut a few hours off waiting at the airport and arrival to Washington, DC.

This trip proved to be a *big year* conquest for birds. Southern Florida afforded the following birds: snowy egret, little blue heron, white ibis, brown pelican, magnificent frigatebird, purple gallinule, turkey vulture, and black vulture. Costa Rica added the following birds to my count: osprey, common hawk, green parakeets, little blue heron, magnificent frigatebird, great green macaw, spotted sandpiper, white-collared manakin, anhinga, turkey vulture, black vulture, great kickadee, yellow-throated toucan, keel-billed toucan, Baltimore oriole, northern jacana, great curassow, cattle egret, and scarlet macaw.

I was also introduced to a new fruit, jackfruit. An interesting flavor, it is described as a combination of banana, apple, and mango. It is a large fruit and obvious when growing on trees. Although used in curries and desserts, it's being explored as a substitute for meat. The fruit is yellow when ripe.

On our travels, we passed through and stayed in the Guanacaste area; the Area de Conservación Guanacaste is a UNESCO World Heritage Site since 1999. For Florida, I visited Everglades National Park, a World Heritage Site designated in 1979. With respect to national parks, I visited in Costa Rica: Arenal Volcano National Park, Caño Negro Wildlife Refuge, Guanacaste National Park, Manuel Antonio National Park, and Tortuguero National Park. I added the United States National Parks of the Everglades, Biscayne, and Dry Tortugas to my checked list.

six-toe cat   Key West marker   red-eyed treefrog

Fort Jefferson of Dry Tortugas   Key West sunrise

river boat cruise   find the Crocodile

scenes from the mountain to ocean   squirrel and capuchin monkey

sea turtle beach   green iguana

sea turtles mating   hanging bridge

animals in the wild

493

Part 2-My Big Year

Chapter 16

Summary

My Travel Big Year One was quite aggressive with travel every month after my retirement in March 2023. Even with only a week or two or five days in between trips, I found myself still excited for the next adventure. The countries visited were a combination of old-world charm to outdoor nature, making each one special. At least at this point, I can't pick a favorite because I felt I learned something new about each one and learning does make adventure more unique. This was the most asked question, which trip was my favorite?

To summarize my accomplishments, I visited 51 UNESCO sites in this year. These 51 sites merely scratch the surface of the 1,223 current sites listed for 2024. I'm not sure that I will make all of them before I *kick the bucket*. I've explored the Colosseum in Italy of the Seven Wonders of the Modern World. I've explored one, the Great Barrier Reef in Australia, of the Seven Natural Wonders of the World.

I encountered one of UNESCO's Representative List of the Intangible Cultural Heritage of Humanity that included several countries inscribed in 2013: Cyprus, Croatia, Spain, Greece, Italy, Morocco, and Portugal. What do these countries have in common? The answer is rather obvious since they all reside on the Mediterranean Sea; their cuisine is largely a Mediterranean diet.

The Mediterranean diet involves a set of skills, knowledge, rituals, symbols and traditions concerning crops, harvesting, fishing, animal husbandry, conservation, processing, cooking, and particularly the sharing and consumption of food. Eating together is the foundation of the cultural identity and continuity of communities throughout the Mediterranean basin. It is a moment of social exchange and communication, an affirmation and renewal of family, group or community identity. The Mediterranean diet emphasizes values of hospitality, neighbourliness, intercultural dialogue and creativity, and a way of life guided by respect for diversity. It plays a vital role in cultural spaces, festivals and celebrations, bringing together people of all ages, conditions and social classes. It includes the craftsmanship and production of traditional receptacles for the transport, preservation and consumption of food, including ceramic plates and glasses. Women play an important role in transmitting knowledge of the Mediterranean diet: they safeguard its techniques, respect seasonal rhythms and festive events, and transmit the values of the element to new generations.

Markets also play a key role as spaces for cultivating and transmitting the Mediterranean diet during the daily practice of exchange, agreement and mutual respect.[125]

So, the citation recognizes not only the cuisine but the environment in which the cuisine is grown, prepared, cooked, and eaten in a social environment, entwining social norms of communication, creativity, respect, and the shared values of community. The Mediterranean diet is a community event. I experienced UNESCO Intangible Cultural Heritage List item for the tango dance in Buenos Aires, Argentina.

The follow-on Volume II provides information on previous trips taken for leisure and work. With this additional knowledge, I broach the topic of international relations and global politics citing theories and opinions sourced from experts, such as Hans Morgenthau, Robert Kaplan, Sir Halford John Mackinder, Samuel Huntington, Zbigniew Brzezinski, Ray Dalio, Jared Diamond, John Mearsheimer, Paul Kennedy, Kenneth Waltz, Michael Pillsbury, Kishore Mahbubani, and of course, Henry Kissinger. The list is not all inclusive. Excerpts from their books are entwined with information gained from other books where pertinent to raise more intriguing questions. This Volume II chapter provides thought-provoking sentiments on the past, present, and future of the world. Traveling with the intent to merge history, culture, and environment creates an intellectual traveler.

I also shed light on the planned future trips for Travel Big Year Two and Travel Big Year Three hoping to complement the globe with regions that I have not yet experienced. Will new knowledge change any pre-conceived opinions that I might have for places in the world? Only learning more with venturing to these locations and learning more on their history, culture, and environment can impact current judgments and attitudes.

Part 2-My Big Year

Part 2-My Big Year

References

Introduction

[1]https://www.nbcnews.com/news/world/taliban-destroyed-afghanistans-ancient-buddhas- now- welcoming-tourists-rcna6307

[2] https://www.unesco.org/en

Chapter 1: Rationale for Bucket List

[3]https://med.stanford.edu/letter/bucket-list/what-is-bucket-list.html

[4] https://en.wikipedia.org/wiki/Kick_the_bucket

[5]https://www.worldhistory.org/article/2257/philo-of-byzantiums-on-the-seven-wonders/

[6]https://education.nationalgeographic.org/resource/seven-wonders-ancient-world/

[7] https://whc.unesco.org/en/list/483

[8] Holy Bible, King James Version, 189

[9] https://whc.unesco.org/en/list/326

[10] https://whc.unesco.org/en/list/252/

Chapter 2: Potential Natural Wonder Bucket List Items

[11]https://www.worldatlas.com/places/the-7-natural-wonders-of-the-world.html

[12]https://www.worldatlas.com/places/the-7-natural-wonders-of-the-world.html

[13] https://www.worldatlas.com/places/the-7-natural-wonders-of-the-world.html

[14] https://www.worldatlas.com/places/the-7-natural-wonders-of-the-world.html

[15] https://ourplnt.com/new-7-wonders-of-nature/

[16] https://whc.unesco.org/en/list/1264

[17] https://whc.unesco.org/en/list/1007

[18] https://ourplnt.com/new-7-wonders-of-nature/

[19] https://ourplnt.com/new-7-wonders-of-nature/

[20] Ernest Hemingway, The Snows of Kilimanjaro, *Esquire* magazine, 1936

Chapter 3: Other Bucket List Points of Interest

[21] https://www.unesco.org/en

[22] https://www.unesco.org/en/iggp/geoparks

[23] https://www.unesco.org/en/articles/unesco-designates-11-new-biosphere-reserves-1

[24] https://peabody.harvard.edu/files/peabody/files/a_museums_purpose_discussionguide.pdf?m=16420242

15

[25] The Pillars of Earth, Ken Follett, Penguin Random House LLC, 1999, xiv-xv

[26] https://en.wikipedia.org/wiki/Architecture_of_cathedrals_and_great_churches

[27]https://www.architecturaldigest.com/story/most-beautiful-churches-around-the-world

[28]https://www.cntraveler.com/gallery/the-most-beautiful-churches-in-the-world

[29]https://www.roadaffair.com/most-beautiful-churches-in-the-world/

[30]https://www.veranda.com/travel/g30732005/beautiful-mosques-in-the-world/

[31]https://www.veranda.com/travel/g34338651/beautiful-temples-in-the-world/

[32]https://www.cntraveler.com/galleries/2014-12-23/hanukkah-travel-synagogues-israel-new-york-   city- buenos-aires-germany

[33]https://www.famouscastles.net/list-of-famous-castles/

[34]https://www.travelpirates.com/captains-log/the-most-beautiful-castles-in-the-world

[35]https://savingcastles.com/10-top-famous-castles-to-visit/

Chapter 4: Background Information for Understanding

[36]https://education.nationalgeographic.org/resource/civilizations/

[37]https://www.britannica.com/topic/empire-political-science

[38]Guns, Germs, and Steel, Jared Diamond, W.W. Norton and Company, 2017, 37

[39]https://www.britannica.com/topic/democracy

[40]https://www.jfklibrary.org/learn/about-jfk/historic-

speeches?gad_source=1&gbraid=0AAAAAD1wgU7- lxfGvv09D5-

fEyCEUBGRg&gclid=CjOKCQjwlMfABhCWARIsADGXdy9wwJTeXeagRo
oWJMgxNPZt5wxq9Viu9Fxp41i3kzFYps   HMNirdE9YaAoEQEALw_wcB

[41]https://www.loc.gov/resource/rbpe.24404500/?st=text

[42]https://winstonchurchill.org/resources/quotes/the-worst-form-
of-government/

[43]   https://www.usatoday.com/story/news/2023/03/10/oligarchy-
government-power- explained/11338810002/

[44] The Revenge of Geography, Robert Kaplan, Random House,
2012, 196

[45]   https://www.usatoday.com/story/news/2023/03/10/oligarchy-
government-power- explained/11338810002/

[46]https://en.wikipedia.org/wiki/Authoritarian_capitalism#:~:text=
Countries%20commonly%20referred%20to

%20as,as%20fascist%20regimes%20and%20military

[47] Leadership, Henry Kissinger, Penguin Press, 2022, 281

[48] Leadership, Henry Kissinger, Penguin Press, 2022, 320

[49] The Road Ahead, Bill Gates, Viking Penguin, 1995, 51

[50]https://www.ias.edu/ideas/2018/schmidtorah#:~:text=ninth%2
0century%20B.C.E.,Who%20wrote%20the

%20Torah%3F,the%20Torah%20itself%20says%20otherwise

[51]https://www.americamagazine.org/faith/2021/06/02/st-peter-
forgotten-tomb-vatican-240779

[52] https://whc.unesco.org/en/news/2156

[53] https://www.worldhistory.org/Protestant_Reformation/

[54] https://www.metmuseum.org/toah/hd/isla/hd_isla.htm

[55] *Fund for Peace 2014 Booklet*, https://www.fundforpeace.org/ , 9

Chapter 5: Portugal

[56] https://whc.unesco.org/en/list/1590/

[57] https://whc.unesco.org/en/list/1387

[58]https://city-of-tomar.com/window-of-the-chapter-house-at-the-convent-of-christ-in-tomar/

[59] https://en.wikipedia.org/wiki/Sedlec_Ossuary

[60] https://whc.unesco.org/en/list/723/

[61] <u>Bucket List: 1000 Adventures Big and Small</u>, Kath Stathers, Universe Publishing, 2017.

Chapter 6: Patagonia, Argentina and Chile

[62] https://www.gocollette.com/en-us/travel-blog/patagonias-big-5-the-wild-wonders-at-the-edge-of-the- world

[63]https://www.swoop-patagonia.com/blog/patagonia-wildlife-the-big-5/

[64]https://www.bbc.com/future/article/20150710-the-gruesome-untold-story-of-eva-perons-lobotomy

[65]https://www.gate1travel.com/small-groups/small-group-americas/2025/small-groups-southamerica-14dsam4dc26.aspx?Brand=DISCOVER

[66]https://www.pbs.org/wnet/nature/blog/flamingo-fact-sheet/

[67]The Origin of Species, Charles Darwin, Bridge-Logos, 2009, 99-100

[68]https://www.pacificbeachcoalition.org/albatross-fun-facts/

[69] Sailing Along Around the World, Joshua Slocum, 63

Chapter 7: Italy

[70]https://www.worldatlas.com/articles/what-is-the-national-dish-of-italy.html

[71]https://fragilestatesindex.org/country-data/

[72]https://www.stmarksbasilica.com/st-marks-square

[73] The Agony and the Ecstasy, Irving Stone, Doubleday and Company, 1961, 591

[74] https://whc.unesco.org/en/list/286

[75] The Agony and the Ecstasy, Irving Stone, Doubleday and Company, Inc., 1961, 747

[76] The Agony and the Ecstasy, Irving Stone, Doubleday and Company, Inc., 1961, 557-558

[77]https://www.britannica.com/place/ancient-Rome

[78] Destinations of a Lifetime: 225 of the World's Most Amazing Places, National Geographic, Washington, DC, 305.

[79] The Pope Who Would Be King: The Exile of Pius IX and the Emergence of Modern Europe, David I. Kertzer, Random House, 2018, p. 6

[80] The Pope Who Would Be King: The Exile of Pius IX and the Emergence of Modern Europe, David I. Kertzer, Random House, 2018, p. 267

[81] The Pope Who Would Be King: The Exile of Pius IX and the Emergence of Modern Europe, David I. Kertzer, Random House, 2018, p. 344

[82]https://smv.org/learn/blog/volcano-mount-vesuvius/

Chapter 8: Seattle, Washington, United States

[83]https://san.com/cc/crime-in-seattle-increases-after-police-budget-cuts/

[84] https://www.museumofflight.org/about/

[85] https://whc.unesco.org/en/list/151

[86]https://www.pikeplacemarket.org/vendor/the-first-starbucks/

[87]https://www.nps.gov/parkhistory/hisnps/npsthinking/famousquotes.htm

[88]https://www.nps.gov/parkhistory/hisnps/npsthinking/famousquotes.htm

Chapter 9: Switzerland

[89]https://www.nato.int/cps/en/natohq/topics_50349.htm

[90] https://whc.unesco.org/en/list/1037

[91]https://www.wilden-mann.ch/en/hotel

[92]https://www.nbcnews.com/world/europe/village-destroyed-swiss-glacier-collapse-rcna209652

Chapter 10: Northern France

[93]https://www.history.com/topics/european-history/bastille-day

[94] https://whc.unesco.org/en/list/80

[95]https://en.chateaudeblois.fr/2464-the-royal-apartments.htm#par17281

Chapter 11: Australia

[96]https://www.australia.com/en-us/things-to-do/food-and-drinks/guide-to-australian-cuisine.html

[97]https://www.brucemunro.co.uk/work/field-of-light/

[98]https://www.afr.com/life-and-luxury/travel/uluru-why-celebrities-struggle-to-describe-it-20170720-gxet2s

[99]https://www.dalailama.com/news/2015/his-holiness-the-dalai-lama-visits-uluru

[100]https://whc.unesco.org/en/list/166

[101] https://whc.unesco.org/en/list/1306

[102]https://www.ifs.tas.gov.au/discover-trout-fishing-in-tasmania

[103] https://whc.unesco.org/en/list/181

[104] https://en.wikipedia.org/wiki/Australian_rules_football

Chapter 12: Alaska, United States and Canada

[105]https://earthquake.usgs.gov/earthquakes/events/alaska1964/

[106] https://www.nps.gov/wrst/index.htm

[107] Destinations of a Lifetime: 225 of the World's Most Amazing

Places, National Geographic, Washington, DC, 197.

[108]https://darrp.noaa.gov/oil-spills/exxon-valdez

[109]https://www.britannica.com/place/Mendenhall-Glacier

[110] https://www.fws.gov/story/zombie-salmon

[111]https://education.nationalgeographic.org/resource/glacier/

Chapter 13: Spain and France

[112]https://www.butterfield.com/get-inspired/seasonal-fare-bordeaux-vs-burgundy

[113]https://www.archdaily.com/877599/10-must-see-gaudi-buildings-in-barcelona

[114] https://whc.unesco.org/en/list/932/

[115] https://en.wikipedia.org/wiki/San_Sebasti%C3%A1n

[116]https://www.guggenheim.org/press-release/guggenheim-museum-among-eight-buildings-by-frank-   lloyd- wright-inscribed-on-unesco-world-heritage-list

[117]https://www.guggenheim-bilbao.eus/en/the-collection/works/the-matter-of-time

[118] https://whc.unesco.org/en/list/379/

Chapter 14: Danube Cruise (Hungary, Slovakia, Austria, Germany, and Czech Republic)

[119]The World of Yesterday, Stephan Zweig, University of Nebraska Press, 2013, 257.

[120]https://thefrenchroomhome.wordpress.com/2020/02/04/ten-of-

the-most-famous-paintings-by- pierre- auguste-renoir/

[121]https://whc.unesco.org/en/list/784/

[122]https://www.bmwgroup-werke.com/regensburg/de.html

Chapter 15: Costa Rica and Southern Florida, United States

[123]https://crie.cr/celebrities-in-costa-rica/

[124]https://thecostaricanews.com/keanu-reeves-enjoyed-his-vacation-in-costa-rica/

Chapter 16: Summary

[125] https://ich.unesco.org/en/RL/mediterranean-diet-00884

Bibliography

Introduction

1. https://www.nbcnews.com/news/world/taliban-destroyed-afghanistans- ancient- buddhas-now-welcoming-tourists-rcna6307

2. https://www.unesco.org/en

Chapter 1: Rationale for Bucket List

1. https://med.stanford.edu/letter/bucket-list/what-is-bucket-list.html

2. https://en.wikipedia.org/wiki/Kick_the_bucket

3. https://www.worldhistory.org/article/2257/philo-of-byzantiums-on-the- seven- wonders/

4. https://www.history.com/articles/seven-wonders-of-the-ancient-world

5. https://education.nationalgeographic.org/resource/seven-wonders- ancient- world/

6. https://www.britannica.com/topic/Pyramids-of-Giza/

7. https://www.worldhistory.org/Great_Pyramid_of_Giza/

8. https://www.britannica.com/topic/lighthouse-of-Alexandria/

9. https://www.worldhistory.org/Lighthouse_of_Alexandria/

10. *The Pyramids and Implementing Project Management Processes*, Dr. Alaa A. Zeitoun and Dr. Ahny W. Helmy.

Part 2-My Big Year

https://www.wcu.edu/pmi/1997/97IN01.PDF

11. https://www.britannica.com/place/Hanging-Gardens-of-Babylon/

12. https://www.worldhistory.org/Hanging_Gardens_of_Babylon/

13. www.britannica,com/topic/Statue-of-Zeus/

14. https://www.worldhistory.org/Statue_of_Zeus_at_Olympia/

15. https://www.britannica.com/topic/Colossus-of-Rhodes/

16. https://www.worldhistory.org/Colossus_of_Rhodes/

17. https://www.britannica.com/topic/Temple-of-Artemis-temple-Ephesus-Turkey/

18. https://www.worldhistory.org/Temple_of_Artemis_at_Ephesus/

19. https://www.britannica.com/topic/Mausoleum-of-Halicarnassus/

20. https://www.worldhistory.org/disambiguation/mausoleum_of_halicarnassus/

21. https://www.britannica.com/list/new-seven-wonders-of-the-world/

22. https://www.thoughtco.com/wonders-of-the-world-new-list-4065228/

23. https://whc.unesco.org/en/list/483

24. https://www.chichenitza.com/

25. https://www.britannica.com/place/Chichen-Itza

26. https://whc.unesco.org/en/list/483

27. https://education.nationalgeographic.org/resource/colosseum/

28. https://www.britannica.com/list/new-seven-wonders-of-the-world/

29. Turn Right at Machu Picchu: Rediscovering the Lost City One, Mark Adams, Dutton Publishing, April 2012

30. https://www.britannica.com/place/Machu-Picchu/

31. https://study.com/academy/lesson/why-is-christ-the-redeemer-considered-   one-of-the-seven-wonders-of-the-world.html#:~:text=Christ%20the%20Redeemer%20statue%20is%20the%20la   r gest%20Art%20Deco%20design,Pedro%20II's%20daughter%2C%20Princess% 2 0Isabel.

32. https://whc.unesco.org/en/list/1100/

33. https://lisbonlisboaportugal.com/lisbon-sights/cristo-rei-christ- statue- lisbon.html

34. https://whc.unesco.org/en/list/326

35. https://www.touristjordan.com/movies-filmed-in-jordan/#:~:text=3)%20Indiana%20Jones%20and%20the,sequence%20was%2 0f ilmed%20at%20Petra.

36. https://www.britannica.com/place/Petra-ancient-city-Jordan

37. https://whc.unesco.org/en/list/252/

38. https://www.britannica.com/topic/Taj-Mahal

39. https://www.britannica.com/topic/Great-Wall-of-China

40. https://www.chinahighlights.com/greatwall/

41. https://www.ce.memphis.edu/1101/interesting_stuff/7wonders.html__

Chapter 2: Potential Natural Wonder Bucket List Items

1. https://www.worldatlas.com/places/the-7-natural-wonders-of-the-world.html

2. https://www.space.com/15139-northern-lights-auroras-earth-facts-sdcmp.html

3. https://www.swpc.noaa.gov/communities/aurora-dashboard-experimental

4. https://oceanservice.noaa.gov/facts/gbrlargeststructure.html

5. https://en.wikipedia.org/wiki/Great_Barrier_Reef

6. https://ourplnt.com/new-7-wonders-of-nature/

7. https://whc.unesco.org/en/list/1264

8. https://www.britannica.com/place/Jeju-Island

9. https://whc.unesco.org/en/list/652

10. https://whc.unesco.org/en/list/1007

11. https://whc.unesco.org/en/list/403/

12. Ernest Hemingway, *The Snows of Kilimanjaro*, Esquire magazine, 1936)

13. https://www.globaladventurechallenges.com/journal/facts-about-sahara-desert

14. https://whc.unesco.org/en/list/1432/

15. https://whc.unesco.org/en/list/39/

16. https://sevenwonders.org/nile-river/

17. https://sevenwonders.org/red-sea-reef/

18. https://sevenwonders.org/serengeti-migration/

Chapter 3: Other Bucket List Points of Interest

1. https://ich.unesco.org/en/lists

2. https://www.unesco.org/en

3. https://whc.unesco.org/en/criteria/

4. https://www.unesco.org/en/iggp/geoparks

5. https://www.unesco.org/en/articles/unesco-designates-11-new- biosphere- reserves-1

6. https://peabody.harvard.edu/files/peabody/files/a museums purpose discuss i onguide.pdf?m=1642024215

7. https://en.wikipedia.org/wiki/List of largest art museums

8. https://www.whatsthediff.org/blog/2019/04/23/whats-the-

difference- between- a-church-chapel-cathedral-and-basilica/

9. *The Pillars of Earth*, Ken Follett, Penguin Random House LLC, 1999

10. https://en.wikipedia.org/wiki/Architecture_of_cathedrals_and_great_churches

11. https://www.architecturaldigest.com/story/most-beautiful-churches- around- the-world

12. https://www.cntraveler.com/gallery/the-most-beautiful-churches-in-the-world

13. https://www.roadaffair.com/most-beautiful-churches-in-the-world/

14. https://www.britannica.com/topic/mosque

15. https://www.veranda.com/travel/g30732005/beautiful-mosques-in-the-world/

16. https://www.veranda.com/travel/g34338651/beautiful-temples-in-the-world/

17. https://www.cntraveler.com/galleries/2014-12-23/hanukkah-travel- synagogues- israel-new-york-city-buenos-aires-germany

18. https://en.wikipedia.org/wiki/List_of_castles

19. https://www.famouscastles.net/list-of-famous-castles/

20. https://www.travelpirates.com/captains-log/the-most-

beautiful-castles-in- the- world

21. https://savingcastles.com/10-top-famous-castles-to-visit/

Chapter 4: Background Information for Understanding

1. https://www.britannica.com/event/Middle-Ages

2. https://www.britannica.com/event/Renaissance

3. https://www.britannica.com/summary/The-Enlightenment-Key-Facts

4. https://www.worldhistory.org/The_Enlightenment/

5. Guns, Germs, and Steel, Jared Diamond, W.W. Norton and Company, 2017

6. https://www.history.com/news/first-earliest-human-civilizations

7. https://education.nationalgeographic.org/resource/civilizations/

8. https://www.britannica.com/topic/empire-political-science

9. https://archive.globalpolicy.org/component/content/article/155- history/25992- empires-in-world-history.htm

10. https://www.britannica.com/topic/democracy

11. https://www.jfklibrary.org/learn/about-jfk/historic-speeches?gad_source=1&gbraid=0AAAAAD1wgU7-IXfGvv09D5-fEyCEUBGRg&gclid=Cj0KCQjwlMfABhCWARIsADGXdy9wwJTeXeagRooWJM g

xNPZt5wxq9Viu9Fxp41i3kzFYpsHMNirdE9YaA0EQEALw_wcB

12. https://www.loc.gov/resource/rbpe.24404500/?st=text

13. https://winstonchurchill.org/resources/quotes/the-worst-form-of-government/

14. https://www.npr.org/sections/money/2022/03/29/10888865 54/how- putin- conquered-russias-oligarchy

15. https://www.usatoday.com/story/news/2023/03/10/oligarch y- government- power-explained/11338810002/

16. The Revenge of Geography, Robert Kaplan, Random House, 2012

17. https://daviscenter.fas.harvard.edu/insights/meet-russias-oligarchs-group- men- who-wont-be-toppling-putin-anytime-soon

18. https://www.usatoday.com/story/news/2023/03/10/oligarch y- government- power-explained/11338810002/

19. https://en.wikipedia.org/wiki/Authoritarian_capitalism#:~:te xt=Countries%20 c ommonly%20referred%20to%20as,as%20fascist%20regimes %20and%20milita r y

20. Leadership: Six Stories in World Strategy, Henry Kissinger, Penguin Press, 2022

21. The Road Ahead, Bill Gates, Viking Penguin, 1995

22. https://www.visualcapitalist.com/cp/mapped-worlds-

government-systems/

23. https://www.ias.edu/ideas/2018/schmidtorah#:~:text=ninth%20century%20B.C.E.,Who%20wrote%20the%20Torah%3F,the%20Torah%20itself%20says%20 otherwise

24. https://www.britannica.com/topic/paganism

25. https://www.britannica.com/topic/polytheism/Forms-of-polytheistic- powers- gods-and-demons

26. https://www.britannica.com/topic/Hinduism

27. https://www.edu.gov.mb.ca/k12/docs/support/world religions/hinduism/belie f s.pdf

28. https://education.nationalgeographic.org/resource/buddhism/

29. https://www.history.com/topics/religion/judaism

30. https://www.britannica.com/topic/Christianity

31. https://www.newadvent.org/cathen/12272b.htm

32. https://www.americamagazine.org/faith/2021/06/02/st-peter-forgotten- tomb- vatican-240779

33. https://www.thevaticantickets.com/vatican-history/

34. https://whc.unesco.org/en/news/2156

35. https://www.worldhistory.org/Protestant Reformation/

36. https://www.metmuseum.org/toah/hd/isla/hd isla.htm

37. https://www.bosphorustour.com/camlica-mosque.html

38. https://www.history.com/news/sunni-shia-divide-islam-muslim

39. https://www.fundforpeace.org/

40. Fund for Peace 2014 Booklet, https://www.fundforpeace.org/

Chapter 5: Portugal

1. http://www.notable-quotes.com/c/culture_quotes.html

2. https://onu.missaoportugal.mne.gov.pt/en/about-portugal/history

3. https://www.britannica.com/place/Portugal/Government-and-society

4. https://www.washingtonpost.com/health/interactive/2023/portugal-us- health- systems-life-expectancy/

5. https://www.architecturaldigest.com/story/heres-a-peek-inside- madonnas- newly-purchased-18th-century-moorish-revival-mansion-in- portugal

6. https://fragilestatesindex.org/country-data/

7. https://free-map.org/

8. The Camino: A Journey of the Spirit, Shirley MacLaine, Atria Books, 2001

9. The Only Way Is West: A Once In a Lifetime Adventure Walking 500 Miles On Spain's Camino de Santiago, Bradley

Chermside, www.bradleychermside.com

10. https://www.britannica.com/place/Santiago-de-Compostela

11. https://artsandculture.google.com/story/a-virtual-visit-to-the-cathedral- of- santiago-de-compostela-cathedral-of-santiago-de- compostela/IQVBcpdeUMCMqw?hl=en-US

12. https://whc.unesco.org/en/list/1590/

13. https://whc.unesco.org/en/list/1387

14. https://www.britannica.com/place/Portugal/History

15. https://www.americamagazine.org/faith/2017/05/10/story-fatima- apparitions- miracles-and-journey-sainthood?gad_source=1&gclid=CjoKCQiAkeSsBhDUARIsAK3tieev6uf6NbdfIk f 8nJ3yhm3_hzVAGPjKErI4jcxMMXrY4DyCtO71nPMaAqPDEALw_wcB

16. https://city-of-tomar.com/window-of-the-chapter-house-at-the-convent- of- christ-in-tomar/

17. https://www.visitevora.net/en/bones-chapel-evora/

18. https://en.wikipedia.org/wiki/Sedlec_Ossuary

19. https://whc.unesco.org/en/list/723/

20. https://www.travelawaits.com/2494140/obidos-portugal/

21. https://www.dailyartmagazine.com/king-pedro-and-ines-de-castro/

22. https://www.earthmagazine.org/article/benchmarks-november-1-

1755- earthquake-destroys-lisbon/

23. https://portugaltravelguide.com/church-ruins-lisbon/

24. https://www.portugal.com/food-drink/the-story-behind-portos-francesinha/

25. Bucket List: 1000 Adventures Big and Small, Kath Stathers, Universe Publishing, 2017

26. https://whc.unesco.org/en/list/

Chapter 6: Patagonia, Argentina and Chile

1. https://myadviceforlife.com

2. https://www.gocollette.com/en-us/travel-blog/patagonias-big-5-the- wild- wonders-at-the-edge-of-the-world

3. https://www.swoop-patagonia.com/blog/patagonia-wildlife-the-big-5/

4. https://www.gocollette.com/en-us/travel-blog/patagonias-big-5-the- wild- wonders-at-the-edge-of-the-world

5. https://emergingdestinations.com/patagonias-big-five-wildlife-list/

6. https://en.wikipedia.org/wiki/Magellanic_penguin

7. The Origin of Species, Charles Darwin, Bridge-Logos, 2009

8. https://www.britannica.com/place/Tierra-del-Fuego-archipelago- South- America

9. https://www.adventure-life.com/patagonia/articles/tierra-del-fuego-culture

10. https://www.newworldencyclopedia.org/entry/Tierra_del_F uego

11. https://www.worldatlas.com/islands/tierra-del-fuego.html

12. https://argentineasado.com/what-foods-is-argentina-known-for/

13. https://www.whychristmas.com/cultures/chile

14. https://en.wikipedia.org/wiki/Politics_of_Argentina

15. https://en.wikipedia.org/wiki/Politics_of_Chile

16. https://fragilestatesindex.org/country-data/

17. https://free-map.org/

18. https://www.bbc.com/future/article/20150710-the-gruesome-untold-story- of- eva-perons-lobotomy

19. https://en.wikipedia.org/wiki/Tango

20. https://ich.unesco.org/en/RL/tango-00258

21. https://www.gate1travel.com/small-groups/small-group-americas/2025/small-   groups-southamerica-14dsam4dc26.aspx?Brand=DISCOVER

22. https://www.pbs.org/wnet/nature/blog/flamingo-fact-sheet/

23. https://www.patagonia-argentina.com/en/fitz-roy-mount/

24. https://lastorres.com/en/torres-del-paine/torres-del-paine-national-park/

25. https://www.lifegate.com/icebergs-grey-glacier-patagonia-

chile

26. https://www.britannica.com/biography/Charles-Darwin/The-Beagle-voyage

27. The Origin of Species, Charles Darwin, Bridge-Logos, 2009

28. Endurance: Shackleton's Incredible Voyage, Alfred Lansing, Carroll & Graf Publishers, 2002

29. The Condor's Feathers: Traveling Wild in South America, Michael Webster, www.septemberpublishing.org, 2022

30. https://www.pacificbeachcoalition.org/albatross-fun-facts/

31. Sailing Along Around the World, Joshua Slocum, 63

32. https://www.unesco.org/en/mab/cabo-de-hornos#:~:text=The%20Cabo%20de%20Hornos%20(Cape,ter ms%20biologic al%20and%20cultural%20diversity.

33. https://www.britannica.com/topic/Yamana

34. https://foreignpolicy.com/2013/03/18/the-last-time-a-papal-intervention- worked-in-south-america

35. https://www.batimes.com.ar/news/argentina/new-tension-between- argentina- and-chile-over-territorial-waters.phtml

36. https://www.iwm.org.uk/history/a-short-history-of-the-falklands-conflict#:~:text=The%20Falklands%20Conflict%20was%20a, and%20cost%20200 v er%20900%20lives.

37. Destinations of a Lifetime: 225 of the World's Most

Part 2-My Big Year

<u>Amazing Places</u>, National Geographic, Washington, DC

38. <u>LlamaDrama</u>, Anna McNuff, 2020

39. <u>https://whc.unesco.org/en/list/</u>

Chapter 7: Italy

1. <u>https://pubmed.ncbi.nlm.nih.gov/29936236/</u>

2. <u>https://www.britannica.com/topic/history-of-Italy</u>

3. <u>https://www.britannica.com/place/Italy/</u>

4. <u>https://www.history.com/this-day-in-history/may-9/aldo-moro-found-dead</u>

5. <u>https://european-union.europa.eu/principles-countries-history/eu-countries/italy_en#:~:text=Italy%20is%20a%20parliamentary%20republic,is%2 0subdivided%20into%2020%20regions</u>

6. <u>https://www.worldatlas.com/articles/what-is-the-national-dish-of-italy.html</u>

7. <u>https://fragilestatesindex.org/country-data/</u>

8. <u>https://free-map.org/</u>

9. <u>https://thecatholicmanreviews.wordpress.com/tag/lucernarium/</u>

10. <u>https://www.britannica.com/topic/Verona-Arena</u>

11. <u>https://estreetshuffle.com/index.php/2018/10/05/where-the-band-was- verona- october-5-2006/</u>

12. https://www.pinkfloydz.com/concerts-tours/roger-waters-dark-side- tour- 2006/roger-waters-dark-side-tour-2006-5-june-italy-verona/

13. https://www.stmarksbasilica.com/st-marks-square

14. https://www.towerofpisa.org/

15. https://whc.unesco.org/en/list/286

16. The Agony and the Ecstasy, Irving Stone, Doubleday and Company, 1961

17. https://dogmatics.wordpress.com/2015/07/31/a-guide-to-catholic- religious- orders/

18. https://www.britannica.com/topic/Carthusians

19. https://www.stdominicchurch.org/dominican-order.html

20. https://www.britannica.com/topic/Jesuits

21. https://whc.unesco.org/en/list/174/

22. https://www.seetheholyland.net/tag/muhraka/

23. https://www.pivada.com/en/michelangelo-buonarroti-the-sistine-chapel- nine- main-scene

24. https://www.britannica.com/place/ancient-Rome

25. https://romeonrome.com/2016/09/the-walls-and-gates-of-rome/

26. https://www.turismoroma.it/en/itineraries/passage-over-tiber- rome%E2%80%99s-seven-most-iconic-bridges

27. Destinations of a Lifetime: 225 of the World's Most Amazing Places, National Geographic, Washington, DC

28. The Pope Who Would Be King: The Exile of Pius IX and the Emergence of Modern Europe, David I. Kertzer, Random House, 2018

29. https://smv.org/learn/blog/volcano-mount-vesuvius/

30. https://www.aljazeera.com/news/liveblog/2025/5/8/white-smoke- emerges- from-sistine-chapel-signalling-new-pope-elected

Chapter 8: Seattle, Washington, United States

1. https://www.brainyquote.com/quotes/john_muir_108391

2. https://en.wikipedia.org/wiki/History_of_Seattle

3. https://www.boeing.com/content/dam/boeing/boeingdotcom/history/pdf/Bo ei ng_Founders.pdf

4. https://fragilestatesindex.org/country-data/

5. https://san.com/cc/crime-in-seattle-increases-after-police-budget-cuts/

6. https://nationalpolice.org/defund-the-police-movement-plays-follow-the-   leader-down-rabbit-hole/?info=EG0101&ad=440929114537&kw=defunding%20p olice%20moveme n t&gad_source=1&gclid=CjoKCQiAq-u9BhCjARIsANLj-s2hTdSv_GVukxGw6UTNfYnEwyFNoQCYl2aClo6klWMRm Zgbgm- FHa4aAgC5EALw_wcB

7. https://free-map.org/

8. https://www.museumofflight.org/about/

9. https://whc.unesco.org/en/list/151

10. https://www.nps.gov/olym/learn/nature/elwha-ecosystem-restoration.htm

11. https://www.pikeplacemarket.org/vendor/the-first-starbucks/

12. https://www.nps.gov/mora/learn/nature/carnivores.htm

13. https://www.zoo.org/savingpenguins#:~:text=Humboldt%20Penguin%20Cons   ervation%20%2D%20Woodland%20Park%20Zoo%20Seattle%20WA

14. https://www.nps.gov/parkhistory/hisnps/npsthinking/famousquotes.htm

Chapter 9: Switzerland

1. https://www.brainyquote.com/quotes/john_muir_380220

2. https://en.wikipedia.org/wiki/Heidi_(1937_film)

3. https://www.britannica.com/place/Switzerland

4. https://www.britannica.com/place/Switzerland

5. https://fragilestatesindex.org/country-data/

6. https://free-map.org/

7. https://vivamost.com/dark-side-chillon-castle-beloved-swiss-castle/

8. <u>Einstein: His Life and Universe</u>, Walter Isaacson, Simon & Schuster Paperbacks, 2007

9. https://whc.unesco.org/en/list/1037

10. https://www.jungfrau.ch/en-gb/jungfraujoch-top-of-europe/

11. https://www.balmers.com/visit-the-jungfrau/

12. https://grindelwald.swiss/en/

13. https://www.wilden-mann.ch/en/hotel

14. https://www.nbcnews.com/world/europe/village-destroyed-swiss- glacier- collapse-rcna209652

15. https://www.rodelbahn.ch/en/uber-uns/

16. https://houseofswitzerland.org/swissstories/history/st-bernard-making- alpine- legend

Chapter 9: Northern France

1. https://www.brainyquote.com/quotes/thomas_paine_163018

2. https://www.britannica.com/topic/history-of-France

3. https://www.britannica.com/event/French-Revolution

4. https://en.wikipedia.org/wiki/Medieval_architecture

5. https://www.britannica.com/event/Normandy-Invasion

6. https://www.history.com/articles/d-day

7. https://fragilestatesindex.org/country-data/

Part 2-My Big Year

8. https://free-map.org/

9. https://www.experienceloire.com/loire-valley-chateaux.htm

10. https://www.history.com/topics/european-history/bastille-day

11. https://www.cathedrale-reims.com/decouvrir-la-cathedrale/historique/lhistoire-de-la- cathedrale

12. https://en.wikipedia.org/wiki/Reims_Cathedral

13. https://www.britannica.com/topic/Chartres-Cathedral

14. https://whc.unesco.org/en/list/81/

15. https://www.britannica.com/biography/Claude-Monet

16. https://www.claude-monet.com/

17. https://www.theartstory.org/artist/monet-claude/

18. https://en.wikipedia.org/wiki/Foie_gras

19. https://ww w.britannica.com/place/Arromanches

20. https://www.memorial-caen.com/

21. https://whc.unesco.org/en/list/80

22. https://www.worldhistory.org/Mont-Saint-Michel/?gad_source=1&gbraid=0AAAAA0ULJo3pLX66-WYIFP4Eq9VJ9A2QO&gclid=CjoKCQjwt8zABhDKARIsAHXuD7YVXZScqOUi b VpBkrP3GXuf-v7leSR8B3aingA1muzrdxW5bJAH_1waAl_FEALw_wcB

23. https://catholicmagazine.news/the-shrine-of-monte-gargano/

24. https://www.theguardian.com/artanddesign/2020/apr/17/the-forgotten-french-tapestry-with-lessons-for-our-apocalyptic-times

25. https://www.raremaps.com/gallery/detail/62228/second-world-war-german-invasion-of-france-rochecotte-ju-anonymous

26. https://en.chateaudeblois.fr/2193-history-and-architecture.htm

27. https://en.chateaudeblois.fr/2464-the-royal-apartments.htm#par17281

28. https://en.wikipedia.org/wiki/Ch%C3%A2teau_de_Chambord

29. https://praywithjillatchartres.com/mary/the-veil-of-mary/

30. <u>Destinations of a Lifetime: 225 of the World's Most Amazing Places</u>, National Geographic, Washington, DC

Chapter 11: Australia

1. https://www.brainyquote.com/quotes/jacques_yves_cousteau_204406?src=t_n ature

2. http://law2.umkc.edu/faculty/projects/ftrials/Bounty/bountyaccount.html

3. https://www.amnesty.org.au/eight-facts-about-indigenous-people-in-australia/?cn=trd&mc=click&pli=23501504&PluID=0&ord={t

imestamp}&gclid

=
CjoKCQiAtOmsBhCnARIsAGPa5yZEAUtE17JcOs18so3XB-

4OnvbY3CoZAjpBjcSpLyEeHKhj9hpY7zwaAsFEEALw_w
cB

4. https://fragilestatesindex.org/country-data/

5. https://free-map.org/

6. https://whc.unesco.org/en/list/154

7. https://www.brucemunro.co.uk/work/field-of-light/

8. https://www.afr.com/life-and-luxury/travel/uluru-why-
    celebrities-struggle- to- describe-it-20170720-gxet2s

9. https://www.dalailama.com/news/2015/his-holiness-the-
    dalai-lama-visits-uluru

10. Destinations of a Lifetime: 225 of the World's Most
    Amazing Places, National Geographic, Washington, DC

11. https://www.dailymail.co.uk/news/article-11913803/Barack-
    Obama- Michelle- Obama-climb-Sydney-Harbour-Bridge-
    without-safety- harnesses.html

12. https://www.bondi38.com.au/the-history-of-bondi-beach-
    sydneys-most-   famous-
    beach/#:~:text=The%20beach%20boasts%20a%201,is%20op
    en%20all%20yer

       %20round

13. https://www.therocks.com/our-story

14. https://whc.unesco.org/en/list/166

15. https://www.sydneyoperahouse.com/our-story/utzon-departs-the-house

16. https://ucmp.berkeley.edu/mammal/marsupial/marsupial.html

17. https://whc.unesco.org/en/list/1306

18. https://abcnews.go.com/Travel/story?id=118765&page=1

19. https://www.thehistorypress.co.uk/articles/the-land-of-the-free- criminal- transportation-to-america/

20. https://www.ifs.tas.gov.au/discover-trout-fishing-in-tasmania

21. https://blighmuseum.wixsite.com/blighmuseum

22. https://whc.unesco.org/en/list/181

23. https://en.wikipedia.org/wiki/St_Patrick%27s_Cathedral,_Melbourne

24. https://en.wikipedia.org/wiki/Australian_rules_football

Chapter 12: Alaska, United States and Canada

1. https://www.brainyquote.com/quotes/albert_einstein_106912

2. https://www.nps.gov/bela/learn/historyculture/the-bering-land- bridge- theory.htm

Part 2-My Big Year

3. https://www.history.com/topics/us-states/alaska

4. https://www.nps.gov/sitk/learn/historyculture/battle1804.htm

5. https://www.history.com/topics/us-states/alaska

6. https://www.archives.gov/milestone-documents/louisiana-purchase-treaty

7. https://fragilestatesindex.org/country-data/

8. https://free-map.org/

9. https://earthquake.usgs.gov/earthquakes/events/alaska1964/

10. https://www.nps.gov/state/ak/index.htm

11. https://earthquake.usgs.gov/earthquakes/events/alaska1964/

12. https://en.wikipedia.org/wiki/Denali%E2%80%93Mount_McKinley_naming_dispute

13. https://www.mprnews.org/story/2025/01/26/alaskans-say-trump-can-change-the-name-of-denali-but-cant-make-people-call-it-mount-mckinley

14. https://www.adn.com/alaska-life/2025/01/21/denali-vs-mckinley-a-brief-history-of-the-long-debate-over-what-to-call-north-americas-highest-mountain/

15. https://mckinleymuseum.org/william-mckinley/

16. https://www.nps.gov/wrst/index.htm

17. <u>Destinations of a Lifetime: 225 of the World's Most Amazing Places</u>, National Geographic, Washington, DC

18. https://www.britannica.com/topic/Trans-Alaska-Pipeline

19. https://www.alaska.gov/Kids/learn/pipeline.htm

20. https://darrp.noaa.gov/oil-spills/exxon-valdez

21. https://www.nps.gov/glba/index.htm

22. https://www.travelalaska.com/Destinations/Parks-Public-Lands/Klondike- Gold-Rush-National-Historical-Park

23. https://www.britannica.com/place/Mendenhall-Glacier

24. https://www.fws.gov/story/zombie-salmon

25. https://education.nationalgeographic.org/resource/glacier/

26. https://www.lifegate.com/icebergs-grey-glacier-patagonia-chile

27. https://www.batimes.com.ar/news/world/united-nations-reports-off-the- charts- melting-of-glaciers.phtml

28. https://www.tourismvictoria.com/plan-your-trip/about-greater-victoria/history?gad_source=1&gclid=CjoKCQjw_sq2BhCUA RIsAIVqmQvqxm c mgufYFS-rfgByLTszf6_eyr89ADBAbeelmIFpwPT75GeYB_YaAkZYEAL w_wcB

29. https://www.history.com/news/canada-independence-from-

britain-france- war- of-1812

30. https://www.butchartgardens.com/media/

Chapter 13: Spain and France

1. https://www.brainyquote.com/topics/culture-quotes

2. https://www.britannica.com/place/Spain/Government-and-society

3. https://www.butterfield.com/get-inspired/seasonal-fare-bordeaux-vs-burgundy

4. https://winefolly.com/deep-dive/a-primer-to-bordeaux-wine/

5. https://winetourismspain.com/wine-regions/catalonia/#:~:text=The%20most%20outstanding%20DO%20is,is%20s h ared%20among%20other%20regions

6. https://fragilestatesindex.org/country-data/

7. https://free-map.org/

8. https://www.foreverbarcelona.com/fascinating-montserrat-history/

9. https://www.archdaily.com/877599/10-must-see-gaudi-buildings-in-barcelona

10. https://whc.unesco.org/en/list/345/

11. https://en.wikivoyage.org/wiki/Carcassonne

12. https://www.historichotels.org/hotels-resorts/hotel-de-la-cite-carcassonne- mgallery-by-sofitel/history.php

13. https://whc.unesco.org/en/list/932/

14. https://www.britannica.com/place/Biarritz

15. https://en.wikipedia.org/wiki/San_Sebasti%C3%A1n

16. https://www.guggenheim-bilbao.eus/en

17. https://www.guggenheim.org/press-release/guggenheim-museum-among- eight- buildings-by-frank-lloyd-wright-inscribed-on-unesco-world-heritage-list

18. https://www.guggenheim-bilbao.eus/en/the-collection/works/the-matter of- time

19. https://bilbaomuseoa.eus/en/home/

20. https://en.wikipedia.org/wiki/Bilbao_Cathedral

21. https://www.afpradomuseum.org/

22. https://www.britannica.com/biography/Hieronymus-Bosch

23. https://whc.unesco.org/en/list/379/

24. https://camino.uk.com/2018/05/31/the-origin-of-tapas/

25. Destinations of a Lifetime: 225 of the World's Most Amazing Places, National Geographic, Washington, DC

Chapter 14: Danube Cruise (Hungary, Slovakia, Austria, Germany, and Czech Republic)

1. https://www.brainyquote.com/topics/culture-quotes

2. https://www.britannica.com/topic/Czechoslovak-history

3. <u>The World of Yesterday</u>, Stephan Zweig, University of Nebraska Press, 2013

4. https://www.britannica.com/event/Arab-Spring

5. https://fragilestatesindex.org/country-data/

6. https://www.free-map.org/

7. https://vajdahunyadcastle.com/history-of-vajdahunyad-castle-budapest/

8. https://www.heritagedaily.com/2020/08/castle-of-vlad-iii-dracula/134890

9. https://www.budapestbylocals.com/st-stephens-basilica/

10. https://thefrenchroomhome.wordpress.com/2020/02/04/ten-of-the- most- famous-paintings-by-pierre-auguste-renoir/

11. https://www.wien.info/en/see-do/sights-from-a-to-z/st-stephens-cathedral-

    359690

12. <u>Destinations of a Lifetime: 225 of the World's Most Amazing Places</u>, National Geographic, Washington, DC

13. https://www.britannica.com/summary/House-of-Habsburg

14. https://www.britannica.com/biography/Richard-I-king- of-England/Imprisonment

15. https://whc.unesco.org/en/list/784/

16. https://simple.wikipedia.org/wiki/Wolfgang_Amadeus_Moz

art

17. https://www.dallassymphony.org/community-education/dso-kids/listen- watch/composers/wolfgang-amadeus-mozart/

18. https://www.britannica.com/biography/Christian-Doppler

19. https://www.britannica.com/place/Passau

20. https://en.wikipedia.org/wiki/Regensburg_Cathedral

21. https://www.bmwgroup-werke.com/regensburg/de.html

22. Kissinger, A Biography, Walter Isaacson, Simon & Schuster Paperbacks, 2005

23. https://www.britannica.com/story/defenestration-pragues-history-of- literally- throwing-authority-out-the-window

24. https://www.iilj.org/publications/the-peace-of-westphalia-1648-as-a- secular- constitution/

25. https://mzv.gov.cz/riyadh/en/information_about_the_czech_republic/brief_h istory_of_the_czech_republic.html

26. https://www.britannica.com/biography/Gavrilo-Princip

27. https://www.terezin.org/the-history-of-terezin

28. https://www.britannica.com/place/Prague-Castle

Chapter 15: Costa Rica and Southern Florida, United States

1. https://www.brainyquote.com/search_results?q=john+muir

2. https://history.state.gov/countries/costa-rica

3. https://www.under30experiences.com/blog/costa-rica-has-run-on-

    100- renewable-energy-for-299-days

4. https://www.worldfuturecouncil.org/100-renewable-energy-costa-rica/

5. https://lowcarbonpower.org/region/Costa_Rica

6. https://www.britannica.com/topic/history-of-Costa-Rica

7. https://www.thelatinamericatravelcompany.com/christmas-in-costa-rica/

8. https://fragilestatesindex.org/country-data/

9. https://free-map.org/

10. https://www.hemingwayhome.com/his-life

11. https://www.trumanlittlewhitehouse.org/

12. https://www.history.com/articles/thomas-edison

13. https://www.melfisher.org/1622-galleons

14. https://www.nps.gov/drto/index.htm

15. https://www.drytortugas.com/national-park-history/

16. https://www.worldanimalprotection.us/latest/blogs/10-facts-about-sloths-natures-slowest-animals/?gad_source=1&gclid=CjoKCQiA7se8BhCAARIsAKn F3ryH6xboLXw9lrlHoumT4BcuS6kypPcTNtlo_-tEVI9uTocF1F8eTM4aAqdbEALw_wcB&gclsrc=aw.ds

17. https://en.wikipedia.org/wiki/Megatherium

18. https://crie.cr/celebrities-in-costa-rica/

19. https://thecostaricanews.com/keanu-reeves-enjoyed-his-vacation-in-costa-rica/

Chapter 16 Summary

1. https://ich.unesco.org/en/RL/mediterranean-diet-00884

www.ingramcontent.com/pod-product-compliance
Lightning Source LLC
Chambersburg PA
CBHW051128120626
46547CB00012B/715